# Rural Dimensions of Welfare Reform

# Rural Dimensions of Welfare Reform

Bruce A. Weber
Greg J. Duncan
Leslie A. Whitener
*Editors*

2002

W.E. Upjohn Institute for Employment Research
Kalamazoo, Michigan

**Library of Congress Cataloging-in-Publication Data**

Rural dimensions of welfare reform : welfare, food assistance, and poverty in rural
America / Bruce A. Weber, Greg J. Duncan, Leslie A. Whitener, editors.
    p. cm.
    "This book presents revised versions of about half of the papers presented at a
conference on the title topic held in May 2000"—summary p.
    Includes bibliographical references and index.
    ISBN 0-88099-239-5 (pbk. : alk. paper) — ISBN 0-88099-240-9 (cloth : alk. paper)
    1. Rural poor—United States. 2. Social service, Rural—United States. 3. Public
welfare—United States. 4. United States. Personal Responsibility and Work
Opportunity Reconciliation Act of 1996. I. Weber, Bruce A. II. Duncan, Greg J.
III. Whitener, Leslie A.

HC110.P6 R855 2002
361.6′8′091734—dc21

2002016815

© 2002
W.E. Upjohn Institute for Employment Research
300 S. Westnedge Avenue
Kalamazoo, Michigan 49007-4686

Cover design by J.R. Underhill.
Index prepared by Nairn Chadwick.
Printed in the United States of America.

# Contents

Foreword     ix

**Introduction: As the Dust Settles: Welfare Reform and Rural America**     1
*Leslie A. Whitener, Bruce A. Weber, and Greg Duncan*

**Part 1:   Welfare Reform, Rural Labor Markets, and Rural Poverty**

**1  Approaching the Limit: Early National Lessons from Welfare Reform**     25
*Sheldon Danziger*

**2  Rural Labor Markets in an Era of Welfare Reform**     51
*Robert M. Gibbs*

**3  Rural America in Transition: Poverty and Welfare at the Turn of the Twenty-First Century**     77
*Daniel T. Lichter and Leif Jensen*

**Part 2:   Welfare Dynamics in Rural and Urban Areas**

**4  Reducing Food Stamp and Welfare Caseloads in the South: Are Rural Areas Less Likely to Succeed Than Urban Centers?**     113
*Mark Henry, Lynn Reinschmiedt, Willis Lewis, Jr., and Darren Hudson*

**5  Seasonal Employment Dynamics and Welfare Use in Agricultural and Rural California Counties**     147
*Henry E. Brady, Mary Sprague, Fredric C. Gey, and Michael Wiseman*

**6  Location and the Low-Income Experience: Analyses of Program Dynamics in the Iowa Family Investment Program**     177
*Helen H. Jensen, Shao-Hsun Keng, and Steven Garasky*

7   **Small Towns and Welfare Reform: Iowa Case Studies of**    201
    **Families and Communities**
    *Cynthia Needles Fletcher, Jan L. Flora, Barbara J. Gaddis,*
    *Mary Winter,* and *Jacquelyn S. Litt*

8   **Where All the Counties Are above Average: Human Service**    231
    **Agency Directors' Perspectives on Welfare Reform**
    *Ann Tickamyer, Julie White, Barry Tadlock,* and
    *Debra Henderson*

Part 3:   **Employment and Family Well-Being**
          **under Welfare Reform**

9   **The Impact of Welfare Policy on the Employment of Single**    257
    **Mothers Living in Rural and Urban Areas**
    *Signe-Mary McKernan, Robert Lerman, Nancy Pindus,* and
    *Jesse Valente*

10  **Welfare Reform in Rural Minnesota: Experimental Findings**    287
    **from the Minnesota Family Investment Program**
    *Lisa A. Gennetian, Cindy Redcross,* and *Cynthia Miller*

11  **Will Attainable Jobs Be Available for TANF Recipients in**    313
    **Local Labor Markets?  Evidence from Mississippi on**
    **Prospects for "Job-Skill Matching" of TANF Adults**
    *Frank M. Howell*

12  **Whose Job Is It?  Employers' Views on Welfare Reform**    345
    *Ellen Shelton, Greg Owen, Amy Bush Stevens,*
    *Justine Nelson-Christinedaughter, Corinna Roy,* and
    *June Heineman*

13  **The Short-Term Impacts of Welfare Reform in Persistently**    375
    **Poor Rural Areas**
    *Mark Harvey, Gene F. Summers, Kathleen Pickering,* and
    *Patricia Richards*

Part 4:   **Food Assistance and Hunger: The Rural Dimension**

14  **Food Stamps in Rural America: Special Issues and**    413
    **Common Themes**
    *Sheena McConnell* and *James Ohls*

**15   The Decline in Food Stamp Use by Rural Low-Income          433
       Households: Less Need or Less Access?**
       *Mark Nord*

**Part 5:   Lessons Learned**

**16   Lessons Learned: Welfare Reform and Food Assistance in       455
       Rural America**
       *Greg Duncan, Leslie A. Whitener,* and *Bruce A. Weber*

The Authors                                                        471

Cited Author Index                                                 477

Subject Index                                                      485

About the Institute                                                501

# Foreword

The Personal Responsibility and Work Opportunity Reconciliation Act of 1996 (PRWORA) changed welfare as we knew it, dramatically altering the social safety net for poor Americans. PRWORA repealed the entitlement welfare program, Aid to Families with Dependent Children, replacing it with a new federal block grant program, Temporary Assistance for Needy Families. The act also introduced program cuts and changes in the nation's food assistance programs. With these changes came new roles, responsibilities, and expectations for low-income families, their communities, and their local governments.

With new opportunities come a great number of challenges to implementing welfare reform. Many issues resulting from welfare reform confront rural and urban areas alike. Meeting work requirements, achieving economic independence, and maintaining family and child well-being are concerns for both rural and urban people. Once employment is secured, ensuring the availability and affordability of child care, transportation, health care, housing, and other support services is needed. However, rural areas have unique demographic, economic, and geographic characteristics that may translate into unique challenges for welfare reform implementation. Compared with urban areas, many rural communities have higher poverty levels, greater unemployment, lower education levels, lower incomes, and longer distances between home, child care, and work sites. Because of lower population density, rural areas tend to have higher costs for services and frequently lack a full range of services. These characteristics all present a unique context in which to implement welfare reform.

In May of 2000, the Economic Research Service of the U.S. Department of Agriculture (USDA), the Northwestern University/University of Chicago Joint Center for Poverty Research, and the Rural Policy Research Institute joined together to sponsor a research conference in Washington, D.C., on the rural dimensions of welfare reform. The Economic Research Service has a long history of distinguished research on rural America and is recognized as an eminent source of knowledge on rural population, labor, and income, and on place-attentive policy research. The Joint Center for Poverty Research is the premier poverty research center in the United States, committed to advancing an understanding of the causes and consequences of poverty and the effect of policies designed to reduce it. The Rural Policy Research Institute is recognized as a major source of policy-relevant analysis on the challenges, needs, and opportunities facing rural America and serves as a catalyst for bringing the rural dimensions of critical policy questions into the policy process. These three nationally recognized policy research organizations blended their resources, with funding from USDA's Food Assistance and Nutrition Research Program, to organize this research conference on the implications of welfare reform for poverty, welfare, and food assistance in rural areas. Over half of the papers presented at the conference are included in this volume. The book assesses the effects of welfare reform on caseloads, employment, earnings, and family well-being in rural and urban areas, and it incorporates both national and state-level analyses in its chapters.

Much of the research and debate over poverty, welfare reform, and food assistance programs has centered on our nation's inner cities. However, although poverty has become more urbanized over the past several decades, almost 60 percent of poor families and almost half of welfare-recipient families live outside central cities. The findings reported in this volume provide a strong empirical basis to help inform the policy debate on the upcoming reauthorization of PRWORA. The most effective policies will be those that recognize America's diversity and the differences in the needs, challenges, and opportunities of both rural and urban people.

Betsey Kuhn, Director
Food and Rural Economics Division
Economic Research Service
U.S. Department of Agriculture

# Introduction

## As the Dust Settles: Welfare Reform and Rural America

Leslie A. Whitener
*Economic Research Service, U.S. Department of Agriculture*

Bruce A. Weber
*Oregon State University* and *Rural Policy Research Institute*

Greg Duncan
*Northwestern University* and *Joint Center for Poverty Research*

The Personal Responsibility and Work Opportunity Act of 1996 (PRWORA) dramatically transformed the federal safety net and the food assistance landscape for low-income households in the United States. Although considerable research has focused on understanding how these reforms are affecting the lives of low-income families, most research to date has focused on urban settings. Yet there is reason to think that welfare reform may not be working as well for the almost 7.5 million people living in poverty in nonmetropolitan areas (Rural Policy Research Institute 2001; Cook and Dagata 1997). America's recent economic boom has left a poorer menu of job options for rural than urban families, and unemployment, underemployment, and poverty levels remain higher in rural than in urban places (Cook and Gibbs 2000).

In May 2000, the Economic Research Service of the U.S. Department of Agriculture, the Northwestern University/University of Chicago Joint Center for Poverty Research, and the Rural Policy Research Institute co-sponsored a research conference to explore the rural dimensions of welfare reform and food assistance policy. This conference brought together some of the nation's leading academic researchers, poverty policy evaluators, rural scholars, and welfare policy experts to review current research on welfare reform outcomes in rural areas. This volume contains revised versions of over half of the papers presented at the conference, selected on the basis of policy relevance, plus one additional paper specifically commissioned for this volume.[1] It represents the first comprehensive look at the spatial dimensions of PRWORA, examining how welfare reform is affecting caseloads, employment, earnings, and family well-being in rural and urban areas.

## REFORMING WELFARE

The Personal Responsibility and Work Opportunity Reconciliation Act (PRWORA) of 1996 is the most significant social welfare legislation in more than 60 years, modifying the nation's cash welfare system and having both direct and indirect effects for food stamps and other federal assistance programs. The long-term guarantee of benefits under a variety of programs has been eliminated in favor of a short-term temporary assistance program to help families get back on their feet. States have been given more flexibility in designing and implementing programs that meet their needs, and individuals have been given added personal responsibility to provide for themselves through job earnings and for their children through child-support payments by absentee parents. The key provisions of PRWORA are summarized in Table 1.

Specifically, the new legislation replaced the entitlement program Aid to Families with Dependent Children (AFDC) with the Temporary Assistance for Needy Families (TANF) program, which is funded through block grants to states. TANF emphasizes moving from welfare to work by imposing a five-year lifetime limit on receiving federal welfare benefits, requiring recipients to participate in work activities within two years of receiving benefits, and penalizing states that have too few recipients in work activities by reducing the federal contribution to their TANF funds. The federal government provides a block grant of fixed size to each state and no longer shares in the cost increases or decreases associated with rising or falling caseloads.

Assessment of the effects of welfare reform in rural and urban areas is complicated by the increased variation among state programs. Diversity in state welfare policies was already under way in the early to

**Table 1  Key Provisions of the Personal Responsibility and Work Opportunity Reconciliation Act of 1996**

Establishes Temporary Assistance for Needy Families (TANF) that
- Replaces former entitlement programs with federal block grants
- Devolves authority and responsibility for welfare programs from federal to state government
- Emphasizes moving from welfare to work through time limits and work requirements

Changes eligibility standards for Supplemental Security Income (SSI) child disability benefits
- Restricts certain formerly eligible children from receiving benefits
- Changes eligibility rules for new applicants and eligibility redetermination

Requires states to enforce a strong child support program for collection of child support payments

Restricts aliens' eligibility for welfare and other public benefits
- Denies illegal aliens most public benefits, except emergency medical services
- Restricts most legal aliens from receiving food stamps and SSI benefits until they become citizens or work for at least 10 years
- Allows states the option of providing federal cash assistance to legal aliens already in the country
- Restricts most new legal aliens from receiving federal cash assistance for five years
- Allows states the option of using state funds to provide cash assistance to nonqualifying aliens

Provides resources for foster care data systems and a national child welfare study

Establishes a block grant to states to provide child care for working parents

Alters eligibility criteria and benefits for child nutrition programs
- Modifies reimbursement rates
- Makes families (including aliens) that are eligible for free public education also eligible for school meal benefits

Tightens national standards for food stamps and commodity distribution
- Reduces the maximum food stamp benefit from 103 percent to 100 percent of the Thrifty Food Plan
- Caps standard deduction at fiscal year 1995 level
- Limits receipt of benefits to three months in every three years by childless able-bodied adults age 18–50 unless working or in training.

mid 1990s through a process that permitted waivers to federal welfare requirements for state experiments or pilot programs. In response to the flexibility provided through waivers and then under TANF, state programs varied widely as governments made their own decisions about eligibility and benefits, time limits, work participation requirements, and other aspects of personal responsibility. State programs differ, for example, on sanctions imposed for noncompliance, the amounts and types of assets that are used in determining eligibility and benefits, the time period for work requirements, and the design of child care and transportation assistance programs (Gallagher et al. 1998; Liebschutz 2000; Nightingale 1997).

An equally important state variant is the level of responsibility assigned to the administration of welfare. Thirty-five states have vested responsibility for policymaking, funding, and administration in the state government, but the remaining 15 states have devolved responsibility to local counties and communities.[2] Liebschutz (2000) argued that this "second-order devolution" leads to heightened discretion for local governments and allows greater flexibility in the types and delivery of services offered to families. Gais et al. (2001) caution that local administration will be difficult unless states create an information infrastructure to help local administrators understand the magnitude and nature of the problems facing families in their areas. This volume helps to capture the diversity of state programs by examining program operation and welfare reform outcomes in 12 predominantly nonmetropolitan states.

In addition, PRWORA has had direct and indirect implications for the Food Stamp program, the largest federal food assistance program and a mainstay of the federal safety net.[3] Although the legislation decentralized the welfare system with block grants to states, the centralization of the Food Stamp program was maintained at the federal level. Directly, the 1996 legislation affected the Food Stamp program by

- reducing the maximum food stamp benefit from 103 percent to 100 percent of the Thrifty Food Plan;
- limiting benefits to 3 months in every 36 months for able-bodied adults without dependents, unless they are working or in training;
- limiting deductions from income when calculating benefits;

- giving states increased powers to reduce or eliminate food stamp benefits if the recipient does not comply with the rules of other public assistance programs; and
- restricting most legal aliens from receiving benefits until they become citizens or work for at least 10 years.

Indirectly, research has suggested that welfare reform has operated in several ways to reduce food stamp participation. A recent review of studies of TANF "leavers" found that many TANF participants who have left the cash welfare program have also stopped receiving food stamp benefits, even though they are likely to still be eligible (Dion and Pavetti 2000). State diversion policies, local office practices, and misinformation about the program may be operating to increase the difficulty for eligible families to enter the Food Stamp program (Wilde et al. 2000). Three of the chapters in this volume address issues related to the effects of welfare reform on food stamp participation and its outcomes.

## UNDERSTANDING THE RURAL CONTEXT

What do we mean by "rural"? Our understanding of the rural context and its importance for assessing policy and program effectiveness is complicated by the lack of a consistent definition of rural. Often when researchers and policy analysts discuss conditions in rural America, they are referring to conditions in nonmetropolitan areas. Metropolitan areas are defined by the Office of Management and Budget to include core counties with one or more central cities of at least 50,000 residents or with an urbanized area of 50,000 or more and total area population of at least 100,000. Fringe counties (suburbs) that are economically tied to the core counties are also included in metropolitan areas. Nonmetropolitan counties are outside the boundaries of metro areas and have no cities with 50,000 residents or more (Figure 1, nonmetro counties shown in black or white). Although most analysts use the terms "nonmetropolitan" and "rural" interchangeably, the official definitions are quite different. According to the Bureau of the Census, *rural areas* are defined as places (incorporated or unincorporated)

**Figure 1  Over 500 Nonmetro Counties Are Classified as Persistently Poor**

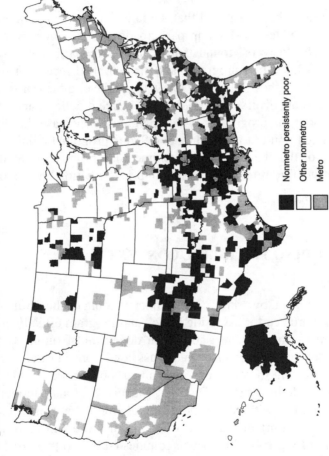

NOTE: *Persistently poor* counties are defined as nonmetro counties with 20% or more of their population in poverty in each of the years 1960, 1970, 1980, and 1990, as measured by the decennial censuses.

SOURCE: Economic Research Service, USDA.

with fewer than 2,500 residents and open territory. *Urban areas* comprise larger places and densely settled areas around them.[4] Most (but not all) of the studies in this volume use the metropolitan/nonmetropolitan classification of counties in their analyses, and most use the terms "rural" and "nonmetropolitan" interchangeably. Readers are encouraged to examine the definition of "rural" used in each chapter.

During the 1990s, the national economy enjoyed an unprecedented period of economic growth. Unemployment rates reached 30-year lows, and employment continued to expand. Efforts by the Federal Reserve Board successfully restrained inflation while sustaining economic growth. Rural areas, in general, shared in the good economic times. Yet, even in the face of strong economic growth, rural labor markets will often follow the improving national patterns, but they will not converge with urban trends. Thus, at the close of the century, nonmetro poverty remained 2 percentage points higher than in metropolitan areas, with over 14 percent of the nonmetro population living below poverty. Unemployment and underemployment remained higher in nonmetro than metro labor markets, and job growth was slower. Nonmetro areas lagged metro areas in both per capita income and earnings per job (Cook and Gibbs 2000). Thus, rural families are facing fewer job options than urban families at a time when large numbers of lower-skilled rural residents will be leaving the welfare rolls and entering the labor force.

Also, many rural areas are characterized by conditions that are likely to impede the move from welfare to work, irrespective of population characteristics or the health of the local economy. As a result of low population densities in rural areas, distances to jobs are often great, creating needs for reliable transportation; key social and educational services may be unavailable or are available only with a long commute; and child care options are fewer and harder to arrange. To the extent that rural and urban areas differ in their support services, policy impacts may vary. Several chapters in this book address issues related to barriers affecting the welfare-to-work transitions for low-income families in rural areas.

Yet, rural America is characterized by diversity. Some areas have participated in the economic progress of the nation, while others have not (Economic Research Service 1995). For example, more than 500 nonmetro counties have been characterized by chronically high levels of poverty and unemployment over the last four decades and offer special challenges for welfare reform (Figure 1).[5] Welfare reform successes in these persistently poor areas may be more difficult to achieve than in many other nonmetro areas because of structural and human capital disadvantages inherent in the history and culture of the areas and the general weakness of their local economies.  A main distinguishing feature of these persistently poor counties is the disproportionate number of economically at-risk people, including racial/ethnic minorities, female-headed households, and high school dropouts (Table 2).  At the same time, the local economies of these areas do less well than other nonmetro places.  Population and employment growth for persistently poor counties fall below that of nonmetro counties as a whole; unemployment and poverty rates are considerably higher; and earnings per job and per capita income are considerably lower.

Persistently poor counties are heavily concentrated in the South, with representation in Appalachia, the Ozark-Ouachita area, the Mississippi Delta, the Rio Grande Valley, and the Native American reservations of the Southwest and Northern Plains.  These chronically poor counties contained 19 percent of the nonmetro population and 32 percent (2.7 million) of the nonmetro poor in 1990.  The nature of the welfare reform challenges facing some of these persistently poor, nonmetro counties is discussed in several of the state studies presented in this volume.

## ASSESSING THE OUTCOMES OF WELFARE REFORM

A major goal of PRWORA is to reduce long-term welfare dependency in favor of employment.  Both cash assistance and food stamp participation have fallen dramatically in recent years (Figure 2). AFDC and TANF caseloads declined 47 percent, falling from a high of 14 million in 1994 to 7.5 million in 1999.  Food Stamp program participation fell from 27.5 million participants in 1994 to 19.4 million participants in 1999, a 30 percent decline.  Most of the decline for these two programs took place from 1996–1998, following the enactment of PRWORA and during a period of unprecedented and sustained national economic growth.  These trends demonstrate the responsiveness of poverty

**Table 2  Counties with Persistent Poverty: Selected Characteristics**

| Characteristic | Counties with persistent poverty | All nonmetro counties |
|---|---|---|
| No. of counties | 535 | 2,276 |
| % of nonmetro population, 1999[a] | 18.5 | 100 |
| Population change[a] (%) | | |
| 1980–90 | –0.16 | 2.69 |
| 1990–99 | 6.15 | 7.61 |
| Annualized employment change[b] (%) | | |
| 1979–89 | 0.5 | 0.9 |
| 1989–99 | 0.8 | 1.1 |
| Unemployment rate[b] (%) | | |
| 1990 | 8.1 | 6.5 |
| 1999 | 7.1 | 5.2 |
| Poverty rate, 1990[c] (%) | 29.1 | 18.3 |
| Black population, 1990[c] (%) | 21.2 | 8.0 |
| Hispanic population, 1990[c] (%) | 7.8 | 4.3 |
| Female-headed households with children, 1990[c] (%) | 7.5 | 5.2 |
| High school dropouts[c] (%) | 14.3 | 11 |
| Earnings per job, 1998[d] ($) | 22,931 | 24,408 |
| Per capita income, 1998[d] ($) | 17,910 | 21,384 |

[a] Bureau of the Census.
[b] Bureau of Labor Statistics, Local Area Unemployment Statistics.
[c] 1990 Census of Population.
[d] Bureau of Economic Analysis.
SOURCE: Calculated by USDA, Economic Research Service.

and caseloads to economic conditions (as measured by unemployment), but they also suggest that a large proportion of the nation's poor has not been participating in the two major federal safety net programs, even before enactment of PRWORA. In 1995, for example, almost 10 million people living in poverty were not receiving food stamps, and over 23 million were not receiving cash assistance under AFDC. Little is known about rural/urban contrasts in caseload responses, especially in states where county unemployment and poverty rates range widely.

**Figure 2  AFDC/TANF and Food Stamp Participants, Persons in Poverty, and Unemployed Persons, 1980–1999**

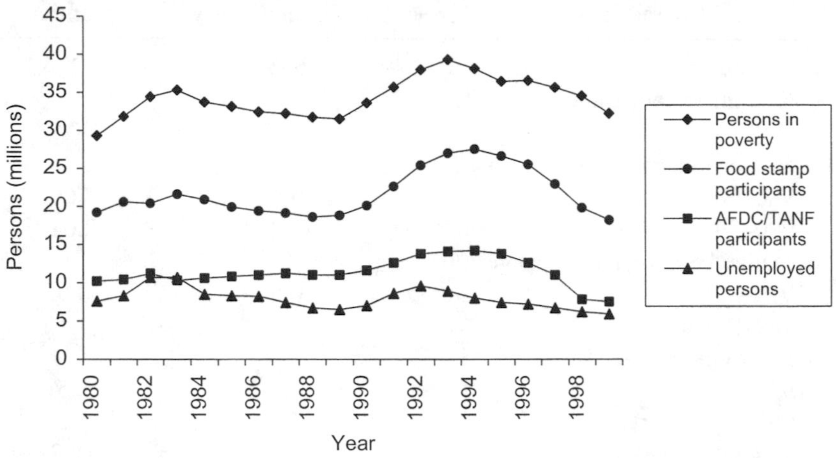

SOURCE: Calculated by ERS based on data from the Bureau of the Census, USDA Food and Nutrition Service, Department of Health and Human Services, and Bureau of Labor Statistics.

Disentangling the influence of a healthy economy and policy changes is important to understanding what lies ahead for federal assistance programs in both rural and urban areas. Several chapters in this volume focus attention on the determinants of changing TANF and food stamp caseloads in rural areas.

A second goal of welfare reform is to increase self-sufficiency of former welfare recipients through employment. National-level studies have suggested that welfare reform is playing a major role in raising the employment rates of single mothers, with some research finding that more than half of mothers leaving the welfare rolls are employed at some time after ending their welfare participation (Cancian et al. 1999; Holzer 1999). Questions about how rural recipients who have left the rolls are faring and if their experience differs from that of their urban counterparts remain unanswered. Can rural welfare recipients find work? Have welfare-to-work transitions improved the economic well-being of rural recipients? Have declines in welfare and food stamp assistance increased food insecurity and hunger for low-income rural families?  Many of the chapters in this volume address these questions. The booming economy of the late 1990s created the best possible environment for former welfare recipients entering the labor market.  However, reductions in caseloads do not mean that all rural and urban families who leave the rolls are making ends meet.  As Lionel Beaulieu, Director of the Southern Rural Development Center, has said, "The measure of success of this legislation should not be tied to the numerical decline in the number of welfare cases.  Rather, it should be linked to how well we have succeeded in offering welfare participants a genuine opportunity to realize substantive improvement in the quality of their family and work life" (Beaulieu 2000).

Although there are reasons to suggest that welfare reform may not be working as well for the one-fifth of the nation's poor living in rural areas, there has been no systematic look at the rural dimensions of welfare reform.  In this volume, leading policy-oriented researchers explore the rural context of welfare reform and food assistance policy and summarize the early results from qualitative and quantitative studies of welfare reform outcomes in rural and urban places.  National-level analyses and information on welfare reform outcomes in 12 individual states are included.  Most of the states are predominantly nonmetropolitan in character, and they represent all four major geographic regions of the country (Figure 3).  Collectively, the chapters provide a sound empirical basis for the design of state policies to increase employment and well-being of low-income families in rural and urban regions.

## ORGANIZATION OF THE BOOK

The remainder of the book is organized into four sections that address issues related to the impacts and outcomes of welfare reform in rural areas.  The first section, "Welfare Reform, Rural Labor Markets, and Rural Poverty," sets a context for the subsequent discussion about policy outcomes.  It provides an overview of the economic and policy environment in which welfare reform has been implemented.

Sheldon Danziger opens this section by summarizing three general lessons learned from studies of welfare reform effects at the national level: 1) earnings and employment have increased since 1996 due

**Figure 3  States Represented in this Volume**

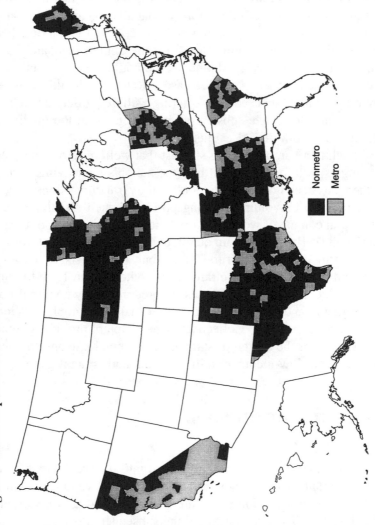

SOURCE: Mapped by Economic Research Service, USDA, using OMB's 1993 metro/nonmetro county designations.

to a combination of favorable economic conditions and federal and state policy changes; 2) there is uncertainty about how welfare reform will play out under less favorable economic conditions; and 3) poverty levels have decreased little despite dramatic caseload declines. Using national Current Population Survey data, Danziger finds similar patterns of work effort, welfare receipt, and poverty for central city, "suburban," and nonmetropolitan working, single mothers with children. Then, based on a panel study of urban single mothers with children who received public assistance, he finds that many welfare recipients face multiple barriers that impede work effort, and that lower work effort is associated with higher poverty status. He suggests that many current recipients who might be willing to work will "hit the time limits" because of their personal barriers, even if favorable economic conditions continue.

Robert Gibbs provides an in-depth examination of the rural labor markets within which rural welfare recipients often begin their transitions into the workforce. His chapter describes the distinctive nature of many rural labor markets, focusing on characteristics that constrain job availability and earnings and thus affect the prospects for the economic success of welfare recipients. He argues that rural labor markets may be better positioned for welfare reform than often supposed because rural and urban job structures appear to be converging. At the same time, however, rural labor markets also face significant welfare reform challenges in terms of higher unemployment and a persistent rural/urban earnings gap. In particular, Gibbs notes that the apparent lack of opportunity for many former welfare recipients to move from their low-wage to higher-paying jobs without additional education is likely to be a serious stumbling block to a sustainable wage.

Daniel Lichter and Leif Jensen provide a detailed national picture of changing rates of poverty, sources of income, and employment among rural and urban female-headed families with children. Using national data from the Current Population Survey, they find similar trends in poverty (including deep poverty), welfare receipt, labor force participation, and earnings among these rural and urban families: employment and earnings have increased and welfare receipt and poverty have declined. Nonetheless, there are disturbingly high rates of poverty among rural working women; one-third of working female heads are in poverty.

A remarkable outcome of the 1996 welfare reform act has been the unprecedented decline in welfare caseloads. The second section of the book, "Welfare Dynamics in Rural and Urban Areas," looks at the changes in caseloads in rural and urban areas of selected states, examines the interaction between welfare use and employment of low-income populations, and explores rural/urban differences in welfare reform barriers and outcomes in selected states.

Mark Henry and others use county-level AFDC, TANF, and food stamp data from Mississippi and South Carolina to examine rural and urban caseload trends within the context of local economic conditions. Their analysis shows no consistent pattern of caseload declines across rural and urban counties in these two states. However, when they control for local economic conditions, incentives facing potential workers, and policy changes, their findings suggest that rural areas will have more difficulty than urban areas in reducing both welfare and food stamp participation rates.

Henry Brady and his coauthors show that welfare use patterns in rural and agricultural counties differ from those in urban counties, largely due to differences in employment patterns and labor market structures. Using a unique combination of administrative data sets from California, they show that seasonality of employment in rural and agricultural counties has led welfare recipients to combine seasonal work with welfare in the off-season, when unemployment rates rise to high levels. With the advent of time limits, these families will have to find other ways to support themselves in the off-season once their welfare benefits have ended. Brady and his coauthors argue that rural and agricultural areas face significant challenges in finding paths from welfare to work for these families who have traditionally had work opportunities for only part of the year.

Helen Jensen and her coauthors use state administrative data to examine why some low-income households who were active in Iowa's Family Assistance Program successfully left public assistance during the 1993–1995 period and why others who left later returned. They find that rural recipients in Iowa are more likely to return to welfare than their urban counterparts during the first two quarters after leaving the program, but after this initial period, rates of return are quite similar in both areas.

Cynthia Fletcher and her colleagues, drawing on state and community interviews with service providers and welfare recipients, examine rural and urban differences in welfare reform barriers and outcomes in seven Iowa communities selected to represent a continuum of rural and urban places. They find important differences across the rural/urban continuum related to accessibility and distance to jobs and support services. For rural families moving from welfare to work, fewer services are available locally, and when they are available, rural families have less access. The accessibility of jobs, job training and education, health care, child care, and emergency services are particularly problematic for recipients in rural areas.

In a qualitative study of local welfare administrators and welfare recipients in rural Appalachian counties in Ohio, Ann Tickamyer and coauthors find that local administrators share the values about responsibility and work that underlie welfare reform but are pessimistic about the prospects for their clients given the barriers they face and the lack of jobs in rural areas. At the same time, welfare administrators work to create interventions that make welfare clients more "work-ready" and are enthusiastic about the local autonomy they have been given in Ohio. Program participants, however, believe that local authority to impose rules has led to some capricious and irrational barriers. Some recipients view the new work-readiness interventions as paternalistic.

A major objective of welfare reform is to increase family well-being in low-income populations through employment. The third section of the book, "Employment and Family Well-Being under Welfare Reform," looks at the impacts of welfare policies on the welfare-to-work transitions of welfare recipients.

Signe-Mary McKernan and her coauthors use the Current Population Survey, as well as data from fieldwork in 12 selected rural areas in 4 states, to assess whether the employment responsiveness of single mothers differs in rural and urban areas. The qualitative fieldwork identifies inadequate transportation, limited employment services, weak labor markets, low education levels, and shortfalls in transitional benefits as problems in rural areas. The quantitative analysis with national data finds that welfare reform is playing a major role in raising the employment of single mothers ages 19–45, but that, contrary to expectations, the gains are approximately as high in rural as in urban areas. However, although additional child care benefits increased urban employment of single mothers, they did not increase the employment of their rural counterparts. For young single mothers with low education, moreover, welfare reform increased employment significantly more in urban than rural areas.

Lisa Gennetian and her colleagues examine the impact of an early pilot welfare reform program, the Minnesota Family Investment Program (MFIP), on employment and earnings of welfare recipients in rural and urban Minnesota. This pilot program required recipients to participate in training, offered a benefit structure to make work pay more, and streamlined benefits by, among other things, cashing out food stamps. Using an experimental analytical design in which they followed MFIP and regular AFDC participants for two years after random assignment, the authors find that MFIP increased employment in both rural and urban counties. The MFIP program had a large and lasting impact on urban participants; its impact on rural participants was smaller and it diminished over time, so that the rural effect was less than half of the urban effect by the second year. MFIP had, moreover, a significant positive impact on earnings in both years for urban participants, but it had no significant impact on rural participant earnings in either year.

"Will there be enough jobs for those leaving welfare?" is a question that has been raised frequently in welfare reform debates. This question has particular salience in rural regions, where unemployment rates are generally higher. Frank Howell assesses the capacity of labor markets in Mississippi to absorb the 1996 cohort of TANF recipients by "matching" their educational credentials with the educational profile needed for projected jobs in each labor market area from 1997–2002. He also assesses the capacity of local labor markets to provide child care. The author concludes that urban labor markets will be better able to provide both "skill-matched" jobs for welfare leavers and child care services than rural labor markets.

Because transitions to jobs are critical to the success to welfare reform, a key question focuses on employers' view of the potential workforce of former welfare participants. Drawing on a survey of 130 Minnesota employers who participated in local welfare-to-work partnerships, Greg Owen and his coauthors first looked at the needs and attitudes of these employers in rural and suburban/urban areas. They find very little difference in attitudes between the areas, concluding that employers generally view lack of "soft skills" as the primary barrier to workforce participation.  Employers also believe their main contribution to welfare reform is their willingness to consider hiring; most employers did not believe it was their responsibility to help participants overcome their barriers.  Owen and his colleagues also interviewed 395 randomly selected participants in the Minnesota Family Investment Program in rural and urban areas to determine perceived barriers to employment and self-sufficiency.  In contrast with employers, welfare recipients in both rural and urban areas tended to cite structural problems such as low wages, lack of child care, and lack of education as primary barriers.

Mark Harvey and coauthors emphasize several dimensions of rural labor markets that are often neglected in more quantitative assessments of welfare reform.  They examine labor market participation and involvement in assistance programs in persistently poor rural counties in Kentucky (Central Appalachia), Mississippi (Lower Mississippi River Delta), Texas (Lower Rio Grande Valley), and South Dakota (Indian reservations) to obtain a qualitative picture of the survival strategies of low-income families under welfare reform.  Information was obtained from national data archives, state administrative data, records of nongovernmental organizations, and interviews with community leaders and welfare recipients.  Their analysis highlights the importance of the local "opportunity structures," the centrality of the household in the labor market strategies of rural women, the central role of the informal economy in rural labor market decisions, and the importance of entrenched local power structures in the operation of rural labor markets.

The decline in food stamp caseloads after welfare reform raised concern about why eligible families are not participating in the Food Stamp program.  The fourth section, "Food Assistance and Hunger: The Rural Dimension," addresses this concern.

Sheena McConnell and James Ohls examine how well the Food Stamp program serves nonmetropolitan households.  They conclude that the program is at least as successful in serving low-income nonmetropolitan households as it is in serving their metropolitan counterparts.  Participation rates are higher in rural areas, and the recent declines in participation rates have occurred primarily in metropolitan areas.  Their survey data suggest a high degree of satisfaction with the program in both metro and nonmetro areas.

Mark Nord uses data from the Current Population Survey Food Security Supplements to examine whether the declines in food stamp use are due to lower levels of food insecurity and hunger or to less access to the Food Stamp program. He finds that food insecurity increased substantially among low-income households not using food stamps, suggesting that the decline in food stamps is due to reduced access. However, because hunger among this population did not increase, he concludes that those who most need food assistance still have access to food stamps. Nonmetropolitan patterns are not substantially different from national patterns.

In the concluding chapter of this book, we summarize the findings of the studies presented in this volume and discuss policy implications and options. We draw several policy lessons for the federal design of welfare and food assistance policy and state implementation of welfare reform and food assistance programs.

In closing, we call attention to a statement taken from the 1995 report, *Understanding Rural America* (Economic Research Service 1995):

> Understanding rural America is no easy task. It is tempting to generalize and oversimplify, to characterize rural areas as they once were or as they are now in only some places. Understanding rural America requires understanding the ongoing changes and diversity that shape it. The economies of individual rural areas differ, as do the resources upon which they are built and the opportunities and challenges they face. Some have participated in the economic progress of the Nation, while others have not. Even among those that have benefited in the past, many are not well positioned to compete in today's global economy. Each of those types of areas has different needs. No single policy can sufficiently address the needs of all.

The U.S. Congress now begins to prepare for the upcoming debate over reauthorization of PRWORA in 2002. The research studies presented in this book will provide a strong empirical basis to help inform the policy debate on reauthorization and will serve to identify some of the welfare challenges and opportunities facing rural people, their families, and their communities.

# Notes

1. Visit the JCPR Web site at <www.jcpr.org> to download conference papers, the executive summary, and other relevant resources and information from the May 2000 conference, "Rural Dimensions of Welfare Reform."
2. For example, Wisconsin's 72 county governments and New York's 57 counties plus New York City are responsible for welfare administration in those states. In contrast, Florida, Mississippi, and Washington have state-centered welfare programs (Liebschutz 2000).
3. See Oliveira (1998) for a more detailed description of the effects of welfare reform on the food stamp and other food-assistance programs.
4. Using population counts from the 1990 Census, there were 50.9 million nonmetro county residents and 61.7 million rural residents in 1990. Thus, when using the nonmetro definition, we are missing some 29 million individuals who live in small rural towns with fewer than 2,500 residents or open territory but are classified as metropolitan residents because they live within the boundaries of a metropolitan county. At the same time, some 36 percent of nonmetro residents live in urban areas with 2,500 residents or more. See The Economic Research Service Web site at <www.ers.usda.gov/briefing/rurality/whatisrural/> for more information on these definitions.
5. The Economic Research Service has identified 535 persistent poverty counties that had poverty rates of 20 percent or higher in 1960, 1970, 1980, and 1990 (Cook and Mizer 1994). Persistently poor counties were not defined for metro counties as part of the ERS typology; therefore, persistently poor counties are all nonmetro. See the Economic Research Service Web site at <www.ers.usda.gov/briefing/rurality/typology/> for more information on these and other county classifications.

# References

Beaulieu, Lionel J. 2000. Comments given at the Research Conference on Rural Dimensions of Welfare Reform: Implications for Welfare, Poverty, and Food Assistance. Cosponsored by the Economic Research Service, the Northwestern University/University of Chicago Joint Center for Poverty Research, and the Rural Policy Research Institute, Washington, D.C., May 4–5.

Cancian, Maria, Robert Haveman, Thomas Kaplan, Daniel Meyer, and Barbara Wolfe. 1999. "Work, Earnings, and Well-Being after Welfare." In *Economic Conditions and Welfare Reform*, Sheldon Danziger, ed. Kalamazoo, Michigan: W.E. Upjohn Institute for Employment Research, pp. 161–186.

Cook, Peggy, and Elizabeth Dagata. 1997. "Welfare Reform Legislation Poses Opportunities and Challenges for Rural America." *Rural Conditions and Trends: Federal Programs* 8(1): 38–47. Available at http://www.ers.usda. gov/publications/rcat/rcat81/rcat81g.pdf.

Cook, Peggy, and Robert Gibbs. 2000. *Rural Conditions and Trends: Socioeconomic Conditions*, 11(2). Available at http://www.ers.usda.gov/publications/rcat/rcat112/contents.htm.

Cook, Peggy J., and Karen L. Mizer. 1994. *The Revised ERS County Typology*. RDRR no. 89, Washington, D.C.: U.S. Department of Agriculture, Economic Research Service.

Dion, M. Robin, and LaDonna Pavetti. 2000. *Access to and Participation in Medicaid and the Food Stamp Program: A Review of the Recent Literature.* Washington, D.C.: Mathematica Policy Research, Inc.

Economic Research Service. 1995. *Understanding Rural America.* Agriculture Information Bulletin no. 710, Washington, D.C.: U.S. Department of Agriculture. Available at <http://www.ers.usda.gov/publications/aib710/>.

Gallagher, L. Jerome, Megan Gallagher, Kevin Perese, Susan Schreiber, and Keith Watson. 1998. *One Year after Federal Welfare Reform: A Description of State TANF Decisions as of October 1997.* Assessing the New Federalism Occasional Paper no. 6, The Urban Institute, Washington, D.C. Available at <http://newfederalism.urban.org/html/occas6.htm>.

Gais, Thomas L., Richard P. Nathan, Irene Lurie, and Thomas Kaplan. 2001. "The Implementation of the Personal Responsibility Act of 1996: Commonalities, Variations, and the Challenge of Complexity." Paper for the conference titled "New World of Welfare: Shaping a Post-TANF Agenda for Policy," Washington, D.C. February 1–2, hosted by the University of Michigan Ford School of Public Policy.

Holzer, Harry. 1999. "Employer Demand for Welfare Recipients and the Business Cycle." In *Economic Conditions and Welfare Reform*, Sheldon Danziger, ed. Kalamazoo, Michigan: W.E. Upjohn Institute for Employment Research, pp. 187–218.

Liebschutz, Sarah F. 2000. "Public Opinion, Political Leadership, and Welfare Reform." In *Managing Welfare Reform in Five States: The Challenge of Devolution*, Sarah Liebshutz, ed. Albany, New York: The Rockefeller Institute Press, pp. 1–24.

Nightingale, Demetra Smith. 1997. *Transportation Issues in Welfare Reform: Background Information.* Washington, D.C.: Urban Institute.

Oliveira, Victor. 1998. "Welfare Reform Affects USDA's Food-Assistance Programs." *FoodReview* 21(1): 8–15. (Available at http://www.ers.usda. gov/publications/jan1998/jan98b.pdf.)

Rural Policy Research Institute.  2001.  *Welfare Reform in Rural America: A Review of Current Research.*  Report P2001-5, Rural Policy Research Institute, Columbia, Missouri.  Available at <http://www.rupri.org/pubs/archive/reports/P2001-5/>.

Wilde, Parke, Peggy Cook, Craig Gundersen, Mark Nord, and Laura Tiehen.  2000.  *The Decline in Food Stamp Program Participation in the 1990's.*  Report FANRR no. 7, U.S. Department of Agriculture, Economic Research Service, Washington, D.C.  Available at <http://www.ers.usda.gov/publications/fanrr7/>.

# Part 1

# Welfare Reform, Rural Labor Markets, and Rural Poverty

# 1

# Approaching the Limit

## Early National Lessons from Welfare Reform

Sheldon Danziger
*University of Michigan*

Welfare reform has been one of the most controversial social poli-cies of recent times. A Democratic president abandoned welfare reform legislation drafted by his administration—the Work and Responsibility Act (announced by President Clinton on June 14, 1994)—and support-ed legislation, the Personal Responsibility and Work Opportunity Rec-onciliation Act (PRWORA) of 1996, crafted by a Republican Congress. PRWORA ended the entitlement to cash assistance for poor families with children and relinquished to the states the authority for decisions about most policies affecting welfare recipients. Within a few years of passage, PRWORA had "ended welfare as we knew it" more decisively than most policy analysts expected when the legislation was signed; welfare caseloads dropped so dramatically that, by the middle of 2000, the number of recipients had fallen below 6 million, about the same number as the late 1960s.

Several early lessons have emerged from dozens of recent studies of PRWORA's effects. In this chapter, I emphasize changes across the nation as a whole; other chapters focus on rural/urban differences. Some of the factors I discuss—for example, caseload declines—are similar in rural and urban areas. Others, however, such as job growth and access, differ.

The first lesson is that economic conditions, federal government policy changes, and state welfare policy changes in the last few years have contributed to increased employment and net earnings. As a re-sult, the dramatic caseload decline has not produced the dire scenario that some analysts predicted. PRWORA has not caused a surge in poverty or homelessness, because most former recipients are finding jobs. Even though many welfare "leavers," as they are called, are not working full-time, full-year, a significant number are earning at least as much as they had received in cash welfare benefits.

Second, because very favorable economic conditions—rapid economic growth, low inflation, and low unemployment—ended in mid 2001, we do not yet know how welfare reform will play out during a recession or even during a period of moderate unemployment rates and slow economic growth. Indeed, because PRWORA placed a five-year, lifetime limit on the receipt of cash assistance, recipients who continue to receive welfare (stayers), and who face greater barriers to employment than those who have already left the rolls, are at risk of hitting their time limits during a recession. At the present time, we do not know whether the possible coincidence of millions of recipients exhausting eligibility for cash assistance during a recession might produce the increased child poverty and extreme hardships that critics predicted PRWORA would cause. Also, we do not know whether Congress and the states might respond to the recession of 2001–2002 by increasing the number of exemptions allowed from or extensions to federal time limits, providing work-for-welfare community service employment, creating state-funded programs for those who exhaust federal benefits, or implementing some mixture of the above.

A third early lesson is that, despite the large caseload reduction, the national poverty rate has fallen rather little. Many who have left welfare for work remain poor and continue to depend on food stamps, Medicaid, and other government assistance; others have left welfare and remain poor but do not receive the food stamp or Medicaid benefits to which they remain entitled. The extent of economic hardship remains high because, given their human capital and personal characteristics, many former and current welfare recipients have limited earnings prospects in a labor market that increasingly demands higher skills. Thus, despite promising early results with respect to declining caseloads and increasing work effort, much uncertainty exists about the long-run prospects for escaping poverty of both welfare stayers and leavers.

In this chapter, I present some evidence that documents these early lessons. In the next section, I place welfare reform in an economic context by reviewing changes in earnings and family incomes over the past several decades. I then analyze early findings regarding welfare reform by using cross-sectional national data on trends in work, welfare receipt, and poverty, as well as panel data from a study that my colleagues at the University of Michigan and I are conducting. I conclude with a discussion of policy implications for the post-PRWORA era.

## THE ECONOMIC ENVIRONMENT

In the late 1990s, many less-skilled and less-educated workers and former welfare recipients continued to have difficulty earning enough to support their families. Despite robust economic recoveries in both the 1980s and the 1990s, the bottom 40 percent of the population has benefited relatively little. The economic prospects for the less-skilled improved after 1993, when the unemployment rate and the poverty rate began falling. The unemployment rate for adult men fell from 6.7 percent in January 1993 to 3.2 percent in September 2000, the lowest male unemployment rate since December 1973. The rate for adult women fell from 6.3 percent in January 1993 to 3.5 percent in September 2000, the lowest female unemployment rate since December 1969. The official poverty rate nationwide fell every year between 1993 and 2000, from 15.1 percent to 11.3 percent.

Nonetheless, the long economic recovery did not benefit the disadvantaged enough to restore their economic well-being to where it stood a quarter century ago. The 2000 poverty rate is still higher than the 1973 rate (11.1 percent) and much higher than the rates of Canada, Japan, and most northern European countries (Jantti and Danziger 2000).

Typically, poverty falls as real per capita income increases during economic recoveries and rises as income falls during recessions. The increases in poverty and income inequality in the late 1970s and early 1980s, however, were so great that it now requires substantially higher real per capita income to achieve the same poverty rate as it did a quarter century ago. The 2000 poverty rate for central city residents, 16.1 percent, is 5.0 percentage points below the 1993 rate (21.5 percent), but about 3.5 points above its 1969 historical low (12.7 percent). Likewise, the 2000 rate for residents of nonmetropolitan areas, 13.4 percent, is about 4 percentage points below its 1993 rate (17.2 percent) and just about at its 1978 historical low (13.5 percent).[1]

Even though per capita income was higher in the late 1990s than in the late 1960s, the average inflation-adjusted wage of production workers was lower. After a continued increase that ended in October 1972, workers' hourly earnings fell 13 percent between 1972 and 1993. Since 1993, earnings have been rising. Average hourly earnings in October 2000 were $13.88 per hour, 7 percent above the rate of October 1993, but still below the October 1972 peak. These data include male and female workers of all ages and with all levels of work experience. Welfare recipients, on average, earned much less than the average wage because they were younger, less-experienced, and had fewer years of schooling and less labor market skills than the average worker.

The trend in women's earnings is somewhat better than that for all workers because the labor market changes of the last three decades have disproportionately hurt less-skilled males. However, a review of trends in the annual earnings of single mothers suggests that a typical welfare recipient is likely to have a difficult time earning enough to support her family. The top line in Figure 1.1 shows median real annual earnings (in 1998 constant dollars) from 1967–1998 for single mothers between the ages of 18 and 64 who report earnings.[2] In 1998, their median annual earnings were $16,352, just about the poverty line for a family of four. The bottom line shows the trend for a single mother at the 20th percentile of the annual earnings distribution and better represents the earnings prospects of welfare recipients, whose educational attainment and skills are significantly lower than those of the median single mother. Over these three decades, annual earnings at the 20th percentile increased 56 percent, from $4,590 to $7,154, with more than half of this increase occurring between 1994 and 1998.

If one focuses only on women who work full-time (data not shown), one finds that a single mother of three children at the 20th percentile, with earnings as her only source of income, would escape poverty only if she worked full-time, full-year. As discussed below, however, most women leaving welfare for work do not work full-time, full-year. Thus, if they are to escape poverty, they must continue to rely on government income supplements, such as food stamps, the Earned Income Tax Credit, and subsidies for day care and health care expenses.

In sum, the longest peacetime economic expansion in history did

**Figure 1.1  Annual Real Earnings of Single Mothers, Ages 18–64, 1967–98 (nonearners excluded)**

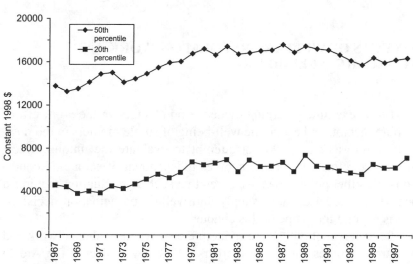

SOURCE: Computations from annual March Current Population Surveys, provided by Deborah Reed, Public Policy Institute of California.

not manage to restore the poverty rate and average wage rate to the levels achieved three decades ago. We have never been wealthier as a nation, but millions of families still have difficulty making ends meet. For single mothers, moving from welfare to work is a necessary, but not sufficient, first step along the path out of poverty. The strong work incentives and work requirements of the 1996 act have, to date, produced only a small decline in the national poverty rate because welfare mothers have relatively low earnings prospects. Despite our national commitment to encouraging work, we have in place a safety net that does little to provide work opportunities for those who have trouble finding a job or working full-time, full-year. This brief review of labor market trends suggests that reducing poverty in the post-welfare-reform era for both single mothers and poor families not receiving welfare requires government to increase income supplements for low earners and provide some employment opportunities for those left behind despite a robust economic recovery.

## EFFECTS OF WELFARE REFORM ON WORK AND ECONOMIC WELL-BEING

I now examine emerging evidence on changes in the work effort, welfare receipt, and economic well-being of single mothers in the post-welfare-reform era.  I do not attempt to evaluate the unique effects of welfare reform on these outcomes independent of economic conditions and other policy changes, given that such an evaluation requires a behavioral model of labor supply and welfare participation decisions that is beyond the scope of this chapter.

Several recent policy and economic changes have shaped work and welfare outcomes for single mothers.  First, by replacing the Aid to Families with Dependent Children program with the Temporary Assistance for Needy Families (TANF) program, PRWORA dramatically reduced the likelihood that a single mother can "choose" to remain a nonworking welfare recipient, even if she finds that the economic benefits of working do not exceed its costs.  There is no longer an entitlement to cash assistance; welfare is a transitional program with cash assistance conditional on the performance of work-related or community service activities.  In most states, a recipient who refuses to take an available, low-wage job will be sanctioned.

On the other hand, many states have expanded policies that allow recipients to combine work and welfare, notably by increasing earnings disregards so that recipients can have some earnings that do not directly offset their welfare benefits (Acs et al. 1998; Gallagher et al. 1998).  Taken together, changes in welfare policy have led more recipients to look for work, have made it more difficult for nonworking recipients to remain on the rolls, and have increased the financial benefit for recipients to work part-time at low-wage jobs (Corcoran et al. 2000; Danziger et al. 2000a).

Other policy changes have increased the returns from work for all low earners.  The minimum wage was increased from $4.25 to $5.15 in 1997, just after welfare reform was implemented.  In 1993, President

Clinton proposed and Congress passed a major expansion of the Earned Income Tax Credit (EITC). In 1998, a working single mother was eligible for a maximum EITC of $2,272 if she had one child and of $3,756 if she had two or more children. The Children's Health Insurance Program (CHIP) of 1997 subsidizes health care for children of the working poor, thereby making jobs that do not provide health care coverage more attractive to women leaving welfare. Finally, as noted above, the labor market in the late 1990s was much tighter than it had been for years, making it easier for welfare mothers to find jobs.

Against this background of state and federal public policy and economic changes, welfare caseloads fell dramatically after the mid 1990s. Some of this decline is undoubtedly due to welfare reform, some to the nonwelfare policy changes, some to the booming economy, and some to the interactions among them (Danziger 1999).

**National Trends by Residence**

Table 1.1 presents March Current Population Survey data for selected years between 1969 and 1998 on trends in the work effort, welfare receipt, median welfare income, and the poverty rate of single mothers ages 18–54 who have at least one child residing with them. Data are shown separately for residents of central cities, residents living in metropolitan areas but not within central cities, and nonmetropolitan area residents. The patterns for each variable are strikingly similar regardless of place of residence. Between 1969 and 1989, work effort, welfare receipt, and the family poverty rate were relatively stable. By 1998, however, work effort had increased substantially, welfare receipt declined dramatically, and poverty declined modestly in most residential groups.

For single mothers who worked (i.e., who reported earnings) at some time during the year, work effort was roughly constant for each residential group in 1969, 1979, and 1989; in 1998, work increased by about 12.5 percentage points for central city residents and by about 8 percentage points for the other groups. In 1998, median earnings were about $14,000 for single mothers residing in central cities and nonmetro areas and about $20,000 for those living in the noncentral city portion of metro areas (earnings data not shown).

The trend in the percentage of single mothers reporting cash wel-

**Table 1.1  Trends in Work, Welfare Receipt, and Poverty for Single
Mothers with Children, by Residence**

| Economic outcome | Central city | Remainder of metro | Nonmetro |
|---|---|---|---|
| Percent reporting earnings during the year | | | |
| 1969 | 64.7 | 74.6 | 73.4 |
| 1979 | 65.5 | 78.2 | 73.4 |
| 1989 | 64.3 | 78.2 | 76.0 |
| 1998 | 76.8 | 86.6 | 84.3 |
| Percent reporting welfare during the year | | | |
| 1969 | 41.2 | 21.1 | 27.3 |
| 1979 | 42.9 | 27.7 | 28.6 |
| 1989 | 41.2 | 21.8 | 28.0 |
| 1998 | 27.9 | 14.0 | 16.5 |
| Median welfare income of recipients ($1998) | | | |
| 1969 | 8,837 | 8,539 | 4,600 |
| 1979 | 6,978 | 6,168 | 4,414 |
| 1989 | 5,048 | 4,454 | 3,423 |
| 1998 | 3,108 | 2,844 | 2,400 |
| Official family poverty rate (%) | | | |
| 1969 | 47.8 | 32.4 | 48.8 |
| 1979 | 48.9 | 28.8 | 40.0 |
| 1989 | 52.2 | 31.6 | 49.3 |
| 1998 | 48.0 | 30.8 | 43.3 |

NOTE: Single mothers include women between the ages of 18 and 54 who are never-
married, divorced, separated, or widowed and reside with at least one child under the
age of 18. Each family is counted once; data are weighted. Because of confidentiality reasons, especially in small states, some observations are listed as "residence not
identified"; those observations are excluded.

SOURCE: Computations by author from March Current Population Survey computer
tapes.

fare receipt at some time during the year was quite similar to earnings trends. Welfare receipt was similar for each residential group in 1969, 1979, and 1989 (the rate of welfare receipt is higher in every year among central city residents); by 1998, it had declined by 13.2 percentage points for central city residents and by about 8–12 points for the other two groups.

Median welfare benefits, adjusted for inflation, fell dramatically over the three decades for all groups. In 1998, annual welfare income for recipients was about $3,100 per year for central city residents, $2,800 for those living in the non-central-city portion of metro areas, and $2,400 for residents of nonmetro areas.

Poverty rates increased some between 1969 and 1989, but by 1998, they were about the same as in 1969 and 1979 for single mothers residing in central cities and somewhat above the 1979 rates for residents of the suburbs and nonmetro areas. Between 1989 and 1998, poverty rates fell, but by a smaller amount than the decline in welfare receipt— by about 4 percentage points for single mothers residing in central cities, 1 point for suburban residents, and 6 points for residents of nonmetro areas.

## Detailed Results from a Post–Welfare Reform Panel Study of Michigan Residents

I now analyze data on work effort and economic well-being following welfare reform from the first two waves of the Women's Employment Study (WES) of the Poverty Research and Training Center at the University of Michigan (see Danziger et al. 2000b for more information on the study). I examine the relationship between human capital and other personal characteristics and work effort, and I evaluate differences in economic well-being between workers and nonworkers.

All respondents were first observed as welfare recipients. The women were systematically selected with equal probability from an ordered list of single mothers with children who received cash assistance in an urban Michigan county in February 1997. To be eligible, they had to be U.S. citizens between the ages of 18 and 54, and be either Caucasian or African American. At the time the sample was drawn, their average number of years of welfare receipt since turning age 18 was 7.3. Interviews were conducted in fall 1997 and in fall 1998. The response rate was 86 percent for the first wave ($N$ = 753) and 92 percent for the second wave of the panel ($N$ = 693 who participated in both waves).  Both interviews lasted approximately one hour.[3]

## Work and welfare outcomes

The study gathered information on a variety of problems that might affect a woman's likelihood of moving into the workforce and finding and a keeping job.  We included traditional human capital measures, such as whether the recipient had completed high school, the extent of her labor force skills, and previous work experience.  We also included measures of a range of mental and physical health problems, access to automobiles, perceptions of previous experiences of discrimination, and other psychosocial and familial attributes.

The fall 1998 interviews, which occurred roughly 20 months after the initial sample was drawn, allow us to evaluate differences between women who are working and those who are not about two years after PRWORA was introduced.  Table 1.2 lists our measures of 14 barriers to employment.  The first five barriers are measured only at wave 1 because any changes in their prevalence are likely to have occurred in response to work effort changes between waves 1 and 2.  For example, if a woman at wave 1 had not performed at least four of the nine work tasks on a previous job, we classified her as having low skills.  The only way for her to have low skills at wave 1 and not at wave 2 was for her to have acquired those skills while working on a job between the two waves.  The next nine barriers are evaluated at both waves; they describe conditions that may be episodic.  In this chapter, a woman is counted as having these barriers only if they were present at both waves.  At wave 1, we found that most of these barriers were negatively and significantly related to the likelihood that a respondent was working at least 20 hours per week (Danziger et al. 2000a).

Most barriers to employment are also correlated with whether or not a woman was working at the time of the wave 2 interview and the extent of her work involvement between the two waves.  The columns in Table 1.3 classify 675 of the 693 women who completed both surveys into one of four mutually exclusive categories based on their work and welfare income status in fall 1998 (the 18 women who are excluded had moved from welfare to the Supplemental Security Income pro-

**Table 1.2  Measures of Employment Barriers**

Education, work experience, job skills, and workplace norms (at wave 1)
1.  Less than a high school education
2.  Low work experience (worked in fewer than 20 percent of years since age 18)
3.  Fewer than 4 job skills on a previous job (out of a possible 9)
4.  Knows 5 or fewer work norms (out of a possible 9)

Perceived discrimination (at wave 1)
5.  Reports 4 or more instances of prior discrimination on the basis of race, gender, or welfare status (out of a possible 16)

Transportation problem (at both waves)
6.  Does not have access to a car and/or does not have a driver's license

Psychiatric disorders and substance dependence within past year (at both waves)
7.  Major depressive disorder
8.  PTSD – Post-traumatic stress disorder
9.  Generalized anxiety disorder or social phobia
10. Alcohol dependence
11. Drug dependence

Physical health problems (at both waves)
12. Mother's health problem (self-reported fair/poor health and age-specific physical limitation)
13. Child health problem (has a health, learning, or emotional problem)

Domestic violence (at both waves)
14. Severe abuse from a partner within past year

gram by fall 1998 and hence were not expected to work).[4]  We define *wage-reliant mothers* as those who reported positive earnings but no cash assistance in the month prior to the interview; they are 43.6 percent of the sample ($N = 294$).[5]  The next group includes *combiners*, women who reported both earnings and cash assistance in the month prior to the interview; they make up 27.1 percent of respondents ($N = 183$). We define *welfare-reliant mothers* as those who reported no income

**Table 1.3 Prevalence of Employment Barriers, by Work and Welfare Status**

| Barrier | All respondents (N = 675) | Wage-reliant[a] (N = 294) | Combiners[b] (N =183) | Welfare-reliant[c] (N = 138) | No work/ no welfare[d] (N = 60) |
|---|---|---|---|---|---|
| Measured at wave 1 (%) | | | | | |
| Less than high school education | 31.2 | 22.8 | 32.2 | 45.7 | 35.6 |
| Low work experience | 14.8 | 9.9 | 11.0 | 27.5 | 20.3 |
| Fewer than 4 skills | 20.6 | 18.0 | 13.7 | 33.3 | 25.0 |
| Fewer than 5 work norms | 9.2 | 7.5 | 11.0 | 11.7 | 6.7 |
| 4+ experiences of discrimination | 13.8 | 11.9 | 11.5 | 18.8 | 18.3 |
| Present at both waves (%) | | | | | |
| Transportation barrier | 30.2 | 21.1 | 27.3 | 52.2 | 33.3 |
| Psychiatric diagnosis[e] | 16.1 | 10.9 | 15.8 | 24.6 | 23.3 |
| Alcohol or drug dependence | 1.3 | 1.4 | 1.6 | 0.7 | 1.7 |
| Health barrier | 10.6 | 8.5 | 5.0 | 19.6 | 16.7 |
| Child health barrier | 10.3 | 7.5 | 8.2 | 17.6 | 13.8 |
| Domestic violence | 6.1 | 3.7 | 7.7 | 8.7 | 6.7 |
| Mean number of barriers (11 total) | 1.5 | 1.2 | 1.4 | 2.3 | 2.0 |

[a] Wage-reliant are mothers relying only on earnings to support their families; they made up 43.6% of sample.
[b] Combiners were those receiving both earnings and welfare; they made up 27.1% of the sample.
[c] Welfare-reliant mothers relied only on welfare (they were not working) and made up 20.4% of the sample.
[d] No work/no welfare were those receiving neither welfare nor earnings from work; they made up 8.9% of the sample.
[e] Coded "1" if respondent had depression, generalized anxiety, or post-traumatic stress disorder at wave 1, and depression, social phobia, or post-traumatic stress disorder at wave 2.
SOURCE: Computations by author from Women's Employment Study.

from earnings in the month prior to the interview, but who reported receiving income from TANF; they represent 20.4 percent of respondents ($N = 138$). The remaining 8.9 percent ($N = 60$) of the sample includes women who were neither working nor receiving TANF benefits in fall 1998.

Table 1.3 shows how women in these work-welfare income categories differ in the prevalence of barriers. The last row shows the mean number of barriers for women in each of the categories. In this table, we combine the separate diagnoses for psychiatric disorders into a single variable and alcohol and substance dependence into a single variable.

The results are quite dramatic. The women who are wage-reliant at wave 2 are much less likely to have most of these barriers to employment, and the women who were not working at wave 2 (right-most two columns) are much more likely to face barriers. The welfare-reliant mothers have the highest prevalence on 10 of the 11 barriers (although some of these differences are not significant). These differences are present for human capital, mental health, and health barriers. For example, 22.8 percent of the wage-reliant have less than a high school degree, compared with 45.7 percent of the welfare-reliant. In addition, 10.9 percent of the wage-reliant met diagnostic screening criteria for at least one of the three psychiatric disorders we asked about at both waves. In contrast, 24.6 percent of the welfare-reliant met such criteria.

These results suggest caution in simply classifying welfare recipients as "stayers" or "leavers" in the aftermath of PRWORA, as has been done in most recent studies. Table 1.3 documents substantial differences in the extent of barriers between leavers who are wage-reliant and those who are not working (no work/no welfare), and substantial difference between stayers who are working (combiners) and those who are not (welfare-reliant). In fact, those who are working (wage-reliant and combiners) and those who are not working (the welfare-reliant and those neither working nor receiving cash assistance) are similar to each other in terms of their mean number of barriers. The former two working groups average 1.2 and 1.4 barriers, respectively, whereas nonworkers average 2.3 and 2, respectively.

Figure 1.2 graphs the relationship between the number of barriers

**Figure 1.2  Persistent Employment Barriers, by Percentage of Months
Worked between Wave 1 and Wave 2**

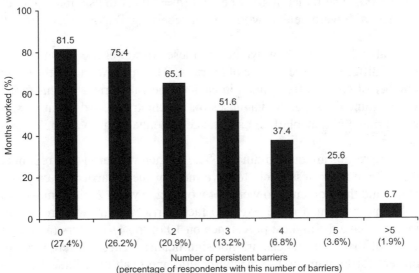

NOTE: The "Number of Persistent Barriers" is a count of wave 1 measures of high
   school education, work experience, skills, work norms, and discrimination; and two-
   wave measures of transportation, mental health, substance dependence, health, child
   health, and domestic violence (see Table 1.3).
SOURCE: Computations by author from Women's Employment Study data.

and the extent of work, measured by the percentage of months a respondent worked between the two surveys.[6] The percentage of months
worked falls from 81.5 percent for respondents who did not have any of
the barriers (27.4 percent of the sample) to only 6.7 percent for the 1.9
percent of the sample with six or more barriers. A respondent with two
barriers worked, on average, in about two-thirds of the months, whereas a respondent with four barriers worked in fewer than two-fifths of
the months. This pattern of declining work as the extent of barriers increases is remarkably similar to the pattern we observed for those who
were working at least 20 hours per week at the first wave of the survey
(Danziger et al. 2000b).

   Despite a booming economy and pressures from state agencies to find jobs, it has been difficult for many of these current and former welfare recipients to stay employed. About two-fifths of respondents worked in every month between the fall 1997 and fall 1998 surveys, whereas 13 percent did not work in a single month. The percentage working in any month between the two waves varied little, ranging from 60 percent to 70 percent. One reason that poverty has not declined as fast as the caseload is that few former recipients are working full-time, full-year. In addition, as the next section shows, poverty among the respondents remains high.

### Financial well-being

Given that a majority of respondents was working in fall 1998, I now evaluate the extent to which "work pays," that is, whether working respondents have higher incomes than nonworking welfare recipients. Respondents were asked to report, for the month before the interview, their work hours, earnings, welfare receipt, and income from a variety of sources. These sources include the earnings of other household members, cash assistance from TANF, food stamps, Social Security and other pension and disability income, Supplemental Security Income (SSI), unemployment compensation, child support, cash contributions from other household members and from outside friends and family, and any other income not previously mentioned.[7] We also asked about expenses for work-related child care and transportation. We also have information on cash assistance received from official records of Michigan's Family Independence Agency.

Table 1.4 presents two measures of mean monthly income and the monthly poverty rate in fall 1998 for respondents, classified by their work/welfare income status in the survey month (see Danziger et al. 2001 for greater detail on financial well-being). Monthly income is the sum of work-based income, welfare-based income, and income from other sources, less work-related child care and transportation expenses. In addition to the reported income sources, we imputed the value of federal taxes paid, the EITC, and the employee's share of Social Security taxes. We imputed the value of federal taxes paid and the value of the EITC received based on respondents' own earnings, unemployment insurance, marital status, and number of children.[8] The employee's share of Social Security taxes is 7.65 percent of reported earnings.[9] Be-

**Table 1.4  Monthly Income and Monthly Poverty Rate, by Work and Welfare Status**

| Receipt in month prior to fall 1998 interview | All respondents (N = 675) | Wage-reliant[a] (N = 294) | Combiners[b] (N =183) | Welfare-reliant[c] (N = 138) | No work/no welfare[d] (N = 60) |
|---|---|---|---|---|---|
| Net income, excluding earnings of household members other than husbands ($) | 1,213 | 1,405 | 1,277 | 892 | 798 |
| Net income, including earnings from all household members ($) | 1,418 | 1,677 | 1,449 | 1,027 | 1,178 |
| Poverty rate using row 1 income concept (%) | 61.2 | 47.4 | 55.3 | 91.1 | 78.6 |
| Poverty rate[e] using row 2 income concept (%) | 53.5 | 38.4 | 50.3 | 83.3 | 68.3 |

[a] Wage-reliant are mothers relying only on earnings to support their families; they made up 43.6% of sample.
[b] Combiners were those receiving both earnings and welfare; they made up 27.1% of the sample.
[c] Welfare-reliant mothers relied only on welfare (they were not working) and made up 20.4% of the sample.
[d] No work/no welfare were those receiving neither welfare nor earnings from work; they made up 8.9% of the sample.
[e] To determine the monthly poverty rate, the official poverty line was divided by 12 and compared with monthly income.
SOURCE: Computations by author from Women's Employment Study data.

fore turning to the results, I discuss differences in receipt of the various income sources.

By definition, all wage-reliant women and all women combining work and welfare had earnings in the interview month, whereas welfare-reliant mothers and those not working and not receiving welfare did not. Wage-reliant mothers earned more per month than did combiners—$987 versus $626 (data not shown). Compared with combiners, wage-reliant mothers were more likely to be working at least 35 hours per week (66 percent vs. 37 percent), and they earned a higher average hourly wage ($7.63 vs. $6.52). Almost every working mother in the sample was eligible for the EITC. We estimate that wage-reliant mothers received, on average, $202 per month; combiners received $191. Federal income and Social Security taxes decreased the earnings of wage-reliant mothers by $142 per month and those of combiners by $78 per month.

Substantial numbers of respondents co-resided with another household member who worked. About 35 percent of wage-reliant mothers, 21 percent of combiners, 17 percent of welfare-reliant mothers, and 52 percent of those neither working nor receiving welfare lived in a household with an additional earner. These other earners, many of whom are husbands or cohabiting partners, earned on average more than the respondents.

All welfare-reliant mothers and combiners, by definition, received TANF benefits that averaged $441 and $275 per month, respectively.[10] Welfare-reliant mothers and combiners were much more likely to receive food stamps than wage-reliant mothers and those not working and not receiving cash assistance—about 90 percent of the former two groups, compared to about half of the latter two groups. The average value of food stamps ranged from $182–$240 across the groups.

Wage-reliant women had higher child care and transportation costs than did welfare-reliant women. The majority of both groups of working mothers (77 percent of wage-reliant mothers and 64 percent of combiners) reported work-related transportation expenses that averaged $74 and $63 per month, respectively. Slightly more than one-quarter of the two groups of working mothers reported out-of-pocket child care expenses that averaged $264 to $316 per month.[11]

Table 1.4 presents two measures of monthly income. First, income from all sources (excluding the earnings of household members other than husbands) is summed, the EITC is added, and income and payroll taxes are subtracted, as are work-related transportation and child care expenses.  This measure does not include the earnings of household members other than husbands because we do not know the extent to which these members actually share their earnings with the respondents. In the second measure of monthly income, these earnings are included.

The average net monthly income (first row) was $1,405 for wage-reliant mothers, $1,277 for combiners, $892 for welfare-reliant mothers, and $798 for those neither working nor receiving welfare.  Adding the earnings of all household members raised these averages to $1,677, $1,449, $1,027, and $1,178, respectively.  Because a larger percentage of the women who neither worked nor received welfare live with another earner who is not their husband, the increase in their income between rows 1 and 2 is greater than the increase for the other three groups.

For both measures, working mothers have a substantial income advantage over welfare-reliant mothers.  When the earnings of household members other than husbands are excluded, average net income for wage-reliant mothers was 58 percent higher than that of the welfare-reliant.  When the earnings of other household members are included, wage-reliant mothers had an average net income that was 63 percent higher than that of the welfare-reliant.  Women combining work and welfare had net incomes (second row) 41 percent higher than those of the welfare-reliant.  Thus, in the post-PRWORA era, it does pay to move from welfare to work.

Table 1.4 also presents the monthly poverty rates for the four groups of respondents (we divide the official 1998 federal poverty threshold for a household of that size by 12).  A large portion of workers remain poor.  When earnings of household members other than husbands are excluded, 47.4 percent of wage-reliant mothers, 55.3 percent of combiners, 91.1 percent of welfare-reliant mothers, and 78.6 percent of those who neither worked nor received welfare were poor.  When earnings of all household members are included, the poverty rates for the wage-reliant, combiners, the welfare-reliant, and those neither working nor receiving welfare fall to 38.4 percent, 50.3 percent, 83.3 percent, and 68.3 percent, respectively.

The good news is that poverty is much lower for both income measures among workers than among nonworkers. In addition, about 80 percent of the wage-reliant mothers earn more than the maximum TANF benefit in Michigan (a state that has above-average benefit levels). The bad news is that poverty remains very high for workers. Also, the annual poverty rate for the wage-reliant and combiners is higher than Table 1.4 indicates because most of them do not work in every month, and hence do not earn this much in every month.[12]

We have not attempted to determine the extent to which these differences in poverty rates are due to welfare policy changes, the very favorable economic climate, or other policy changes. In Michigan, however, the decision of the state to allow recipients an earnings disregard (the first $200 of monthly earnings does not reduce welfare benefits; welfare is reduced by 80 cents for every additional dollar earned) and the absence of a time limit have encouraged women to combine work and welfare. Women whose earnings would have disqualified them from cash assistance a decade ago can now receive some welfare benefits. Even if the cash benefit amount is small, its receipt increases the likelihood that a respondent will continue to receive food stamps and Medicaid. In addition, the tight labor market has made it easier for respondents to get and keep jobs. Nonetheless, most working respondents are not escaping poverty on their paychecks alone, and a substantial fraction of the wage-reliant and combiners continue to receive government assistance (e.g., TANF, food stamps, EITC), or to rely on cash contributions from friends and family, or both.

Several implications concerning welfare reform follow from these findings. First, in a booming economy, most welfare recipients can find some work and many can escape poverty. In addition, the economic incentives now in place are in accord with the goals of policy planners—on average, wage-reliant mothers and those combining work and welfare are economically better off than welfare-reliant mothers. Second, these results suggest that more attention should be paid to factors that prevent some of the welfare-reliant from finding steady employment. The new economic incentives and the increased pressure to leave the welfare rolls make it unlikely that many welfare-reliant mothers are rejecting work and choosing to stay on welfare. Rather, as shown in Table 1.3 and Figure 1.2, many of them have multiple problems, such as poor physical or mental health or lack of job skills, which prevent them from getting and keeping jobs even when unemployment rates are low.

Third, in the aftermath of welfare reform, many welfare-reliant mothers are at high risk of losing their welfare benefits owing to impending sanctions or time limits. In many states, mothers combining work and welfare are also at risk of losing benefits owing to impending time limits. Now that it is economically beneficial to move from welfare to work, there remains a need for policies to make work pay enough so that a greater percentage of working mothers can escape poverty and for enhanced policies to help welfare-reliant mothers move into regular jobs or into subsidized employment.

## POLICY IMPLICATIONS

In 1959, Robert J. Lampman testified to the Joint Economic Committee of Congress that

> [a] more aggressive government policy could hasten the elimination of poverty and bring about its virtual elimination in one generation. A program directed against poverty should be of several parts. The basic part should be one of insuring high levels of employment and increasing average product per worker. This should be supplemented by special private and public programs for those groups who do not readily share in the benefits of economic progress . . . Almost a fifth of the nation's children are being reared in low-income status, and it is critical in the strategy against poverty that these children have educational opportunities that are not inferior to the national average. The costs of such a program would be offset by positive gains in terms of both economic and human values. (Lampman 1959, pp. 4–5)

Unfortunately, 40 years later, the very same aggressive policies are needed if our generation is to "hasten the elimination of poverty." Despite unprecedented prosperity, more than one-fifth of the nation's children are now being reared in poverty. Despite self-accolades about our compassion, as a nation we do not even discuss, much less pursue, an "aggressive policy" to "hasten the elimination of poverty."

Declining employer demand for less-skilled workers means that their wage rates remain low and poverty stays high even when labor markets are tight.  Additional policy responses are required if we are to ensure that a single mother working full-time at the minimum wage will have an income above the poverty line, after accounting for taxes paid, work-related expenses, and tax credits received.   Policies to achieve this goal can be implemented if we are willing to spend government funds on them.

Any social welfare system produces errors of commission and omission.  The pre-1996 welfare system did provide cash assistance to some recipients who could have made it on their own in the labor market.  Some welfare recipients were unwilling to look for a job, others turned down job offers because the wages were low or because they did not provide health insurance.  Others chose to stay at home to care for their children.  The 1996 law reflects the expectations of policymakers and taxpayers that anyone offered a minimum-wage job should accept it.  Indeed, the law allows states to curtail benefits for anyone who does not search for work or cooperate with the welfare agency.

However, the law does not reflect the fact that finding a job has become more difficult for less-skilled workers over the past three decades.  The early results from welfare reform reviewed here suggest that many recipients are likely to reach time limits without finding stable jobs even if economic conditions remain as favorable as they were at the end of the 1990s.  They will be terminated from cash assistance even if they are willing to work, either because they cannot find any employer to hire them or because their personal attributes make it unlikely that they can work steadily.  This problem will increase during recessions and will persist even in good economic times because employers continue to escalate their demands for a skilled workforce.

Because I support a work-oriented safety net, I am not suggesting a return to the pre-1996 welfare status quo.  Welfare recipients and the unemployed should have the personal responsibility to look for work.  However, if they diligently search for work without finding a job, assistance should not be terminated.  At a minimum, those who are willing to work but unable to find jobs should be offered an opportunity to perform community service in return for continued welfare benefits.  A more costly option, but one that would have a greater antipoverty impact, would be to provide low-wage public service "jobs of last resort" (see Danziger and Gottschalk 1995, Chapter 8).

Data from the panel study from a Michigan county also suggest that many welfare recipients face multiple barriers to employment— e.g., health and mental health problems, low education, and low job skills. Some will need greater access to treatment and social services before they can even take advantage of community service employment. Many could benefit from relatively modest changes in current work-first programs, such as increased emphasis on and support for job retention services.

For people who are able to find jobs, the key elements of a policy to "make work pay and end poverty as we know it" are expanded wage supplements, refundable child care tax credits, extensions of transitional Medicaid, and a higher minimum wage. The Earned Income Tax Credit, which was substantially expanded in 1993, has done much to offset the decline in real wages for workers at the bottom of the earnings distribution who work year-round and who have children (Ellwood 1999). Further increases in the EITC, for example for married couples, absent fathers, and families with three or more children, would make the federal income tax more progressive and increase the EITC's already large antipoverty impact. Several states have adopted their own EITCs for families with children, something other states should consider, especially those that continue to impose income and high sales taxes on the working poor.

Many of the working poor spend a substantial portion of their earnings on child care. The Dependent Care Credit (DCC) in the federal income tax should be made refundable; doing so would raise the disposable income of low-income working families who spend substantial sums on child care but who do not benefit from the way this nonrefundable credit is currently structured.

In addition, in the Michigan study, almost one-third of welfare leavers had no health insurance for themselves in fall 1998; they had exhausted their transitional Medicaid benefits and were either not covered by their employer or could not afford the monthly payments. Extending transitional Medicaid further or expanding CHIP to include parents who are former welfare recipients would help address this problem. Finally, the minimum wage should be increased. Congress has seemed ready to adopt such an increase since 1999, although it had not acted by early 2001.

The 1996 welfare reform increased work expectations and demands for personal responsibility on the part of welfare recipients. Now it is time to increase demands on government for mutual responsibility. What is required if we are to reduce poverty as well as welfare dependency is an increased willingness to spend public funds to develop a work-oriented safety net.

# Notes

This research was supported in part by grants from the Charles Stewart Mott, Joyce, and John D. and Catherine T. MacArthur foundations and by Grant No. R24-MH51363 from the National Institute of Mental Health. Nath Anderson, Nancy Collins, and Elizabeth Oltmans provided valuable research assistance; Nath Anderson, Scott Allard, Colleen Heflin, Rucker Johnson, Kristin Seefeldt, and Bruce Weber provided helpful comments on a previous draft.

1. In a time-series regression analysis (not shown), the nonmetro poverty rate is estimated to be more responsive to increases in national per capita income than is the central city poverty rate. The central city rate is more responsive to changes in the national unemployment rate.
2. These data are based on computations from the March Current Population Surveys by Deborah Reed, Public Policy Institute of California. The sample includes unmarried female heads of household with at least one co-resident child under 18, who were in the civilian labor force and had at least $1 of earnings. Students, those whose primary job is unpaid, and the self-employed are excluded.
3. A third interview was fielded during fall/winter 1999/2000, with a response rate of 91 percent; a fourth interview in fall 2001 had a 90 percent response rate.
4. Wave 2 has data on 79 percent of the original sample, i.e., the product of the wave 1 and the wave 2 response rates: $0.86 \times 0.92$.
5. Our use of income sources during a single month may overstate well-being differences across the groups if earnings are less stable than welfare income. We examined alternative classifications in which mothers were considered wage-reliant and welfare-reliant only if they were in these categories for three consecutive months. The results do not differ much from those presented here.
6. The number of months between a respondent's wave 1 and wave 2 interviews ranged from 8 to 16 months (each survey period lasted about four months). The mean number of months between interviews was 11.6.
7. Supplemental Security Income (SSI) reported by respondents and included in Table 1.4 was received by their children or another household member; respondents who received SSI on their own are excluded from the analyses.
8. We estimated the monthly EITC and monthly federal income taxes by using monthly income sources as proxies for annual income (i.e., we multiply monthly income from own earnings and unemployment insurance by 12 months). The

credit was calculated using only respondent's earned income and our estimates of adjusted gross income (which includes unemployment insurance). Eligibility was determined by the number of children and amount and source of income. We assumed that no untaxed earned income, interest and dividends, student loan interest, or scholarship income was received, and no IRA deductions were paid by respondents. We assumed income reported in the category of "disability, pension or social security income" reflected Social Security benefits or pension income of other household members and is therefore nontaxable to the respondent. We assumed that respondents file returns with themselves and their children as a single tax unit and excluded other household members' income if the respondents were not married. If they were married, we included husband's earnings.

9.  We also adjusted for state income taxes and for the credit, which Michigan provides working renters through the state income tax. Danziger et al. (2001) describe each income source, tax, tax credit, and expense category.

10. We used administrative data for TANF income rather than self reports, because the latter tend to be too low for women whose rent or utilities are vendored (i.e., paid directly to the landlord or utility company). For example, in fall 1998, almost 15 percent of welfare recipients had their rent vendored. On the other hand, for some respondents, the administrative record value of the TANF benefit is too high. Because the state pays benefits "prospectively," a woman who just starts a job or increases her hours of work, will later have her TANF payment adjusted downward and the state would recover the overpayment.

11. The percentage of working mothers who reported child care expenses were low because many received subsidized child care and/or relied upon friends and family members or had no young children. In Michigan, child care subsidies are available for all welfare recipients and for working families whose incomes fall below 85 percent of the state's median income. Child care costs were higher for wage-reliant mothers than for combiners, in part, because the former worked, on average, 6 more hours per week on all jobs.

12. The wage-reliant and combiners worked in almost 75 percent of the months between February 1997, when the sample was drawn, and the wave 2 survey. Annual poverty rates would be somewhat lower for those not working at wave 2 because they worked in about 25 percent of the months over this period.

# References

Acs, Gregory, Norma Coe, Keith Watson, and Robert Lerman. 1998. *Does Work Pay? An Analysis of the Work Incentives under TANF*. Washington, D.C.: The Urban Institute.

Corcoran, Mary, Sandra K. Danziger, Ariel Kalil, and Kristin Seefeldt. 2000. "How Welfare Reform Is Affecting Women's Work." *Annual Review of Sociology* 26: 241–269.

Danziger, Sandra K., Mary Corcoran, Sheldon Danziger, and Colleen Heflin. 2000a. "Work, Income and Material Hardship after Welfare Reform." *Journal of Consumer Affairs* 34: 6–30.

Danziger, Sandra K., Mary Corcoran, Sheldon Danziger, Colleen Heflin, Ariel Kalil, Judith Levine, Daniel Rosen, Kristin Seefeldt, Kristine Siefert, and Richard Tolman. 2000b. "Barriers to the Employment of Welfare Recipients." In *Prosperity for All? The Economic Boom and African Americans*, R. Cherry and W. Rodgers, eds. New York: Russell Sage Foundation, pp. 239–277.

Danziger, Sheldon, ed. 1999. *Economic Conditions and Welfare Reform.* Kalamazoo, Michigan: W.E. Upjohn Institute for Employment Research.

Danziger, Sheldon, and Peter Gottschalk. 1995. *America Unequal.* Cambridge, Massachusetts: Harvard University Press.

Danziger, Sheldon, Colleen Heflin, Mary Corcoran, and Elizabeth Oltmans. 2001. "Does It Pay to Move from Welfare to Work?" University of Michigan working paper, available at <www.ssw.umich.edu/poverty/pubs.html>.

Ellwood, David. 1999. "The Impact of the Earned Income Tax Credit and Other Social Policy Changes on Work and Marriage in the United States." Working paper, Harvard University, Cambridge, Massachusetts.

Gallagher, L. Jerome, Megan Gallagher, Kevin Perese, Susan Schreiber, and Keith Watson. 1998. *One Year after Welfare Reform: A Description of State Temporary Assistance for Needy Families (TANF) Decisions as of October 1997.* Washington, D.C.: Urban Institute Press.

Jantti, Markus, and Sheldon Danziger. 2000. "Income Poverty in Advanced Economies." In *Handbook on Income Distribution*, Vol. 1, A.B. Atkinson and F. Bourguignon, eds. Amsterdam: Elsevier Science, pp. 309–377.

Lampman, Robert J. 1959. "The Low-Income Population and Economic Growth." U.S. Congress, Joint Economic Committee, Study Paper no. 12. Washington, D.C.: U.S. Government Printing Office.

# 2

# Rural Labor Markets in an Era of Welfare Reform

Robert M. Gibbs
*Economic Research Service, U.S. Department of Agriculture*

The 1996 welfare reform act placed employment in the formal workforce at the center of the nation's official response to poverty among families with working-age adults. In doing so, current welfare reform efforts necessarily emphasize the role of local labor markets as the means to escape poverty rather than as a prime contributor to its persistence. For many, the difference is not merely a semantic one, as increased willingness in some states to spend public funds on work supports for low-income welfare recipients attests (Long et al. 1998; National Rural Development Partnership 1998). Welfare reform has led to increased recognition that the ability to move people out of poverty relies largely on the ability of labor markets to generate a sufficient number of good jobs (Pavetti and Acs 1997; Gottschalk 2000).

Thus, reform has also re-energized attempts to understand the characteristics and processes that create and sustain low-wage, low-skill labor markets (Kaye and Nightingale 2000). The implications of this sea change are particularly important in rural America, where the share of workers in the low-wage, low-skill labor market is well above the nation's, and where past efforts to reduce poverty often confronted deep-rooted social and economic resistance (Gibbs and Parker 2000).[1] Recent rural economic trends suggest that solutions will not be easy. Despite a decade of steady economic expansion, rural labor market outcomes—job growth, unemployment rates, earnings, and wage progression among them—typically fall below the national average, and most show no signs of convergence. On average, it remains slightly harder

51

to get a job, and much harder to get a good-paying job, in a rural community.

This chapter describes the distinctive characteristics that constrain job availability and earnings in many rural labor markets and, in turn, affect the prospects for the economic success of welfare recipients. Crucial differences in rural and urban labor markets exist, particularly the limitations that low levels of formal education and rural job structures place on workers' upward occupational and wage mobility. Low pay and limited career ladders are endemic among rural people who feel the effects of welfare reform most acutely: i.e., women with less education or who belong to a racial or ethnic minority.

We begin with a brief overview of rural labor trends, which show improvement in some measures of labor force well-being during the 1990s. However, the rural trends also fail to converge with national indicators, especially during the urban-biased expansion of the late 1990s. The roots of enduring rural differences are found in the inherent qualities of small, sparse populations historically associated with extractive industries (mining and forestry, for example). Rural geography and history continue to shape labor markets in the form of a spatial division of labor reflected in their low education levels and relatively few opportunities for career advancement compared with complex urban skill and occupational hierarchies.

The second section of the chapter examines the implications of these distinctive rural features for job availability and family-sustaining earnings, particularly among women and minorities. We find a substantial overlap between areas where welfare reform is likely to affect a large share of the population and where jobs are relatively scarce. These areas also tend to be marked by low average earnings and a relative lack of good-paying jobs for less-educated adults, especially for rural women without a college education. Finally, the labor market prospects for less-educated, rural workers in an increasingly service-oriented economy are discussed.

## RECENT TRENDS IN THE RURAL LABOR FORCE

The steady expansion of the U.S. economy over the past 10 years provides the best possible conditions for welfare reform to move individuals into sustaining employment. Although rural employment growth has slowed since 1995, it remained robust enough at the end of 2000 to maintain downward pressure on unemployment. Rural unemployment rates have closely tracked the national decline since 1992 with few exceptions and, as of the fourth quarter of 2000, hovered just above 4 percent (Figure 2.1).

Economists have noted the generally modest upswing in earnings during the 1990s expansion, despite the lowest unemployment rates in 30 years. Statistics drawn from the Current Population Survey indicate a 10 percent gain in average weekly earnings between 1990 and 1999, after adjusting for inflation, for both rural and urban workers, a gain that is sizable by the standards of the previous decade. However, a similar measure, average earnings per nonfarm job, derived from data developed by the Bureau of Economic Analysis, shows that real rural earnings have changed little since the beginning of the 1990s (Figure 2.2).[2] Still, although the two data sources disagree slightly on trends, both show a persistently large gap of 25–30 percent between rural and urban earnings levels, which has changed little since the early 1980s. A portion of the gap is probably explained by lower costs of living in rural areas. A recent study, however, found that cost-of-living differences probably account for no more than half of the nominal earnings gap (Nord 2000).

Together, trends in unemployment and earnings point to the continuing distinctiveness of rural labor markets. In the face of strong eco-

**Figure 2.1  Unemployment Rates by Urban/Rural Status, 1991–99**

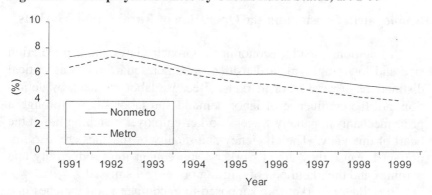

SOURCE: Calculated by ERS using data from the Bureau of Labor Statistics.

**Figure 2.2  Earnings per Nonfarm Job by Urban/Rural Status, 1991–99**

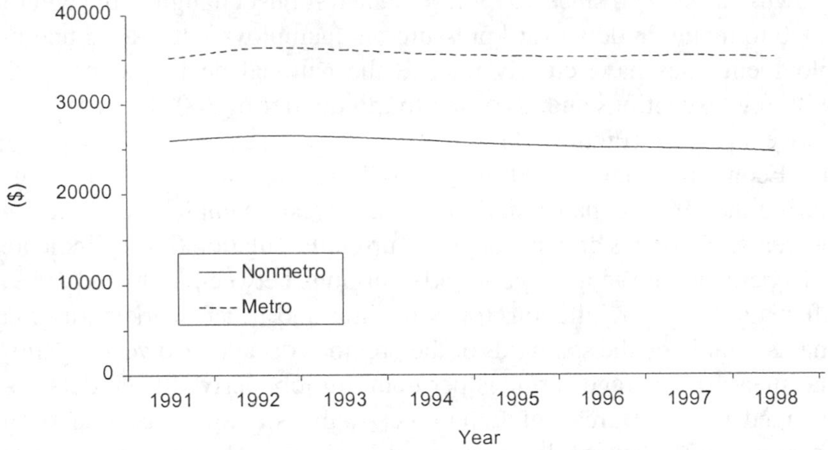

SOURCE: Calculated by ERS using data from the Bureau of Labor Statistics.

nomic growth, rural labor market outcomes have followed improving national patterns, without necessarily converging with urban levels. Moreover, a comparison of aggregate rural and urban trends presents a conservative view of the rural predicament with respect to welfare reform. Many of the demographic and economic groups most at risk of unemployment and low or stagnant earnings are found in disproportionate numbers in rural areas. Likewise, the overwhelming majority of high-unemployment or low-earnings counties are rural.

## Employment Density and the Operation of Rural Labor Markets

A traditional spatial economics approach views small population size and low employment densities (jobs per square mile) as critical distinctions of rural labor markets. Because labor markets, by definition, are the confluence of labor demand and labor supply through a price mechanism, namely wages, worker-employer matching lies at the heart of this view. The efficiency and quality of matches are also important because they affect workers' subsequent job productivity and earnings and the likelihood of quitting or being dismissed.

Rural labor markets are supposed to encourage good matches in a

number of ways.  Rural job seekers are considered more likely to find
employers (and vice versa) through informal methods—such as word
of mouth—than are those in urban labor markets, and searchers and
employers in rural areas are more likely to have personal knowledge of
one another with which to assess the quality of the match.  Because the
number of job openings at any given time is likely to be smaller in a rural labor market area, searchers can canvass and compare a larger share
of openings (Doeringer 1984; Rungeling, Smith, and Scott 1976).

Limited job openings in rural areas, however, may also constrain
the "goodness of fit" between worker and employer, and may require
the job searcher to look further afield or go without a new job for a
longer period of time.  Urban labor markets offer a wider variety of
jobs and a larger share with specialized skill requirements that are well
suited to particular individuals.  The small size of many rural labor
markets, on the other hand, means that the types of jobs available may
be less varied.  In addition, rural employers may give undue weight to
their personal "knowledge" of a job applicant.  With fewer employers
in a local labor market, a worker can be more easily marked as a problem employee.  Identifying problem workers improves productivity to
the extent that poor performers are less likely to find jobs, but it is troubling when searchers are rejected unfairly, as when recent labor force
entrants are denied sufficient opportunity to develop consistent work
habits.  In any event, the net effect of low job density on worker-employer matches is unclear.  This is unfortunate for rural welfare policy
analysts and points to an unmet need for research that applies rural job
search theory specifically to the low-wage, low-skill workforce (Goldstein and Gronberg 1984; Doeringer 1984).

Well-matched workers are more productive and, on average, earn
higher wages.  Rural wages are typically lower than urban wages, but
the impact of low density on worker-employer matches plays only a
small part in low rural wages.  Of greater importance are the forces that
generate rural/urban differences in economic activity and, therefore, in
the types of workers found in each.  Contemporary attempts to explain
the rural/urban division of labor draw mostly on variants of the urban
hierarchy or core-periphery models of regional economies.[3]  A widely
accepted version of this model views cities as engines of skills development.  The same processes of "cumulative causality" that give rise to
urban centers encourage skill specialization, linked in labor economics

with higher productivity. At the same time, cities usually serve their regions or nations as the hub of communication and transportation networks, promoting the labor functions associated with administration and other headquarter operations in manufacturing and services (Glaeser and Maré 1994; Lucas 1988).

These functions, and the jobs that accompany them, are less common in rural economies. Furthermore, rural goods and service production are geographically distant from the sources of innovation and initial product development. Rural production is often more routinized, demanding less training or education. Over time, rural areas have retained a relatively large share of the nation's low-skill, low-technology industries and less-skilled occupations (McGranahan and Ghelfi 1998; Norton and Rees 1979).

**Education and Rural Labor Supply**

The quintessential rural traits of low employment density and remoteness are inseparable from the historical reliance on natural resource-based, extractive industries, especially farming, but also mining, lumbering, and fishing. Although employment in these industries often entailed mastering a complex set of skills, they rarely required much formal education. Over time, differences in educational attainment became a hallmark of rural and urban economic divergence (Killian and Beaulieu 1995).

The oft-repeated assumption that rural education levels have for the most part caught up with urban levels is, in fact, overly optimistic. Table 2.1 compares decennial census data on rural and urban education attainment from 1960 to 1990. The 1990 census shows that only about one in eight rural adults over age 25 has a college degree, compared with more than one in five urban adults. The ratio of adults without a high school diploma to college graduates is nearly two to one in rural areas, compared with near parity in urban areas.

What is most remarkable about the rural/urban difference in education is its persistence despite 40 years of economic restructuring. Whether the difference is increasing is a matter of perception. On the one hand, Table 2.1 shows a widening rural/urban gap in college graduation through 1990, based on the simple difference in rural and urban rates. However, the rate of increase in the share of adults with a college

**Table 2.1  Urban and Rural Educational Attainment, 1960–99, for Persons 25 Years Old and over (%)**

| Year | <High school | | HS graduate | | Some college | | Graduate college | | Total | |
|---|---|---|---|---|---|---|---|---|---|---|
| | Metro | Nonmetro | Metro | Nonmetro | Metro | Nonmetro | Metro | Nonmetro | Metro | Nonmetro |
| 1960 | 56.8 | 66.1 | 25.5 | 21.7 | 9.2 | 7.1 | 8.5 | 5.1 | 100.0 | 100.0 |
| 1970 | 45.4 | 55.9 | 31.8 | 28.6 | 11.2 | 8.5 | 11.6 | 7.0 | 100.0 | 100.0 |
| 1980 | 31.3 | 41.7 | 34.5 | 35.0 | 16.5 | 12.5 | 17.7 | 10.8 | 100.0 | 100.0 |
| 1990 | 23.1 | 31.2 | 28.7 | 34.8 | 25.9 | 21.2 | 22.3 | 12.8 | 100.0 | 100.0 |
| 1991[a] | 15.2 | 20.3 | 31.6 | 39.7 | 25.3 | 24.1 | 27.9 | 15.9 | 100.0 | 100.0 |
| 1999[a] | 11.4 | 13.4 | 30.4 | 41.5 | 27.8 | 28.0 | 30.4 | 17.1 | 100.0 | 100.0 |

[a] Current Population Survey.
SOURCE: Census of the Population, 1960, 1970, 1980, and 1990, unless otherwise noted.

degree since 1960 is identical (not shown). On the other hand, although the high school noncompletion gap seems to have narrowed slightly, the decline in the high school dropout rate has generally been faster in urban areas.

Comparable statistics from the 1999 Current Population Survey indicate substantial rural/urban convergence in the 1990s and that parity is fast approaching in the share of those without a high school diploma and those who are college graduates. The number of rural adults without a high school diploma has remained fairly steady during this period because of a balance between the labor force entry of young adults who are better educated than the previous generations (shown in the last row of Table 2.1) and the influx of less-educated, older adults from urban areas.

## Industrial Structure and Skill Requirements in Rural Labor Markets

Rural industrial change has largely mimicked changes in urban America over the last quarter century, but with a lag. The decline in employment in extractive industries—predominantly mining and agriculture—continued, although the rate of decline in agriculture has leveled off as its share of the rural workforce fell below 10 percent. By the late 1990s, the number of job openings in these industries was small enough to make them unlikely avenues for entry-level workers (with the exception of international migrants in some cases).

The main story, of course, is the transition from manufacturing to service employment, which occurred in both rural and urban economies. In the mid 1970s, manufacturing employed about 19 percent of both the rural and urban labor forces. In contrast to the precipitous decline in urban manufacturing employment beginning with the recessions of the early 1980s, rural manufacturing has declined gradually. As a result, 16 percent of the rural labor force remained employed in manufacturing by 1998, as opposed to 11 percent in urban areas. In many counties in the rural South, especially, manufacturing is an important source of jobs for men and women without a college education.

Nonetheless, services are now the source of slightly more than half of rural jobs and two-thirds of urban jobs. The transition has had rather different implications for men and women. As happened in urban centers, the growth of the rural service economy paralleled and reinforced the mass entry of women in the formal labor market. Today, services and trade provide 73 percent of rural women's total employment, compared with 39 percent of men's. Despite the disproportionate importance of manufacturing in the rural economy, rural women are only slightly more likely than urban women to work in that industry (13 percent vs. 10 percent).

The rise of the service sector is a boon for women's labor force participation, because many service-related jobs are more likely to be part-time or seasonal and allow women to integrate formal market work into the still-pervasive demands of maintaining a household and rearing children. Yet this flexibility is a double-edged sword, given that part-time employment is often involuntary and often includes fewer non-wage benefits than full-time work. In rural areas, women are relatively concentrated in retail trade, which has the lowest average pay of any major industry.

Although the broad outlines of rural industrial structure have come to more closely resemble urban structure, skill requirements within industries often differ substantially across rural/urban lines (Table 2.2). The sharpest contrasts are evident in the share of workers holding college degrees. Nearly one in four urban manufacturing workers, for example, has at least a bachelor's degree compared with fewer than one in ten rural manufacturing workers. Similarly large rural/urban gaps exist in almost every major industry. For the least-educated workers (those without high school diplomas), rural/urban differences are often slight, or even show higher rural education levels, as is the case for farming, wholesale and retail trade, and personal services. Although not directly discernible from Table 2.2, it is also true that the employment distributions by industry for less-educated rural and urban workers are quite similar, with somewhat greater employment in manufacturing among less-educated rural workers.

Skill differences between rural and urban workforces have also become more muted, as seen in employment distributions among occupations (Table 2.3). Urban workers are much more likely to be in managerial and professional occupations and less likely to be employed in noncraft, blue-collar occupations. However, other distinctions are less finely drawn. For workers without a high school diploma, rural/urban differences are negligible and mainly reflect differences in industrial

**Table 2.2  Education by Industry, 1999 (%)**

| Industry | Less than high school | | College graduate | |
|---|---|---|---|---|
| | Rural | Urban | Rural | Urban |
| Farming, forestry, fishing | 22.7 | 34.8 | 13.6 | 14.2 |
| Mining | 16.9 | 11.4 | 6.8 | 35.6 |
| Construction | 20.2 | 20.0 | 6.1 | 11.2 |
| Manufacturing | 17.5 | 13.9 | 8.8 | 24.5 |
| Trans., comm., utilities | 12.5 | 7.3 | 11.2 | 22.1 |
| Wholesale trade | 9.9 | 10.4 | 14.8 | 26.1 |
| Retail trade | 20.9 | 21.7 | 8.5 | 13.3 |

NOTE: Numbers represent the share of workers 25 and older in each industry with the stated education level.
SOURCE: Current Population Survey.

structure. Rural less-educated workers are more likely to work in blue-collar occupations, many concentrated in manufacturing. Urban less-educated workers are more often engaged in the administrative support, clerical, sales, and service occupations typical of the service sector.

## RURAL LABOR MARKETS AND WELFARE REFORM: IMPLICATIONS FOR JOB AVAILABILITY

An abundance of job openings is the first condition for ensuring that welfare recipients have the opportunity to make a successful transition into the labor force. Ideally, one would measure job availability by looking at job vacancy rates. These data are unavailable at the national level, and unemployment rates are typically used as a proxy. Many macroeconomists believe that national (and by extension, rural) unemployment in the late 1990s rested near the lowest rate possible without encouraging inflation, providing the best possible conditions for labor force entrants (Council of Economic Advisers 2000, p. 92). For this reason, economists have generally concluded that most welfare

**Table 2.3  Employment Distribution by Major Occupation Groups, 1999 (%)**

| Occup. Group | All employed | | Employed, less than high school | |
|---|---|---|---|---|
| | Rural | Urban | Rural | Urban |
| Managerial and professional | 22.2 | 32.0 | 4.2 | 4.8 |
| Technical | 2.7 | 3.3 | 0.4 | 0.5 |
| Administrative, clerical, sales | 22.7 | 26.6 | 14.0 | 18.6 |
| Craft | 13.2 | 10.4 | 15.7 | 14.5 |
| Other blue-collar occup. | 19.2 | 12.5 | 32.2 | 27.2 |
| Services | 14.3 | 12.7 | 23.8 | 28.3 |
| Farming | 5.7 | 1.8 | 9.7 | 6.1 |
| Total | 100 | 100 | 100 | 100 |

SOURCE: Current Population Survey.

recipients will find employment readily and without creating significant supply-demand imbalances (Lerman, Loprest, and Ratcliffe 1999; Bartik 1998; Burtless 1998).

The marginally higher unemployment rates in rural labor markets imply that rural welfare recipients will have about the same difficulty finding a job as urban recipients, and will perhaps have less difficulty than those in urban centers where welfare use is concentrated. Two points are necessary, however, to give a more complete picture of rural job availability. First, the likelihood of being unemployed varies considerably according to a person's demographic and human capital characteristics, such as race and educational attainment (Table 2.4). Unemployment rates are higher for the less educated and for racial and ethnic minorities, but only slightly higher for women (with the exception of Hispanic women). Unemployment rates for rural black men and women with at most a high school diploma are at or near 10 percent, more than twice the rate of whites. Aggregate unemployment rates, therefore, may not provide an accurate picture of the difficulty the welfare population will have finding a job, given that they are disproportionately nonwhite and less-educated than average.

Second, unemployment rates vary widely across counties.  In 1999, 325 counties, most of them rural, had unemployment rates greater than twice the national average of 4 percent.  These high-unemployment rural counties are characterized by little or no urbanization, remoteness from urban areas, very low education levels, and a large share of minority residents.  Because many of the same characteristics are associated with persistent poverty and consistently high use of welfare programs, a substantial number of counties where the need for jobs is greatest owing to welfare reform are the same counties with the lowest job availability (Figure 2.3).

Moreover, the relationship between worker characteristics and employers' location decisions is self-reinforcing.  Low-education, high-poverty counties are unattractive to many prospective employers who need sufficiently large pools of well-trained workers.  In the rural South, for instance, manufacturers are now eschewing traditional low-wage, low-skill areas in favor of a better educated—and presumably more trainable—workforce (McGranahan 1999).  Without substantial investments in human capital development, these counties face one or more scenarios over the next few years: the lack of jobs will cause wages to fall further and entice some types of new employment; job seekers will search elsewhere for better prospects, either through commuting or migration; or job seekers will retreat from the formal labor market altogether.

**Table 2.4  Rural Unemployment Rates for Ages 20 and over, by Education and Demographic Group, 1999 (%)**

|          | All | HS grad or less |
|----------|-----|-----------------|
| All      | 3.9 | 5.0 |
| White    | 3.2 | 4.1 |
| Black    | 8.6 | 9.7 |
| Hispanic | 5.9 | 6.4 |
| Women    | 4.1 | 5.5 |
| White    | 3.4 | 4.6 |
| Black    | 9.0 | 10.0 |
| Hispanic | 7.3 | 8.0 |

SOURCE: Current Population Survey.

Figure 2.3  Nonmetro AFDC and Unemployment Rates, 1996

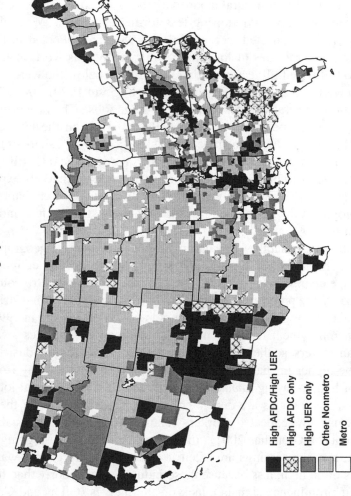

High AFDC/High UER

High AFDC only

High UER only

Other Nonmetro

Metro

NOTE: "High" refers to the top quartile of rural counties ranked by the estimated share of families using Aid to Families with Dependent Children or by the annual average unemployment rate.

SOURCE: Produced by the ERS using data from the U.S. Department of Commerce.

## Sustainable Earnings in Rural Labor Markets

Although less-educated workers in some rural counties will have difficulty finding jobs, the problem of low earnings is more widespread. The distribution of jobs in rural labor markets, as noted above, is heavily weighted toward work requiring less formal education. Wage declines among less-educated workers in the 1980s are reflected in the persistent high rural rates of low-wage work, defined as work that, if performed full-time full-year, would yield earnings below the weighted average poverty level for a family of four ($16,655 in 1999). In 1979, 24 percent of the rural workforce held low-wage jobs. The proportion climbed to nearly one-third by the mid 1980s. Only in the last few years has low-wage employment declined significantly as a share of total rural employment. However, in 1999, at 27 percent, the rate still exceeded the rate in 1979. Low-wage work in urban labor markets experienced a similar rise and fall over time, but always at a lower share of total employment than in rural areas; the urban rate stood at just under 20 percent in 1999.

As with job availability, low earnings show a distinctive geographic pattern. The Economic Research Service (USDA) recently delineated low-wage counties, defined as the top 20 percent of nonmetro counties ranked by the proportion of wage-and-salary workers in industries with average earnings below the four-person poverty threshold in 1995. Just as unemployment rates are higher on average for counties away from urban centers, so the share of employment in low-wage industries tends to be higher in sparsely populated, remote counties, away from clusters of higher-paying managerial, professional, and technical jobs. Few low-wage counties are dependent on manufacturing, since these industries pay low-educated workers relatively well and offer stable employment (McGranahan 2001). In areas where farming or logging is important, average earnings are often low and the share of low-wage workers is often high, less because these industries pay poorly than because their prominence signals a lack of alternatives (Gibbs and Cromartie 2000).

Unlike counties with high unemployment, however, low-wage counties do not significantly overlap counties with high welfare use, except for a few counties in the lower Mississippi Delta and scattered counties with large minority populations in Georgia, Texas, New Mexico, and South Dakota (Figure 2.4). Low-wage counties with the lowest rates of welfare use are located in the Great Plains, where low-wage workers are less likely to be the family's sole wage earner and where outmigration is a more common alternative to economic deprivation than in other regions (Gibbs and Cromartie 2000).

During the 1980s, attention was focused on demand-side reasons for the lack of good-paying jobs and for lower wage levels in rural areas. Researchers noted that real rural earnings fell by 12 percent while urban earnings rose by 1 percent between 1979 and 1989, even as educational attainment rose in both areas. The increase in skills required by rural employers appeared to be outpaced by the rate of human capital growth. Employers also continued to seek out pools of low-skill, low-cost labor, dampening the growth of high-skill jobs and causing a large outflow of the best-educated to urban areas (McGranahan and Ghelfi 1991).

In the 1990s, interest in the association between low educational attainment and low earnings in rural areas has re-emerged as the rural economy prospered relative to its earlier performance. This association takes on a special character in rural areas where low-wage jobs are concentrated. Historically, the relatively large supply of workers with low education depressed earnings. For example, a typical worker without a high school diploma earned 19 percent less in a low-education county than in a high-education county, in part because competition for available low-skill jobs is usually stiffer in the former.[4] Moreover, social scientists have recently explored the ability of large concentrations of high-skill, high-education workers to augment the productivity, and therefore the earnings, of individual workers in urban areas (Rauch 1993; Jovanovic and Rob 1989). To the extent that this principle operates in low-skill, low-wage labor markets as well, many rural workers are likely to enjoy very little, if any, productivity enhancement.

An examination of 1999 earnings data shows that the economic and demographic changes of the 1990s altered earlier earnings/education relationships (Table 2.5). Rural average weekly earnings are, for the most part, lower than urban earnings, even after controlling for education levels. The most important exception is rural adults who did not complete high school. Their average earnings are almost equal to those of similar urban workers. In fact, cost-of-living differences may mean that many rural high school dropouts can achieve a higher stan-

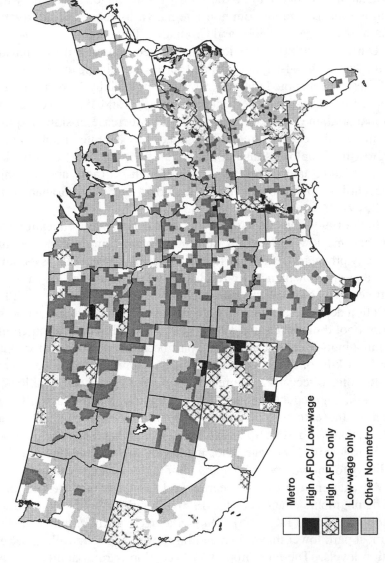

Figure 2.4 Nonmetro AFDC and Nonmetro Low-Wage Counties, 1996

Metro

High AFDC/ Low-wage

High AFDC only

Low-wage only

Other Nonmetro

SOURCE: Produced by the ERS using data from the U.S. Department of Commerce.

**Table 2.5  Average Weekly Earnings by Education and Demographic Group (age 25 and older) 1999**

| Group | All ($) | High school graduate ($) | Less than high school ($) | Less than high school (as % of poverty) |
|---|---|---|---|---|
| Rural | | | | |
| All | 513 | 459 | 364 | 1.11 |
| White | 532 | 472 | 384 | 1.17 |
| Black | 390 | 374 | 295 | 0.90 |
| Hispanic | 405 | 417 | 338 | 1.03 |
| Women | 407 | 345 | 257 | 0.78 |
| White | 418 | 351 | 262 | 0.80 |
| Black | 338 | 303 | 241 | 0.74 |
| Hispanic | 327 | 320 | 254 | 0.78 |
| Urban | | | | |
| All | 645 | 507 | 364 | 1.11 |
| White | 696 | 532 | 411 | 1.25 |
| Black | 519 | 441 | 330 | 1.01 |
| Hispanic | 467 | 448 | 333 | 1.02 |
| Women | 521 | 403 | 279 | 0.85 |
| White | 547 | 412 | 301 | 0.92 |
| Black | 473 | 383 | 278 | 0.85 |
| Hispanic | 398 | 370 | 256 | 0.78 |

NOTE: "White" and "Black" categories exclude Hispanics.
SOURCE: Current Population Survey.

dard of living, a possibility also suggested by the influx of persons with low education from urban to rural areas.

Given the high rates of high school noncompletion among welfare recipients, this comparison initially suggests that many rural recipients will fare at least no worse than urban recipients in securing a sustaining wage. However, aggregate earnings estimates are potentially misleading for those workers most likely to be affected by welfare reform. Table 2.5 shows that average weekly earnings for rural women, especially minority women, fall well below the rural average. Rural women without high school diplomas can expect to earn $257 per week on average, or the equivalent of $13,364 annually, 22 percent below the four-person poverty threshold of $16,655. Rural black women earn $241 per week, 26 percent below the four-person equivalent. Even this measure overstates likely earnings over time, because many women are working part-time and may not hold a job 52 weeks out of the year.

A stated goal of welfare reform is to promote financial independence. The need for auxiliary work supports became clearer as PRWORA was implemented by states and localities in 1997. Implicit in the provision of public assistance for child care, transportation, and employment counseling, for example, is the assumption that recipients who go to work will gain skills, general and specific, in entry-level jobs and eventually leverage them for better pay. Yet, how likely is it that rural workers with limited education can move into better-paying jobs?

It should be noted here that the four-person poverty threshold, which translates into slightly more than $8 an hour on a full-time basis in 1999, is not necessarily adequate for true financial independence even in low-cost areas. The "living wage" movement, which developed just as the public policy link between poverty reduction and work tightened, seeks to establish local minimum wages that more accurately reflect the earnings necessary to sustain a basic standard of living than does the current federal minimum wage ($5.15/hour). Living wages are usually calculated based on either the official poverty threshold or local family budgets. Most recent studies that employ the latter method place the living wage in the $9–$20 per hour range depending on family size, with the exception of very large cities (Zimmerman and Garkovich 1998; Bernstein, Brocht, and Spade-Aguilar 1999). If we (somewhat arbitrarily) establish a $12 per hour threshold for a sustainable wage in rural areas, then about 20 percent of all jobs held by rural workers without college experience can be classified as "sustainable." Only 14 percent of the jobs held by similarly situated women offer that pay, however.

These figures apply to current rural workers; they may not be appropriate for estimating the wage prospects of those required to go to work under PRWORA. An alternative approach is to calculate the share of low-skill jobs—those requiring limited formal education and most likely to be held by new entrants—that are in occupations typically paying at least $12 an hour (Table 2.6).[5] Nearly two-thirds of all rural jobs are in low-skill occupations, compared with just over half of urban jobs. The percentage of low-skill employment among predomi-

**Table 2.6 Share of Low-skill and "Good" Jobs by Rural/Urban Status (%)**

| Group | All low-skill | Jobs that require short-term on-the-job training | "Good" jobs as share of all low-skilled jobs | "Good" jobs as share of all short-term, on-the-job training jobs |
|---|---|---|---|---|
| Rural |  |  |  |  |
| All | 65.5 | 36.6 | 23.2 | 13.4 |
| Predominantly women | 58.5 | 42.0 | 2.0 | 2.0 |
| Urban |  |  |  |  |
| All | 55.8 | 33.0 | 23.2 | 11.9 |
| Predominantly women | 54.2 | 40.2 | 3.5 | 2.9 |

NOTE: "Good" = jobs in occupations with average earnings above $12/hour for workers with no college.
SOURCE: Bureau of Labor Statistics.

nantly female-held occupations is lower, particularly in rural areas. Considering only occupations that require short-term (fewer than 90 days) on-the-job training, about one-third of both rural and urban jobs fall into this category; the rate for such occupations held mainly by women is higher, around 40 percent. Only a small share of these low-skill jobs can be described as "good paying." Among predominantly female-held occupations, the share of these jobs that pay well is extremely low (2 to 4 percent), suggesting that wage progression will be quite difficult for the majority of welfare recipients who enter the labor force.

## POLICY IMPLICATIONS

Rural labor markets continue to be distinguished from urban markets by lower levels of human capital and a larger share of employment in extractive and manufacturing industries. The small populations and low employment densities that typify rural labor markets reinforce these characteristics and discourage prospective or expanding employers. Rapid spatial diffusion of new information and communications technologies can mitigate, but not negate, the need for a substantial on-site pool of skilled labor, nor can it fully counter the lack of physical infrastructure and services often arising from the high per-unit provision costs in rural areas.

Despite these inherent limitations, rural America as a whole in the 1990s saw employment gains in line with national trends. Conclusions about rural earnings are sensitive to the data source used, but in general, changes in rural real earnings during the period follow overall patterns. In fact, rural labor markets may be better positioned for welfare reform than is often assumed because rural and urban job structures appear to be converging. Urban and rural industry and occupation mixes are becoming more alike; aggregate rural unemployment rates are usually within a few tenths of a point of urban rates; earnings for rural high school dropouts are as high as those for urban dropouts; and the share of good-paying jobs among low-skill occupations is not substantially different in rural and urban areas.

However, rural labor markets also face substantial welfare reform challenges. Many rural counties still have very high unemployment rates, and a high proportion of those entered the PRWORA era with large welfare caseloads. Furthermore, the rural/urban earnings gap is a conservative indicator of the challenge faced by rural labor markets to provide sustainable earnings. The average earnings of women and minorities fall well below the rural average, and for those without a high school diploma, annual earnings from a full-time, full-year job are usually below the four-person poverty threshold. In addition, although the rates of "good" jobs in rural and urban areas among low-skill occupations are similar, both are extremely low for occupations held predominantly by women. Because welfare reform is most likely to affect women, the apparent lack of opportunity to move up the job ladder without additional education is a critical stumbling block.

What do the structural economic changes under way in rural areas imply for the less-skilled, low-paying sector of the labor force? On the one hand, the slow decline in manufacturing employment is closing the historical avenues that led to sustained earnings and stable employment for many of these workers. The poverty rate of full-time manufacturing workers without a high school diploma is one-third that of other similar full-time workers. Employment declines have accelerated since the mid 1990s, with little chance for reversal despite the entry of a few high-visibility manufacturers into labor market areas accessible to rural workers.

On the other hand, the growth of service and retail trade is often portrayed as leading to an inevitable decline in living standards among low-wage, low-skill workers. Service-sector earnings in rural areas have fallen farther behind manufacturing wages since the early 1980s, increasing the chance of a long-term deterioration in wages for workers who might formerly have become machine operators but are now sales clerks or cashiers. Nevertheless, in some areas, service employment is the only alternative to a loss of jobs. For two-earner households, particularly those with young children, service employment may provide the means for women (and some men) to contribute to the household's income while juggling the dual demands of home and workplace. Single-earner households—those most likely to be affected by welfare reform—are more likely to find themselves performing the same juggling act but facing greater economic hardship as a result of the transformation of local economies from manufacturing-based to service-based.

With a few significant exceptions, federal industrial and employment policies assume the primacy of market forces to determine the spatial location of economic activities. Although states are more active in fashioning interventions that encourage the location of large plants within their borders, they play a minor role in aggregate employment changes over time. For the foreseeable future, most rural areas—those outside easy commuting distance to urban centers and without abundant natural amenities—will not see large-scale changes in the nature of the local economy. Where such changes do occur, the benefits for less-educated workers are often small.

For these workers, policies that encourage skills acquisition and additional education are critical to reducing long-term supply-and-demand mismatches in low-wage labor markets. Because most of these workers are women or minorities, or both, it is equally important to ensure that their talents and skills are fully used and that past occupational channeling that locked workers into low-wage jobs is avoided. Finally, it should be noted that low-skill jobs will continue to be a significant part of the economy in almost all local labor market areas, rural and urban, for many years to come. For the workers who participate in these markets, a safety net of work supports, wage floors, and assistance during employment transitions will remain a key component of any set of policies aimed at improving the well-being of the disadvantaged and the marginalized in U.S. society.

# Notes

1. "Rural" and "urban" are used throughout the chapter to denote "nonmetropolitan" and "metropolitan" counties as defined in 1994 by the Office of Management and Budget.
2. Earnings per job from the Bureau of Economic Analysis is based on data from establishments located in nonmetro counties and counts all jobs including those held by self-employed workers, whereas the CPS data is based on a household survey and includes (in this analysis) only wage and salary workers. A significant number of these workers, however, may work in metro areas.
3. Bloomquist, Gingeri, Tomaskovic-Devey, and Truelove (1993) provided an excellent discussion of theoretical frameworks for understanding rural/urban differentiation in employment structures.
4. A "low-education" county is defined as being in the top quartile of rural counties ranked by the share of workers without a high school diploma; a "high-education" county is in the bottom quartile. The statistic is derived from an analysis of the

1990 Public Use Microsample files prepared from decennial census data by the U.S. Census Bureau.

5. Low-skill jobs are defined here as being in occupations that typically require no formal education, but 3–12 months of on-the-job training are required to become proficient (Bureau of Labor Statistics).

# References

Bartik, Timothy J. 1998. "Displacement and Wage Effects of Welfare Reform." Paper presented at the Joint Center for Poverty Research conference "Labor Markets and Less-Skilled Workers," held in Washington, D.C., November 5–6, 1998.

Bernstein, Jared, Chauna Brocht, and Maggie Spade-Aguilar. 1999. *How Much Is Enough? Basic Family Budgets for Working Families.* Washington, D.C.: Economic Policy Institute.

Bloomquist, Leonard E., Christina Gringeri, Donald Tomaskovic-Devey, and Cynthia Truelove. 1993. "Work Structures and Rural Poverty." In *Persistent Poverty in Rural America.* Rural Sociological Society Task Force on Persistent Rural Poverty. Boulder, Colorado: Westview Press.

Burtless, Gary. 1998. "Can the Labor Market Absorb Three Million Welfare Recipients?" *Focus* 19(3): 1–6.

Doeringer, Peter B. 1984. "Internal Labor Markets and Paternalism in Rural Areas." In *Internal Labor Markets*, Paul Osterman, ed. Cambridge, Massachusetts: MIT Press, pp. 271–289.

Council of Economic Advisers. 2000. *Economic Report of the President.* Washington, D.C.: U. S. Government Printing Office.

Gibbs, Robert, and John B. Cromartie. 2000. "Low-Wage Counties Face Locational Disadvantages." *Rural Conditions and Trends* 11(2): 18–26.

Gibbs, Robert, and Timothy Parker. 2000. "Rural Low-Wage Employment Rises among Men." *Rural Conditions and Trends* 1(2): 9–17.

Glaeser, Edward L., and David C. Maré. 1994. "Cities and Skills." Working paper no. 4728, National Bureau of Economic Research, Washington, D.C.

Goldstein, G.S., and T.J. Gronberg. 1984. "Economies of Scope and Economies of Agglomeration." *Journal of Urban Economics* 16(1): 91–104.

Gottschalk, Peter. 2000. "Work as a Stepping Stone for Welfare Recipients: What Is the Evidence?" In *The Low Wage Labor Market: Challenges and Opportunities for Economic Self-Sufficiency*, Kelleen Kaye and Demetra Smith Nightingale, eds. Washington, D.C.: U.S. Department of Health and Human Services, Office of the Secretary, Assistant Secretary for Planning and Evaluation, pp. 157–170.

Jovanovic, Boyan, and Rafael Rob. 1989. "The Growth and Diffusion of Knowledge." *Review of Economic Studies* 56: 569–582.

Kaye, Kelleen, and Demetra Smith Nightingale. 2000. *The Low Wage Labor Market: Challenges and Opportunities for Economic Self-Sufficiency.* Washington, D.C.: U.S. Department of Health and Human Services, Office of the Secretary, Assistant Secretary for Planning and Evaluation.

Killian, Molly Sizer, and Lionel J. Beaulieu. 1995. "Current Status of Human Capital in the Rural U.S." In *Investing in People: The Human Capital Needs of Rural America*, Lionel J. Beaulieu and David Mulkey, eds. Boulder, Colorado: Westview Press, pp. 23–48.

Lerman, Robert I., Pamela Loprest, and Caroline Ratcliffe. 1999. *How Well Can Urban Labor Markets Absorb Welfare Recipients?* ANF Policy Brief A-33, Washington, D.C.: Urban Institute.

Long, Sharon K., Robin Kurka, Shelley Waters, and Gretchen Kirby. 1998. *Child Care Assistance under Welfare Reform: Early Response by the States.* ANF Occasional Paper no. 13. Washington, D.C.: Urban Institute.

Lucas, Robert E., Jr. 1988. "On the Mechanics of Economic Development." *Journal of Monetary Economics* 22: 3–42.

McGranahan, David A. 1999. "The Geography of New Manufacturing Technology: Implications for the Nonmetropolitan South." *Southern Rural Sociology* 15: 85–104.

———. 2001. "New Economy Meets Old Economy Education Policy in the Rural South." *Rural America* 15(4): 19–27.

McGranahan, David A., and Linda M. Ghelfi. 1991. "The Education Crisis and Rural Stagnation in the 1980's." In *Education and Rural Economic Development: Strategies for the 1990's.* ERS Staff Report no. AGES 9153. Washington, D.C.: Agriculture and Rural Economy Division, Economic Research Service, U.S. Department of Agriculture, pp. 40–92.

———. 1998. "Current Trends in the Supply and Demand for Education in Rural and Urban Areas." In *Rural Education and Training in the New Economy: The Myth of the Rural Skills Gap*, Robert M. Gibbs, Paul L. Swaim, and Ruy Teixeira, eds. Ames: Iowa State University Press, pp. 131–172.

National Rural Development Partnership. 1998. *Child Care and Transportation Strategies for Rural Communities: Meeting the Welfare Reform Challenge.* Welfare Reform Task Force, Washington, D.C., September.

Nord, Mark. 2000. "Does It Cost Less to Live in Rural Areas? Evidence from New Data on Food Security and Hunger." *Rural Sociology* 65(1): 104–125.

Norton, R.D., and J. Rees. 1979. "The Product Cycle and the Spatial Decentralization of American Manufacturing." *Regional Studies* 13: 141–151.

Pavetti, LaDonna, and Gregory Acs. 1997. *Moving Up, Moving Out or Going Nowhere? A Study of the Employment Patterns of Young Women.* Washington, D.C.: Urban Institute.

Rauch, James, E. 1993. "Productivity Gains from Geographic Concentration of Human Capital: Evidence from the Cities." *Journal of Urban Economics* 34: 380–400.

Rungeling, Brian, Lewis H. Smith, and Loren C. Scott. 1976. "Effectiveness of Rural Job Search Methods." *Monthly Labor Review* 99(4): 27–30.

Zimmerman, Julie N., and Lori Garkovich. 1998. *The Bottom Line: Welfare Reform, the Cost of Living, and Earnings in the Rural South.* Welfare Reform Information Brief no. 2, Southern Rural Development Center, Mississippi State, Mississippi.

# 3

# Rural America in Transition

## Poverty and Welfare at the Turn of the Twenty-First Century

Daniel T. Lichter
*The Ohio State University*

Leif Jensen
*Pennsylvania State University*

The passage of the Personal Responsibility and Work Opportunity Reconciliation Act (PRWORA) of 1996 ended the nation's largest cash assistance program (Aid to Families with Dependent Children [AFDC]) and replaced it with Temporary Assistance for Needy Families (TANF). The new legislation has sought to end dependence on public assistance by "promoting job preparation, work and marriage." To early critics of the bill, "the end of welfare as we know it" was a legislative calamity, one that would bring new material hardships and social injustice to America's most vulnerable and innocent population—children living with low-income, single mothers. These early fears have not materialized. Rather than rising, the poverty rate among America's children, although still high, fell in 1998 to its lowest level (18.9 percent) in almost 20 years.

Welfare reform happened at a propitious time. The United States began the twenty-first century in the midst of its longest economic expansion in modern economic history. The average unemployment rate of 4.2 percent in 1999 reached its lowest point in 30 years, while inflation remained low, at 2 percent to 3 percent per annum. Single mothers entered the labor force in record numbers, and welfare caseloads dropped by about 50 percent since 1993. After stagnating for decades, inflation-adjusted earnings also began to rise in the late 1990s, even among the least educated and skilled, and the rise in income inequality halted or even reversed. Optimism about the strong economy, along with the ride upward in the stock market, fueled public confidence in America's economic future.

Unfortunately, the national euphoria sometimes caused us to forget that all people and places did not share in the benefits of recent economic growth and rising personal incomes. National statistics tend to hide growing spatial inequality and "pockets of poverty" in an increasingly urban, bicoastal, and high-tech U.S. economy. Indeed, with federal devolution (including state welfare reform) and regional economic restructuring, some observers fear a growing economic, social, and cultural balkanization (Lobao, Rulli, and Brown 1999; Massey 1996). By almost any standard, for example, rural America continues to be an economic backwater, and it faces new challenges in today's increasingly global and high-tech economy (Andrews and Burke 1999; Purdy 1999). Unlike urban America, rural America has been buffeted by a periodically depressed farm economy; a shift away from extractive industries (such as timber and mining, especially in Appalachia); severe competition from cheap labor overseas in the manufacturing sector; in the southern "black belt," the continuing economic legacy of the old slave and plantation economy; and, on Indian reservations, government policy regarding tribal affairs and governance (Duncan 1992; Marks et al. 1999).

Rural problems are largely invisible to many Americans. Most people reside in or around heavily populated metropolitan cities and therefore are exposed largely to urban culture and values, urban media and marketing, and urban problems and politics. The apparent lack of public awareness about rural issues is reflected in the new welfare bill and its goal to reduce the welfare dependency of poor, single mothers. It is largely a product of an urban political and cultural legislative agenda: to reduce the dependence of poor and disproportionately minority single mothers and their children on government "handouts" by promoting work and reducing unmarried childbearing. However, the family circumstances, labor market conditions, and barriers to maternal employment (i.e., stigma, lack of adequate child care) are decidedly different in rural than in urban America. How have single mothers with children fared over the past decade in rural America? Have they been largely bypassed by a strong urban economy? Have single mothers and children—the prime targets of state welfare reform—been helped or hurt economically?

In this chapter, we examine the economic trajectories and changing sources of income among female-headed families during the recent period of economic expansion and welfare policy changes. We have three specific objectives. First, we evaluate trends in nonmetropolitan (nonmetro) and metropolitan (metro) poverty rates among female-headed families between 1989 and 1999. Second, we examine recent changes in the "income packaging" of poor and nonpoor female heads with children. Are they more reliant on earnings and less dependent on welfare income today than in the pre-TANF period? Third, we evaluate the ameliorative effects of public assistance and work on poverty rates among female-headed families. Is welfare income more or less likely than in the past to lift poor, rural families out of poverty, and are employed female heads of household more or less likely to be poor? We use pooled data from the March annual demographic supplements (1989–1999) of the *Current Population Survey*.

## RURAL POVERTY AND WELFARE REFORM TODAY

In 1968, the President's National Advisory Commission on Rural Poverty reported that "[r]ural poverty is so widespread, and so acute, as to be a national disgrace" (U.S. National Advisory Commission on Rural Poverty 1968). Over 30 years later, this conclusion rings less true. The nonmetro poverty rate in 1967 was 20.2 percent, roughly twice the rate of metro areas (U.S. Bureau of the Census 1999a). Today, the nonmetro poverty rate is 14.4 percent, a figure only slightly higher than the metro rate of 12.3 percent and less than the rate in metro central cities (18.5 percent). America's rural population has experienced substantial reductions (roughly one-third) in the official poverty rate over the past three decades. Moreover, predominantly rural states—Iowa (2.5 percent), New Hampshire (2.7 percent), and South Dakota (2.9 percent)—enjoy some of the lowest unemployment rates in the country (U. S. Bureau of Labor Statistics 2000). Clearly, rural residents have, on balance, caught up with the rest of the nation on several key policy indicators of economic well-being. Such optimism, however, should not distract from evaluating other behavioral adaptations (e.g., doubling-up, migration, welfare dependence) to time-limited welfare among the people left behind, including low-income, single mothers in rural areas.

## Rural Pockets of Poverty

The immediate and longer-term consequences of rural welfare reform are ambiguous, largely because they are likely to be different for different geographic and demographic segments of the population (Marks et al. 1999). Economic indicators based on statistical averages for people, often classified based on increasingly outdated or obsolete geographic concepts (like nonmetro or rural), may hide growing spatial inequality within and between metro and nonmetro areas. Indeed, the current period of massive federal devolution, regional economic restructuring, and economic bifurcation has coincided with growing economic and cultural diversity in America, including emerging spatial inequalities among geographic areas.

This is clearly reflected in large differences in income and poverty across the states. Not surprisingly, among the six states with the highest average poverty rates during 1997–1999, five were predominantly rural states, including New Mexico (poverty rate of 20.8 percent), Louisiana (18.2 percent), Mississippi (16.7 percent), West Virginia (16.7 percent), and Arkansas (16.4 percent). These figures are played out in the 1999 Kids Count project, which ranked the rural states of Mississippi, Louisiana, New Mexico, and Alabama as the nation's worst on 10 measures of children's well-being (Annie E. Casey Foundation 2000). These are also states with heavy concentrations of rural minorities, who suffer disproportionately high rates of poverty.

Accelerated inequality also may now be occurring in nonmetro areas, but with decidedly less attention or policy concern. Income and employment differences have grown between thriving rural population growth centers (e.g., based on recreational development or other natural amenities) and other persistently poor and economically depressed backwater regions and rural ghettos (e.g., the Mississippi Delta, Appalachia, and the lower Rio Grande Valley) (Lyson and Falk 1992; Fossett and Seibert 1997; Harvey et al., in this volume, p. 375). Growing spatial inequality is reflected in the emergence of "rural ghetto communities," "pockets of poverty," and "persistent low-income areas" (Brown and Warner 1989; Weinberg 1987). Some depressed rural communities have become the "dumping grounds" for urban refuse, prisons, and low-level radioactive materials (Fitchen 1991; Duncan and Lamborghini 1994).

The result is that current low unemployment rates in many rural states often coincide with substantial economic hardship in small towns and the countryside. In Iowa, for example, the low average unemployment rate of 2.2 percent masks the fact that the highest unemployment rates are found in thinly populated areas of the state and those dependent on agriculture (Conger and Elder 1994). For example, Decatur County, a largely rural and agricultural area in south central Iowa, had an unemployment rate of 5.1 percent in 1998 (Burke et al. 1999). In rural West Virginia, unemployment rates also are well above state and national averages, especially in many depressed coal mining regions, such as McDowell, Clay, and Webster counties, where as many as one in five men are without jobs and looking for work (McLaughlin, Lichter, and Matthews 1999).

**Rural Workers and Rural Labor Markets**

Rural labor markets and workers are different in ways that, on the surface, militate against achieving the stated welfare-to-work goals in the 1996 welfare bill. One point of view stresses the chronic problem of rural human resource development, including the historically low levels of education and job skills among rural workers. The other side locates the problem in labor market structure and processes (e.g., globalization) and the absence of good rural jobs—those that pay a decent or family wage—in the new information economy (Flynt 1996; Lichter, Johnston, and McLaughlin 1994).

To be sure, rural areas suffer from chronic shortages of human capital (Jensen and McLaughlin 1995). This problem has been exacerbated by longstanding patterns of migration of the "best and brightest" from nonmetro to metro areas (Lichter, McLaughlin, and Cornwell 1995; Garasky 2000). Among those at the prime age for working and building a family (ages 25–44), only 16.3 percent of nonmetro persons in 1998 had attained a bachelor's degree or higher (U.S. Bureau of the Census 1999b). In metro areas, the comparable rate was 29.1 percent.

For the population aged 18 and older, almost one-quarter of the non-metro population failed to complete high school, compared with 16 percent in metro areas.

These educational deficits in rural areas are striking, especially in persistently poor regions.  In the 399 counties of Appalachia, for example, more than 30 percent of the population over age 25 has less than a high school education (McLaughlin, Lichter, and Matthews 1999).  In Kentucky—the heart of Appalachia—60 percent or more of that population in five rural counties did not complete high school.  Out-migration has fueled the problem.  Between 1985 and 1990, economically distressed counties in Appalachia experienced a net out-migration rate of 3.81 per 100 among those with a college education and a net in-migration rate of 3.09 among high school dropouts.  Migration patterns have reinforced existing patterns of spatial inequality (Lichter, McLaughlin, and Cornwell 1995; Nord, Luloff, and Jensen 1995).

The problem, however, cannot be easily reduced to poorly skilled or unproductive workers alone.  The currently low unemployment rates suggest that rural residents suffer less from having no jobs than from having jobs that pay poorly.  The unfavorable sectoral mix of industries (i.e., extractive, low-wage manufacturing, etc.) places even the most skilled and educated rural workers at a competitive disadvantage.  Rural workers are less likely to be unionized.  They also are often dependent on single industries or companies for employment, which subjects them to the unexpected vicissitudes or downturns in the local economy.  Not surprisingly, compared with metro areas, a larger percentage of the rural poor include a working head, while a disproportionate share of workers in nonmetro areas are poor (Lichter and McLaughlin 1995; Brown and Hirschl 1995).  At every level of education, average earnings and income are lower in nonmetro than in metro areas (Rural Sociological Society Task Force on Persistent Rural Poverty 1993; Jensen and McLaughlin 1995).  Findeis and Jensen (1998) reported that, in 1993, the rate of underemployment (i.e., unemployment, involuntary part-time employment, and low-income workers) was 22.6 percent in nonmetro areas, 21.5 percent in metro central cities, and 15.6 percent in the suburban ring.  The substantive implication is clear: rural residents suffer less from unemployment than from myriad forms of underemployment (Lichter and Costanzo 1987).  Now, more than ever, it is important to monitor the labor force experiences of poor and single mothers, those most affected by time-limited welfare reform, low job skills or experience, and depressed rural labor market conditions.

## Rural Families

The PRWORA legislation seeks to balance the right of welfare receipt with the recipient's obligation to behave responsibly—to stay in school, to avoid premarital pregnancy and childbearing, and to work. Indeed, an explicit goal of the welfare bill is to discourage childbearing and child rearing outside of two-parent families. Based on the conventional wisdom of strong family and kinship ties in rural America, the assumption—an inappropriate and often erroneous one—is that these welfare provisions may be less germane for rural areas. At the same time, rural women and children have not been immune to the larger cultural and societal forces that arguably have undermined traditional family life (McLaughlin, Gardner, and Lichter 1999). As in urban cities, the past two decades have brought more teen childbearing, more female headship, more unmarried cohabitation, and more divorce (Lichter and Eggebeen 1992; Jensen and Eggebeen 1994).

Such unexpected similarity between contemporary nonmetro and metro families is easily demonstrated. In 1998, nearly one in five (i.e., 19.8 percent) of all U.S. families with children lived in nonmetro areas (U.S. Bureau of the Census 1998). Female-headed families are nearly proportionately represented in nonmetro areas (18.4 percent). Despite considerably different racial, cultural, and economic environments, rural families are more like urban families (in structure) than they are different. Moreover, the mean number of children per female-headed family was 1.87 in nonmetro areas and 1.83 in metro areas.

Clearly, the common view of a unique, even idyllic, rural family life is inappropriate. Racial breakdowns support much the same conclusion. Among whites, 17.3 percent of metro families and 17.4 percent of nonmetro families were headed by females; the corresponding figures for blacks were 54.1 percent and 46.2 percent; for Hispanics, the figures were 25.5 percent and 21.3 percent. These data reveal familiar racial differences, but they also reinforce a clear message of substantial, overall rural/urban similarity within specific racial and ethnic groups.

The question is not whether "pro-family" welfare policies are appropriately targeted to unmarried mothers and children.  Rather, it is whether state TANF proposals will naively or unwittingly embrace the conventional wisdom of traditional rural family life and therefore direct their program energies and allocate their funds (i.e., provisions for day care, transportation services, and abstinence programs) disproportionately to big city populations at the expense of rural areas.

This would be unfortunate.  Child poverty rates were higher in rural than urban areas (24.4 percent vs. 22.3 percent) in 1996, while rates of "affluence" revealed the opposite pattern, with 24.8 percent of nonmetro children and 39.2 percent of metro children living in families with incomes 300 percent or more above the poverty threshold (Dagata 1999).  Poverty rates among rural children living with single mothers are higher than in urban areas (Lichter and Eggebeen 1992), and a larger percentage of poor children are in "deep poverty," that is, living in families with incomes below 50 percent of the poverty threshold (Dagata 1999).  Furthermore, the ameliorative effect of public assistance (the ability of welfare income to lift families with children above the poverty line) is lower in rural than in urban areas (Jensen and Eggebeen 1994).  The policy implication is clear.  Welfare policy has historically been less appropriately targeted and less effective in rural areas. Whether the same conclusion now applies in the new welfare policy environment is uncertain.  What is clear is that rural women and children have been overrepresented among the poor and underrepresented among those receiving government income assistance.

## DATA

This study examines recent changes in poverty and income packaging (including welfare receipt and income) in the United States over the past decade.  We use pooled data from the March Current Population Survey (CPS) from 1989 through 1999.  Each March demographic supplement of CPS includes nationally representative information on the civilian, noninstitutionalized population residing in approximately 60,000 housing units each year.

The 1990s represent an important period in U.S. economic history. It includes an economic downturn and (comparatively) high unemployment at the beginning of the decade, ending with subsequent economic expansion and low unemployment later in the 1990s.  Welfare caseloads also rose significantly (before 1993) and then declined even more rapidly as the decade progressed.  The 1990s also brought significant new legislation, including increases in the minimum wage, rapid expansions in the Earned Income Tax Credit (EITC), the end of AFDC, and the implementation of state TANF programs.  Between 1992 and 1996, many states also actively experimented with public assistance programs through the federal welfare waiver process (Schoeni and Blank 2000).

Our analyses center on female-headed families, although we also include some comparative information on other family types.  Female-headed families with children are the primary "targets" of the new welfare legislation; they receive the overwhelming share of public assistance and they have historically experienced exceptionally high rates of poverty.  They also represent an increasing share of all family households, and, unlike in the 1960s, most poor children today in the United States now live in female-headed families (Lichter 1997).

The analytic advantage of the March CPS is that it provides comparable social and economic data from year to year.  For our purpose, we can distinguish between families residing in metro and nonmetro areas.  Metro areas include one or more economically integrated counties that meet specific population size thresholds (e.g., including a large city [a central city] of 50,000 or more).  Nonmetro is a residual category.  In 1998, the Census Bureau estimated a nonmetro population of 55 million, or 20.3 percent of the U.S. population.

How best to measure poverty has been a topic of much debate.  The official poverty income threshold (for families of various sizes) can be criticized on a number of counts: it miscalculates family economies of scale (i.e., equivalence scales); it fails to take into account in-kind government transfers (e.g., food stamps); it does not account for geographic variations in cost of living or consumption; it is based on family rather than household income; and it does not adjust for taxes or other nonconsumption expenditures, such as child support payments (Citro and Michael 1995; Short et al. 1999).  How such issues distort rural-urban comparisons is difficult to tell, although the available evidence suggests that the cost of living is lower in rural areas, if housing costs are adjusted (Nord 2000).  At the same time, data from the 1998 Consumer Expenditure Survey indicate that rural residents spend a larger percentage of their incomes on food, utilities, transportation, and health care than their metro counterparts (U. S. Bureau of Labor Statistics 2000; see also discussion by Nord 2000).

We cannot resolve such long-standing debates here. For our purposes, we mainly restrict our analyses to the official poverty measure, which is the basis of eligibility for a number of government programs and is available annually in the March CPS files. We recognize the limitations of our approach and, therefore, include caveats when appropriate, as well as relevant supplemental data (e.g., adjustments for the EITC or food stamps).

A complete description of poverty measurement is provided elsewhere (U.S. Bureau of the Census 1999b). Poverty income thresholds are based on annual money income in the calendar year that preceded the March CPS interview; for example, the March 1999 survey asks about income from various sources in 1998. We focus on income from earnings and government transfers (including welfare recipients). Compared with administrative records, most survey data—including data from the CPS—typically underestimate the extent of welfare participation, although the substantive implications of such bias appear to be minor (Schoeni and Blank 2000).

## FINDINGS

### Trends in Family Poverty

#### Differences between metro and nonmetro areas

We begin by reporting official poverty rates for primary families with children younger than age 18 (Figure 3.1). We also track adjusted poverty rates that include the additional income received from the EITC. These data show that poverty among families with children generally rose in the late 1980s and early 1990s, peaked in 1994, and then began to decline, reaching its lowest level in 1999. This was true in both nonmetro and metro areas, using both the official and EITC-adjusted poverty rate.

These data also indicate that welfare reform has not resulted in in-

**Figure 3.1  Poverty (adjusted and unadjusted) by Year and Residence, 1989–99**

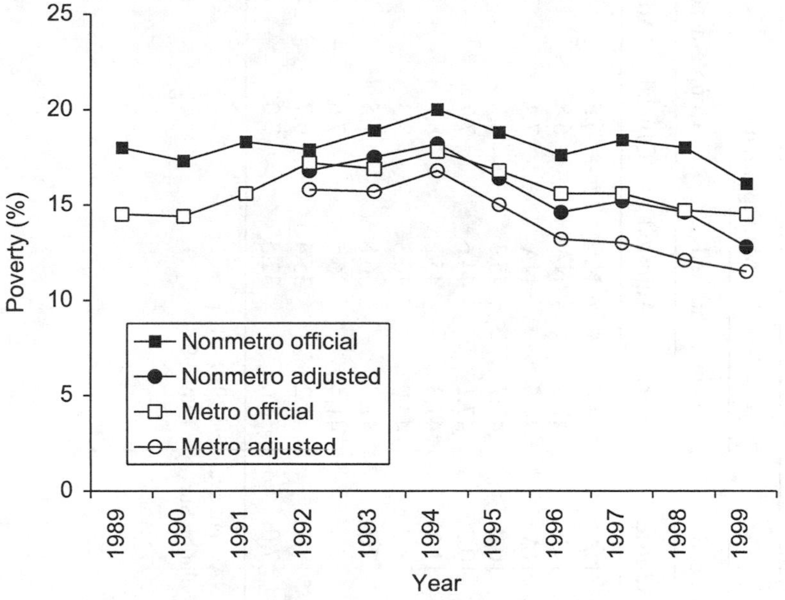

NOTE: Official poverty rate adjusted for earned income credit.  Not available in 1989–1991.

creased poverty among single-parent families with children, as many earlier critics of PRWORA had expected.  Indeed, poverty rates have declined since the welfare bill was passed in 1996.  Although family poverty rates remain higher in nonmetro than in metro areas, there is little indication that the economic well-being of rural families with children has diverged significantly from their metro counterparts.  In 1999, the EITC-adjusted poverty rate in nonmetro areas was slightly more than 10 percent higher than in metro areas.  In 1994, when poverty rates were at their peak, the nonmetro EITC-adjusted poverty rate exceeded the metro rate by 8.3 percent.

### Poverty among female-headed families

As shown in Table 3.1, poverty rates among nonmetro female-headed families have been very high historically (well above 40 per-

**Table 3.1 Primary Family Poverty Rates by Headship Status and Residence, 1989–99 (%)**

| | Nonmetropolitan | | | | Metropolitan | | | |
| | Female-headed | | Couple-headed | | Female-headed | | Couple-headed | |
| CPS Year | Official | Adjusted[a] | Official | Adjusted[a] | Official | Adjusted[a] | Official | Adjusted[a] |
|---|---|---|---|---|---|---|---|---|
| 1989 | 53.1 | NA | 10.7 | NA | 44.0 | NA | 6.5 | NA |
| 1990 | 48.6 | NA | 10.5 | NA | 42.1 | NA | 6.8 | NA |
| 1991 | 50.9 | NA | 11.2 | NA | 44.6 | NA | 7.4 | NA |
| 1992 | 50.4 | 48.6 | 10.9 | 10.0 | 47.7 | 45.1 | 8.0 | 7.1 |
| 1993 | 48.6 | 46.4 | 11.9 | 10.7 | 47.1 | 44.6 | 7.7 | 6.9 |
| 1994 | 50.2 | 47.3 | 12.5 | 11.1 | 47.3 | 45.3 | 8.7 | 8.0 |
| 1995 | 52.9 | 48.1 | 10.4 | 8.7 | 44.0 | 40.3 | 8.3 | 7.1 |
| 1996 | 44.8 | 39.5 | 9.7 | 7.5 | 41.8 | 36.8 | 7.5 | 6.1 |
| 1997 | 48.5 | 42.5 | 9.5 | 7.5 | 41.4 | 36.5 | 7.6 | 5.8 |
| 1998 | 47.5 | 39.5 | 9.8 | 7.7 | 41.2 | 35.4 | 6.7 | 5.2 |
| 1999 | 42.4 | 35.0 | 9.3 | 7.0 | 38.6 | 32.5 | 7.0 | 5.0 |

[a] Official poverty rate adjusted for earned income tax credit.  NA = not available 1989–91.
SOURCE: Original computations from the March Current Population Surveys, 1989–99.

cent) and typically have exceeded the poverty rates of married-couple families by a factor of 4 or 5. Although the 1989–1999 nonmetro poverty trend for female-headed families is more volatile than the trend for all families (Figure 3.1), it generally points to lower poverty in the post-welfare-reform era than in the years immediately preceding reform. The official poverty rate for female-headed families in nonmetro areas dropped nearly 13 percent between 1997 and 1999, from 48.5 percent to 42.2 percent. The comparable decline in metro areas was less than 7 percent. Whether the decline is due mostly to welfare reform is debatable. Compared with the pre-TANF period, official poverty rates also declined after 1996 among married-couple families, despite the fact that such families typically are ineligible for transfer income under the new welfare bill.

Table 3.1 also includes poverty estimates adjusted for the EITC. Not surprisingly, these adjusted estimates amplify the observed downward trends in poverty; that is, the downward trend in poverty is stronger in light of the expansion of EITC since 1992. For example, the adjusted poverty rate in nonmetro areas declined from 48.6 percent in 1992 to 35 percent in 1999 among female-headed families. This 28 percent reduction in adjusted poverty rates in nonmetro areas exceeds the 16 percent reduction observed when using the official poverty rate. Moreover, even after EITC adjustments, the poverty rate remains higher in nonmetro than metro areas, both among female-headed families and families headed by married couples. Despite prognostications to the contrary, we find little evidence that the economic well-being of nonmetro and metro areas diverged since the implementation of TANF.

### Sources of Income and Income Packaging

#### Earnings, public assistance income, and food stamps

Our next objective is to examine the changing sources of income in poor, female-headed families. Table 3.2 lists the percentage of all poor single mothers with earnings, public assistance, and food stamps for both nonmetro and metro areas. It also lists the median income received from each source.[1]

These data suggest several conclusions. Perhaps the most striking is that the percentage of poor female heads with earnings rose sharply

**Table 3.2  Percentage Receiving and Median Receipt of Earnings, Public Assistance and Food Stamps for Poor, Single Female–Headed Families with Children by Residence, 1989–99**

| Residence/Year | Earnings (%) | Earnings Median ($) | Public assistance (%) | Public assistance Median ($) | Food stamps (%) | Food stamps Median ($) |
|---|---|---|---|---|---|---|
| Nonmetropolitan | | | | | | |
| 1989 | 62.9 | 3,835 | 65.0 | 4,092 | 73.3 | 1,922 |
| 1990 | 59.1 | 4,995 | 53.6 | 3,786 | 65.9 | 2,366 |
| 1991 | 58.1 | 5,126 | 60.1 | 3,892 | 78.0 | 2,357 |
| 1992 | 59.8 | 5,026 | 61.4 | 3,673 | 74.8 | 2,394 |
| 1993 | 57.3 | 3,485 | 62.3 | 3,728 | 75.6 | 2,606 |
| 1994 | 55.3 | 4,258 | 64.7 | 3,920 | 79.4 | 2,301 |
| 1995 | 59.0 | 4,399 | 60.5 | 3,960 | 76.1 | 2,448 |
| 1996 | 62.5 | 4,599 | 59.1 | 3,979 | 70.4 | 2,541 |
| 1997 | 68.4 | 5,194 | 50.2 | 3,740 | 71.2 | 2,406 |
| 1998 | 66.2 | 5,562 | 49.5 | 3,583 | 65.7 | 2,437 |
| 1999 | 71.5 | 6,131 | 40.5 | 3,216 | 57.3 | 2,400 |
| Metropolitan | | | | | | |
| 1989 | 47.7 | 4,134 | 68.6 | 5,374 | 73.0 | 2,342 |
| 1990 | 45.5 | 5,258 | 66.4 | 5,269 | 72.1 | 2,449 |
| 1991 | 47.7 | 4,490 | 70.9 | 5,193 | 77.0 | 2,544 |
| 1992 | 46.8 | 5,134 | 66.9 | 5,220 | 73.3 | 2,729 |
| 1993 | 48.5 | 4,833 | 67.5 | 4,753 | 76.3 | 2,556 |
| 1994 | 46.5 | 4,306 | 68.5 | 4,981 | 78.3 | 2,558 |
| 1995 | 50.8 | 5,168 | 65.1 | 5,319 | 76.8 | 2,640 |
| 1996 | 53.7 | 5,348 | 61.9 | 4,894 | 73.1 | 2,695 |
| 1997 | 56.2 | 5,194 | 59.6 | 4,737 | 70.6 | 2,493 |
| 1998 | 63.5 | 5,586 | 50.6 | 4,291 | 65.4 | 2,437 |
| 1999 | 65.4 | 5,862 | 48.7 | 3,768 | 62.2 | 2,376 |

SOURCE: Original computations from the March Current Population Surveys, 1989–99.

in nonmetro areas after the mid 1990s, and especially after PRWORA. Although 59 percent had at least some earnings at mid decade, more than 70 percent reported earnings by 1999. This is a remarkable up-swing in a short period of time, especially because it occurred at the same time that poverty rates among female-headed families also de-clined.

The evidence that more poor women are working today than in the past has multiple interpretations, some benign, others less so. The be-nign view is that low-income female heads are now "playing by the rules" by seeking economic independence through employment. The welfare bill has accomplished its goal of moving a significant share of poor mothers into the labor force. The less benign view is that, despite working more, a large share of nonmetro single mothers and their chil-dren remain poor, and they are poor even as their average real earnings increased from $3,835 to $6,131 across the 1989–1999 period.

Poor rural women are arguably doing their part. The government's response, however, is reflected in the declining percentage of poor, nonmetro female heads who receive public assistance, from 65 percent in 1989 to 40.5 percent in 1999, and the declining real dollar value of welfare income (from $4,092 to $3,216 between 1989–1999). Food stamp receipt among the poor also declined during the past decade, from 73.3 percent in 1989 to 57.3 percent in 1999, although the median dollar value of food stamp receipt inched upward. Clearly, these wo-men remain poor because any gains from work have been offset by losses from public assistance income. Of course, we recognize that some of the employment and earnings increases reflect salutary re-sponses to other government policy initiatives, including the EITC.

For the most part, these rural trends in "income packaging" mirror national and metro patterns. The results nevertheless indicate clear and persistent differences between metro and nonmetro single female heads in their reliance on earnings and welfare. Poor, rural, single mothers are more likely than their urban counterparts to have earnings (71.5 percent vs. 65.4 percent in 1999) and the average dollar value of their earnings is greater ($6,131 vs. $5,862).[2] They are less likely to receive public assistance income (40.5 percent vs. 48.7 percent) and food stamps (57.3 percent vs. 62.2 percent). The dollar value of public as-sistance also is slightly lower for rural single mothers ($3,216 vs. $3,768). Rural single mothers are more likely than their metro counterparts to "play by the rules," yet a higher percentage were poor in 1999 (42.4 percent vs. 38.6 percent).

Based on available evidence, it is perhaps premature to make strong conclusions about different effects of PRWORA in metro and nonmetro areas. However, the early figures are instructive and are worth monitoring, especially as the full implications of PRWORA are revealed in the years ahead. Between 1996 and 1999, the percentage of poor female heads with earnings increased by 22 percent in metro areas and by 14 percent in nonmetro areas. The receipt of public assistance among poor female heads dropped by 21 percent in metro areas and by 31 percent in nonmetro areas. For metro areas, this means that declines in welfare receipt have been matched by similar increases in employment. The story is different in rural areas. The large drop in welfare receipt swamps the comparatively small increases in employment growth (i.e., 31 percent vs. 14 percent). The apparent policy implication is that rural mothers are leaving welfare without corresponding increases in work.

### Income packaging

The preceding analyses provided information about income from various sources. However, as shown in Figure 3.2, the sources of income can be packaged differently over time and place among nonmetro, poor, female-headed families. If welfare reform has had an impact on poor, female-headed families, we should expect that earnings represent an increasing share of family income, while welfare income will decline, on average.

The results confirm this expectation. For poor, female-headed families with children, earnings, on average, accounted for 34.9 percent of family income in 1989, while public assistance income represented 45 percent of money income. Ten years later, earnings provided a substantially larger share of family income (54.1 percent) than did public assistance income (30.5 percent). Clearly, poor, single mothers living in rural areas are less likely to be dependent on welfare income.

In general, trends in income packaging—more reliance on earnings and less on welfare—are observed in both nonmetro and metro areas (data not shown). Both metro and nonmetro areas experienced a 20 percentage point increase in the share of income from earnings over the

**Figure 3.2  Income Packaging among Poor, Nonmetropolitan, Single Fe-
male–Headed Families with Children, 1989–99**

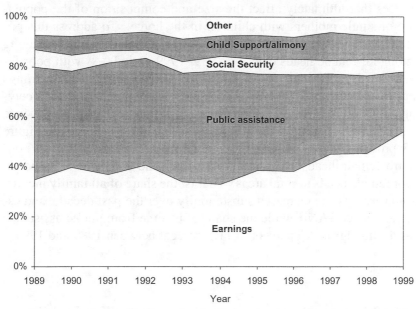

1989–1999 period.  However, there are also several interesting metro/
nonmetro differences.  For example, welfare income is much lower as a
percentage of family income among rural (versus urban) poor, female-
headed families with children (23.8 percent for rural mothers vs. 32
percent in 1999 for urban mothers).  Despite efforts to insure child support payments from so-called "deadbeat dads," child support (and alimony) constituted a very small share of family income in 1999, although this figure is slightly higher than observed in the late 1980s.  In
rural areas, however, child support and alimony accounted for roughly
twice the share of family income as in metro areas (9.4 percent vs. 4.5
percent), and this differential has grown over the past decade.  One explanation is that rural single mother families with children are more
likely to be products of divorce rather than nonmarital childbearing.
Divorced fathers are more likely than never-married fathers to be involved with their children, to be employed, and to make child support
payments (Garfinkel and Oellerich 1989).

Our results on income packaging among poor women must be interpreted with caution. They reflect, at least in part, changes over time in the choices all female heads make regarding work and welfare, choices that ultimately affect the size and composition of the population of single mothers with children in the home. To address this potential endogeneity problem, we have also examined income packaging among all female heads over the 1989–1999 period. As with poor female heads, the share of all nonmetro female heads with earnings reached its peak in 1999 (at 85.9 percent), while the proportion receiving public assistance (22.1 percent) or food stamps (31.3 percent) were at their nadir, at least for the period considered here. Moreover, Figure 3.3 provides the cumulative shares of income by source for all nonmetro female heads. These data reinforce the conclusions based on poor female heads in rural areas. That is, the share of all family income from earnings has increased substantially over the past decade, and especially since TANF, while the share of income from public assistance has declined from 25 percent to 11.3 percent between 1989 and 1999.

**Figure 3.3  Income Packaging among All Nonmetropolitan, Single Female–Headed Families with Children, 1989–99**

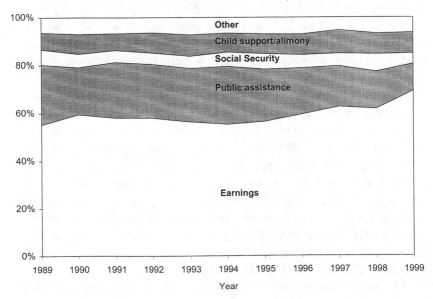

## The Ameliorative Effects of Public Assistance and Work

### Economic well-being among single mother families

The declining welfare receipt and share of family income from public assistance suggest that the ameliorative effects of public assistance—whether it lifts families above the poverty threshold—may have declined over the past decade (Jensen and Eggebeen 1994). It also begs the question of whether an increasing share of poor, female heads are poorer in absolute terms (e.g., declines in the median income-to-poverty ratio). To address this issue, we calculate, for each female-headed family, the ratio of family income to the appropriate poverty income threshold (IPR).[3]  Figure 3.4 charts the median IPR for all single mother families and for the poor in both nonmetro and metro areas. We also present a measure of deep poverty, which is defined by the percentage

**Figure 3.4  Income-to-Poverty Ratio for Female-Headed Families with Children, by Residence, 1989–99**

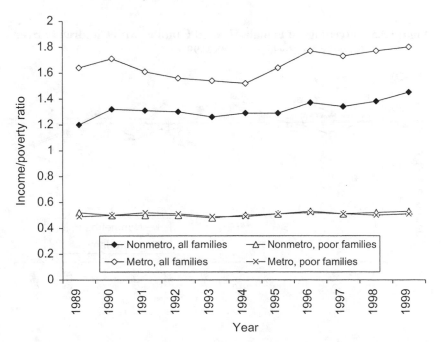

of all single mother families that are living below 50 percent of the official poverty threshold (Figure 3.5).

In general, the IPRs for all single mother families have increased
slightly since the mid 1990s, both in nonmetro and metro areas. For
example, in 1994, rural female heads had family incomes that were
1.29 times their poverty rates, a figure lower than that observed in
metro areas. This means that the average income of female heads was
29 percent higher than the poverty income threshold. By 1999, the income-to-poverty ratio had climbed to 1.45 in nonmetro areas and to
1.80 in metro areas. If we adjust for the EITC, these figures increase
slightly to 1.55 and 1.88. Although rural female heads are worse off
than their metro counterparts, they nevertheless have more family-size-
adjusted income after TANF than before.

The situation among the poor, single mothers is different. Regardless of residence, the average income of poor, single, female heads
showed no improvement, remaining at roughly 0.50 throughout the
1989–1999 period. This also means that poor, female-headed families
fell farther behind the average female-headed family income over the

**Figure 3.5  Percentage of Female-Headed Families with Children in Deep
Poverty, by Residence, 1989–99**

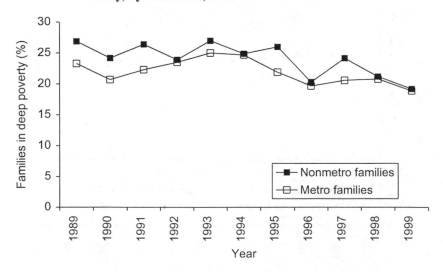

decade; that is, inequality increased among female-headed families. At the same time, the rate of deep poverty declined over this period, from 26.9 percent in 1989 to 19.2 percent in 1999 among nonmetro female heads, and from 23.3 percent to 18.9 percent among metro female heads (Figure 3.5). Because most deeply impoverished female heads are not employed, any adjustments for EITC have little or no effect on our estimates.

### Public assistance income and poverty

To what extent has public assistance income, both before and after TANF, improved the economic well-being of female family heads? In Table 3.3, we evaluate the ameliorative effects of public assistance. Among those whose income without welfare (public assistance and Supplemental Security Income (SSI)) is below the official poverty threshold, we calculate the percentage whose income when including welfare assistance with post-welfare income falls above that threshold (data column 1). In a similar way, we also calculate the ameliorative effects of public assistance income on deep poverty (data column 2); that is, for families with incomes below one-half the official poverty threshold when welfare income is excluded, we calculate the percentage that rise above the deep-poverty line when welfare income is added back in with other income. Finally, we estimate the percentage of the pre-welfare-income poverty gap (i.e., the difference between the poverty threshold and pre-welfare income) that is closed by public assistance (data column 3). This measure is restricted to those whose pre-welfare income is less than the official threshold, and it is forced to equal 100 percent when post-welfare income exceeds the poverty threshold.

The time trends indicate that the ameliorative effects of public assistance income have not only been modest, but may have deteriorated slightly since PRWORA. For example, among nonmetro female heads, the ameliorative effect of public assistance on poverty grew over much of the early 1990s, peaking at 6.6 percent in 1996. The appropriate interpretation is that 6.6 percent of those whose pre-welfare income was below the official poverty income threshold were lifted from poverty by the receipt of welfare income. By 1999, the ameliorative effect of public assistance had declined to 4 percent. This finding apparently re-

**Table 3.3  Ameliorative Effects of Public Assistance among Female-Headed Families with Children, 1989–99 (%)**

| CPS year | Nonmetropolitan | | | Metropolitan | | |
|---|---|---|---|---|---|---|
| | Pre-welfare poor lifted above poverty | Pre-welfare deeply poor lifted above deep poverty | Pre-welfare poverty gap closed | Pre-welfare poor lifted above poverty | Pre-welfare deeply poor lifted above deep poverty | Pre-welfare poverty gap closed |
| 1989 | 4.3 | 29.2 | 28.6 | 4.9 | 35.0 | 32.6 |
| 1990 | 3.6 | 27.4 | 23.3 | 5.4 | 36.6 | 32.6 |
| 1991 | 2.4 | 27.3 | 24.2 | 5.9 | 36.0 | 33.7 |
| 1992 | 4.7 | 30.4 | 24.1 | 3.5 | 33.7 | 30.1 |
| 1993 | 4.2 | 24.0 | 24.4 | 5.5 | 31.5 | 30.6 |
| 1994 | 4.4 | 33.4 | 28.9 | 6.4 | 33.9 | 31.8 |
| 1995 | 5.4 | 31.7 | 26.1 | 6.3 | 33.5 | 31.3 |
| 1996 | 6.6 | 35.3 | 27.5 | 7.7 | 35.8 | 31.5 |
| 1997 | 4.6 | 28.8 | 22.2 | 6.4 | 32.6 | 28.6 |
| 1998 | 3.9 | 26.3 | 21.0 | 5.7 | 26.2 | 24.0 |
| 1999 | 4.0 | 28.0 | 17.5 | 6.0 | 26.5 | 22.8 |

SOURCE: Original computations from the March Current Population Surveys, 1989–99.

flects the declining percentage who receive assistance, and continuing declines in the amount of public assistance received by poor, female-headed families.

The ameliorative effects of public assistance on poverty have generally been smaller in nonmetro than metro America. The nonmetro disadvantage is seen most clearly with the first (poverty threshold) and third (poverty gap) measures of amelioration. For example, in nonmetro areas, the poverty gap measure declined by 36 percent between 1996 and 1999, while in metro areas the decline was 28 percent. The ameliorative effects of public assistance on deep poverty also were substantial and favored metro residents until the late 1990s. In 1999, a larger percentage of nonmetro than metro female heads were brought out of deep poverty by the receipt of public assistance.

Our results must be interpreted in light of significant expansions over the last decade in the EITC. For example, if we treat the EITC as public assistance income, 20.6 percent (rather than 4 percent) of nonmetro, poor female heads are lifted out of poverty, and 33.1 percent (rather than 28 percent) are no longer deeply impoverished. The percentage of the pre-welfare poverty gap that is closed increases dramatically, from 17.5 percent to 47.1 percent if EITC is treated as public assistance. More important, the ameliorative effects of public assistance (including EITC) increased substantially over the past decade. Whereas 8.1 percent of rural female heads were lifted from poverty in 1992 as a result of public assistance and EITC, 20.6 percent were helped out of poverty in 1999. This is nearly identical to the figure observed in metro areas (21 percent). When TANF income is considered along with income supports (through EITC), the improving salutary effects on poverty are clear.

### Work and poverty

As we have shown, female heads of household in rural areas are less dependent on welfare income, now more than any time in recent memory. Many have moved successfully from welfare to work. However, what are the ameliorative effects of maternal employment on poverty in rural areas? Does employment lift them out of poverty? We address this question in Table 3.4, which lists poverty rates for working and nonworking single female heads. As with the measure of annual

**Table 3.4  Official and Adjusted Poverty Rates by Work Status and Residence among Single Female–Headed Families with Children, 1989–99**

| CPS Year | Official poverty rate by work status | | | | Adjusted[a] poverty rate by work status | | | |
|---|---|---|---|---|---|---|---|---|
| | All workers | | | Non-workers | All workers | | | Non-workers |
| | Total | FT/FY[b] | Other | | Total | FT/FY[b] | Other | |
| Nonmetropolitan | | | | | | | | |
| 1989 | 40.2 | 17.7 | 66.5 | 89.1 | NA | NA | NA | NA |
| 1990 | 36.0 | 13.9 | 63.4 | 87.6 | NA | NA | NA | NA |
| 1991 | 37.8 | 15.0 | 63.0 | 89.0 | NA | NA | NA | NA |
| 1992 | 37.0 | 16.9 | 58.0 | 88.1 | 34.5 | 14.1 | 55.9 | 88.1 |
| 1993 | 34.7 | 11.3 | 61.2 | 88.3 | 31.7 | 8.8 | 57.6 | 88.3 |
| 1994 | 35.4 | 13.0 | 61.0 | 89.5 | 31.5 | 9.6 | 56.5 | 89.5 |
| 1995 | 40.2 | 15.6 | 64.5 | 85.3 | 33.6 | 9.1 | 57.9 | 85.3 |
| 1996 | 33.7 | 13.7 | 55.7 | 85.6 | 26.9 | 6.5 | 49.4 | 85.6 |
| 1997 | 39.0 | 16.3 | 62.9 | 85.5 | 31.5 | 9.1 | 55.0 | 85.5 |
| 1998 | 38.1 | 16.9 | 67.6 | 80.1 | 27.8 | 8.6 | 54.6 | 80.1 |
| 1999 | 35.0 | 17.4 | 62.9 | 78.8 | 26.1 | 8.3 | 54.4 | 78.8 |
| Metropolitan | | | | | | | | |
| 1989 | 26.6 | 8.9 | 55.2 | 87.2 | NA | NA | NA | NA |
| 1990 | 24.3 | 8.3 | 47.8 | 85.8 | NA | NA | NA | NA |
| 1991 | 27.9 | 7.6 | 56.3 | 86.1 | NA | NA | NA | NA |
| 1992 | 29.7 | 10.5 | 56.8 | 89.1 | 26.0 | 7.8 | 51.7 | 89.1 |
| 1993 | 29.5 | 10.0 | 57.4 | 87.9 | 25.9 | 7.9 | 51.8 | 87.9 |
| 1994 | 29.3 | 10.7 | 54.0 | 85.9 | 26.4 | 8.4 | 50.2 | 85.9 |
| 1995 | 28.4 | 11.0 | 54.5 | 86.5 | 23.4 | 7.1 | 47.9 | 86.5 |
| 1996 | 27.4 | 12.9 | 51.3 | 83.9 | 20.7 | 6.6 | 43.9 | 83.9 |
| 1997 | 28.0 | 9.0 | 57.7 | 84.4 | 21.6 | 4.0 | 49.0 | 84.4 |
| 1998 | 30.6 | 10.8 | 61.2 | 83.3 | 23.2 | 6.2 | 49.6 | 83.3 |
| 1999 | 29.2 | 12.1 | 54.8 | 82.1 | 21.7 | 5.5 | 46.1 | 82.1 |

[a]  Official poverty rate adjusted for earned income tax credit.  NA = not available.
[b]  FT/FY = full-time, full-year.
SOURCE: Original computations from the March Current Population Surveys, 1989–99.

income and poverty, employment status in the March CPS is based on work-related activities during the previous year. For our purposes, we distinguish between those working full-time, full-year, those working part-time or part-year (other), and those not working at all.[4]

These data yield several general observations. First and foremost is the fact that work clearly matters in the economic lives of rural single mothers (Table 3.4, left-most four columns). In 1999, for example, the poverty rate among all working female heads was 35 percent, compared with 78.8 percent among their nonworking counterparts in nonmetro areas. The poverty rate among full-time, full-year working single mothers was still high (17.4 percent), but it was substantially lower than for nonworkers and part-time workers. Not surprisingly, the benefits from work are even greater if we adjust income upward for the EITC. Such adjustments suggest that only 8.3 percent of nonmetro female heads who worked full-time were poor in 1999. Interpreted differently, the EITC cuts the official poverty rate in half.

Our results also indicate that the economic benefits from employment have changed very little over the 1990s in nonmetro areas. The poverty rate among rural employed single moms fluctuated between roughly 35 percent and 40 percent over the past decade. That poverty rates remained constant among workers, amid an overall decline in poverty, suggests that recent declines in poverty among all female heads largely resulted from increasing labor force participation rather than from increased remuneration from work. At the same time, the poverty rate among nonworkers, although typically exceeding 80 percent, has trended downward slightly since welfare reform. One interpretation is that the "truly disadvantaged" are more likely to be helped today—albeit only marginally more so—in the currently tougher welfare environment.

Although some additional analyses (not reported) reveal that a larger share of poor nonmetro than metro female heads are working (68.6 percent of poor nonmetro vs. 62.2 percent of poor metro) and working full-time (21 percent vs. 15.4 percent), this does not result from greater incentives or remuneration from work in rural areas. In fact, work tends to pay less in nonmetro areas (Table 3.4). For each year, poverty rates are higher among rural, working, female heads than among their urban counterparts, although this differential has declined somewhat over the past decade. In 1999, 35 percent of working, rural single mothers were poor compared with 29.2 percent in metro areas. For full-time workers, the figures were 17.4 percent and 12.1 percent, respectively, in nonmetro and metro areas. Although the poverty rate among working female heads was nearly 20 percent higher in nonmetro than metro areas, this represents substantial convergence since 1989 when the nonmetro rate was over 50 percent higher than the metro rate. Declines in the urban advantage are not altered appreciably if we adjust income upward for the EITC.

## DISCUSSION AND CONCLUSION

The PRWORA of 1996 ended the nation's largest cash assistance program (AFDC) for needy, single-parent families. Many of the early forecasts about the putative effects of the new legislation on poor children have not materialized. Indeed, most indicators of "success" have painted a rather rosy picture: declining welfare caseloads, a dip in poverty rates for female-headed families with children, and rising labor force participation rates (and, supposedly, rising economic independence) among unmarried mothers with children. The question today is largely one of identifying specific population groups that have been helped or hurt most by state welfare reform policies (i.e., TANF).

In this spirit, our goal has been to evaluate recent economic trends among America's largely forgotten rural families and children. Specifically, we have focused on changes in labor force behavior and welfare participation of rural, single mother families, who often remain invisible in the national debate about welfare reform. However, rural mothers—especially poor single mothers—face many barriers to employment that seem incongruent with current legislative mandates that emphasize time limits on receipt and that require recipients to find work or face sanctions. Whether such an agenda is practical or realistic in isolated rural areas is an empirical question, one that we have taken up in this chapter. Indeed, the longstanding problems of limited job skills and education, depressed labor markets, poor transportation, and inadequate child care pose serious barriers to adequate employment among many rural women (Rural Sociological Task Force on Persistent

Rural Poverty 1993). They also may vitiate against successful welfare reform in rural areas.

Our analysis, however, revealed some unexpected, but welcome, surprises during the period since PRWORA; trends that provide reasons for optimism about the state of rural America. In general, rural mothers and their children have not been "left behind" in the new welfare policy and economic environment. For the most part, recent trends in rural poverty, earnings, and welfare receipt have followed national patterns. During the past decade, but especially since welfare reform was introduced nationally in 1996, rural poverty rates (including deep poverty) have declined among female-headed families, rates of welfare receipt have dropped dramatically, and labor force participation has increased along with average earnings. Moreover, the income of all rural, female-headed families with children increased, on average, over the past few years, and even more if we add income from the EITC. The early, gloomy forecasts have not matched the empirical record, at least not to date. Instead, our data have provided a measure of hope for rural families, and, more important, have indicated that the "new" economy and the "end of welfare" have not seriously undermined the economic gains made by rural women over the past generation or more.

Our data nevertheless also tell the familiar story of persistent rural-urban inequality in the lives of single mothers and their children (Friedman and Lichter 1998; Tickamyer and Duncan 1990). About 7.5 million poor people live in rural areas, and rural poverty rates continue to exceed those in urban areas (Dalaker 1999). In 1999, for example, about 42 percent of rural, female-headed families were poor, and about one-half of these had incomes less than one-half the poverty threshold. This happened even though the share of rural female heads who were employed grew and continued to exceed their urban counterparts. In addition, rural/urban differences in poverty occurred despite higher average earnings among rural female heads; median earnings of rural women were about $6,131 in 1998, compared with $5,862 among urban women. More than most, rural single mothers have played by the new rules seeking to balance welfare receipt with personal responsibility and work. The problem today for most poor rural mothers is finding a good job that pays a living wage. Over one-third of working rural female heads are in poverty, a rate higher than at any time during the period examined here. Increases in poverty rates among working, rural, female heads occurred hand-in-hand with the rising proportion of poor female heads who are employed. It also occurred despite increases in the minimum wage and expansions to the EITC.

As in the past, rural poverty today is reinforced by comparatively low and declining rates of rural welfare receipt and the low dollar value of welfare transfers. As we have shown here, welfare reform clearly has been associated with the aggregate movement from welfare to work in rural areas. Over the past ten years, the proportions of rural single mothers with earnings from work increased dramatically. It is also true, however, that the rise in the proportion with earnings has not kept pace with the large decrease in the proportion with welfare income since the passage of PRWORA. This pattern was not apparent among metro female heads; for them, the drop in welfare receipt was offset almost entirely by the growth in earnings. Compared with metro female heads, welfare reform has hurt rural women; they have been removed from welfare without a proportionate increase in employment. This fact accounts for the larger share of family income among rural female heads that derives from employment. It also explains why the ameliorative effects of public assistance on rural poverty have declined.

Our results, supporting both optimistic and pessimistic interpretations of welfare success, seemingly provide something for everyone. As such, they also suggest a cautious approach to the evidence. Neither unbridled optimism nor pessimism about current trends can be projected into the short- or long-term future, for several reasons. Indeed, the next few years will be especially telling, as the "hardest cases" and other nonworking, welfare-dependent mothers run up against time limits for welfare receipt, or if the economy slows down and unemployment creeps up to pre-1994 levels. Moreover, static measures of welfare "success" or "failure," such as those reported here, are incomplete. Aggregate annual statistics do not represent a fixed or unchanging population but are the net product of transitions into and out of poverty and welfare dependence. Behavioral data (i.e., individual data on poverty transitions) will be required to measure the changing extent and etiology of individual adaptations to rural welfare reform, especially among hard to serve cases.

We should also be mindful that our baseline results apply to non-metro areas as a whole; we have not examined recent changes for particular rural regions, nor have we identified differences or similarities across historically disadvantaged racial or ethnic groups such as Native Americans or blacks (Swanson 1996). Rural minorities are "doubly disadvantaged" (Jensen and Tienda 1989; Saenz and Thomas 1991). Although our focus on employment and poverty has clear interpretive advantages (in terms of data availability over time) for rural policy, conventional measures may be less indicative today of the quality of rural life or of economic hardship generally. Underemployment is especially common in rural areas (Findeis and Jensen 1998), and income-based measures of family poverty may be seriously flawed, especially if the new family realities in our increasingly multicultural society are ignored. "Doubling up," adoption and fosterage, unmarried cohabitation, and multigenerational households are sometimes viewed with a jaundiced eye, a cause rather than a consequence of the problem. They might also be regarded as family survival strategies, as symptoms of poverty, or as "safety nets" for some poor women.[5] Whether rural family behavioral responses to welfare reform differ from the rest of the nation remains unclear (Struthers and Bokemeier 2000).

Finally, our results are not meant to pit the policy and economic interests of rural and urban America against each other. The paradox today is that the forces of geographic balkanization and of globalism have occurred simultaneously. In fact, throughout this century, rural and urban areas have become increasingly integrated, culturally, politically, and economically. New information technologies (radio, television, and the internet), transportation innovations, and mass production and mass marketing bind rural and urban people and communities together and reinforce interdependence (and dependence, in some instances). For rural America, ignored or forgotten economic and social problems tend to become America's urban problems. The urban migration of displaced rural blacks from southern agriculture to northern cities, or poor whites from depressed mining areas of Appalachia, are obvious historical cases in point. This spatial relationship is hardly asymmetric. Examples include the encroachment of urban residential and commercial activity on the rural hinterland, the expansion of urban-based corporate agriculture and other business interests in rural communities, and the delivery of health and social services (e.g., medical services, social welfare, job services, etc.), which often tax the resources of urban-based government providers. What is good (or bad) for rural America is good (or bad) for urban America, and vice versa. Rural and urban communities and people increasingly share a common destiny.

## Notes

This research was supported by a Population Research Center Core Grant (P30 HD28263-01) from the National Institute of Child Health and Human Development to the Population Research Institute, Pennsylvania State University; by a National Research Initiative grant from the U.S. Department of Agriculture (NRICGP 98-35401-6157); and by the Russell Sage Foundation. We thank Karin Garver and J. Brian Brown for technical assistance, and Calvin Beale and Greg Duncan for helpful comments.

1.  Median income for a given source is calculated on the basis the population of female householders with positive income from that source. For each year, median income is calibrated in 1998 dollars, using the CPI-U.
2.  The higher average earnings among nonmetro, poor, female heads is more likely to reflect greater labor supply than higher wage rates. In fact, the 1999 CPS indicates that nonmetro poor women worked, on average, 25 weeks during the previous year, compared with 21.3 weeks for metro poor women.
3.  If two families of different sizes have the same family income, the IPR will be lower (appropriately so) for the larger family than the smaller family because more income is needed to exceed the poverty income threshold. Thus, the income-to-poverty ratio provides a useful family-size-adjusted measure of family income. It is based on the income equivalency scales implicit in the poverty thresholds for families of different sizes.
4.  Keep in mind that these data are presented for each CPS year, which means that work and poverty refer to the previous year. For example, the poverty changes reported here between 1996 and 1997 actually took place 1995 and 1996.
5.  Our analysis has been restricted to primary female heads with children; it does not include children and their unmarried mothers who move in with grandparents or other relatives.

## References

Annie E. Casey Foundation. 2000. *2000 KIDS COUNT Data Book*. Available on-line at <http://www.aecf.org/kidscount/kc2000>.
Andrews, David, and Raymond L. Burke. 1999. "A Crisis in Rural America." *America* 181(13): 8–11.

Brown, David L., and Thomas A. Hirschl. 1995. "Household Poverty in Rural and Metropolitan-Core Areas in the United States." *Rural Sociology* 60: 44–66.

Brown, David L., and Milred Warner. 1989. "Persistent Low-Income Nonmetropolitan Areas in the United States." *Policy Studies Journal* 19:22–41.

Burke, Sandra Charvat, Willis Goudy, Margaret Hanson, and Michael Blank. 1999. "Employment and Unemployment in Iowa's Counties, 1980–1998." Available on-line at <http://www.iowa.org/communities/>.

Citro, Constance F., and Robert T. Michael. 1995. *Measuring Poverty: A New Approach*. Washington, D.C.: National Academy Press.

Conger, Rand D., and Glen H. Elder, Jr. 1994. *Families in Troubled Times: Adapting to Change in Rural America*. New York: Aldine de Gruyter.

Dagata, Elizabeth. 1999. "The Socioeconomic Well-Being of Rural Children Lags that of Urban Children." *Rural Conditions and Trends* 9(2): 85–90. Available on-line at <http://www.ers.usda.gov/epubs/pdf/rcat/rcat92/rcat92o.pdf>.

Dalaker, Joseph. 1999. *Poverty in the United States: 1998*. U.S. Census Bureau, Current Population Reports, Series P60-207, Washington, D.C.

Duncan, Cynthia. 1992. *Rural Poverty in America*. New York: Auburn House.

Duncan, Cynthia M., and Nita Lamborghini. 1994. "Poverty and Social Context in Remote Rural Communities." *Rural Sociology* 59: 437–461.

Findeis, Jill L., and Leif Jensen. 1998. "Employment Opportunities in Rural Areas: Implications for Poverty in a Changing Policy Environment." *American Journal of Agricultural Economics* 80: 1000–1007.

Fitchen, Janet M. 1991. *Endangered Spaces, Enduring Places: Change, Identity, and Survival in Rural America*. Boulder, Colorado: Westview Press.

Flynt, Wayne. 1996. "Rural Poverty in America." *Phi Kappa Phi Journal* 76: 32–42.

Fossett, Mark A., and M. Therese Seibert. 1997. *Long Time Coming: Racial Inequality in the Nonmetropolitan South, 1940–1990*. Boulder, Colorado: Westview Press.

Friedman, Samantha, and Daniel T. Lichter. 1998. "Spatial Inequality and Poverty among American Children." *Population Research and Policy Review* 17(2): 91–109.

Garasky, Steven. 2000. "Understanding the Employment Experiences and Migration Patterns of Rural Youth and Young Adults." Working paper no. 143, Joint Center for Poverty Research, Chicago, Illinois.

Garfinkel, Irving, and Donald Oellerich. 1989. "Noncustodial Fathers' Ability to Pay Child Support." *Demography* 26(2): 219–233.

Jensen, Leif, and David J. Eggebeen. 1994. "Nonmetropolitan Poor Children and Reliance on Public Assistance." *Rural Sociology* 59: 45–65.

Jensen, Leif, and Diane K. McLaughlin. 1995. "Human Capital and Nonmetropolitan Poverty." In *Investing in People: The Human Capital Needs of Rural America*, Lionel J. Beaulieu and David Mulkey, eds. Boulder, Colorado: Westview Press.

Jensen, Leif, and Marta Tienda. 1989. "Nonmetropolitan Minority Families in the United States: Trends in Racial and Ethnic Economic Stratification, 1959–1986." *Rural Sociology* 54: 509–532.

Lichter, Daniel T. 1997. "Poverty and Inequality among Children." *Annual Review of Sociology* 23: 121–145.

Lichter, Daniel T., and Janice Costanzo. 1987. "Nonmetropolitan Underemployment and Labor Force Composition." *Rural Sociology* 51: 329–344.

Lichter, Daniel T., and David J. Eggebeen. 1992. "Child Poverty and the Changing Rural Family." *Rural Sociology* 57: 151–172.

Lichter, Daniel T., and Diane K. McLaughlin. 1995. "Changing Economic Opportunities, Family Structure, and Poverty in Rural Areas." *Rural Sociology* 60: 688–706.

Lichter, Daniel T., Gail M. Johnston, and Diane K. McLaughlin. 1994. "Changing Linkages between Work and Poverty in Rural America." *Rural Sociology* 59: 395–415.

Lichter, Daniel T., Diane K. McLaughlin, and Gretchen T. Cornwell. 1995. "Migration and the Loss of Human Resources in Rural Areas." In *Investing in People: The Human Capital Needs of Rural America*, L.J. Beaulieu and D. Mulkey, eds. Boulder, Colorado: Westview Press.

Lobao, Linda, Jamie Rulli, and Lawrence A. Brown. 1999. "Macrolevel Theory and Local-Level Inequality: Industrial Structure, Institutional Arrangements, and the Political Economy of Redistribution, 1970 and 1990." *Annals of the Association of American Geographers* 89: 571–601.

Lyson, Thomas A., and William W. Falk. 1992. *Forgotten Places*. Lawrence: University of Kansas Press.

Marks, Ellen L., Sarah Dewees, Tammy Ouellette, and Robin Koralek. 1999. *Rural Welfare to Work Strategies: Research Synthesis*. Calverton, Maryland: Macro International, Inc.

Massey, Douglas S. 1996. "The Age of Extremes: Concentrated Affluence and Poverty in the Twenty-First Century." *Demography* 33: 395–412.

McLaughlin, Diane K., Erica L. Gardner, and Daniel T. Lichter. 1999. "Economic Restructuring and Changing Prevalence of Female-Headed Families in America." *Rural Sociology* 64: 394–416.

McLaughlin, Diane K., Daniel T. Lichter, and Stephen A. Matthews. 1999. *Demographic Diversity and Economic Change in Appalachia.* Final report, Appalachia Regional Commission, Washington, D.C.

Nord, Mark. 2000. "Does It Cost Less to Live in Rural Areas? Evidence from New Data on Food Security and Hunger." *Rural Sociology* 65: 104–126.

Nord, M., A.E. Luloff, and Leif Jensen. 1995. "Migration and the Spatial Concentration of Poverty." *Rural Sociology* 60: 399–415.

President's National Advisory Commission on Rural Poverty. 1968. *Rural Poverty in the United States.* Washington, D.C.: U.S. Government Printing Office.

Purdy, Jedediah. 1999. "The New Culture of Rural America." *The American Prospect* (December 20): 26–31.

Rural Sociological Society Task Force on Persistent Rural Poverty. 1993. *Persistent Poverty in Rural America.* Boulder, Colorado: Westview Press.

Saenz, Rogelio, and John K. Thomas. 1991. "Minority Poverty in Nonmetropolitan Texas." *Rural Sociology* 56: 204–223.

Schoeni, Robert F., and Rebecca M. Blank. 2000. *What Has Welfare Reform Accomplished? Impacts on Welfare Participation, Employment, Income, Poverty, and Family Structure.* Santa Monica: Rand Corporation.

Short, Kathleen, Thesia Garner, David Johnson, and Patricia Doyle. 1999. *Experimental Poverty Measures, 1990 to 1997.* Current Population Reports P60-205, Washington, D.C.

Struthers, Cynthia B., and Janet L. Bokemeier. 2000. "Myths and Realities of Raising and Creating Family Life in a Rural County." *Journal of Family Issues* 21: 17–46.

Swanson, Linda (ed.). 1996. *Racial/Ethnic Minorities in Rural Areas: Progress and Stagnation, 1980–90.* Agricultural Economic Report no. 731, Rural Economy Division, Research Service, U.S. Department of Agriculture, Washington, D.C.

Tickamyer, Ann R., and Cynthia M. Duncan. 1990. "Poverty and Opportunity Structure in Rural America." *Annual Review of Sociology* 16: 67–86.

U.S. Bureau of the Census. 1998. *Household and Family Characteristics: March 1998.* Current Population Reports, P20-515, Washington, D.C.

U.S. Bureau of the Census. 1999a. *Money Income in the United States: 1998.* Current Population Reports, P60-206, Washington, D.C.

U.S. Bureau of the Census. 1999b. March 1999 Current Population Survey. Available on-line at <http://www.census.gov/hhes/poverty/poverty98/table5.html>.

U.S. Bureau of Labor Statistics. 2000. *1998 Consumer Expenditure Survey.* Available on-line at <http://stats.bls.gov/csxstnd.htm>.

U.S. National Advisory Commission on Rural Poverty. 1968. *Rural Poverty in the United States: A Report by the President's National Advisory Commission on Rural Poverty.* Washington, D.C.: Government Printing Office.

Weinberg, Daniel H. 1987. "Rural Pockets of Poverty." *Rural Sociology* 52: 398–408.

# Part 2

# Welfare Dynamics in Rural and Urban Areas

# 4

# Reducing Food Stamp and Welfare Caseloads in the South

## Are Rural Areas Less Likely to Succeed Than Urban Centers?

Mark Henry
*Clemson University*

Lynn Reinschmiedt
*Mississippi State University*

Willis Lewis, Jr.
*Clemson University*

and

Darren Hudson
*Mississippi State University*

As this volume attests, welfare reform is likely to have different effects in different areas of the country. We consider how the distribution of cash assistance and food stamps across urban and rural areas may affect caseload change in the South. Some trends suggest that rural areas face more difficulty in reducing caseloads than urban areas; other trends do not. In this chapter, we provide a statistical test of rural/urban differences in capacity to reduce caseloads. Spatial effects are captured by contrasting caseload trends over time in metropolitan (urban) counties and nonmetropolitan (rural) counties in two southern states, Mississippi and South Carolina.[1]

A rural/urban difference in rates of program participation might be expected if barriers to moving off public assistance are more difficult to overcome in rural counties than in urban counties.[2] Moreover, there may be a link between the decline in welfare (Aid to Families with Dependent Children [AFDC] or Temporary Assistance for Needy Families [TANF]) caseloads and the recent declines in the Food Stamp program participation. Zedlewski and Brauner (1999), for example, found that those exiting welfare (beginning in 1995) leave the Food Stamp program at higher rates than families that had not been on welfare.

To test for location effects on caseload change, we use an empirical model that controls for trends in the vitality of the local (county) economy, trends in the "opportunity costs" (e.g., minimum-wage earnings, cash assistance, and the Earned Income Tax Credit) to the welfare recipient of not entering the workforce, and changes in welfare policy in each state. Findings from these tests indicate that reducing both welfare and food stamp participation rates will be more difficult in rural counties than in urban counties in these southern states.

## WHY METROPOLITAN/NONMETROPOLITAN CASELOAD ANALYSIS?

Urban and rural areas have very different kinds of economies. Rural areas tend to have a larger share of jobs in "routine" manufacturing, those further down the product life cycle. Many rural areas are dominated by a single industry, such as manufacturing, farming, or extractive industries, while urban economies offer jobs in a wide range of trade and services sectors. Because welfare caseloads can be affected by both the vitality of the economy and the kinds of economic sectors that are growing, diversified urban economies may have an advantage over rural areas in reducing caseloads.[3] In terms of work support services, rural areas lack professional child care facilities and public transit for daily commuting. Both services are much more likely to be available in urban than in rural counties. Each of these urban/rural differences suggests that reducing caseloads in rural counties will be a more difficult task than in urban counties, given the strength of the local economy and the policy regime in effect.[4]

## Why Look at Caseload Changes?

We take a slightly different approach to studying welfare participation than the approaches in much of the previous research. Modeling caseloads, as we do here, instead of examining exit rates of welfare participants (e.g., in leaver studies) has the advantage of capturing both entry and exit effects of changes in welfare policy (Moffitt 1999, pp. 96–97). Looking only at the exit population says little about how potential entrants respond to new policy, to the strength of the local economy, or to the opportunity cost of not entering the workforce.[5]

Because our goal is to test for urban/rural differences in caseloads over time, ignoring how potential entrants affect caseload changes assumes away much of the problem of understanding why caseloads increase or decline. A focus on total caseload change not only captures how policy, the local economy, and opportunity costs affect potential entrants, but also offers insight into related issues. Figlio and Ziliak (1999, p. 18), for example, note that if welfare caseloads are strongly associated with the rate at which the economy is growing, state fiscal problems may arise when the economy weakens. When the economy enters a recession, state TANF payments can be expected to rise sharply. States that have not set up a reserve fund from recent TANF block grant funds will be faced with difficult choices on work assistance program cutbacks and the need to raise new revenues.[6]

## Why Within-State Caseload Analysis?

Most analyses of caseload change have used panel studies across states and years.[7] Caseload changes appear to be sensitive both to the strength of the state economy and to the changing incentives embodied in the welfare reforms in each state. Using within-state analysis allows us to capture the effect of local county labor market conditions on welfare and food stamp participation decisions by households residing in that county. By tracking caseload changes in cash assistance programs and the Food Stamp program over time and across counties within a state, we also test for the effects of policy changes and for rural/urban differences in caseload changes. The welfare policy changes we examine include the adoption by South Carolina of the Family Independence

Act of 1996, under the TANF umbrella.[8]  In Mississippi, several counties obtained waivers from AFDC rules in 1995, and TANF was instituted statewide in 1997.[9]  The Food Stamp program changes in 1997, as mandated under the Personal Responsibility and Work Opportunity Reconciliation Act (PRWORA), reduced eligibility for some families but mainly reduced benefit levels for all and required coordination with TANF sanction rules (Zedlewski and Brauner 1999, pp. 4–8).

## RECENT TRENDS: MISSISSIPPI AND SOUTH CAROLINA[10]

### Mississippi Caseloads

The number of welfare and food stamp cases (household units) has declined dramatically since October of 1991 (see Figures 4.1 and 4.2). In the pre-TANF period (October 1991 through September 1996), the number of AFDC/TANF cases averaged 53,272 per month across all counties.  This average caseload in the post-TANF period (October 1996 through April 1999) declined to 31,123 cases, a decline of 43.8 percent.  Although not as significant, average county food stamp caseloads declined 25.1 percent in the post-TANF period (190,659 cases to 142,732 cases).  Caseload trends for three county groupings based on degrees of ruralness (Ghelfi and Parker 1997) are constructed: metropolitan counties (MET); nonmetropolitan (rural) counties adjacent to metropolitan counties (ADJ); and nonmetropolitan counties not adjacent to a metropolitan county (NONADJ).  In Figures 4.1 and 4.2, AFDC/TANF and food stamp caseload trends are compared with monthly unemployment rates for each spatial grouping.

### Welfare

Since the beginning of fiscal year (FY) 1992 on October 1, 1991, the number of AFDC/TANF cases (households) has declined steadily for all three groups of counties, metropolitan, rural adjacent, and rural nonadjacent (Figure 4.1).  Only in metropolitan counties was there a slight increase in cases from October 1991 through roughly mid July 1993.  Over the remainder of the time, cases have steadily dropped in all three county classifications.  Comparing average monthly caseloads

**Figure 4.1  Mississippi AFDC/TANF Caseloads and Unemployment Rates, 1991–99**

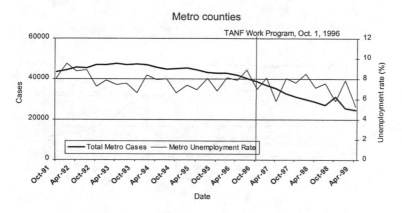

Metro counties

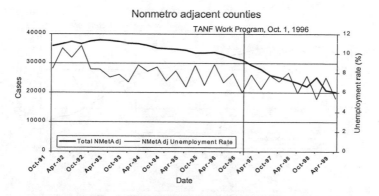

Nonmetro adjacent counties

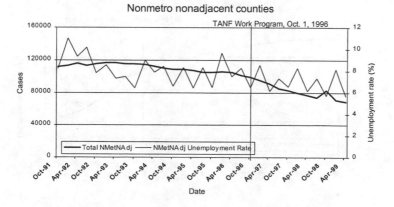

Nonmetro nonadjacent counties

**Figure 4.2  Mississippi Food Stamp Caseloads and Unemployment Rates, 1991–99**

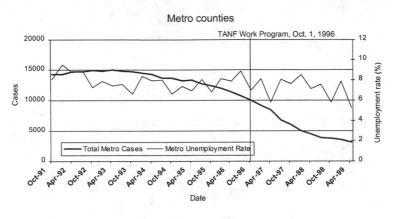

Metro counties

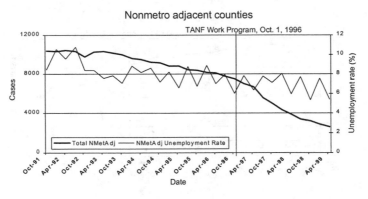

Nonmetro adjacent counties

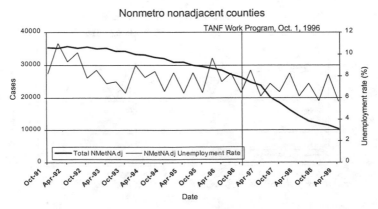

Nonmetro nonadjacent counties

in the pre- and post-TANF periods indicates that MET counties experienced a decline of 51.6 percent in caseloads (from 13,589 to 6,573), while ADJ caseloads fell by 43.5 percent (from 9,361 to 5,291), and NON-ADJ county caseloads fell by 40.6 percent (from 32,422 to 19,259).

Unemployment rates have also declined somewhat over the time period, reflecting the overall robustness of the state and national economies (Figure 4.1). However, there does not appear to be any clear correlation between welfare caseload changes and unemployment rates beyond the fact that both have fallen over time. Also, there are no sharp differences across the three county groupings in welfare cases and unemployment trends.

The rural/urban share of caseload numbers has changed somewhat over the 1990s. The rural share of total state caseloads increased from 59 percent to 62 percent, the rural adjacent county share remained essentially unchanged, and the metropolitan share dropped by almost 4 percent. These figures may reflect the barriers in rural areas to successful welfare-to-work transitions reported by Beeler et al. (1999).[11]

### Food stamps

As with welfare caseloads, food stamp caseloads have been declining, but at a significantly lower rate (Figure 4.2).[12] Food stamp trends reveal little correlation to fluctuations in unemployment rates. Mean monthly food stamp declines from the pre- to post-TANF periods were roughly half as great as those for welfare cases: 28 percent for metropolitan; 27 percent for rural adjacent; and 23 percent for rural nonadjacent areas. In contrast to welfare cases, where the rural share of total cases increased after welfare reform, food stamp shares of the total caseload by county groups remained essentially unchanged.

## South Carolina Caseloads

### Welfare

The number of welfare caseloads in South Carolina (household units) also declined steadily after the implementation of the Family Independence Act (FIA) in October 1996 (Figure 4.3). The monthly average caseloads across all counties in South Carolina declined from 47,610 in the pre-TANF period (January 1990 through September

**Figure 4.3  South Carolina AFDC/TANF Caseloads and Unemployment Rates, 1990–99**

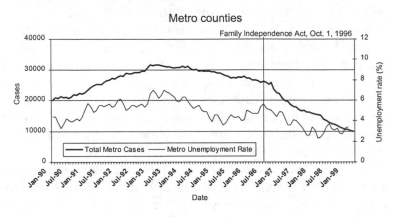

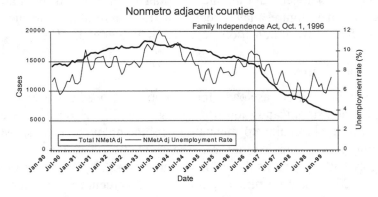

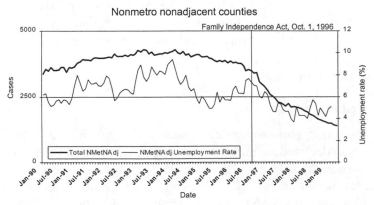

1996) to 32,566 during the post-TANF period (October 1996 through August 1998), a decline of 31.6 percent. The monthly caseload trend in metropolitan counties shows a sharp decline (29.1 percent) in the post-TANF period after October 1, 1996. The caseload declined from an average caseload of 27,280 in the pre-TANF period to 19,344 after TANF. Similar downturns are evident in rural counties adjacent to metropolitan counties and nonadjacent rural counties; each area experienced average caseload declines of about 35 percent from the pre- to post-TANF period averages.[13]

In South Carolina, metropolitan counties have the highest welfare caseloads, while in Mississippi, rural counties have the most welfare cases. Moreover, unlike in Mississippi, the trends in Figure 4.3 also suggest that the robustness of the local economies is correlated with changes in caseloads since the FIA was implemented. In each county group, the mean unemployment rate has declined since October 1996.[14] Although unemployment rates have been lower in metropolitan counties than in rural counties, the rates have fallen sharply across all county types since late 1996. Figure 4.3 suggests that strength in the local economy (lower unemployment rates) is associated with reduced welfare caseloads. When unemployment rates rise, welfare cases increase (as they did in the early 1990s). This local economy effect on caseloads seems to have been in play both before and after the state's TANF plan was implemented in October 1996. After 1996, the rural share of cases fell from 43 percent to 41 percent while the metropolitan share increased from 57 percent to 59 percent.

### Food stamps

In contrast to the dramatic declines in welfare caseloads since 1993, South Carolina food stamp caseloads have remained stable even as unemployment rates dipped in the mid 1990s. There is also no apparent reduction in caseloads after the FIA—especially in the rural counties (Figure 4.4). The number of food stamp caseloads is three to four times the number of cash assistance cases, suggesting an ongoing need for this form of support even as welfare caseloads have plunged over the 1990s.

In metropolitan counties, the number of food stamp caseloads in the 1990s fluctuated around 80,000 households each month. The trends

**Figure 4.4  South Carolina Food Stamp Caseloads and Unemployment
Rates, 1990–99**

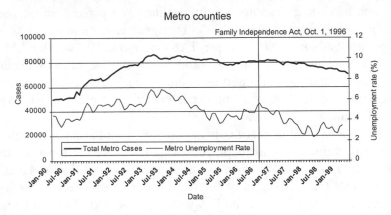

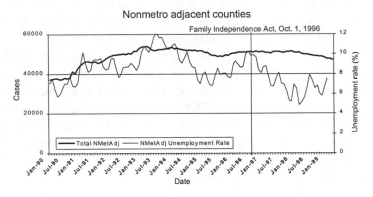

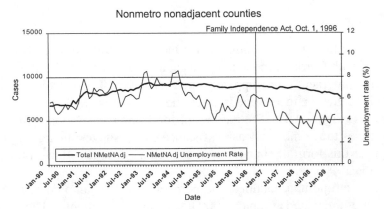

in Figure 4.4 suggest that food stamp caseloads vary with the unemployment rate in metropolitan counties—with perhaps the beginning of a downward trend appearing in 1997. In rural adjacent counties, about 50,000 households received food stamps in the 1990s. The number of caseloads did not deviate much from this level throughout the decade. Even more apparent is the lack of correlation between changes in the rural nonadjacent unemployment rate and the number of food stamp cases. In these rural counties, food stamp caseloads hovered around 10,000 even as the unemployment rate dropped from over 8 percent to about 4 percent.

The mean number of metropolitan county food stamp caseloads declined by about 3 percent from the pre-FIA to the post-FIA period. In rural counties, the decline was about 1 percent. These results differ sharply from the 31.6 percent decline seen in the cash assistance cases after the FIA was implemented. Because the FIA does not end food stamp eligibility and many of the jobs taken by former FIA clients are in entry-level, service-sector jobs, it is not surprising that many former welfare clients draw on food stamps to help cover the basic costs of living.[15] It appears that rural households may have a more long-term need for food stamp assistance than households in metropolitan counties. This may be due to a more attractive mix of job opportunities (and earnings potential) in metropolitan counties than in rural counties. Or, it may reflect differing demographic characteristics of urban and rural low-wage households that suggest more persistent need for food stamp assistance in rural areas.

A key finding in the pre- and post-FIA caseloads by county type is that rural counties in South Carolina do not seem to be at a disadvantage in reducing caseloads. The state share of caseloads in rural counties is smaller after the FIA than before. However, population and the associated resident labor force may also be growing faster in metro counties than in rural counties. If so, the caseloads per capita may be increasing in rural areas relative to urban areas. A summary of surveys of former FIA clients presented in Reinschmiedt et al. (1999) indicated that inadequate public transportation and child care continue to be barriers to reducing welfare caseloads in Mississippi. However, without a rural-urban distinction in the South Carolina leaver surveys, it is unclear whether these barriers are worse in rural or urban counties.

## CASELOAD CHANGES: TESTS FOR A "RURAL DISADVANTAGE"

Some caseload trends in Mississippi and South Carolina suggest that there are more severe barriers to moving off public assistance and more need for food assistance in rural counties relative to urban counties; other trends do not. We examine the "rural disadvantage" hypothesis using econometric models of caseload change along the lines of those developed by the Council of Economic Advisers (1999).[16] The formal model is presented in the appendix.

The dependent variable in this model is the caseload participation rate—the number of caseloads in a county divided by the county labor force.[17] Because a county with a larger population (and labor force) will have more caseloads than less densely populated counties, a proper test for rural-urban differences must control for the size of the county labor force (or population). Using caseload participation rates achieves this control.

To explain why caseload participation rates may have changed over time, three groups of "explanatory variables" are used in the regression model. These include opportunity cost variables, TANF and the economy variables, and region identifiers to test for rural/urban differences in caseload participation rates, holding other factors constant.

### "Opportunity Cost" Variables[18]

The first opportunity cost variable, the value of the Earned Income Tax Credit (EITC), has been assigned an important role in reducing caseloads by Ellwood (2000). Its value changed substantially over the 1990s, giving more incentives to welfare recipients to join the workforce. These changes are proxied by the average maximum EITC for taxpayers with children for each year, 1990–1999. As the value of the EITC increases, caseloads should decline because the earned income forgone by remaining on welfare increases.

The second opportunity cost variable is the monthly value of state minimum wage divided by the maximum monthly AFDC/TANF cash assistance benefit for a family of three. Because many former welfare clients begin work in the low-wage segment of the labor market, changes in the minimum wage serve as a good proxy for the expected wage income for former welfare participants who enter the labor market. By comparing this expected wage income from working to the cash assistance forgone by leaving welfare, welfare recipients can estimate the expected net income benefits from voluntarily leaving AFDC/TANF.

**TANF and the Economy Variables**[19]

Several welfare policy variables are constructed to test for the effect that TANF reforms have had on changes in caseloads, holding constant opportunity costs, the strength of the county economy and urban-rural location of the welfare recipients. Tests of the effect of the TANF reforms at the county level in the two states are made using three variables. First, a simple test for a discrete change in caseloads before and after TANF is made. This discrete effect—independent of the strength of the local economy—might arise from aspects of the TANF reforms that reflect new sanction rules, time limits, and efficiencies or "cultural" reforms in how the local welfare agencies provide services to welfare clients under TANF versus AFDC.

A second welfare policy variable tests the proposition that TANF reforms are likely to reduce caseloads only in conjunction with a robust county economy that provides job opportunities to former welfare clients. Simply put, welfare reform may provide a host of incentives to exit welfare but if no jobs are available, one would not expect the caseloads to decline. To test this hypothesis, we create two interaction variables. If the TANF reforms reduce caseloads mainly when the unemployment rate is falling, then the interaction variable will have a positive parameter (increasing the expected positive parameter value for the unemployment rate variable in the TANF period compared to the AFDC period).

The role of the local economy in caseload change is also captured in a second variable, the employment growth rate for the county. Employment growth is a good indicator of how well the local economy is generating new jobs for welfare leavers and those who might be new entrants to the welfare program. In contrast, the unemployment rate reflects household decisions on labor force participation and underlying population change as well as local job generation. Faster local job growth should reduce welfare caseloads; a negative parameter is expected for the employment growth variable. As before, if TANF reforms are most effective when jobs are more plentiful, then the interaction effect between local employment growth rates and TANF should be significant, and the parameter estimate should be negative. Faster job growth is expected to reduce welfare caseloads and caseloads are expected to decline faster in the post-TANF period under this scenario.

## Regions Used to Test for Rural/Urban Differences in Caseload Change

We estimate several regression models to reflect alternative ways to define "rurality" using *alternative* dummy variables representing location effects. In the first regression, a simple indicator variable identifies counties as either metropolitan or nonmetropolitan. The second regression tests for a "remote" rural disadvantage by dividing the nonmetropolitan counties into a group adjacent to metro counties and nonmetropolitan counties not adjacent to metropolitan counties. Welfare participants in counties more distant from urban job centers may have less access to jobs than welfare participants in counties near urban counties.

A third regression divides the nonmetro counties into one of four economic base groups: farm, manufacturing, government, or other, the last including services and nonspecialized (Ghelfi and Parker 1997). Positive parameters on these dummy variables would indicate that counties in these classes are less likely to reduce welfare participation rates than are urban counties, given the same vitality of the local economy, opportunity cost of not working, and policy regime. This is a way to control for "industry mix" effects on welfare participation that Bartik and Eberts (1999) found to be useful in explaining changes in welfare caseloads.

In addition, each state was divided into functional economic regions (economic areas developed in Johnson 1995). These regions have an urban center and rural hinterland that are connected by substantial within-region commuting. Regions with a booming urban center that offers jobs to residents in proximate rural areas are expected to have more success in reducing rural caseloads than other regions. Including economic area region variables also provides control for the type of urban center: government-dominated urban areas such as Columbia, South Carolina, and Jackson, Mississippi; manufacturing-dominated regions such as the Greenville-Spartanburg metro center along the I-85 growth corridor from Charlotte to Atlanta; and resort-tourism service oriented urban areas such as Charleston, South Carolina, and the Mississippi Gulf Coast.

### Food stamps model

The food stamps model is similar to the welfare caseload model used by the Council of Economic Advisors (CEA) for two reasons. First, across most states, there has been a strong correlation between food stamps and AFDC/TANF caseload changes. Second, important changes in food stamp policy took effect in 1997 (Zedlewski and Brauner 1999). Following a suggestion in Wallace and Blank (1999), we use AFDC/TANF caseloads per capita as a variable in explaining food stamp caseloads in one model, recognizing that this raises endogeneity problems.

However, unlike the CEA model that is estimated among states, the level of nominal cash assistance benefits is approximately constant among counties in South Carolina and Mississippi—about $200 per month. Thus, we cannot test for the effects of varying benefits levels among counties as the CEA does among states. Instead, the ratio of the minimum wage monthly equivalent to the benefit level was used as one proxy for the changing opportunity cost to welfare caseloads to staying on AFDC/TANF.

### RESULTS

The key findings from estimating the regression equations are summarized in Table 4.1 for both AFDC/TANF and food stamps. The county welfare caseload participation rate (county caseloads divided by county labor force) is the dependent variable in columns 1 and 2 of the table, while the county food stamp caseload participation rate is the dependent variable for columns 3 and 4.

**Table 4.1 Determinants of Welfare and Food Stamp Caseloads in South Carolina and Mississippi, 1990–99**

| | Direction of influence on | | | |
| | AFDC/TANF | | Food stamps | |
| Explanatory variables | S.C. | Miss. | S.C. | Miss. |
|---|---|---|---|---|
| Opportunity cost | | | | |
| Ratio of minimum wage to benefits | – | – | – | – |
| Value of the Earned Income Tax Credit | – | – | – | – |
| TANF and the economy | | | | |
| TANF (welfare reform alone) | ns | ns | ns | – |
| TANF × employment growth | – | – | – | – |
| Employment growth (lagged) | mixed | – | mixed | – |
| TANF × unemployment rates | + | | | + |
| Unemployment rates (lagged) | + | | | + |
| Region | | | | |
| 1) Rural | + | + | + | + |
| 2) Rural – adjacent | + | + | + | + |
| Rural – not adjacent | + | + | + | + |
| 3) Rural – farm | + | + | + | + |
| Rural – manufacturing | + | ns | + | + |
| Rural – government | ns | ns | ns | + |
| Rural – other | + | + | + | + |
| 4) "Persistent poverty" in S.C. | + | | + | |
| "Delta" in Miss. | | + | | ns |

NOTE: Dependent variable is ln(caseloads/labor force). Nonsignificant regression parameter at the 0.05 level is denoted "ns." Regression parameters significant at least at the 0.05 level are denoted "+" for a positive relationship between increasing the value of the explanatory variable and increasing caseloads (for details, see Henry et al. 2000). Variables that have some positive and some negative effects are indicated as "mixed." Blank cells indicate that the variable was not used in the regression. "Region" effects are comparisons between the rural category and the metropolitan counties in the state.

**Opportunity Costs, Policy Reforms, and the Economy: How Did They Affect Welfare Caseloads in Mississippi and South Carolina?**

The effect on AFDC/TANF caseloads from the "opportunity costs" and "TANF and the economy" variables are reported in data columns 1 and 2 of the first two sections of Table 4.1. For the two "opportunity cost" variables—increases in the minimum wage relative to AFDC/TANF benefits and a higher EITC, increasing the EITC and the minimum wage relative to cash assistance reduces welfare participation as expected. These results are statistically significant across all models estimated for South Carolina and Mississippi.[20]

A second consistent finding is that TANF policy impacts on caseloads occur in conjunction with a strong local economy. Although the TANF indicator variable is not significantly different from zero[21] in either state, the interaction of TANF with the local economic variables was important in explaining caseload. This suggests that TANF incentives to leave welfare (or not join the welfare program) are effective if the local economy is generating local job opportunities. This finding is consistent with Ellwood (2000), who argued the TANF effect may be strongest where a robust local economy offers more low-wage jobs to former welfare clients.

In South Carolina, lower unemployment rates reduce caseloads, and the effect of lower unemployment rates on caseloads is about twice as strong after TANF than before. Employment growth rate effects are more mixed for South Carolina. Prior research (e.g., Council of Economic Advisers 1999) indicates that employment growth affects welfare participation decisions but that there is a lag between the labor market signal and caseload changes. In South Carolina and Mississippi, faster employment growth reduces caseloads as expected, but there is about a three-month lag between a stronger local economy and caseload declines. Although faster job growth reduces welfare caseloads, the job growth impact of caseloads has been stronger since TANF. However, the employment growth effects are more mixed than those for the unemployment rate. The four-quarter lag in employment growth has a positive effect on caseloads. This suggests in-migration to fast-growing counties by low-wage households that are seeking jobs but still drawing welfare benefits for a period. During the post-TANF period, however, the four-quarter lagged employment growth turns negative or neutral.

The Mississippi findings for local economic and policy effects on caseloads are similar to those for South Carolina. In Mississippi, the one-quarter and four-quarter lagged job growth effects were negative, as expected. The one-quarter lag interaction with TANF also contributed to strong declines in welfare caseloads, while the four-quarter lag interaction effect was neutral. The Mississippi results also indicate that both a strong economy and the implementation of welfare reform have contributed to declines in welfare participation rates.

## Is There a Rural Disadvantage in Reducing Welfare Caseloads?

Findings indicate a strong metropolitan advantage in reducing the rate of welfare participation rates in both South Carolina and Mississippi, other things being equal, as shown in data columns 1 and 2 of the "Region" section of Table 4.1. Welfare caseload participation rates are higher in nonmetro counties than metro counties after controlling for local economic vitality, TANF policy effects, and the rising opportunity cost of staying on welfare. The results suggest a slightly higher disadvantage in the more remote South Carolina and Mississippi rural counties (those not adjacent to a metro county).

Spatially configuring counties according to predominant economic activity produced mixed results for the two states. Farm-based economies in both South Carolina and Mississippi had higher rates of welfare participation relative to other counties. Beyond this common element, other economy types showed varying differences from the metro base. In South Carolina, where most rural counties are manufacturing or service or mixed economies, there was little difference from the nonmetro average effect. The lower salary, predominantly service-mixed rural economies in Mississippi had greater numbers of welfare cases than metro counties.

Economic region effects are also associated with welfare participation in both states. In South Carolina, the reference region is the I-85 growth corridor in the northwest corner of the state. It is dominated by a diverse manufacturing sector, with BMW, Hitachi, and Michelin providing a high profile for international investors, and the region has a rapidly expanding service sector serving a growing population. Other regions, with the exception perhaps of the Charlotte (North Carolina) spillover region, are likely to have higher rates of welfare participation than the I-85 growth corridor. The Midlands and Low Country regions include many of the persistent poverty counties in South Carolina and are part of the set of counties with persistent poverty that run across the Southeast. It appears that rural counties in these economic regions will have the most difficult time reducing welfare caseloads.

In Mississippi, the Jackson-based metro region and surrounding area was used as a reference. Three regions differed significantly from the base. Two regions had lower levels of welfare participation—a corridor of development activity paralleling an interstate highway from Jackson to Meridian; and an area in which the economy has undergone rapid growth in light industry, particularly upholstered furniture manufacturing. A third region differing significantly from the metro base was the high-poverty region of the Mississippi Delta, which had notably higher numbers of welfare cases.[22] This region depends heavily on production agriculture and is plagued by limited employment opportunities and the full range of socioeconomic problems accompanying persistent poverty across the Black Belt region of the South.

Several general conclusions can be inferred from the Mississippi and South Carolina cash assistance findings. One is that a strong economy, represented here by variables measuring unemployment rates and employment growth rates, has contributed significantly to the caseload declines observed from 1991–1999. Second, TANF program changes have not significantly affected caseloads, holding other things constant, unless accompanied by strong local economies. As noted, the relatively short time elapsed since the passage and implementation of the PRWORA may be a factor in this finding. Over time and as economic conditions change, these program initiatives may have a more significant impact.

Finally, this research shows that spatial issues are important to understanding caseload changes. Specifically, the results show that the caseload participation rates are significantly higher in nonmetropolitan areas, all else the same, and farm-dependent areas face the most difficult challenges in reducing caseloads. This finding suggests that rural areas may experience unique problems and face additional obstacles in the implementation of PRWORA not encountered in more urbanized areas.

## Food Stamp Participation in South Carolina and Mississippi

Results for food stamp participation in South Carolina and Mississippi are presented in data columns 3 and 4 of Table 4.1. They differ somewhat from the cash assistance results. This is not surprising given the smaller changes in food stamp caseloads compared with the dramatic reductions in AFDC/TANF over the period under review.[23] We find that higher minimum wages and increases in the EITC in both states tend to lower total food stamp participation. However, when looking at those only receiving food stamps without cash assistance (the residual cases), the relationships reverse in South Carolina. A possible reason for the reversal is that residual cases view the higher minimum wage and higher EITC benefits and food stamps as a "work support package." As the minimum wage and EITC increased, fewer people entered welfare but more signed on for food stamps.

Focusing on the South Carolina "residual" food stamp cases, TANF, by itself, has a negative, but insignificant, impact on food stamp caseloads and seems to have only a weak effect during quarters when employment is growing. Faster employment growth lagged four quarters seems to increase the food stamp caseloads. This suggests that there is in-migration to high employment growth counties, with added demand for food stamps at least for a time. Employment growth in the most recent quarter reduces food stamp caseloads. It may be that not enough time has passed between this quarterly signal of job growth in a county and subsequent immigration of food stamp participants.

In Mississippi, relative to the welfare caseload results, the effects on food stamp caseloads were considerably smaller. This is expected given the eligibility link between food stamp benefits and income as well as other eligibility requirements. That is, as income levels increase, individuals can remain eligible for some level of benefits as long as they remain below the 130 percent poverty level and meet other necessary requirements.

Differing from South Carolina, the effect of TANF implementation is highly significant and negative in all the Mississippi food stamp models, indicating that program changes have contributed to declining

food stamp participation.  This finding, although not necessarily anticipated, is not surprising for two reasons.  First, addressing food stamp
and TANF interrelationships, Zedlewski and Brauner (1999) found that
about one-third of families leaving food stamps were no longer eligible
based on their current income, meaning that almost two-thirds were
leaving for some reason other than income thresholds.  They found that
former welfare recipients left the Food Stamp program more often than
their non-welfare counterparts regardless of income level.  Roughly 84
percent of those receiving TANF in Mississippi also received food
stamps over the time period evaluated.  Second, although not likely as
important to Mississippi as to border states such as Texas and California, the denial of food stamps to immigrants beginning in 1997 was a
major policy change that nearly coincides with implementation of
TANF.

The impact of employment growth lagged one- and four-quarters
on food stamps paralleled the findings for welfare caseloads.  Again,
the fourth-quarter lag was not significant.  Unemployment lagged 12
months and the lagged unemployment–TANF interaction terms were
both highly significant and both had positive signs, indicating that lower unemployment rates reduce food stamp caseloads.  Although highly
significant, the post-TANF program unemployment effect is considerably weaker in the post-TANF timeframe.

## Is There a Rural Disadvantage in Reducing
## Food Stamp Caseloads?

Except for the case of the lone government-dependent county in
South Carolina, all rural counties in both states, regardless of location
or economic base, fare worse than metropolitan counties in reducing
the rate of food stamp participation.  Mirroring the South Carolina welfare caseload results, counties in the economic regions outside the I-85
manufacturing belt depend more on the Food Stamp program to supplement incomes of the working poor.  Economic regions in Mississippi also showed results similar to the welfare caseload analyses.  Farm-
based counties had higher food stamp participation rates, although the
Delta region showed no significant difference in food stamp participation rates relative to the urban reference.

## SUMMARY

Evidence presented here suggests that, for these two southern states, rural areas will have more difficulty than urban areas in reducing both cash assistance and Food Stamp program participation, all else the same.  In Mississippi, rural counties with a strong orientation toward farming and those in the Delta region are likely to face the greatest difficulty in reducing cash assistance caseloads.  Farm-based rural counties in Mississippi face the most difficulty in reducing food stamp participation rates.  In South Carolina, it is the set of rural counties that lie between Columbia and the coast that are least likely to reduce dependence on welfare and food stamps.

Why the rural disadvantage exists is an open question.  It may mean that improved rural transit linking rural residents to urban employment growth areas is needed to reduce rural caseloads.  More widely available child care, job training, and other assistance in rural areas may be needed.  Because rural clients tend to be dispersed, rural efforts to reduce barriers to leaving welfare are likely to be more expensive on a case-by-case basis than in urban centers.

One important qualifier to the evidence presented in this chapter is worth emphasizing.  Unlike other areas in the country, South Carolina and Mississippi have few, if any, metropolitan areas with urban core counties that have a concentration of poverty and TANF dependence.  Given the evidence in Smith and Woodbury (1999) that urban core cities do worse than suburbs or nonurban areas in providing jobs for low-wage labor, a test for caseload change between rural and the urban core would be useful but best undertaken in states that have larger metropolitan areas.

Finally, most of the employment growth in both Mississippi and South Carolina has been concentrated in urban counties and rural counties along the Atlantic and Gulf coasts.  The most remote rural counties have not benefited as much from state economic growth, suggesting that both economic development programs and "barrier" programs to provide transit, child care, and job training are needed to reduce the rate of welfare participation in rural Mississippi and South Carolina.  As caseloads rise in the next recession, under the TANF rules, states will have three choices: "cut people off even though jobs may not be available, relax the time limits, or provide some form of subsidized work for those that cannot get private employment" (Ellwood 2000, p. 193). States like South Carolina and Mississippi, with pockets of rural poverty, may be under substantial fiscal stress when they are faced with rising needs to support low-income households during a time when state revenues are not growing and the TANF block grant is fixed.

# Notes

1. Analysis within a state has several advantages over cross-state analyses. The low-wage labor market conditions that welfare recipients confront are more closely reflected in local county data than state averages. Second, the institutional framework—political, social, and economic—is likely to be more consistent among counties in a given state than among 50 states.

2. Henry, Barkley, and Brooks (1996) examined a South Carolina case study illustrating the rural spatial mismatch between where new entry-level jobs are growing and where low-income households are located. Alternatively, Smith and Woodbury (1999) found that low-wage job growth may be favorable to the employment prospects of former welfare recipients in nonurban areas; urban suburbs are likely to fare best, and central cities the worst in offering low-wage job opportunities.

3. Bartik and Eberts (1999, p. 139) found that three state "industrial mix" variables are important to understanding caseload changes among states.

4. Possible differences in caseload change across multicounty regions, each with an urban core and rural hinterland, are also explored in this chapter.

5. Moffitt and Ver Ploeg (1999) provided an overview of data and methodological issues for evaluating welfare reform and a review of selected state and local evaluation projects.

6. These choices are explored in Pavetti (1999).

7. Bartik and Eberts (1999) is an exception as metropolitan areas are considered in one set of models. In addition, Wallace and Blank (1999) and Figlio and Ziliak (1999) estimated models with monthly data at the state level.

8. Given new federal flexibility in administering state AFDC in the mid 1990s, South Carolina began to transform its AFDC program in January 1996 (prior to the passage of the federal PRWORA) with new training and education programs for adult AFDC recipients. Anticipating the PRWORA, South Carolina had transformed AFDC into its version of TANF, the Family Independence (FI) program, by October 1996. Three key features of the FI program distinguish it from AFDC: 1) Individuals are required to seek work before becoming eligible for the FI program, whereas income criteria were sufficient under AFDC; 2) A time limit of 2 years within a 10-year span, with a total lifetime limit of 5 years; and 3) under FI, failure of an adult client to comply with FI requirements can result in both

the adult recipient and the entire family losing benefits. Although this is a more severe noncompliance feature compared with AFDC, the FI program also allows spouses to participate in FI just as in the more stringent AFDC Unemployed Parent eligibility provision.

9. The process of welfare reform in Mississippi began in 1993 with the passage of legislation to implement statewide changes and demonstration projects to address the needs of the state's low-wage population through increased work opportunities, supportive services for adults, and required school attendance and health care for children. This legislation, the Mississippi Welfare Restructuring Program Act of 1993, was amended in the 1994 legislative session, allowing the state to request waivers, later granted by HHS, HCFA, and USDA, to implement the amended reforms. In December 1994, Mississippi began its pilot Welfare Reform Demonstration Project along with the work program component, WorkFirst, in six counties. The pilot program made benefits contingent on fulfilling a work requirement and was virtually identical to the federal TANF legislation in 1996. Development of the existing state plan for TANF implementation began with the approval of an initial state plan to take advantage of TANF block grant funds available beginning October 1, 1996. The Mississippi legislature passed and the governor signed House Bill 766 in March 1997, authorizing the Mississippi Department of Human Services (MDHS) to implement the TANF Work Program (TWP) and other reforms throughout the state. TWP replaces the old Job Opportunity and Basic Skills (JOBS) program and focuses on the immediate placement of nonexempt TANF recipients in private-sector, full-time jobs. Key features differentiating TWP from JOBS are: TWP focuses on immediate job placement, whereas the JOBS program focused on long-term preparation for work; TWP has a full family TANF sanction for noncompliance that existed with the JOBS program. TWP has a 5-year lifetime limit on the receipt of benefits and provides a 160-hour job search program, including a 20-hour job readiness-training program for adult TANF recipients.

10. This section draws from Reinschmiedt et al. (1999).

11. Key findings in this leaver study are summarized in Reinschmiedt et al. (1999).

12. The spike that occurred in all three groupings in October 1998 resulted from a special disaster one-month issuance of food stamps associated with a hurricane.

13. South Carolina has 16 MSA counties, 24 rural adjacent counties, and 6 nonadjacent rural counties.

14. Unemployment rates are the weighted means for each county type.

15. However, Zedlewski and Brauner (1999) found that former welfare clients exited the FSP at a greater rate than those not receiving AFDC/TANF in 1995–1997.

16. Rector and Youssef (1999, p. 1) found that states with "stringent sanctions and immediate work requirements . . . are highly associated with rapid rates of caseload decline," while "the relative vigor of state economies, as measured by unemployment rates, has no statistically significant effect on caseload decline." However, this is a distinctly minority finding. Most analysts find that robust economic growth is important to reducing welfare caseloads. The Council of Economic Ad-

visers (1999), Figlio and Ziliak (1999), Wallace and Blank (1999), Bartik and Eberts (1999), and Moffitt (1999) each found that stronger state economies have the expected effect of reducing participation in welfare programs. Bartik and Eberts (1999) found that use of the unemployment rate alone as an indicator of the robustness of the local (state) economy failed to explain recent dramatic declines in caseloads or late 1980s increases in caseloads despite low unemployment rates. They concluded that other features of the local labor market—employment growth rates and some industry mix variables—also need to be included in the measurement of the robustness of the local economy. They resolve the riddle of rising caseloads in the late 1980s in the face of lower unemployment rates by noting the decrease in demand for low-skill labor during the same period. The rapid decline in caseloads in the late 1990s is most likely explained by new TANF policy given that indicators of local labor demand fail to explain the decline. Rector and Youssef (1999) provided support for this view for the January 1997 to June 1998 period. Specifically, they assert that an increase in the severity of penalties for noncompliance with TANF regulations across states has been a major force in reducing welfare caseloads in the late 1990s. Recent Council of Economic Advisors (1999) results also support an important policy impact from TANF.

17.  County labor force and monthly estimates of population were used as alternative bases for calculating the caseload participation rates. There is virtually no difference in the empirical estimates using the two divisors.

18.  Ellwood (2000) made several observations about how means-tested benefits in the welfare system (AFDC/TANF and food stamps) and income support programs for working, low-wage households, especially the Earned Income Tax Credit (EITC), have changed since the early 1990s to provide powerful incentives to leave welfare. First, the real value of welfare benefits in the median state is now about half the 1970 level. Second, the EITC benefits expanded dramatically in the early 1990s. Third, there is expanded support for child care and Medicaid coverage for children of a single parent working full-time at the minimum wage. In one comparison, a single parent working full-time at the minimum wage in 1986 would gain total real "disposable" income of $2,005 in 1996 dollars—about a 24 percent gain over AFDC and lose all Medicaid coverage by leaving AFDC. By 1997, the same parent would gain real disposable income of $7,129 and lose Medicaid coverage for adults only by leaving TANF for a full time minimum wage job. This gain roughly doubles the disposable income of the working parent in 1997 in the median state. Chernik and McGuire (1999, pp. 278–280) also argued that the EITC has substantially increased the benefits of moving from no work to at least part-time work. The percentage gain in real disposable income when a welfare recipient moves from welfare to work is likely to be even larger in most southern states given their low levels of TANF benefits compared with the rest of the nation. As the minimum wage is increased and cash assistance from a state's TANF program declines in real terms, there will be further increases in the cost to the welfare recipient of staying on welfare. This "pull" effect is apparent before considering how "push" incentives from new sanction rules for noncom-

pliance with TANF rules or time limits might affect the household decision to leave welfare. This is also before any consideration of caseload impacts from the demand side of the labor market for low-wage households—the strength of the local economy—or the variation in availability of work support services (public transit, child care, and job training) across localities.

19.  Studies find that welfare policy reform has contributed to the reduction in caseloads, although the business cycle caseload effect has been stronger over the periods studied than the impact of welfare policy reform. In part, the relatively weak policy effect may be associated with the short time period over which the new policies have been in place. Although waivers from AFDC were implemented by some states in the early 1990s, in most states TANF was "activated" in October 1996, leaving only two complete years of data on how TANF recipients have responded to the new rules and incentives. The two-consecutive-years-on TANF rule would, in most states, not have been binding on most recipients until late 1998 at the earliest. Indeed, the Council of Economic Advisors (1999) report was a follow-up to the earlier Wallace and Blank (1999) analysis to address this time series issue. The most recent CEA study found that the welfare policy impacts accounted for about one-third of the caseload decline from 1996–1998.

20.  Complete regression results are available from Henry et al. (2000).

21.  The associated $p$ values are in the 0.2 or above range. Tables with detailed statistical properties are available on request.

22.  Howell, in this volume, also examines caseload data in Mississippi, with outwardly different results. However, Howell makes the point that the single labor market area (LMA) with the most TANF recipients is Jackson. He also shows, however, that the Delta *region* (which includes more than one LMA) does indeed have more TANF cases than the Jackson LMA. In addition, and more important, Howell compares actual caseloads, while the findings in this chapter (Henry) are based on a regression analysis in which other factors that might differ between the regions is held constant. Therefore, holding all else constant between the regions, the caseload would be predicted to be higher in the Delta than the Jackson LMA.

23.  The lagged unemployment and its interaction with TANF are deleted to allow use of the random effects approach in the food stamps models displayed in columns 3 and 4 of Table 1.

24.  Data for the CEA study are annual calendar years from 1976–1998 on all states and the District of Columbia for 1,173 observations (Council of Economic Advisers 1999, pp. 10–13).

25.  The models estimated for South Carolina and Mississippi differ from the CEA model in variables, data used, and in estimation strategy. First, counties and months are used as the panel (rather than states and years). Because it is the strength of the local county economy (rather than the state average) that would seem most relevant in welfare clients' job searches, the use of county data seems proper. The CEA study uses the number of caseloads in a case divided by state population on an annual basis. However, the SC-MS data are across counties and months so there is no population estimate available to us as a denominator in the rate calculation. Accordingly, the county labor force by month is used as a proxy

for the size of the local population, and the dependent variable is the log of case-loads/labor force. Although the size of this is a practical necessity given that county population data by month are not available, county working-age population and labor force are likely to be highly correlated. Second, the South Carolina–Mississippi model uses both unemployment rates and employment growth rates as suggested by Bartik and Eberts (1999) to capture the vitality of the county economy in offering work to welfare clients. Interaction effects of the unemployment rate and the employment growth rates with TANF are used to determine whether the policy effects from TANF are influenced by the economic conditions facing welfare recipients. Third, opportunity costs of not working are proxied both by the ratio of the minimum wage to welfare benefits and by changes in the Earned Income Tax Credit. Fourth, there are several tests, using the "region" variables, for the effects of a rural location on welfare and food stamp participation rates. With metropolitan counties as the reference group, region effects are reflected across several alternative dimensions within each state.

26. The CEA model uses a county-specific time trend variable to control for "unobserved factors, such as family structure and other policies that may be correlated with the observed variables" (Council of Economic Advisers 1999, p. 12). A time trend is not used in the South Carolina–Mississippi models for two reasons. First, the location effects in the models should reflect the cross-sectional county social and demographic characteristics that may be omitted. Second, these county characteristics are unlikely to change rapidly over the period of this analysis. Under these circumstances, including a time trend (whether quadratic or linear) will add little control for omitted local characteristics and could reduce the information content in the remaining regressors. A second change from the CEA model revolves around the choice of using a fixed effects (like the CEA model) or a random effects approach to the panel data regressions. This is, in part, a matter of testing for the appropriate model (Greene 2000, pp. 576–577). The Hausman test for orthogonality between the random effects and the regressors is used to limit regressors to those that are consistent with the theoretical expectations from the caseload literature and that do not violate the assumption that the individual effects are not correlated with the regressors in the model. As noted below, the Hausman test was sensitive to the regressors included (most notably in the Mississippi welfare panel data) but generally supported the use of the random effects model for the panel data. The use of cross-sectional dummies for region effects also makes the random effects approach to the panel data estimations attractive. Estimating fixed-effects models was problematic because of the collinearity between cross-section dummies and the region dummies. Finally, the discussion in Wallace and Blank (1999) and Figlio and Ziliak (1999) concerning the merits of the CEA model identified several econometric issues that were taken into account when developing our model. First, the random effects models address the use of first differences as opposed to levels. In Parks (1967), the time-series data were transformed using a first-order autoregressive parameter estimated for each county. In Fuller and Battese (1974), data are transformed using constants derived from the estimators for each of the variance components. Assuming the error

terms are heteroscedastic and contemporaneously correlated, Parks also employs a GLS procedure to adjust for each potential problem. In sum, the estimation strategy for the SCM model is a two-step process. First, use the Hausman test for the random effects assumption that the error term effects are uncorrelated with the other variables in the model. Second, both the Fuller and Battese (1974) and the Parks (1967) GLS models are estimated to gauge the sensitivity of results to alternative assumptions about the error term.

27. "The 1989 classification system of nonmetro counties, known as the ERS typology, is designed to provide policy-relevant information about diverse rural conditions to policymakers, public officials, and researchers. The classification is based on 2,276 U.S. counties (including those in Alaska and Hawaii) designated as nonmetro as of 1993. The typology includes six mutually exclusive economic types: five types (farming, mining, manufacturing, government, and services) reflect dependence on particular economic specializations; a sixth type, termed non-specialized, contains those counties not classified as having any of the five economic specializations" (Cook and Mizer 1994, p. 4).

# APPENDIX

Data sources for the South Carolina caseloads are from reports PC100R03, PC100R17, MR410, and MR420, Division of Information Services, South Carolina Department of Social Services. Mississippi AFDC/TANF and food stamp administrative data are from the Division of Economic Assistance, Mississippi Department of Human Services. Data for the county employment, labor force, and unemployment rates by month are from the Employment Security Commissions of South Carolina and Mississippi. County identifiers are from the Beale code, U.S. Department of Agriculture (Ghelfi and Parker 1997). Earned Income Tax Credit and minimum wage data are from Council of Economic Advisers (1999).

## A WELFARE CASELOADS REGRESSION MODEL

One econometric specification developed by the Council of Economic Advisers (1999) forms the foundation for the regression model in Equation 1 used to test for region effects on caseload change.[24] Discussions of the merits of the CEA model in Wallace and Blank (1999) and Figlio and Ziliak (1999) are used to address estimation issues.

(1)  $\ln R_{ct} = B_0 + \ln \text{EITC} B_{\text{EITC}} + \ln \text{WAGETOBEN}_{ct} B_{wb} + \text{TANF}_{ct} B_{\text{tanf}}$

$\quad\quad + \text{UNEMPLOYMENT}_{ct} B_{u} + \text{TANF} \times \text{UNEMPLOYMENT}_{ct} B_{tu} + \text{EGROW} B_{eg}$

$\quad\quad + \text{TANF} \times \text{EGROW} B_{teg} + \text{REGION} B_{reg} + \gamma_c \, \gamma_t + \varepsilon_{ct}$

where

the dependent variable is caseload participation rates,
$\ln R_{ct}$ = log of the ratio of caseloads to the labor force in county $c$ for month $t$,
$\gamma_c$ = county effects (modeled as an error components term),
$\gamma_t$ = month effects (modeled as an error components term),[25] and
$\varepsilon_{ct}$ = random error.

## Explanatory Variables

### Opportunity cost regressors

ln EITC = log of the average of the maximum earned income tax credit for tax-payers with one child and with more than one child for each year 1990 to 1999

ln WAGETOBEN = log of the ratio of the value of state minimum wage as a monthly amount (30 hours of work per week for 4.33 weeks) to the maximum monthly benefit for a family of three on AFDC/TANF

### TANF and the economy regressors

TANF = dummy variable = 1 for year and month TANF was in effect for a county; otherwise 0

UNEMPLOYMENT = county unemployment rate (lagged two years to ameliorate endogeneity with current labor force)

TANF×UNEMPLOYMENT = interaction effect between unemployment rate lagged two years and TANF

EGROW = employment growth rate in the county (most recent quarter and four-quarter lag)

TANF×EGROW = interaction effect between lagged employment growth rates and TANF

### Region effects used to examine rural/urban differences in caseload change.

Three regressions are estimated to reflect three alternative ways to define "rurality" using *alternative* dummy variables representing location effects.

Group 1 (Rural disadvantage)
    Regional group 1 identifies counties as either metropolitan or nonmetropolitan.

NONMET = dummy variable = 1 for all nonmetropolitan counties and 0 for other counties

Group 2 (Remote rural disadvantage)
    Group 2 is the set of nonmetropolitan counties divided into those that are adjacent to a metro county and those that are not. Welfare participants in counties more distant from urban job centers may have less access to work opportunities than welfare participants in counties near urban counties.

ADJ = dummy variable = 1 nonmet counties adjacent to metro counties and 0 for other counties

NONADJ = dummy variable =1 for nonmet counties not adjacent to metro and 0 for other counties

Group 3 (Rural industry mix effect)

Group 3 divides the nonmetro counties into one of four economic base groups: farm, manufacturing, government, or other (services and nonspecialized), from Ghelfi and Parker (1997). Positive parameters on these dummy variables would indicate that counties in these classes are less likely to reduce welfare participation rates than are urban counties, given the same vitality of the local economy, opportunity cost of not working, and policy regime. This is a way to control for "industry mix" effects on welfare participation that Bartik and Eberts (1999) found to be useful in explaining changes in welfare caseloads. In addition, each state was divided into functional economic regions (BEA Component Economic Areas developed in Johnson 1995). These regions have an urban core and rural hinterland that are connected by substantial within-region commuting. Regions with a booming urban core that offer jobs to residents of proximate rural areas are expected to have more success in reducing rural caseloads than other regions. Including BEA region dummies also provides some control for the type of urban center—government-dominated urban areas such as Columbia, South Carolina, and Jackson, Mississippi; manufacturing-dominated regions like the Greenville-Spartanburg metro center along the I-85 growth corridor from Charlotte to Atlanta; and resort-tourism service-oriented urban areas such as Charleston, South Carolina, and the Mississippi Gulf Coast.[26]

FRM = dummy variable = 1 for farm dependent rural counties. Farming contributed a weighted annual average of 20 percent or more labor and proprietor income from 1987–1989.[27]

MFG = dummy variable for manufacturing dependent rural counties and 0 for other counties; manufacturing contributed a weighted annual average of 30 percent or more labor and proprietor income from 1987–1989.

GOV = dummy variable for government dependent rural counties and 0 for other counties; government activities contributed a weighted annual average of 25 percent or more labor and proprietor income from 1987–1989.

OTH = dummy variable for rural counties not dependent on farming, manufacturing, or government and 0 for other counties. These counties were either services-dependent (service activities contributed weighted annual average of

50 percent or more labor and proprietor income from 1987–1989) or nonspecialized (counties not classified as a specialized economic type from 1987–1989).

# References

Bartik, Timothy J., and Randall W. Eberts. 1999. "Examining the Effect of Industry Trends and Structure on Welfare Caseloads." In *Economic Conditions and Welfare Reform*, Sheldon H. Danziger, ed. Kalamazoo, Michigan: W.E. Upjohn Institute for Employment Research.

Beeler, Jesse D., Bill M. Brister, Sharon Chambry, and Anne L. McDonald. 1999. *Tracking of TANF Clients: First Report of a Longitudinal Study.* Jackson, Mississippi: Millsaps College, Center for Applied Research.

Chernik, Howard, and Therese J. McGuire. 1999. "The States, Welfare Reform, and the Business Cycle." In *Economic Conditions and Welfare Reform*, Sheldon H. Danziger, ed. Kalamazoo, Michigan: W.E. Upjohn Institute for Employment Research.

Cook, Peggy J. and Karen L. Mizer. 1994. *The Revised ERS County Typology: An Overview.* Rural Development Research Report no. 89, Economic Research Service, U.S. Department of Agriculture, Washington, D.C.

Council of Economic Advisers. 1999. *The Effects of Welfare Policy and the Economic Expansion on Welfare Caseloads: An Update.* Washington, D.C.: Council of Economic Advisors.

Department of Social Services, State of South Carolina. 1998. *June 1998 Report, Survey of Former Family Independence Program Clients, Cases Closed during April through June 1997.* Columbia, S.C.: South Carolina Department of Social Services.

Ellwood, David T. 2000. "Anti-Poverty Policy For Families in the Next Century." *Journal of Economic Perspectives* 14(1): 187–198.

Figlio, D., and J. Ziliak. 1999. "Welfare Reform, the Business Cycle, and the Decline in AFDC Caseloads." In *Economic Conditions and Welfare Reform*, Sheldon H. Danziger, ed. Kalamazoo, Michigan: W.E. Upjohn Institute for Employment Research.

Fuller, W.A., and Battese, G.E. 1974. "Estimation of Linear Models with Crossed-Error Structure." *Journal of Econometrics* 2: 67–78.

Ghelfi, Linda, and Timothy Parker. 1997. "A County-Level Measure of Urban Influence." *Rural Development Perspectives* 12(2): 32–41. Economic Research Service, U. S. Department of Agriculture, Washington, D.C.

Greene, William H. 2000. *Econometric Analysis.* Fourth ed. New York: Prentice-Hall.

Henry, M., W. Lewis, L. Reinschmiedt, and Darren Hudson. 2000. "Reducing Food Stamps and Welfare Caseloads in the South: Are Rural Areas Less Likely to Succeed Than Urban Centers?" Working paper 188, Joint Center for Poverty Research, Northwestern University and University of Chicago. Available at <www.jcpr.org>.

Henry, Mark S., D. Barkley, and K. Brooks. 1996. *Coastal Zone Rural Economic Development through Enhanced Linkages to a Resort Growth Center: The South Carolina Low Country and Hilton Head Island.* Research Report 96-1, Department of Agricultural and Applied Economics, Clemson University, South Carolina.

Johnson, Kenneth P. 1995. "Redefinition of the BEA Economic Areas." *Survey of Current Business* 75(2): 75–80.

Mississippi Department of Human Services. 1997. *Mississippi State Plan (Amended): Temporary Assistance for Needy Families (TANF).* March 20.

Moffitt, Robert A. 1999. "The Effect of Pre-PRWORA Waivers on AFDC Caseloads and Female Earnings, Income, and Labor Force Behavior." In *Economic Conditions and Welfare Reform*, Sheldon H. Danziger, ed. Kalamazoo, Michigan: W.E. Upjohn Institute for Employment Research.

Moffitt, Robert A., and Michele Ver Ploeg, eds. 1999. *Evaluating Welfare Reform: A Framework and Review of Current Work.* Washington, D.C.: National Academy Press.

Parks, R.W. 1967. "Efficient Estimation of a System of Regression Equations when Disturbances Are Both Serially and Contemporaneously Correlated." *Journal of the American Statistical Association* 62: 500–509.

Pavetti, LaDonna A. 1999. "What Will the States Do When Jobs Are Not Plentiful?" In *Economic Conditions and Welfare Reform*, Sheldon H. Danziger, ed. Kalamazoo, Michigan: W.E. Upjohn Institute for Employment Research.

Rector, Robert E., and Sarah E. Youssef. 1999. *The Determinants of Welfare Caseload Decline.* Report no. 99-04, Heritage Foundation, Washington, D.C., May 11.

Reinschmiedt, L., M. Henry, B. Weber, E. Davis, and W. Lewis. 1999. "Welfare and Food Stamps Caseloads in Three States: Rural-Urban Contrasts." Report no. P 99-10, University of Missouri, Rural Policy Research Institute, Columbia, Missouri.

Smith, David M., and Stephen A. Woodbury. 1999. "Low Wage Labor Markets: The Business Cycle and Regional Differences." *The Low-Wage Labor Market: Challenges for Economic Self-Sufficiency.* Available at <http://aspe.hhs.gov/hsp/lwlm99/smith.htm>.

Wallace, G., and R. Blank. 1999. "What Goes Up Must Come Down? Explaining Recent Changes in Public Assistance Caseloads." In *Economic Conditions and Welfare Reform*, Sheldon H. Danziger, ed.  Kalamazoo, Michigan: W.E. Upjohn Institute for Employment Research.

Zedlewski, Sheila R., and Sarah Brauner. 1999. "Declines in Food Stamp and Welfare Participation: Is There a Connection?" Discussion paper 99-13, The Urban Institute, Washington, D.C.

# 5
# Seasonal Employment Dynamics and Welfare Use in Agricultural and Rural California Counties

Henry E. Brady
*University of California, Berkeley*

Mary Sprague
*University of California, Berkeley*

Fredric C. Gey
*University of California Data Archive
and Technical Assistance*

Michael Wiseman
*George Washington University*

Welfare participation exhibits significant seasonality in agricultural counties and most rural counties in California. The number of welfare recipients in these counties increases dramatically from summer to winter. Labor market factors drive this seasonality. Welfare rolls contract and expand with seasonal employment and unemployment, leading to a pattern in which a significant fraction of the caseload population works in the summer and receives welfare in the winter.

Different employment sectors drive seasonality in welfare participation among counties. Agricultural employment is primarily responsible for welfare seasonality in agricultural and mixed counties (counties with moderate agricultural employment and a small rural population). In rural counties, the most important sectors vary from one county to another, but they are primarily agriculture, manufacturing, trade, service, and construction and mining. Reductions in the welfare caseload between winter and summer provide a significant fraction of the workforce in these seasonal sectors in many agricultural and rural counties.

The new Temporary Assistance for Needy Families (TANF) legislation and the California WORKs programs emphasize work and time limits for welfare recipients. Although California's time limits do not necessarily remove an entire family from aid, they do substantially reduce the degree to which welfare can provide income for seasonal workers beyond the time-limit period. What will happen to these seasonal workers under the new legislation? One possibility is that they will move elsewhere to find year-round work, forcing seasonal industries to either find their labor elsewhere or bid up the price of their labor. Other possibilities involve the enactment of government policies to protect these workers. Welfare time limits could be modified in those areas with significant seasonal unemployment, or unemployment insurance could be extended to seasonal workers.

Considering the great importance of seasonal workers to industries in agricultural and rural California counties, California policymakers must take into account the plight of seasonal workers combining welfare with work under the new welfare legislation and act accordingly. National policymakers should also be concerned with this distinct population because California's caseload composes about one-fifth of the national caseload. Although our findings on the prevalence and importance of seasonal welfare populations are based on California data, we expect that seasonal workers who combine welfare with work also exist in agricultural and rural areas outside California because seasonal jobs are often characteristic of these areas (Tickamyer 1992).

## PAST RESEARCH

Our work is at the intersection of two different bodies of research. One is how movements on and off welfare are affected by labor markets; the second is how the dynamics of welfare are affected by the different kinds of economies found in rural, agricultural, and urban areas.

**Interaction of Welfare and Labor Market Dynamics**

Welfare is inextricably linked with labor market conditions. A primary path onto or off welfare is a change in a household's attachment to the labor force, a change in income, or a change in the need for income. Families typically enter welfare when the head of the household loses his or her job, when the family breaks up and loses its primary wage earner, or when the demand for income increases because of the addition of a child. Families usually leave welfare when the head of the household gets a job, when marriage (or some other domestic arrangement) brings an earner into the household or makes it possible for the formerly single parent to get a job, or when children leave home. Attachment to the labor force and income, in turn, obviously depend on the local demand for labor, but most of the welfare literature has neglected the role of local labor markets because of the difficulty in linking information about local labor conditions to welfare entrances and exits. Hoynes (1996) noted that studies using survey data focus more on conditions affecting labor supply, such as welfare recipients' education or states' welfare benefit levels, than on demand-side factors such as the unemployment rate, the wage level, or the number of job openings.

Studies that include labor market variables typically use only state-level economic conditions, such as the unemployment rate, in part because confidentiality restrictions limit the information about the location of welfare recipients on most surveys. These studies often find that labor market conditions have little or no impact on individual entrances and exits from welfare. State-level economic conditions, however, are probably too highly aggregated to capture an individual's employment opportunities. The few studies that use labor market conditions at the county or county-group level find mixed results. These studies (Fitzgerald 1995; Harris 1993; Sanders 1992) mainly rely on variation in economic conditions across areas to identify labor market effects because of the limited timespan covered by most surveys. As a result, estimates of labor market effects are biased if area characteristics associated with labor market conditions are excluded from the model, such as lower-skilled workers living in areas with poorer labor markets.

Using a relatively new, rich individual-level administrative data set, Hoynes (1996) addressed many flaws of the earlier studies, finding that local economic conditions have a significant effect on welfare exits. With six years of monthly data (1987–1992) on approximately 100,000 welfare cases in California, Hoynes modeled the probability that a person will leave welfare in a given month. She found that higher unemployment rates, lower employment growth, lower employment-to-population ratios, and lower wage growth have a significant, negative impact on the probability that a person will leave welfare, which leads to longer welfare spells (lengths of time on welfare). Hoynes also found that African Americans, residents of urban areas, and two-parent households are more responsive to changes in labor market conditions, whereas teen parents and refugee groups are less responsive.

Hoynes's results provide strong support for the notion that employment conditions affect welfare participation decisions for individuals and households. Additional support is provided by related studies on aggregate welfare caseload trends. In two recent papers using state panel data to model caseload dynamics, economic growth was identified as the major contributor to caseload decline from 1993 to 1996 (Council of Economic Advisers 1997; Ziliak et al. 1997). Blank's caseload model (1997), which also used annual state-level panel data but was more fully specified than most other models, suggested that the state unemployment rate has a significant, positive effect on both the one-parent caseload (formerly called AFDC-Basic) and two-parent caseload (formerly called AFDC-Unemployed Parent).

Rather than focusing only on the aggregate caseload, a few studies model two flows that compose changes in the caseload level: new case openings and case closings (Albert 1988; Bluestone and Sumrall 1977; Brady and Wiseman 1998; Congressional Budget Office 1993, Appendix B). Considering the components separately is important because their determinants are likely to differ and thus have different policy implications.

The most comprehensive model of both case openings and closings is by Brady and Wiseman for California with monthly data from 1972–1996. In the Brady and Wiseman model, the economic variables appear to have a much larger influence on two-parent cases than on one-parent cases. For one-parent cases, the only economic effect that is statistically significant is the negative impact of female potential earnings on entries to welfare. Among two-parent cases, the unemployment rate has a significant, positive effect on entries and significant, negative effect on exits. The other significant effects for two-parent cases are the negative effect of both employment growth and minimum wage on entries to welfare, as well as the unexpected negative effect of female potential earnings on exits.

These aggregate caseload studies provide strong evidence for the importance of economic variables for welfare dynamics, but they typically involve such large geographic areas (entire states) and aggregate data (monthly or annual caseloads) that the nuances of local labor markets, especially the differences among urban, agricultural, and rural labor markets, are obscured.

## Differences in Welfare and Employment Dynamics by Type of Area

Past work has shown that a larger fraction of the population in nonmetropolitan areas receives welfare than in metropolitan areas (see, for example, Fuguitt, Brown, and Beale 1989), perhaps because of greater poverty in rural areas. A higher level of welfare recipiency has also been documented over the past two decades among women of childbearing age in California's agricultural areas and rural far northern and mountainous areas than in its more urban areas (MaCurdy, Mancuso, and O'Brien-Strain 2000). These nonmetropolitan areas also have higher levels of poverty (Lichter, Johnston, and McLaughlin 1994), which accounts for the higher level of welfare recipiency, but the number of welfare recipients per poor household is actually lower in these agricultural and rural areas than in metropolitan areas. The Rural Policy Research Institute (1999) also finds a lower rate of reliance on public assistance among U.S. households living below 125% of the poverty level in nonmetropolitan areas than in urban areas and the suburbs.

Another difference among areas is the average length of time spent receiving welfare. Event-history analyses show that welfare recipients in urban areas have, on average, longer welfare spells than recipients in nonurban areas (O'Neill, Bassi, and Wolf 1987; Rank and Hirschl 1988; Fitzgerald 1995; Porterfield 1998; Jensen, Keng, and Garasky, in this volume, p. 177). In these studies, the authors suggest that the difference is due to greater stigma attached to welfare receipt in rural areas than in urban areas, given that anonymity is less in rural areas.

Urban/rural variations in employment conditions are an obvious source of these differences in welfare receipt. Rural areas have a higher level of underemployment (Findeis and Jensen 1998). The underemployed include low-income workers ("working poor"), involuntary part-time workers, and unemployed individuals who want to work. The higher percentage of working poor in rural areas is largely due to the limited work opportunities in these areas. According to Tickamyer (1992), jobs in rural areas tend to pay low wages, and many jobs are part-time or seasonal (e.g., agriculture and construction). She found that poverty is lower in rural areas with diversified labor markets than in rural areas with narrow, resource-based labor markets such as agriculture and mining. Linking welfare to employment, Porterfield (1998) found that rural families are more likely than families in urban counties to go on welfare because of a decrease in earnings but are less likely to exit welfare because of an increase in earnings.

A few studies focused specifically on welfare and employment dynamics in areas in California. Taylor, Martin, and Fix (1997) examined California's agricultural areas, arguing that farm employment increases welfare use. With 1990 Census data, regression equations for farm employment, poverty, immigration, income, and welfare use in rural towns were simultaneously estimated. The authors concluded that, largely through its demand for cheap immigrant labor, farm employment increases poverty levels in agricultural areas, leading to increased welfare demand. Hoffmann and Fortmann (1995) examined welfare and employment interactions in California's 31 "forest counties."[1] Using Granger causality tests on monthly data for 11 years, they found that employment helps drive the two-parent welfare caseload in about half of the forest counties.

In MaCurdy, Mancuso, and O'Brien-Strain's (2000) study of California's welfare caseload trends, the counties classified by the authors as resource-based (counties in their farm belt and northern and mountain regions) have both higher and more cyclical welfare caseloads (except for child-only caseloads) and unemployment. By comparing time trends of caseload, demographic, and economic data, the authors suggest that the primary factors that drive welfare caseloads in California (economic conditions, birth rates, and immigration) vary by region. According to the study, in the resource-based regions, economic conditions explain a great deal of the two-parent welfare caseload trends, and nonmarital birth rates explain much of the one-parent caseload trends.

Taken together, these studies demonstrate the greater prevalence of welfare receipt in nonmetropolitan areas, the importance of labor market factors for welfare receipt in general, and the effect of resource-based employment on welfare use in nonmetropolitan areas. What they do not provide is a detailed picture of the seasonal link between welfare receipt and resource-based employment across different kinds of counties.

## OUR STUDY

We use data on California counties to study welfare dynamics in urban, mixed, agricultural, and rural areas. California counties are worth studying because they are so big and so diverse and because they compose a significant fraction of the total welfare population in the United States. The combined population of the 15 California counties we classify as agricultural is larger than the population in each of 21 states. In addition, the value of agricultural production in California is somewhat larger than that of the four agricultural states of Iowa, Kansas, Missouri, and Nebraska combined. The combined population of the 17 counties classified as rural is approximately the same or larger than the population in seven other states.[2] The total welfare population in California is about one-fifth of the nation's total, and it averaged over 2.3 million people each month in 1997. The number of persons on welfare in California agricultural counties alone during each month of 1997 averaged over 325,000.

By using monthly welfare and industry employment data for California spanning 10 years, our study provides much greater detail (relative to past studies) on the impact of local labor markets on welfare participation over time. With our fourfold typology of California counties, we are able to show how counties with different kinds of economies have different welfare patterns.

We first develop our typology of four kinds of California counties. We then describe aggregate welfare and employment dynamics in each type of county. These results strongly suggest that rural and agricultural counties have significant cyclical dynamics that distinguish them from urban counties. Finally, we summarize regression and event-history models that demonstrate the strong link between employment cycles and welfare cycles. We end with a discussion of the policy implications of these results.

**Classification of Counties**

The heart of our enterprise is an analytically powerful way to classify places. There are many ways to do this, but we focus on economic and geographic characteristics because there are good reasons to believe they are especially important for the dynamics of welfare. Economic characteristics matter because they determine the types and number of jobs that are available. The role of geography is less clear, and there is a long-standing debate about what makes rural areas different from urban ones. Nevertheless, there is ample empirical evidence that welfare receipt and welfare dynamics differ between rural and urban areas. For welfare recipients, the major geographic factors affecting them are probably the limited choices of jobs in nonurban areas and the dependence on labor markets that are subject to greater seasonal fluctuations than those in urban areas.

To develop a meaningful typology combining economic and geographic factors, we collected data on the economic, geographic, and demographic characteristics of counties, such as percentage of rural population, population density, unemployment rates, and percentage of farm and agricultural services employment. We then used factor analysis and other data reduction techniques to recognize groups of counties with similar characteristics.

Based on this analysis, we found that a useful classification scheme follows from the clusters produced when we place each of California's 58 counties on a plot of percentage rural by percentage farm and agricultural services employment.[3] Four clusters of counties appear when this is done (Figure 5.1). The 15 counties with more than 11.5 percent agricultural employment (to the right of the vertical dashed line on Figure 5.1) are considered agricultural. Their geographic distribution can be seen in Figure 5.2. They are, not surprisingly, predominantly in California's agricultural Central Valley.

**Figure 5.1  California County Typology**

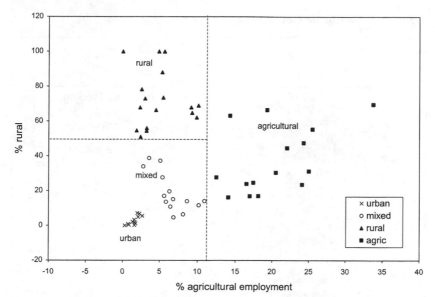

Counties with less than 11.5 percent agricultural employment fit into three categories, depending on their level of urbanization. Those counties with more than 50 percent rural population (above the horizontal dashed line on Figure 5.1) and less than 11.5 percent agricultural workers are labeled rural. These 17 rural counties fall along the northwestern, northern, and eastern edges of the state.

The remaining counties are less than 50 percent rural and have low levels of farm and agricultural workers. They fall into two groups. Twelve counties in the lower left-hand corner of Figure 5.1 are all highly urbanized, with negligible farming employment. These urban counties include four southern counties that compose the metropolitan Los Angeles and San Diego regions and seven counties that constitute the San Francisco Bay area. Sacramento County in the Central Valley is also heavily urbanized because the state capital is located there.

The residual category, "mixed," consists of the remaining 14 counties. Most of these counties have between 5 percent and 11.5 percent agricultural employment and less than 20 percent rural population. They are primarily located around the major urban areas, although a

**Figure 5.2  California County Map**

few stand alone and are centered on moderately sized cities with populations between 27,000 and 85,000.

The 12 urban counties compose approximately 73 percent of the population and 71 percent of the welfare caseload in California. The 14 mixed counties make up approximately 16.5 percent of population and 14.7 percent of welfare cases. The 17 rural counties contain 2 percent of the population and 1.8 percent of the welfare caseload. The 15 agricultural counties contain 8.8 percent of the population and a disproportionately large share of the welfare population, 12.8 percent of the caseload.

Our typology is not the only way to classify California counties. The U.S. Department of Agriculture has developed two widely used county typologies: Beale codes and Economic Research Service (ERS) economic function types. Beale codes classify counties along a rural-urban continuum. Economic function types of the ERS classify counties according to their major industry. Our typology combines the geographic approach of the Beale codes with the economic approach of the ERS function types. To a very large extent, our classification system accords with the alternative classifications; the typologies agree where we would expect them to agree. The greatest differences between our typology and the alternative ones are that ours is much less likely to classify counties as metropolitan, and it has a less stringent requirement for calling a county "agricultural" than the ERS requirement for "farming" counties.

## WELFARE AND EMPLOYMENT DYNAMICS
## BY COUNTY TYPE

In this section, we show that systematic differences in welfare and employment dynamics exist across county types. Using the typology developed in the previous section, we find that both the level and annual variability of welfare use are higher in agricultural and rural counties than in urban counties. The greater variability in welfare participation among the nonurban counties is due largely to significant seasonality in those counties' welfare caseloads. We show that welfare use increases during the winter months and decreases during the summer months in the agricultural and rural counties.

After establishing that distinct welfare patterns exist across county types, we find that differences in employment patterns across county types largely drive the variation in welfare patterns. More specifically, higher rates of unemployment in the agricultural and rural counties help explain the higher welfare use in these counties compared with urban counties. The substantial seasonality in welfare participation among agricultural counties is largely explained by seasonality in employment in the agriculture and manufacturing sectors. In rural counties, the seasonality in welfare use is explained not only by employment in the agriculture and manufacturing sectors, but also by employment in the trade, service, and construction and mining sectors.

## Welfare Dynamics by County Type

To examine differences in welfare dynamics by county type, we rely on county caseload data collected by the State of California's Department of Social Services.[4] These monthly data span a 12-year period from July 1985 to August 1997. Because our focus is on the average county within a county type, our statistics at the county-type level (such as welfare participation by county type) are simple averages among counties within each county type, rather than weighted averages that take into account the different population of each county.[5]

Over the 12-year period of our data set, both the level and annual variability of welfare participation are higher in agricultural and rural counties than in urban counties.[6] Summary statistics of these data are shown in Table 5.1.[7] Among the four types of counties, agricultural counties have the highest percent of the population on aid (10.3%) and the most annual variation (0.39%) in the percent receiving aid. Urban counties have the lowest percent of the population receiving aid (5.7%) and the lowest yearly variation (0.08%). Mixed and rural counties fall in between on both measures.

The greater variability in welfare participation among the nonurban counties is due largely to significant seasonality in those counties' welfare caseloads. These counties experience more welfare participation in the winter months than in the summer months.[8] This seasonality is most apparent when considering the dynamics of entry to welfare (the

**Table 5.1 Level and Variability of Welfare Participation and Unemployment by County Type**

| County type | Level | | Variability | |
| --- | --- | --- | --- | --- |
| | On aid (%) | Unemployment rate (%) | S.D. of % on aid[a] | S.D. of unemp. rate[a] |
| Agricultural | 10.3 | 14.0 | 0.39 | 2.8 |
| Rural | 7.1 | 9.6 | 0.33 | 2.5 |
| Mixed | 6.6 | 8.1 | 0.17 | 1.1 |
| Urban | 5.7 | 5.5 | 0.08 | 0.5 |

NOTE: The measures of variability are based on the standard deviation of monthly figures within a year. They are calculated as the average across all years of the standard deviation within a year.

[a] S.D. = standard deviation.

number of cases entering in a given month) and terminations (the number of cases leaving in a given month). We examine these dynamics for both subprograms of California's welfare program: the unemployed parent program (U) for families with two parents, and the family group program (FG) for families with an absent parent, usually a father.[9] There is seasonality for both types of cases, but it is more pronounced among the U cases.

Figure 5.3 plots the average of the net number of new cases (entries minus terminations) divided by population (in thousands) for U cases by calendar month and county type. Thus, the vertical axis is the net number of new cases per 1,000 population. Figure 5.3 clearly shows the much greater seasonal variability in nonurban counties relative to urban counties. The net effect of this variability is a drop in the caseload in nonurban counties over the summer and an increase during the winter. The line for urban counties is almost flat (ranging from zero to 0.05), while the line for agricultural counties ranges from –0.20 to 0.35. Rural counties are almost as variable as the agricultural counties, and mixed counties are, as we might expect, in between urban counties and agricultural/rural counties.

The same plots for FG cases (absent parent) are shown in Figure 5.4. With only one parent available to work, there has always been much less workforce participation in the FG cases than the U cases, so

**Figure 5.3  Net New Cases by County Type and Calendar Month ("U" cases)**

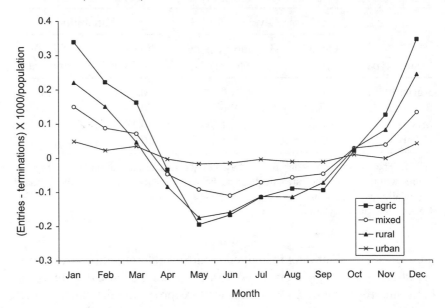

we would expect them to be much less sensitive to employment conditions. Figure 5.4 depicts the monthly changes in the net number of new cases (entries minus terminations) divided by population for agricultural and urban counties. As we would expect, the variation in these series is less than in the U cases, but the pattern is similar. Although there is substantial variability for urban counties, it does not seem to be seasonal, whereas the variability for agricultural counties is clearly seasonal. Seasonality also exists for both mixed and rural counties, but it is greater for rural counties.

**Unemployment Dynamics by County Type**

Can the differences in welfare dynamics by county type be explained by differences in employment dynamics? We use monthly labor force data by county from 1985–1997 to begin to answer this question; these data are from the State of California's Employment Development Department (2000). Both the level and annual variabili-

**Figure 5.4  Net New Cases by County Type and Calendar Month
       ("FG" Cases)**

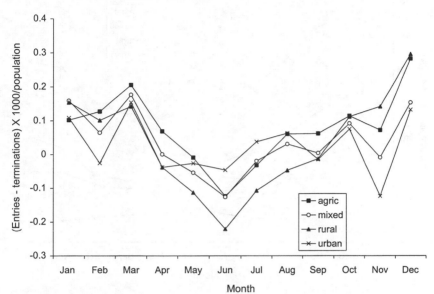

ty of the unemployment rate are higher in agricultural and rural counties than in urban counties over the time period of our data.

Table 5.1 includes summary statistics of the unemployment data as
well as the welfare participation data.  The statistics for both the level
and variability of unemployment and welfare participation are lowest
for urban counties, highest for agricultural counties, and fall in between
for rural and mixed counties.  This comparison of the unemployment
and welfare patterns by county type reveals a strong, positive relationship between the levels of unemployment and welfare participation.
The relationship is in the expected direction, given that an increase in
unemployment is likely to increase the welfare caseload, and a decrease
is likely to lower the welfare caseload.  There is also a strong, positive
relationship between annual variability of both unemployment and
those on aid.  In counties where more people cycle on and off unemployment, more people also cycle on and off welfare.

Employment figures also help explain the seasonality of welfare
dynamics in rural and agricultural counties.  As shown in Figure 5.5,

**Figure 5.5  Unemployment Rate by County Type and Calendar Month**

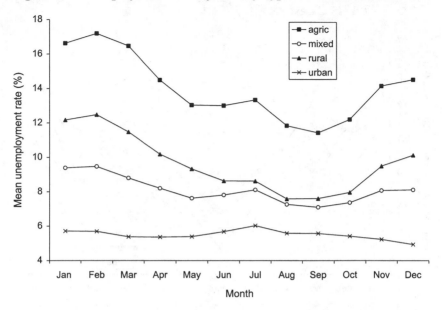

for nonurban counties, unemployment is higher in the winter months and lower in the summer months, corresponding to the seasonal pattern of welfare participation shown earlier.  To quantify the amount of seasonal change in unemployment by county type, we subtract the unemployment rate at its lowest point in the year from its highest point in the year.  Change in unemployment is highest for agricultural counties, a 5.8 percentage point change, from 17.2 percent unemployment in February to 11.4 percent unemployment in September.  The change in unemployment for rural and mixed counties is 4.9 and 2.4 percentage points, respectively.

## Employment Dynamics by Industry across County Types

To investigate further the relationship between yearly employment and welfare variability by county type, we turn to monthly employment data for 1985–1997 for eight mutually exclusive and exhaustive economic sectors: agriculture, manufacturing, trade, services, government, construction and mining, transportation and public utilities, and finance, insurance and real estate. It is important to move from aggregate employment to industry employment so policymakers know which employment sectors drive welfare dynamics and can tailor policies accordingly. For example, if employment in the sector serving tourists is highly seasonal and a large share of total employment, policymakers can work with employers in the tourism industry to devise policies providing employment to these workers in the off season. The industry data are collected by the State of California's Employment Development Department.[10] These monthly, county-level data are for industries classified by the Standard Industrial Classification (SIC) code.

For employment within a specific industry to help explain welfare seasonality, the employment also must exhibit seasonality. In addition, because people are more likely to exit welfare when they are employed, the seasonal pattern for employment must be the reverse of the pattern for welfare participation. Therefore, employment must be higher in the summer months and lower in the winter months. To assess whether an industry's employment helps explain welfare seasonality, we plot each industry's average employment (as a percentage of the civilian labor force) for the 12-year time period by calendar month.

Table 5.2 summarizes the extent to which each employment sector can help explain seasonal welfare participation in each county type. For each sector and county type, the table includes the difference in the percent employed between the summer month with the most employment and the winter month with the least employment.[11] Table 5.2 also shows the potential impact of an employment sector on welfare variability by indicating "little," "some," or "a lot."

Two of the eight employment sectors—the transportation and public utilities sector and the finance, insurance and real estate sector—show negligible, if any, seasonality across the four county types, even when broken down separately by county. Employment in these two sectors (as a percentage of total employment) remains essentially constant over the course of the year.

Service-sector employment also appears flat when averaged over each county type, but further examination reveals significant seasonality for two counties, Trinity and Mariposa. The service sector includes employment in hotels, amusements, and recreation services, and both

**Table 5.2  Difference in Employment between Summer Month with Highest Employment and Winter Month with Lowest Employment, by Employment Sector and County Type (%)**

| County type | Farming | Manufacturing | Trade | Construction & mining | Service | Transportation & public utilities | Finance, insurance & real estate | Government |
|---|---|---|---|---|---|---|---|---|
| Urban | 0.2 | 0.4 | −1.0 | 0.4 | 0.8 | −0.1 | 0.0 | −1.1 |
| Mixed | 2.3 Some | 1.0 Some | −0.7 | 0.6 | −0.4 | 0.3 | −0.1 | −1.8 |
| Agricultural | 7.7 A lot | 1.1 Some | −0.9 | −0.3 | −0.5 | 0.3 | −0.1 | −2.3 |
| Rural | 1.2 Some | 1.0 Some | 1.3 Some | 1.1 Some | −0.8 Little | 0.3 | −0.1 | −2.0 |

NOTE: The potential impact of an employment sector on welfare variability is indicated by "little," "some," or "a lot." Except for the "Government" column, cells with no word below the value are sectors with little seasonal variability (less than 1%).

Mariposa (where Yosemite Park is located) and Trinity (with the Trinity Alps, Lake, and River) have substantial summer tourism.

Employment dynamics in a fourth sector, government, exhibit substantial seasonality; however, the seasonal pattern is in the wrong direction. Employment in the government sector, like welfare participation, is higher in the winter months and lower in the summer months. The large drop in government employment among all four county types during July and August is primarily due to the loss of employment for public school teachers in those months. This sector does not affect welfare dynamics.

Employment in the remaining four sectors can help explain the seasonal welfare participation in nonurban counties, as summarized in Table 5.2. For each sector, employment is higher in the summer months than the winter months for at least one nonurban county type.

Consider farming and agricultural employment displayed by county type in Figure 5.6. The substantial seasonality in farm employment

**Figure 5.6  Agriculture Employment by County Type and Calendar Month**

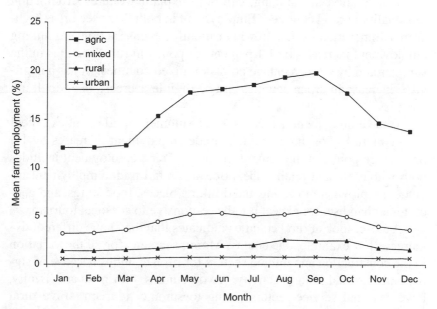

can go a long way toward explaining some of the variability in welfare caseloads for agricultural counties. To quantify the amount of annual turnover in agricultural employment by county type, we calculate the difference in agricultural employment between its lowest and highest points in the year. The change in agricultural employment is highest for agricultural counties: a 7.7 percentage point change, from 12.1 percent of total employment in January to 19.8 percent in September. The annual turnover for mixed, rural, and urban counties is 2.3, 1.2, and 0.2 percentage points, respectively. These changes in agricultural employment from summer to winter for agricultural and mixed counties are the highest among the eight employment sectors.

The second employment sector that may contribute to the variability in welfare participation in agricultural and rural counties is manufacturing, which includes the manufacture of both durable and nondurable goods. There is an increase in manufacturing employment during the summer months for each county type. The annual turnover in manufacturing employment is approximately 1 percentage point for agricultural, mixed and rural counties, and a much smaller amount for urban counties.

Along with manufacturing, employment in two other sectors, trade and construction and mining, can help explain welfare participation seasonality in rural counties. Employment in both these sectors is higher in summer months than in winter months. Construction and mining employment increases by 1.1 percentage points in rural counties in the summer and by 0.6 percentage points in mixed counties. It has a negligible increase in urban counties and negligible decrease in agricultural counties.

Trade employment decreases in the summer for all counties except rural counties. For those counties, trade employment increases by 1.3 percentage points in the summer months. Trade employment includes both wholesale and retail trade. Because retail trade employment includes employment in eating and drinking places, food stores, and general merchandise, we expect it to be responsive to seasonal tourism.

A closer look at rural counties indicates that they have different dynamics. For example, one county, Mono, accounts for all the variation in the construction and mining sectors for rural counties because of significant seasonal mining activity. Two counties, Mariposa and Trinity, have seasonal service sectors owing to summer tourism. Five rural counties drive the farming figures, and three drive the manufacturing figures. Thus, within the rural counties, we can distinguish six types. Farming and trade counties (Del Norte and Lake), farming and manufacturing (Lassen, Mendocino, and Siskiyou), service (Mariposa and Trinity), construction, mining, and trade (Mono), nonfarm mixed (Amador, Calaveras, Plumas, and Tuolumne), and three counties with no seasonality (El Dorado, Inyo, and Nevada).

In summary, the seasonality of welfare use in agricultural counties can apparently be largely explained by seasonality of agricultural and manufacturing employment. During the summer months, agricultural employment increases 7.7 percentage points and manufacturing employment increases by about 1.1 percentage points, for a total increase in employment of almost 9 percentage points in the summer. In rural counties, the welfare seasonality can be attributed to employment in the agricultural, manufacturing, trade, and construction and mining sectors. Employment in each of these sectors increases during the summer months by between 1 and 1.3 percentage points, for a total increase in employment of about 5 percentage points in the summer. The service sector also matters in two rural counties.

## LINKING EMPLOYMENT DYNAMICS TO WELFARE DYNAMICS

The data presented in the last section suggest a strong link between employment and welfare dynamics, but they do not provide the kinds of proof that multivariate statistical methods can provide. In a separate paper (Brady et al. 2000), we have developed a complete statistical model of welfare entries and terminations for both FG and U cases using aggregate California county data and a statistical model of terminations for FG and U recipients using individual-level data for California counties. These models reach the same conclusions, and they provide us with substantial assurances that there are strong links between employment and welfare. We will briefly describe both statistical models and their main findings, and then we will present some of the implications of the aggregate-level estimations.

Our aggregate and individual-level specifications linking welfare use to employment patterns were guided by a theoretical model of welfare entrances and exits. Our model considers entrances and exits from welfare to be the result of a stochastic process within the relevant at-risk population in which different subpopulations have different chances of entering or exiting welfare. These chances depend on employment conditions, benefit levels, and other factors that affect the use of welfare.

Based on the theoretical model, we developed a time-series, cross-sectional, aggregate-level model for explaining welfare entries and exits, a model that included lagged dependent variables, current and lagged values of independent variables (such as employment in various sectors and birth rates), fixed effects for each county and time period, and corrections for heteroscedasticity and auto-correlation. This model showed that a substantial amount of the variation in entries and exits could be explained by the ups and downs of employment. As expected, employment had a greater effect on welfare participation for U cases than FG cases. Regarding specific employment sectors, agriculture employment had a large, significant effect on both entries and exits for U cases and on exits for FG cases in agricultural counties. In rural counties, retail employment helped explain variation in welfare exits for both FG and U cases and variation in entries for U cases. Employment in other sectors also helped explained both entries and exits for U cases in rural counties.

With the individual-level data—a 1 percent sample of welfare recipients in all California counties—we estimated a discrete time hazard model for terminations. In our model, the exit rate is a linear function of the explanatory variables of age, county employment variables, spell duration effects, and calendar month and county fixed effects. Our individual-level results largely mirror the aggregate-level results. We also find that the average welfare recipient in either a rural or agricultural county has both more and shorter welfare spells than the average welfare recipient in an urban county. A person in an agricultural or rural county is, therefore, more likely than a person in an urban county to go on welfare in a given year; however, once on welfare, he or she is more likely to exit welfare before an urban welfare recipient who began welfare at the same time.

Rather than report all of the details of these estimations, we will simply present some of their implications. Figure 5.7 considers the im-

**Figure 5.7   Effect of an Increase in Demand for Agricultural Labor on
Welfare Caseload and the Potential Agricultural Labor Force**

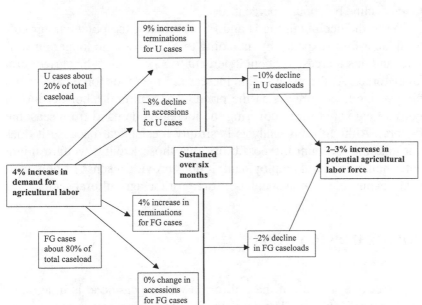

pact on the U and FG caseload of a 4 percent change in the agricultural
employment rate and the resulting impact on the labor available for the
agricultural labor force. The data in this figure are calculated from the
models described above, and the information we have about the variation in agricultural employment and the distribution of FG and U cases
in California.

The figure begins at the left-hand side by assuming a change in the
demand for agricultural employment of 4 percent. In fact, the change
from peak to trough is 8 percent, but this amounts to an average increase of about 4 percent over six months. This change affects both the
U and FG caseload, but the 20 percent of the caseload that is U cases is
affected the most. Terminations of U cases increase by 9 percent with a
4 percent change in agricultural employment. Entries to welfare also
decline by 8 percent. Over the course of six months, this leads to a decline in U caseloads of about 10 percent. The 80 percent of the caseload that is FG is affected less by an increased demand for agricultural

labor, but terminations for FG cases still increase by 4 percent; entries, however, do not seem to be affected.  The net result is that FG case-loads decline by about 2 percent.

With the decline in the U and FG caseloads, the potential agricultural labor force expands by including those who are no longer on welfare, and this increase is about 2 percent to 3 percent of the agricultural labor force.  At the margin, this increase in the labor force can have a highly significant impact on the price of agricultural labor because it goes a long way toward covering the increased demand from seasonal factors.  Although this analysis is simply mechanical because it does not take into account the possibility that those leaving welfare might enter nonagricultural employment, it does provide a sense of how welfare has provided a seasonal labor force for the agricultural sector.

## POLICY IMPLICATIONS

Over one-seventh of the California welfare caseload is in agricultural or rural counties.  The number of welfare recipients in these counties increases dramatically from the summer to the winter.  The total caseload affected by seasonal factors doubles if mixed counties are included with agricultural and rural counties.

The seasonality in welfare receipt is driven by labor market factors.  In agricultural and mixed counties, farming employment is primarily responsible for seasonality.  In agricultural counties, the changing demand for agricultural labor from winter to summer leads to a reduction in the welfare caseload that could supply 2 to 3 percent of the total agricultural workforce.  In rural counties, the most important sectors vary from one county to another, but they are primarily agriculture, manufacturing, trade, service, and construction and mining.  Reductions in the welfare caseload between the winter and the summer provide a significant fraction of the workforce in these sectors in some rural counties.

The new TANF legislation and the California WORKs program emphasize work and time limits for welfare recipients.  Although California's time limits do not necessarily remove an entire family from aid, they do substantially reduce the degree to which welfare can provide income for seasonal workers beyond the time-limit period. What will happen to these seasonal workers under the new legislation?

One answer is that the seasonal workers will stay where they are and simply find other ways to combine summer employment with winter unemployment. This will almost certainly mean that many will have annual incomes below the poverty level. Another answer is that these people might get new jobs with less seasonality or move elsewhere. This will probably happen for some workers, but workers often have difficulty moving from either one job to another or one location to another (Council of Economic Advisers 1990). Furthermore, if a large number of seasonal workers do move to other areas, then seasonal industries must either find their workforce elsewhere or bid up the price of their labor.

Another answer is that welfare time limits might be modified in those areas with significant seasonal or persistent unemployment. This would allow seasonal workers to combine welfare with work and to have enough income to lift them out of poverty. This approach, however, means that the government will be subsidizing the workforce for seasonal employers and that it will be providing incentives for workers to remain in areas with high unemployment rates. It will also extend people's involvement in a stigmatizing social welfare program.

Still another answer might be to extend unemployment insurance (UI), or some variant of it, to seasonal workers. Currently, UI is seldom available to these workers either because their work is not covered originally or because they cannot stay employed long enough to qualify for UI benefits. An unemployment insurance scheme would be less stigmatizing than welfare, and it would involve employers in providing part of the subsidy for its seasonal workers through the traditional experience rating method of funding UI. Unfortunately, it seems likely that many seasonal employers would balk at helping to fund such a program.

# Notes

1. According to the authors, forest counties are those that in 1980 had a forest coverage of more than 50 percent or those in which 3 percent or more of the 1980 county wages came from forest sector industries and in which timber was cut commercially.

2. The counties classified as mixed have a combined population that is greater than the population in each of 40 states. Meanwhile the combined population of the counties classified as urban is about one-third larger than any other state.

3. Percent rural figures are from the Bureau of the Census (1992), *Census of Population and Housing, 1990.* They indicate the percent of the population who lives in rural areas, defined as all areas except places of 2,500 or more population incorporated as cities, villages, and towns. Percent farm and agricultural services employment figures are for 1993, from the U.S. Bureau of Economic Analysis.

4. The data used for this and other welfare analysis at the aggregate level is the California Department of Social Services series, *Public Welfare in California.* This data series provides monthly information by county on total aid payments, number of children and people receiving aid, and number of cases, exits, and entries.

5. Two counties, Sutter and Yuba, have been combined in our data set because some industry data were unavailable for each county separately until 1994. In addition, we have excluded from our data set the two counties with the smallest populations, Alpine and Sierra. They have been omitted because a large portion of the variability in their welfare and employment rates is driven by idiosyncratic factors that are averaged out over very small populations.

6. Welfare participation, or percentage on aid, is calculated as the total number of people on aid divided by the population.

7. The variability numbers, which are based on the standard deviation of monthly figures within a year, measure the amount of variation in the percentage of the population on aid within a year. They are calculated as the average across all years of the standard deviation for welfare participation within a year.

8. We define summer months as May through October and winter months as November through April.

9. FG cases comprised, on average, more than four-fifths of the welfare caseload in each county type over the time period of our data set. The proportion of the welfare caseload comprised of UP cases ranged from about one-seventh in urban counties (13.8%) to one-fifth in agricultural counties (19.6%). Compared with other states, California has a disproportionate share of its caseload comprised of two-parent families; only 7 percent of the national caseload consisted of these families in 1996. More than half of all two-parent cases (54%) were in California in 1996 (U.S. House of Representatives 1998). Within both the FG and U welfare subprograms, some cases are child-only cases, cases in which adults (usually parents) are excluded from the household size calculation used to determine welfare benefits. In our analysis these cases are not distinguished from cases with aided

parents, because we believe adults associated with both types of cases face similar economic incentives.

10. The data were largely obtained from the Employment Development Department's web site at <www.calmis.ca.gov/htmlfile/subject/indtable.htm>. Some data missing from the web site were obtained from the State of California's "Annual Planning Information" publications. When data were unavailable on the web site and in the publications, quarterly ES-202 data were used.

11. For each county type, employment is averaged across counties of that type for each month, and then the difference is taken between the highest summer and the lowest winter month.

# References

Albert, Vicky N. 1988. *Welfare Dependence and Welfare Policy: A Statistical Study*. New York: Greenwood Press.

Blank, Rebecca. 1997. "What Causes Public Assistance Caseloads to Grow?" Working paper, Northwestern University.

Bluestone, Barry, and James Sumrall. 1977. *Public Assistance Dynamics: Testing Alternative Theories of AFDC Growth*. SWRRI Publication no. 24, Social Welfare Regional Research Institute, Boston College.

Brady, Henry E., Mary Sprague, Fredric C. Gey, and Michael Wiseman. 2000. "The Interaction of Welfare-Use and Employment Dynamics in Rural and Agricultural California Counties." Paper for the 2000 National Association for Welfare Research and Statistics conference.

Brady, Peter, and Michael Wiseman. 1998. "Establishing a Baseline: Caseload Dynamics in California before PRWORA." Working paper.

Bureau of the Census. 1992. *Census of Population and Housing, 1990* [computer files]. Washington, D.C.: U.S. Department of Commerce. Inter-university Consortium for Political and Social Research, Ann Arbor, Michigan (distributor), 1993.

Congressional Budget Office. 1993. "Forecasting AFDC Caseloads, with an Emphasis on Economic Factors." Washington, D.C.: Congressional Budget Office.

Council of Economic Advisers. 1990. "The U.S. Council of Economic Advisers on Labor Shortages, Worker Mobility, and Immigration." *Population and Development Review* 16: 193–198.

———. 1997. "Explaining the Decline in Welfare Receipt, 1993–1996." Technical Report. Available at <http://www.whitehouse.gov/WH/EOP/CEA/welfare/technical_report.html>.

Findeis, Jill L., and Leif Jensen. 1998. "Employment Opportunities in Rural

Areas: Implications for Poverty in a Changing Policy Environment." *American Journal of Agricultural Economics* 80: 1000–1007.

Fitzgerald, John. 1995. "Local Labor Market and Local Area Effects on Welfare Duration." *Journal of Applied Policy and Management* 14(1): 43–67.

Fuguitt, Glenn V., David L. Brown, and Calvin L. Beale. 1989. *Rural and Small Town America.* New York: Russell Sage Foundation.

Harris, Kathleen. 1993. "Work and Welfare among Single Women in Poverty." *American Journal of Sociology* 99(2): 317–352.

Hoffman, Sandra A., and Louise Fortmann. 1995. *Poverty in California's Forest Counties: A Preliminary Time Series Analysis with Special Reference to AFDC Caseloads.* Report prepared for the Strategic Planning Program, California Department of Forestry and Fire Protection.

Hoynes, Hilary Williamson. 1996. "Local Labor Markets and Welfare Spells: Do Demand Conditions Matter?" Working paper no. 5643, National Bureau of Economic Research, Cambridge, Massachusetts.

Lichter, Daniel T., Gail M. Johnston, and Diane K. McLaughlin. 1994. "Changing Linkages between Work and Poverty in Rural America." *Rural Sociology* 59(3): 395–415.

MaCurdy, Thomas, David Mancuso, and Margaret O'Brien-Strain. 2000. *The Rise and Fall of California's Welfare Caseload: Types and Regions, 1980–1999.* San Francisco: Public Policy Institute of California.

O'Neill, June A., Laurie J. Bassi, and Douglas A. Wolf. 1987. "The Duration of Welfare Spells." *Review of Economics and Statistics* 69: 241–248.

Porterfield, Shirley L. 1998. "On the Precipice of Reform: Welfare Spell Durations for Rural, Female-Headed Families." *American Journal of Agricultural Economics* 80: 994–999.

Rank, Mark R., and Thomas A. Hirschl. 1988. "A Rural-Urban Comparison of Welfare Exits: The Importance of Population Density." *Rural Sociology* 53: 190–206.

Rural Policy Research Institute. 1999. *Rural America and Welfare Reform: An Overview Assessment.* Report P99-3, Rural Policy Research Institute, Columbia, Missouri.

Sanders, Seth. 1992. "Preliminary Evidence on Human Capital Production and Welfare Participation." Chapter 3 of an unpublished Ph.D. dissertation, University of Chicago.

State of California Employment Development Department. 2000. *Employment by Industry Data.* Sacramento, California. Available at <http://www.calmis.ca.gov/htmlfile/subject/indtable.htm>.

State of California Department of Social Services. *Public Welfare in California* series (July 1985 to October 1997). Sacramento, California.

Taylor, J. Edward, Philip L. Martin, and Michael Fix.  1997.  *Poverty amid Prosperity: Immigration and the Changing Face of Rural California.* Washington, D.C.: Urban Institute Press.

Tickamyer, Ann R.  1992.  "The Working Poor in Rural Labor Markets: The Example of the Southeastern United States."  In *Rural Poverty in America,* Cynthia M. Duncan, ed.  Westport, Connecticut: Auburn House.

U.S. House of Representatives, Committee on Ways and Means.  1998.  *1998 Green Book.*  Washington, D.C.: U.S. Government Printing Office.

Ziliak, James P., David N. Figlio, Elizabeth E. Davis, and Laura S. Connolly.  1997.  "Accounting for the Decline in AFDC Caseloads: Welfare Reform or Economic Growth?"  Discussion paper no. 1151-97, Institute for Research on Poverty, University of Wisconsin, Madison.

# 6

# Location and the
# Low-Income Experience

## Analyses of Program Dynamics in the Iowa
## Family Investment Program

Helen H. Jensen, Shao-Hsun Keng, and Steven Garasky
*Iowa State University*

In 1993, the state of Iowa, through waivers, implemented reforms creating the Family Investment Program (FIP), a program similar to the Temporary Assistance for Needy Families (TANF) created under the Personal Responsibility and Work Opportunity Reconciliation Act (PRWORA). The goals of FIP (helping program recipients leave poverty and become self-supporting) parallel the intent of TANF and PRWORA (Holcomb et al. 1998; Iowa Department of Human Services 1996). FIP merged and coordinated several existing programs and tied support for job training, education, child care, and transportation more directly to income transfers. Iowa has had to change FIP very little to meet current federal guidelines. Thus, Iowa provides over seven years of experience under a program with rules and incentives similar to those instituted nationwide in 1996.

The federal changes to welfare policies and programs raise questions about how rural families receiving assistance are faring under work requirements and time limits on cash assistance. Not well understood is whether rural welfare recipients face a more difficult transition from welfare to sustained employment given the challenges facing some rural areas.

This chapter examines the dynamics of welfare participation during the pre-TANF period of Iowa's reform (1993–1995), and specifically how program, demographic, and macroeconomic factors relate to return to welfare after leaving among program participants. Reasons for returning to welfare are examined over time, with specific attention given to local labor market conditions and to metropolitan and non-metropolitan locations (various classifications). Iowa received a waiver to enact many of the key provisions of TANF during the period of our study, including provisions to encourage recipients to enter job training and the labor market. We use a unique data set composed of linked state administrative records. These data are ideal for longitudinal analyses (analyses spanning a period of time, rather than a cross section at a point in time) because key variables are available monthly. The data can also track location (including location changes) among the FIP households.

We first provide some background to Iowa's welfare program, review previous research, and discuss the aspects of geographic differences that may influence the FIP experience. Next, we outline the main features of the administrative data and discuss the benefits and drawbacks of using administrative data for research purposes. We then describe the dynamics of FIP participation. We develop a model and examine the distribution of the first exit from cash assistance and incidence of returning to welfare. We conclude by drawing several policy implications from our findings.

## BACKGROUND

Throughout the 1990s, rural states enjoyed the benefits of a healthy economy. In Iowa in the latter half of the decade, for example, the statewide unemployment rate remained well below the national rate: 95 of the 99 Iowa counties had unemployment rates below the national rate of 4.1 percent in 1999. Iowa's economic success, however, was not uniform across the state. County-level unemployment rates in Iowa in 1999 ranged from 1.7 percent (Warren County) to 4.5 percent (Butler County); among the seven counties with the highest unemployment rates, all but one was predominantly rural (Iowa Department of Workforce Development 2000). In the more rural counties, manufacturing jobs have absorbed much of the workforce leaving farming. However, since 1993, most of Iowa's population growth has been in the state's 10 metropolitan counties (Eathington, Swenson, and Otto 2000).

During the 1990s, caseloads for Aid to Families with Dependent Children (AFDC)—later FIP—and the Food Stamp program both peaked around the time of the FIP waiver implementation. Since early 1994, the caseloads for both programs have declined relatively steadily (Figure 6.1). Interestingly, while nonmetro unemployment rates in Iowa remain generally higher than metro rates, both nonmetro and metro counties have seen similar reductions in cash assistance and Food Stamp program participation.

Most studies of former welfare recipients have found that between half and three-quarters of parents are employed shortly after they leave the welfare rolls (Parrott 1998). However, wages are low, typically less than $8.00 per hour and often less than $6.00 per hour. As a result, studies measuring earnings over three-month periods find earnings levels well below poverty.

Much of the policy debate over welfare reform has centered on the plight of poor urban families. Although poverty has become more ur-

**Figure 6.1  AFDC/TANF and Food Stamp Caseloads in Iowa, 1990–98**

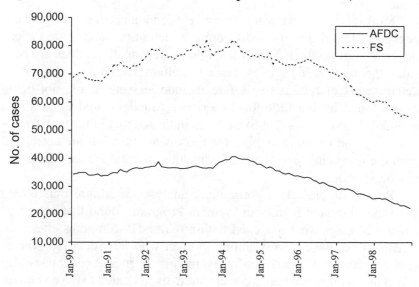

SOURCE: Iowa Department of Human Services.

banized over the past several decades, most poor and welfare recipient families live outside central cities, and many live outside metropolitan areas altogether. Some evidence suggests that rural workers may face substantially greater employment and self-sufficiency barriers than urban workers. In nonmetropolitan areas, poor families are already more likely to be working and more likely to be underemployed (working part-time, earning low wages, or unemployed) than are poor families in metro areas (Findeis and Jensen 1998). In Iowa, average nonfarm earnings in rural counties are below those in metropolitan and other nonmetropolitan counties (i.e., urban nonmetropolitan areas). Nationwide, average rural manufacturing earnings are 68 percent below national levels; in the service sector, rural earnings are 49 percent of the U.S. average (Eathington, Swenson, and Otto 2000).

The majority of the early literature finds that lower participation rates in and higher exit rates from cash assistance programs are associated with greater nonwage income, higher wage rates, more years of schooling, fewer children, good health, and being white. Moreover, these studies also show a "negative duration dependence"; that is, as the time on welfare lengthens, exit rates decline; and the longer a person remains off assistance, the lower the likelihood that they will return.

Moffitt (1992), reviewing the concepts and measures of welfare dependence, found that the most common definition of welfare dependence focuses on the length of a single welfare spell but does not consider the high reentry rates among welfare recipients. Important determinants of returns to welfare include less education, not being married, and having little job experience (Sandefur and Cook 1997; Brandon 1995). Cao's (1996) analyses indicated that initial welfare dependency and return to welfare for those who have left are correlated with the recipient's age, years of education, marital status, ethnic origin, and region.

Born et al. (1998), in preliminary analyses of administrative data from the Maryland Family Investment Program, found that nearly 20 percent of cases were reopened within the first 3–6 months after exit. Reentry rates were lowest among women who left for a job (versus leaving because of marriage, for example). Born and colleagues also found that women whose exits were short-lived tended to have younger children than those women who managed to remain off the program. Reidy (1998) examined the role of noncash benefits for those leaving AFDC. One result is that those who leave AFDC but continue to claim noncash benefits (including food stamps) are more likely to return to AFDC than others who leave both AFDC and other noncash benefit programs at the same time.

The limited information on differences between rural and urban areas in welfare participation (e.g., Porterfield 1998) shows that those in urban areas have longer spells on welfare than those in rural or smaller urban locations. Different labor market opportunities, household and individual characteristics (including human capital differences) as well as costs of working (i.e., logistics of transportation or child care services) are possible reasons for these differences. The shorter spells on welfare in rural areas may also be due to lack of program information and stigma attached to public assistance (Porterfield 1998). Porterfield also found that rural families (relative to urban) are more likely to enter welfare due to decreases in earnings or income, but urban families are more likely to exit welfare owing to earnings or increases in income.

Metro and nonmetro areas may differ in labor market and job opportunities. Davis, Connolly, and Weber (1999) pointed to the spatial mismatch that has occurred as seekers of jobs in small markets meet with less success and employers in other markets have a difficult time finding the types of employees they need. The greater prevalence of underemployment in nonmetro areas, typified by low-wage employment, involuntary part-time work, or "discouraged" workers, may explain part of the inconsistency between relatively low unemployment rates in many areas and continued low incomes (Findeis and Jensen 1998).

The current study examines the effects and outcomes of an assistance program quite similar to the TANF programs that have been established in many states. The early experiences with FIP in Iowa allow us to examine the experiences of individuals and families who left FIP in the two-year period following its introduction. We study why some low-income households successfully leave public assistance while others who leave return. We examine a specific set of families that were enrolled and active in FIP at the time of the newly enacted changes in the system.

## DATA

Iowa was one of the first states to link administrative data across programs to support program administration and policy analysis. In 1995, a project was designed to develop administrative data systems for research purposes. The product of this effort was a three-year longitudinal data file (April 1993–March 1996) that matches and merges FIP, Medicaid, food stamps, child support, and quarterly earnings records for all FIP recipients during this period. FIP, food stamps, and Medicaid represent the key assistance programs for low-income families; child support and earnings are the key sources of nonpublic assistance income. The data include amounts (e.g., program benefits, child support received, and earnings) and dates (e.g., program exit and reentry). Because the data are not subject to problems of respondent recall or respondent bias, administrative data are preferred over survey data in many respects. The data are linked for all residents receiving FIP in April 1993. Observations (cases) are added to the file as they enter FIP; cases are followed throughout the data period, even after exiting FIP.

We supplement the administrative data in two ways. First, we classify each county as metro (counties in metropolitan areas); urban nonmetro (nonmetro counties with at least one urban population of 20,000 or more); small town/rural adjacent (counties with no urban population more than 20,000 and adjacent to a metro area); or small town/rural nonadjacent (counties not adjacent to a metro area). All categories are derived from Butler and Beale (1994). The last three categories can be combined into a nonmetro group. Second, we merge monthly county unemployment rates and county income per capita to account for the effect of local economic conditions in our analyses. Monthly county unemployment rates are available from Iowa Workforce Development.

We create a two-year panel data set, beginning in October 1993 (the start of the FIP program) and ending September 1995. All cases identified as receiving FIP benefits in October 1993 ($N = 38{,}632$) are included in the panel. No samples are drawn for these analyses. We count 22,080 FIP exits among the cases, where an exit is defined as being inactive (i.e., no benefits) for two months in a row. After deleting cases with missing information other than educational attainment, the total is reduced to 32,309 cases.  Of these, 17,159 (53 percent) were metro cases and 15,150 (47 percent) were nonmetro cases.

Although the Iowa linked data set includes detailed information on child support collections, FIP participation, and quarterly wage earnings, the household and demographic variables are limited.  Available information includes the case head's educational attainment, age, marital status, ethnic origin, gender, disability status, and county of residence.  The number of children in the household also is available.

Unfortunately, it is not mandatory to provide educational attainment when applying for FIP, and about half of our observations have missing data on education.  Further, the missing data are not randomly distributed throughout the data set.  Because deleting nonrandom missing data would lead to biased estimates and a loss of information, we employed a multiple imputation procedure (Rubin 1987) to compensate for the missing educational attainment data.  The multiple imputations find that, for the two-year period, there were 6,593 (40.5 percent) cases with no high school degree, 9,436 (57.9 percent) cases with at least a high school degree for two years, and 270 (1.6 percent) cases that experienced a change in education (received a high school degree) some time during the two-year period.

## FIP PARTICIPATION

We next examine how the families fared during the initial period of the FIP program and whether there were differences in how the families fared in metro and nonmetro areas.  As noted, the data are on cases active in October 1993.  Across the two-year period, the overall FIP caseload initially increased and then fell.  Some evidence suggests that the initial caseload increase resulted from the more generous FIP income disregards and the stronger support programs that were introduced in 1993 (Fraker et al. 1998).

Table 6.1 provides descriptive information on FIP cases, both total and divided by metro and nonmetro areas.  Several economic and program variables are compared between December 1993 (the end of first quarter) and September 1995 (the end of the last quarter).  Just over half of the total 32,309 cases were in metro areas.  Of the cases, 91 per-

**Table 6.1  Selected Demographic Variables for Metro and Nonmetro FIP Cases, Dec. 1993 and Sept. 1995**

| Variables | Total | | Metro cases | | Nonmetro cases | |
|---|---|---|---|---|---|---|
| | Dec. 1993 | Sept. 1995 | Dec. 1993 | Sept. 1995 | Dec. 1993 | Sept. 1995 |
| Quarterly wage income ($) | 2,998 | 3,883 | 2,781 | 3,575 | 3,223 | 4,207 |
| Share with quarterly wage income (%) | 55 | 69 | 52 | 67 | 58 | 72 |
| Quarterly child support ($) | 164 | 459 | 162 | 435 | 166 | 480 |
| Share with quarterly child support (%) | 29 | 36 | 26 | 32 | 32 | 41 |
| Share of FIP participation (%) | 100 | 50 | 100 | 51 | 100 | 49 |
| Share receiving food stamps (%) | 89 | 55 | 90 | 57 | 87 | 53 |
| Number of children | 2.20 | 2.27 | 2.2 | 2.31 | 2.14 | 2.23 |
| Share living in metro counties (%) | 53 | 53 | 100 | 97 | 0 | 4 |
| Local unemployment rate (%) | 3.74 | 3.26 | 3.48 | 2.97 | 4.04 | 3.58 |
| Share with high school degree or above (%) | 61 | 63 | 58 | 61 | 64 | 66 |
| Share married (%) | 20 | 23 | 15 | 18 | 24 | 29 |
| Share with female head (%) | 91 | | 92 | | 89 | |
| Share white (%) | 85 | | 76 | | 94 | |
| Number of observations | 32,309 | 32,309 | 17,159 | 17,159 | 15,150 | 15,150 |

NOTE: Tests for the differences between periods show all are statistically significant at the 1% level.

cent of the case heads were female.  The nonmetro cases were more likely to have a case head who was married, was white and who had at least a high school degree.

In both metro and nonmetro areas, nearly half of the active FIP cases in October 1993 were active at the end of the two-year period (51 percent for metro and 49 percent for nonmetro areas).  Food stamps had similar participation patterns by September 1995 (57 percent of metro cases were active and 53 percent of nonmetro cases), although participation remained slightly higher than the FIP participation.  In the first quarter of the observation period (December 1993), 52 percent in metro areas and 58 percent in nonmetro areas were earning wage income.  Two years later, nearly two-thirds of the case heads had earnings from wages, with a slightly higher rate (72 percent) reported for nonmetro cases.  Among those with wage income, average earnings were higher in nonmetro areas in both periods.  This suggests a difference in jobs or a difference in work effort (i.e., more hours worked) by those in nonmetro areas.

The percentage of cases receiving child support also increased during this period; again, a relatively higher share of households in nonmetro areas received child support, and the average amount of child support received was higher in nonmetro areas.  In both areas, the percentage with a high school degree increased, as did the percentage who reported being married.  In sum, in addition to improvements in the overall economy during the two-year period (as measured by unemployment rates), other indicators also improved.

The FIP population is a relatively mobile one: 11.5 percent moved from their original county of residence at least once during the two-year period (analysis not shown).  In metro areas, 7 percent of cases moved to another county; in nonmetro areas, 16.6 percent of cases moved.  Of those who moved from the metro area, nearly 22 percent had moved back to the original county at the end of two years, compared with nearly 15 percent of those in nonmetro counties.  The evidence suggests that FIP recipients in metro areas are more likely to stay (or return) to their "home" county compared with nonmetro recipients.  (Of course, they may move within the county, and the metro areas have more housing and different location options.  We were unable to evaluate this possibility.  Also, there is greater availability of public housing options in metro areas.)

If labor resources were fully mobile, we would expect that as FIP participants moved to obtain a job, their FIP status would change. Table 6.2 shows the FIP status before and after moving to another county for metro and nonmetro moves during the period. The FIP status during the quarter preceding each move was compared with the FIP status during the first quarter in the new location (each observation is a move). There were 5,068 moves in total, 1,629 with metro as the original county of residence and 3,439 with nonmetro as the originating county. For those originally living in metro counties, moves were evenly distributed between moves to metro and to nonmetro locations. Relatively more active cases stayed active and inactive cases stayed in-

**Table 6.2  FIP and Employment Status after Moving to Another County, Oct. 1998–Sept. 1995**

|  | To metro | | To nonmetro | |
|---|---|---|---|---|
|  | Active | Inactive | Active | Inactive |
| Moves from metro (N=1,629) | | | | |
| Active | 100 | 52 | 116 | 44 |
| % employed before | 66 | 54 | 66 | 61 |
| % employed after move | 75 | 75 | 69 | 66 |
| Inactive | 72 | 562 | 75 | 608 |
| % employed before | 68 | 48 | 61 | 53 |
| % employed after move | 75 | 65 | 76 | 69 |
| Total (percent of total) | 172 (11) | 614 (38) | 191 (12) | 652 (40) |
| % employed before | 67 | 49 | 64 | 54 |
| % employed after move | 75 | 66 | 72 | 69 |
|  | | | | |
| Moves from nonmetro (N=3,439) | | | | |
| Active | 114 | 68 | 353 | 199 |
| % employed before | 70 | 60 | 62 | 69 |
| % employed after move | 79 | 69 | 74 | 74 |
| Inactive | 64 | 577 | 224 | 1,840 |
| % employed before | 69 | 53 | 67 | 59 |
| % employed after move | 78 | 71 | 80 | 76 |
| Total (percent of total) | 178 (5) | 645 (19) | 577 (17) | 2,039 (59) |
| % employed before | 70 | 54 | 64 | 59 |
| % employed after move | 79 | 71 | 77 | 76 |

active, irrespective of the destination county type. For those originally living in nonmetro counties, over three-fourths (17 percent and 60 percent) of cases moved to nonmetro areas. Again, the moves were not associated with big shifts in FIP status.

A relatively large share of moves resulted in employment in the quarter after the move, as shown in Table 6.2. Despite the status in FIP, nearly three-fourths of moves had case heads employed after the move, although the employment rates varied among the different groups shown in the table. Nearly 69 percent of moves from metro counties were employed after the move, compared with 75 percent of moves from nonmetro counties. The highest rates of employment after the move was for moves from nonmetro counties to nonmetro counties. One caveat to these results is that there is some lag in employment reporting in the system.

We next examined the time spent (in months) receiving FIP in each of the two years (1993 and 1995).[1] In metro areas, 15.6 percent of recipients had relatively short spells during the first year (0–6 months on FIP in the first year); 64.3 percent remained on FIP during the full 12 months. The distribution of cases is similar for nonmetro areas, with slightly more (17.1 percent) receiving assistance for 6 months or fewer, and 61 percent remaining on for the full first 12 months.

The extremes in our data are those who do not participate in FIP at all during the second year ("long-term leavers"), and those who participate in FIP all 24 months observed (the "hard-core"). Approximately one-fourth (24.4 percent) of all metro cases and a slightly larger percentage of the nonmetro cases did not participate in FIP at all during the second year. In contrast, 38 percent of metro cases and 35 percent of nonmetro cases remained on FIP all 24 months of the two-year period.

Table 6.3 compares differences in the groups among the four geographic locations between the beginning and the end months of the two-year period. To start, we compare those not participating in FIP in the second year across the four geographic areas. For this group, employment rates (receipt of wage income) were relatively high (ranging from 74 percent to 84 percent) during both years, although in all areas, the percentage with wage income fell between the first and second year. This may be because of increases in marriage rates or child support for this group. The highest rates of employment were in the small towns/rural adjacent areas, areas that have benefited from strong

**Table 6.3  Comparison of Selected Demographic Variables for Different Locations and Participation Patterns: Oct. 1993 to Sept. 1995 (October 1993 base year)**

| | Metro | | | | Urban nonmetro | | | |
| --- | --- | --- | --- | --- | --- | --- | --- | --- |
| | No partic. in 2nd yr. $N = 4,183$ (24.4%) | | Participate all 24 mos. $N = 6,541$ (38.1%) | | No partic. in 2nd yr. $N = 1,356$ (24.8%) | | Participate all 24 mos. $N = 2,035$ (37.2%) | |
| Variables | Yr. 1 | Yr. 2 | Yr. 1 | Yr. 2 | Yr. 1 | Yr. 2 | Yr. 1 | Yr. 2 |
| Annual wage income ($) | 10,478 | 14,665*** | 7,671 | 8,504*** | 11,317 | 16,119*** | 9,148 | 10,070** |
| Share employed (%) | 79 | 74*** | 63 | 74*** | 79 | 78 | 66 | 77*** |
| Annual child support ($) | 1,323 | 2,279*** | 377 | 394*** | 1,419 | 2,381*** | 372 | 391** |
| Share having child support (%) | 42 | 43 | 38 | 40*** | 48 | 51 | 42.9 | 47.7*** |
| Share with food stamps (%) | 88 | 26*** | 93 | 92** | 88 | 28%*** | 93.5 | 93.8 |
| Number of children | 2.04 | 2.04 | 2.33 | 2.44*** | 2.01 | 2.01 | 2.22 | 2.32** |
| Share high school or above[a] (%) | 61 | 63* | 56 | 58** | 65 | 67 | 60 | 61 |
| Share married (%) | 19 | 20 | 13.2 | 13 | 23 | 25 | 21.7 | 22 |
| Quarters worked | 2.50 | 2.62*** | 1.85 | 2.24*** | 2.53 | 2.77*** | 1.95 | 2.38*** |
| Proportion w/move to another county | 0.03 | | 0.03 | | 0.05 | | 0.05 | |

**Table 6.3 (continued)**

| Variables | Small town/rural adjacent | | | | Small town/rural nonadjacent | | | |
|---|---|---|---|---|---|---|---|---|
| | No partic. in 2nd yr. N = 4,183 (24.4%) | | Participate all 24 mos. N = 6,541 (38.1%) | | No partic. in 2nd yr. N = 1,356 (24.8%) | | Participate all 24 mos. N = 2,035 (37.2%) | |
| | Yr. 1 | Yr. 2 | Yr. 1 | Yr. 2 | Yr. 1 | Yr. 2 | Yr. 1 | Yr. 2 |
| Annual wage income ($) | 13,033 | 17,758*** | 9,796 | 11,176*** | 12,578 | 17,487*** | 9,369 | 10,771*** |
| Share employed (%) | 84 | 81* | 69 | 76*** | 82 | 78** | 68 | 75*** |
| Annual child support ($) | 1,430 | 2,462*** | 389 | 418** | 1,409 | 2,521*** | 386 | 421*** |
| Share having child support (%) | 47 | 49 | 46 | 47 | 54.8 | 55 | 47 | 51** |
| Share with food stamps (%) | 86 | 30*** | 86.9 | 86.6 | 85 | 28*** | 89 | 88 |
| Number of children | 2.07 | 2.1 | 2.18 | 2.27* | 2.05 | 2.04 | 2.2 | 2.27 |
| Share high school or above[a] (%) | 68 | 70 | 62 | 65* | 70 | 71 | 66 | 68 |
| Share married (%) | 28 | 29 | 24 | 24 | 25 | 26 | 24 | 24 |
| Quarters worked | 2.79 | 2.93** | 2.12 | 2.43*** | 2.69 | 2.81 | 2.07 | 2.39*** |
| Proportion w/move to another county | 0.09 | | 0.10 | | 0.10 | | 0.10 | |

NOTE: *** = significant at the 1% level; ** = significant at the 5% level; * = significant at the 10% level.
[a] The average of five imputation data sets is reported.

growth in jobs and available jobs in metro areas. For those earning wage income, earnings were higher in the second year. The lowest average wage income was reported in metro areas.

Child support receipt also increased in all areas among those not participating in FIP in the second year (Table 6.3). The average rate of growth in annual child support was over 68 percent in all of the areas. Receipt of food stamps decreased, falling from participation levels above 85 percent in the first year to between 26 percent and 30 percent of cases in the second year. Note, however, that even with no FIP participation, up to 30 percent of the cases received food stamp assistance in the second year.

The experience for those on FIP for all 24 months was very different. These cases had lower employment rates, although even during the first year between 63 percent and 69 percent of cases had some wage income. The lowest labor force participation rates were reported in metro areas. Employment rates rose in the second year, with the most rapid increases occurring in metro and urban nonmetro counties. The number of quarters worked also increased for these households. The annual wage income increased; however, the increase was both at a level and rate of increase lower than for those who were not receiving FIP by the second year. Again, the lowest wage income was reported in metro areas.

Rates of child support for the hard core FIP cases increased as well in all areas. The annual levels of child support received were greatest in small town/rural nonadjacent areas. Food stamp assistance was relatively common, and the highest food stamp participation rates occurred in metro counties (with rates of 92–93 percent).

In sum, in all geographic areas, there were changes in labor market activity for FIP households during the two-year period: the average number of quarters worked increased for all groups. Increased work by the hard-core group may be attributed to success in meeting FIP's program goals. In looking across geographic areas, the lower wage income levels and child support in metro areas is striking, especially compared with the two most rural locations. Among those on FIP for the full 24 months, those in metro areas received the lowest wage income and near the lowest levels of child support. Both wages and child support grew relatively more for those in the two most rural areas.

# WELFARE EXIT AND RETURN

We next examine return to welfare after leaving by looking at the duration of the first exit spell. We discuss the methods of analysis in the following sections.

## Definitions of Variables

We analyze the first exit spell to gain a better understanding of reasons for return to welfare. An exit occurs when a FIP recipient leaves the program for at least two consecutive months. Hence, an exit spell ranges from 2–23 months in our data. We require two consecutive months with no FIP benefits to avoid counting individuals as "exiting" due to administrative delays, or not receiving benefits in the short term because they are, for example, only eligible for less than $10.[2] If the first exit spell lasts only one month, we choose the next valid exit spell.

There are 18,382 exit spells in our sample of 32,309 cases. The distribution of spells for the metro and nonmetro areas are similar. Twenty-five percent of the exit spells are complete before the end of our sample period; the remaining spells are right-censored (that is, we do not observe a return within the two-year period of the data). The average length of all exit spells is 11 months. The average length of the complete spell (one observed to begin and end during the 24 months of data) however, is six months. This result indicates that, for those who returned to FIP, the time they are out of the program is relatively short.

## Estimation Procedure

To examine the likelihood of reentry to welfare, we grouped the exit spells into eight mutually exclusive intervals, based on the length of the spell. Each time interval was defined over three months (i.e., 0–3 months, 4–6 months, etc.), and the observation for each interval was whether the case stayed off of FIP or reentered the program. For each time period, we evaluated the likelihood of reentry. (For more detailed description of the estimation procedure, see the appendix.)

This approach allows for the effects of the predictor variables to vary across time intervals, but it requires the effect to be constant within the time interval. The variables that are allowed to vary over time include quarterly potential wage, quarterly child support collections, marital status, number of children, an indicator of the food stamp participation in the previous quarter, an indicator of the area of residence (metro county vs. nonmetro county), and the quarterly local unemployment rate. Time invariant variables are gender and race (white or nonwhite).

Because wage income is an important predictor of FIP participation, and because decisions regarding labor force and FIP participation are jointly determined, we use an instrumental variable approach to control for the endogeneity. The observed wage income in the quarter with highest reported wage income was used in predicting the potential wage income. The instruments for the potential wage include age, education, local unemployment rate, quarter, gender, income per capita of the county of residence, share of county population with a college degree, and an indicator of residing in a metro county.

## Empirical Results

Based on the analysis of all cases, as well as of metro and nonmetro cases, we identify several important factors affecting FIP reentry (Table 6.4). First, the effects of some variables are similar across the geographic areas. This includes whether the family received food stamps and the number of children in the household. The effect of other variables differed between the two areas, including the effects of demographics (marital status and gender), local unemployment, and the potential wage. With the data combined, living in a metro county decreases likelihood of return to welfare for those who have exited from cash assistance, although this result is not statistically significant.

For all areas, higher quarterly wage income reduces the likelihood of return to welfare. This result is statistically significant for all cases and for nonmetro. In other words, the chance that a person will return to cash assistance falls as potential earnings increase. Similarly, receiving child support lowers the probability of reentering FIP in a given interval. The magnitude of the estimated effects indicates that child support is more important in remaining off welfare than wage income. Interestingly, a higher (current) unemployment rate does not increase

**Table 6.4  Estimated Coefficients of Likelihood to Return to Welfare,
Oct. 1993–Sept. 1995**

| Independent variables[a] | All cases | Metro cases | Nonmetro cases |
|---|---|---|---|
| Potential (predicted) wage | –0.06** | –0.04 | –0.07** |
| Child support | –0.52*** | –0.55*** | –0.49*** |
| Local unemployment rate | –0.02 | 0.03 | –0.04** |
| Receipt of food stamps (0,1) | 0.61*** | 0.62** | 0.6** |
| White (0,1) | 0.02 | 0.0003 | 0.12 |
| Married (0,1) | –0.02 | –0.13** | 0.06 |
| Male (0,1) | –0.16*** | –0.23** | –0.11* |
| Number of children | 0.1*** | 0.089*** | 0.1*** |
| Metro location | –0.06 | | |
| Number of observations | 18,382 | 9,492 | 8,890 |

NOTE: *** = significant at the 1% level; ** = significant at the 5% level;
    * = significant at the 10% level.
[a]  Binary variables for the time periods were also included; all were statistically significant.

the probability of reentry. The estimated effect is statistically significant only for nonmetro areas.

Receiving food stamps in the previous quarter is positively associated with return to FIP. This result is consistent with that found by Reidy (1999) in Illinois. The result suggests that the Food Stamp program provides a safety net for those most at risk of return to FIP. Being married decreases the likelihood of returning to FIP in metro areas; the effect is not statistically significant in nonmetro areas. Cases headed by men are less likely to return to FIP than are those headed by women, and this effect is stronger in metro than in nonmetro areas. Race does not affect the reentry rates. As would be expected, families with more children are more likely to return to welfare.

Figure 6.2 shows the predicted reentry rate over the length of an exit spell. The rate is estimated at the sample means of the explanatory variables. The predicted reentry rate decreases as the exit spell lengthens, supporting other studies that show a negative relationship between

**Figure 6.2  Predicted Likelihood of Reentry by County of Residence**

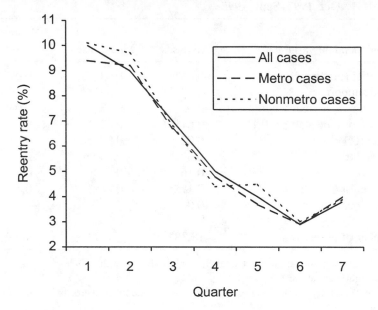

the reentry rate and length of the time off of assistance.  In the first quarter, the probability of return is 9.3 percent in metro areas and 10.1 percent in nonmetro areas.  By the end of the sixth quarter, the likelihood decreases to 2.9 percent for metro areas and 3 percent in nonmetro cases.  The probability of return falls throughout the spell (except the last quarter).  Although the rates differ in the first quarters, when metro cases are less likely to return than those in nonmetro areas, for longer spells, the chance of return is very similar.

## DISCUSSION

We examined the dynamics of welfare participation and the initial experience of welfare reforms in Iowa.  More than 60 percent of the FIP recipients we followed in this study left the program at some point during the two-year period.  Although improvements in the Iowa economy account for a share of the exits, our results provide some evidence that Iowa's reform of its welfare program may have helped reduce the FIP caseloads as well. Differences were also evident between metro and nonmetro areas.

The analysis shows that between the first and last quarters in the study period, some of the households saw marked economic improvements. Higher earnings were found for many in nonmetro areas. Food assistance programs continued to offer assistance to the households and seemed especially important during periods of transition. However, many of those receiving support from the Food Stamp program returned to FIP. There was a relatively high degree of mobility among FIP participants, especially for those in nonmetro areas. The moves were not primarily associated with a concurrent departure from FIP.

What is most apparent, though, is that although some households are able to leave FIP, others experience greater difficulties in achieving self-sufficiency. Thirty-seven percent of FIP cases in our data remained on FIP for the full two years. Several indicators suggest that those in metro areas in Iowa were more dependent on FIP; they were less likely to earn wages or collect child support, and they received lower wages and less child support. Under TANF, the five-year lifetime limit on receiving benefits may affect this group most directly. They may be without assistance if state governments can exempt only 20 percent of their caseloads from the time limit, as the federal law requires.

Looking at the return to welfare by those who left FIP, the data suggest that FIP recipients who returned to the program did so quickly (the average time off welfare is six months). Among FIP recipients, those in metro areas are less likely to leave FIP compared with those in nonmetro areas, but once they leave, metro recipients are less likely to return right away. The multivariate analysis of likelihood of return to FIP shows that, after the first two quarters, there is little difference in the likelihood of returning between metro and nonmetro locations.

The reasons for the differences (and similarities) are likely to be complex, and we are only beginning to understand the experience of those who leave FIP (and food stamps) through closer examination of administrative and survey data. Characteristics of the "leavers," as they are called, may differ across geographic areas. Perhaps metro recipients do not leave FIP until they have very good economic prospects. Once they have left, they remain off FIP longer and are less likely to return immediately. There may also be differences in nonparticipation among those eligible for FIP; administrative data can provide only very limited evidence of this.

The lessons learned here provide a preliminary indication of what we can expect from a state TANF program. Iowa's experience suggests that human capital, marriage, child support, and the number of children are major determinants of welfare dependence. Food assistance programs provide significant support to those most at economic risk. Programs and policies designed to enhance education, encourage marriage, provide and impose job training and job search, and further enforce child support are likely to be most effective in helping families achieve economic self-sufficiency, in both metro or nonmetro areas.

The empirical analyses for this study were conducted using state administrative data. Having the opportunity to use administrative data for research is a mixed blessing. These data allowed for analyses that could not have been conducted with survey data. On the other hand, they have their own challenges and limitations relative to survey data that cannot be ignored. We addressed one of these challenges—the problem of missing data for a key explanatory variable (educational attainment)—in detail in another study (Keng, Garasky, and Jensen 2000). Here, we took advantage of the ability to track location change and the dynamics of active program participation. Research based on administrative data complements traditional survey-based research.

## Notes

1. Note that our data are left censored. That is, we do not have information about the case and case members prior to April 1993. Further, for these analyses, we do not make use of information prior to the start of the FIP program, October 1993.
2. Program rules are such that an FIP program participant eligible for a cash benefit of less than $10 in a given month does not receive a cash benefit that month, but continues to remain eligible for, and must participate in, all other aspects of the program as if she or he had received a cash benefit.

# APPENDIX

# ESTIMATION PROCEDURE

A semiparametric proportional hazard model with time-varying covariates is applied to our grouped duration data (Prentice and Gloeckler 1978; Kiefer 1990). The advantage of the semiparametric method is that the baseline hazard is nonparametric and is estimated along with the coefficients of the explanatory variables using a maximum likelihood procedure. We grouped the exit spells by duration into eight mutually exclusive time intervals: that is, reentry occurs in one of the following intervals $[0, 4), [4, 7), \ldots , [22, \infty)$, where a month is the unit of the measurement. The exit intervals are defined as $[0, a_1), [a_1, a_2), \ldots , [a_i, \infty)$. The probability of an exit spell ending in interval $i$ is equivalent to the probability that a spell survives to interval $i - 1$ and fails in interval $i$. Hence, the probability is given by

$$(1) \quad \text{Prob}(a_{i-1} \leq T < a_i) = (1 - P_{a_i}) \prod_{j=1}^{i-1} P_j,$$

where $j = 1, \ldots , 7$.

We treat survival or failure (reentry) in each time interval as an observation. As a result, each FIP case contributes $i$ observations to the likelihood function where $i$ is the interval in which reentry takes place. For exit spells censored in a given interval, we assume that censoring occurs at the beginning of the interval. Given a sample with $N$ individuals, where $k = 1, \ldots , N$, the likelihood function is given as

$$(2) \quad L(\theta) = \prod_{k=1}^{N} (1 - P_{a_{ik}})^d \prod_{j=1}^{i-1} P_{a_{jk}},$$

where $d = 0$ if the individual is still at risk and $d = 1$ if reentry occurs.

To estimate the likelihood function, we use a proportional hazard function $\lambda(t, X_t) = \lambda_0(t)\phi(\beta, X_t)$, where $\lambda_0(t)$ is the baseline hazard function, $\phi(\beta, X_t) = \exp(\beta' X_t)$, $\beta$ is a vector of coefficients, and $X_t$ is a set of regressors. Instead of specifying the functional form for the baseline hazard, the semiparametric method estimates the baseline hazard function for each time interval. The resulting log likelihood function can be rewritten as follows:

$$(3) \quad \log L * (\theta) = \sum_{k=1}^{N} \{ 1 - \exp[-\exp(r_{ik} + \beta' X_{tk})] \} - \sum_{k=1}^{N} \sum_{j=1}^{i-1} \exp(r_{jk} + \beta' X_{jk}),$$

where $\theta = (r_1, r_2, \ldots, r_m, \beta)$

**(4)**   $r_{ik} = \log[-\log\delta_i]$

$$\delta_i = \exp\left[-\int_{i-1}^{i} \lambda_0(s)ds\right].$$

$\delta_i$ is the conditional survival probability in interval $i$ when $\beta'X_i$ is equal to zero.

# References

Born, Catherine E., Pamela J. Caudill, Christopher Spera, and John F. Kunz. 1998. "A Look at Life after Welfare." *Public Welfare* 56: 32–37.

Brandon, Peter David. 1995. "Vulnerability to Future Dependence among Former AFDC Mothers." Discussion paper no. 1055-95, Institute for Research on Poverty, University of Wisconsin, Madison.

Butler, Margaret A., and Calvin L. Beale. 1994. *Rural-Urban Continuum Codes for Metro and Nonmetro Counties, 1993*. Staff report AGES9425, Agriculture and Rural Economic Division, Economic Research Service, U.S. Department of Agriculture, Washington, D.C.

Cao, Jian. 1996. "Welfare Recipiency and Welfare Recidivism: An Analysis of the NLSY Data." Discussion paper no. 1081-96, Institute for Research on Poverty, University of Wisconsin, Madison.

Davis, Elizabeth E., Laura S. Connolly, and Bruce A. Weber. 1999. "Employment Outcomes for Low-Income Adults in Rural and Urban Labor Markets." Paper presented at the annual meeting of the American Agricultural Economics Association, August.

Eathington, Liesl, David A. Swenson, and Daniel M. Otto. 2000. "Nonfarm Employment Change in Iowa from 1987 to 1997." Department of Economics. Iowa State University. Available at <http://www.econ.iastate.edu/research/abstracts/NDN0075.html>.

Findeis, Jill L., and Leif Jensen. 1998. Employment Opportunities in Rural Areas: Implications for Poverty in a Changing Policy Environment." *American Journal of Agricultural Economics* 80(5): 1000–1007.

Fraker, Thomas M., Lucia A. Nixon, Jonathan E. Jacobson, Anne R. Gordon, and Thomas J. Martin. 1998. *Iowa's Family Investment Program: Two-Year Impact*. Document no. PR98-61, Mathematica Policy Research, Princeton, New Jersey, December.

Holcomb, Pamela A., LaDonna Pavetti, Caroline Ratcliffe, and Susan

Riedinger. 1998. *Building an Employment-Focused Welfare System: Work First and Other Work-Oriented Strategies in Five States.* Report submitted to the U.S. Department of Health and Human Services, Office of the Assistant Secretary for Planning and Evaluation, by The Urban Institute under Contract No. HHS-100-95-0021, June.

Iowa Department of Human Services. 1996. *FIP: The Family Investment Program.* Des Moines: Iowa Department of Human Services.

Iowa Department of Workforce Development. 2000. *Labor Market Information: Monthly Unemployment Rate.* Available at <http://www.state.ia.us/government/wd/>, April 1.

Keng, Shao-Hsun, Steven Garasky, and Helen H. Jensen. 2000. "Welfare Dependence, Recidivism, and the Future for Recipients of Temporary Assistance for Needy Families (TANF)." Working paper 00-WP 242, Center for Agricultural and Rural Development, Iowa State University. Available at <http://www.card.iastate.edu/>.

Kiefer, Nicholas M. 1990. "Econometric Methods for Grouped Duration Data." In *Panel Data and Labor Market Studies*, J. Hartog, G. Ridder, and J. Theeuwes, eds. New York: North-Holland.

Moffitt, Robert A. 1992. "Incentive Effects of the U.S. Welfare System: A Review." *Journal of Economic Literature* 30(March): 1–61.

Parrott, S. 1998. *Welfare Recipients Who Find Jobs: What Do We Know about Their Employment and Earnings?* Center on Budget and Policy Priorities, Washington, D.C. Available at <http://www.cbpp.org>, November.

Porterfield, Shirley L. 1998. "On the Precipice of Reform: Welfare Spell Durations for Rural, Female-Headed Families." *American Journal of Agricultural Economics* 80(5): 994–999.

Prentice R.L., and L.A. Gloeckler. 1978. "Regression Analysis of Grouped Survival Data with Application to Breast Cancer Data." *Biometrics* 34: 57–67.

Reidy, Mairead. 1998. "The Dynamics of AFDC, Medicaid, and Food Stamps: A Preliminary Report." Working paper, Joint Center for Poverty Research, Chicago.

Rubin, Donald B. 1987. *Multiple Imputation for Nonresponse in Surveys.* New York: John Wiley & Sons.

Sandefur, Gary D., and Steven T. Cook. 1997. "Duration of Public Assistance Receipt: Is Welfare a Trap?" Discussion paper no. 1129-97, Institute for Research on Poverty, University of Wisconsin, Madison.

# 7

# Small Towns and Welfare Reform

## Iowa Case Studies of Families and Communities

Cynthia Needles Fletcher, Jan L. Flora, Barbara J. Gaddis,
Mary Winter, and Jacquelyn S. Litt
*Iowa State University*

Since passage of the Personal Responsibility and Work Opportunity Reconciliation Act (PRWORA) in 1996, public discussion of welfare reform and most research efforts to assess the effects of new policies have focused on urban areas. Major studies and frequent newspaper headlines have portrayed the dimensions of welfare reform in Los Angeles, Miami, Boston, and other urban settings (e.g., Burton et al. 1998; Quint et al. 1999). Little attention is being paid to the consequences of the new policies for rural families and communities.

The reasons for this oversight of the rural dimensions of welfare reform are diverse:

- the invisibility of rural poverty and rural welfare recipients, and the erroneous view that poverty is more pervasive in urban than rural areas;
- the difficulty of addressing many different circumstances (rural poverty occurs under more diverse circumstances across communities than is true for urban poverty), coupled with the small absolute number of poor people in rural communities;
- an urban bias in federal government agencies such as Health and Human Services; and
- perhaps equally important, the view among rural residents that hard work leads to financial success and, therefore, poverty is an indicator of lack of effort (Vidich and Bensman 1968). Poverty and welfare status are often seen as caused by character flaws

(an individual problem) rather than as problems having systemic roots (a social problem) (Ryan 1972).

This chapter draws on data from the Family Well-Being and Welfare Reform in Iowa project, a mixed-method longitudinal study of welfare reform in seven communities. The goal of the project is to understand how families and communities are affected by welfare reform. Although the interviews with state and community informants were conducted approximately 6–12 months after passage of PRWORA, and the story has continued to unfold since that time, many of the institutional issues identified in this round of research are ones with which policymakers are still grappling. A series of semiannual, in-depth interviews with families has allowed the study team to continue to monitor effects from the welfare recipients' viewpoints and to track changes that are occurring in the seven communities.

The next section provides a conceptual interpretation for analyzing rural/urban differences in welfare reform's implementation and impacts. It is followed by a brief description of the social, economic, and policy context at the time PRWORA was implemented in Iowa. This description draws on findings from the project's state-level case study. Findings from seven community case studies and a qualitative study of recipient families living in the same communities are reported in the fourth section. By drawing on interviews with key informants in community organizations as well as with recipient families, a rich understanding of the personal and contextual issues of welfare reform in rural Iowa comes to light. It is a complex story that suggests that, although there are many overall similarities, policies and procedures for implementing welfare reform must bear in mind rural-urban differences. The three embedded components of the study complement one another and help clarify the policy issues facing a rural state and its communities. In the final section of the chapter, we discuss specific recommendations for welfare policy and program design.

## CONCEPTUAL CONSIDERATIONS

The principal unit of analysis is the community because, we argue, communities are the primary environments in which welfare reform policies play out. Historically, sociologists—rural sociologists, in particular—have argued that three elements were embodied in the concept of community: location, social and economic systems, and common identity (Flora et al. 1992, p. 14). Thus, a community was a geographic unit with a set of social institutions that provided for the daily needs of its inhabitants. Because frequent and multiple types of social interaction occurred within that community, people developed a common identity and some degree of value consensus. Rural areas, it was argued, developed a greater sense of community than urban places (Tönnies 1963).

Today, these assumptions about rural/urban differences are increasingly questioned. It is becoming less true that rural people live, work, and shop within the same geographic community, even if that community is relatively remote. In this sense, the information age is merely an extension of the transformation in means of transportation and communication brought about by the industrial revolution (Allen and Dillman 1994). Still, it can be argued that those with the least resources in the society have the least access to transportation and communications technology, while the more affluent are becoming less location-bound with respect to access to jobs, social and commercial services, and leisure activities (Fitchen 1991).

Understanding how these tendencies play out in the rural-urban context for welfare recipients and those in transition from welfare to work is the subject of this chapter. Drawing on a transaction costs framework (Williamson 1975), we explore the extent to which the benefits of labor force participation are limited by a number of greater transaction costs in rural compared with urban areas. An obvious cost is the time and effort that rural welfare recipients must spend in travel to jobs and to support services.

## THE IOWA CONTEXT

To provide a backdrop for understanding the context of welfare reform, we review population trends, labor market shifts, and the political landscape in Iowa. The information in this section is based on personal interviews with key informants—legislators, state government agency personnel, representatives of the private sector, nonprofit organizations, and advocacy groups—as well as the reports, memos, and documents shared by the informants during the interviews.

## Population Trends

Iowa's economic base and much of its population are moving from strictly rural areas to urban areas in the state. During the 1990s, the state's population growth rate was 0.5 percent per year, while the nation as a whole grew by about 1 percent per year (Table 7.1). Slow growth in the 1990s reversed a trend of population loss in the state during the 1980s. Although the total state population grew, nearly half of Iowa's 99, primarily rural, counties experienced population loss during this decade (Goudy, Burke, and Hanson 1999). We follow the contemporary

**Table 7.1  Iowa State Characteristics**

| Characteristic | Iowa | U.S.A. |
|---|---|---|
| Population | | |
| Population (1996)[a] | 2,848,033 | 265,179,411 |
| Percent rural (1990)[b] | 39.4 | 24.8 |
| 1990–1995 Growth[c] (%) | 2.3 | 5.6 |
| Economic | | |
| 1996 Per capita income[d] ($) | 22,330 | 24,436 |
| 1995–1996 Median household income[e] (%) | 34,888 | 35,287 |
| Children in poverty, 1998[f] (%) | 15.5 | 18.9 |
| Persons poor, 1997[g] (%) | 9.6 | 13.3 |
| 1997 Unemployment rate[h] (%) | 3.3 | 5.4 |

[a] Bureau of the Census (1998).
[b] U.S. Bureau of the Census; http://www.census.gov/population/censusdata/urpop 0090.txt.
[c] Goudy and Burke (1996). Change is calculated for the 1989–94 period in Iowa and for the 1990–95 period for the U.S.A.
[d] Bureau of the Census (1998). Regional Accounts Data, Table 4; http://www.bea. doc.gov/bea/dr/spitbl-d.htm.
[e] U.S. Bureau of the Census; http://www.census.gov/hhes/income/income96/in96 med1.html.
[f] U.S. Bureau of the Census (1999, March); http://www.census.gov/macro/031999/ pov/new25_003.htm.
[g] U.S. Bureau of the Census (1998, March); http://www.census.gov/macro/031998/ pov/toc.htm.
[h] Department of Commerce (1997, October); Statistical Abstract of the United States 1997, p. 401.

convention of equating the term *rural* with nonmetropolitan (defined as places of less than 50,000 and open country situated outside metropolitan areas), and *urban* with metropolitan areas.[1] The stability and the vitality of Iowa's rural communities are a growing concern. The state lags the nation in per capita and median household income levels, but it experienced very low unemployment rates and a tight labor market in the late 1990s. Despite a healthy economy, 15.5 percent of Iowa's children live in poverty (Table 7.1).

## Labor Market Shifts

In the past three decades, Iowa's employment structure has shifted away from high-wage manufacturing to lower-wage service and value-added agricultural processing jobs. The latter, although not minimum wage jobs, pale in comparison with the traditional manufacturing jobs they replaced. Iowa's average earnings per job have increased slightly over the past decade; however, the state's position relative to the rest of the United States has eroded. Nonfarm jobs in Iowa earned just 81 percent of the U.S. average in 1997 compared with 84 percent in 1987. This persistent erosion in labor earnings is "profoundly worse" in Iowa's nonmetropolitan areas (Eathington, Swenson, and Otto 2000). In real terms, average nonfarm earnings in the state peaked in the late 1970s. Within Iowa, metro earnings per job (identified by place of work, not place of residence of the worker) have paid, on average, at least $5,000 more per year than jobs in nonmetro counties (Figure 7.1).

Eathington and her colleagues' analysis of job growth over the past decade showed a "discernable qualitative difference in many of the kinds of jobs that are being created across the state," (p. 29) with higher-quality jobs concentrated in the state's metropolitan counties. Earnings trends during this period suggest a growing gap between metro and urban-nonmetro jobs on the one hand and rural adjacent and nonadjacent jobs on the other. In general, if the worker is able and willing to commute to the metropolitan area, job opportunities for residents of adjacent rural counties are undoubtedly greater than for those living in counties not adjacent to a metropolitan county. As shown later, commuting can be problematic for those seeking to move from welfare to work. Whether a wage differential exists specifically for low-skilled workers in rural Iowa compared with those in urban areas should be ex-

**Figure 7.1  Iowa Nonfarm Earnings per Job by County Type, 1969–97 (1997 $)**

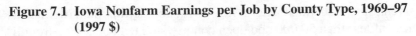
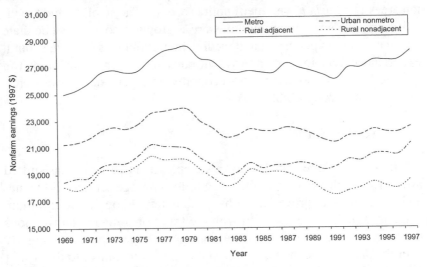

SOURCE: Regional Economic Information System, U.S. Bureau of Economic Analysis. Earnings adjusted for inflation using price indices for gross domestic product and personal consumption expenditures from the National Income and Product Accounts.

amined. Although Jensen, Keng, and Garasky (in this volume, p. 177) find that welfare recipients in rural Iowa report higher total quarterly wage income relative to their urban counterparts, available data do not allow the researchers to explore whether this difference is due to differences in wage rates, work effort, or the location of jobs held by the welfare recipients.

Since passage of PRWORA in 1996, Iowa has experienced relatively low unemployment rates, and it is generally accepted that anyone who wants to work can find a job. Low unemployment rates, however, mask a precarious situation for many low-skilled workers and their families in Iowa, particularly in its rural areas. Low wage scales, multiple job-holding, few worker benefits, and little job stability characterize economic activity in Iowa's rural communities. Iowa has the sixth-highest rural multiple job-holding rate in the nation, with one in 10 workers holding down more than one job (Parker 1997). Besser (1998) showed that about half of Iowa's rural firms in the retail trade and service sectors (where many of the entry-level jobs for welfare recipients are located) provide health care benefits to their full-time workers. Health care benefits to part-time workers are much more scarce; about 9 percent of private-sector, part-time workers are covered (Besser 1998, p. 34). Because most welfare recipients are low-skilled, single women with one or more children, they are less likely than other low-skilled individuals to be able to hold down two (or more) low-wage jobs to make ends meet.

## Policy Reforms

Iowa was an early adopter of welfare reform, implementing an Aid to Families with Dependent Children (AFDC) waiver program in late 1993, following broad, nonpartisan support in the legislature. Iowa's waiver, named the Family Investment Program (FIP), was structured to shift the focus of welfare from ongoing cash assistance to self-sufficiency, with incentives to work (for early results of the FIP program, see Jensen, Keng, and Garasky, p. 177). These incentives included generous income disregards, transitional Medicaid, and child-care subsidies that would cushion the move from welfare to self-sufficiency. In addition, families were required to complete a plan to move off welfare as defined by a flexible, individualized contract between the recipient and the state. Noncompliance with the requirements of the contract resulted in the loss of benefits.

The administration of Iowa's social welfare programs is highly centralized. Income maintenance workers in local Department of Human Services (DHS) offices determine eligibility and cash benefit levels by using uniform guidelines established by the state. DHS contracts with the Iowa Department of Workforce Development (IWD) to deliver job training to FIP clients through Iowa's job training program, PROMISE JOBS (Promoting Independence and Self-Sufficiency through Employment, Job Opportunities, and Basic Skills). Relatively few changes were made in FIP to comply with PRWORA.

Three major challenges face the state's welfare reform initiatives as PRWORA is implemented, according to state welfare administrators and policymakers interviewed. One involves a debate over the proper balance of education and training and workforce attachment. A second stems from the disproportionate number of recipients who remain on welfare and experience multiple employment barriers.  The third relates to the adequacy of Iowa's service delivery system at the local level. Iowa enjoys its reputation as an education state, so the tension has become more focused as some decision makers question the federal restrictions on the funding of postsecondary education.  As an Iowa Workforce Development administrator said, "We are not interested in moving people from FIP to working poor status." A representative of the private sector criticized the current "work first" approach, however, as contrary to the state's philosophy of human investment: "The state now wants to 'invest' in rickety old cars to take people to minimum wage jobs rather than putting those dollars into postsecondary education for welfare recipients."

Program administrators view the implementation of a 60-month lifetime limit on FIP benefits as a serious challenge for many of the recipients who remain on the welfare rolls.  Iowa's FIP caseload decline mirrors the national trend.  After peaking in 1994 at 40,659 cases, fewer than 30,000 were on the FIP rolls in 1997, and only 19,407 households were receiving cash benefits in early 2000 (Figure 7.2).  Approximately half of Iowa's FIP cases reside in metropolitan areas.  A shift toward a more "difficult-to-serve" population raises questions about the state's desire to reduce government staff and spending for a caseload that likely will require more attention and resources.

Finally, the changing expectations of the welfare system raise questions about the adequacy of Iowa's service delivery system at the local level.  Although state officials have been pleased with the 1993 policy reforms, they argue that changes in the thinking at the state level have been slow to "trickle down" to county offices.  Overcoming inertia in the various departments of state government has required great effort, and devolution has yet to be, as one state agency administrator put it, "internalized" either at the state or local level.  Program eligibility determination remains a function of DHS income maintenance staff, while developing and implementing a plan to move from welfare to work is the province of IWD's PROMISE JOBS workers.  Discussions of changes in staffing patterns and service delivery have moved slowly. In an effort to provide some flexibility at the local level, the state initiated family and community self-sufficiency grant programs to help local DHS offices address personal or community-wide systemic barriers to employment.

**Figure 7.2  Total (regular and unemployed parents) Family Investment
Program Caseload in Iowa, 1993–2000**

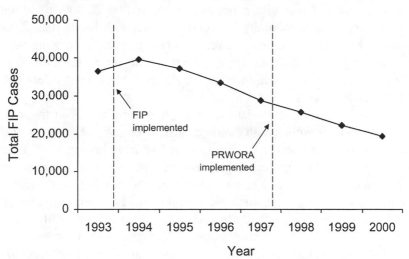

SOURCE: Iowa Department of Human Services, Report Series A-1, January caseloads.

## THE COMMUNITY CONTEXT OF WELFARE REFORM: UNDERSTANDING RURAL/URBAN DIFFERENCES

The fundamental view underlying the project is that the effects of welfare reform—whether positive, negative, or mixed—will be felt initially and directly by welfare recipients, the communities in which they live, and the institutions that provide direct services to needy families. Our study took place in seven communities (all county seats): Marshalltown (Marshall County), Mount Ayr (Ringgold County), Storm Lake (Buena Vista County), Hampton (Franklin County), Manchester (Delaware County), Fort Madison (Lee County), and Cedar Rapids (Linn County). Cedar Rapids, a metropolitan community, was included as a comparison point with the rural (nonmetropolitan) communities. The communities were selected along a rural/urban continuum with a range in population size, the presence or absence of a sizable Hispanic population, a location adjacent or nonadjacent to a metropolitan area, and geographic dispersion throughout the state. The six rural study sites vary in population from Marshalltown, a manufacturing town in central Iowa with a population exceeding 25,000, to Mount Ayr, a very rural community in southern Iowa with fewer than 2,000 people. Marshalltown, Storm Lake, and Hampton have growing numbers of Hispanic residents. Among the six rural study sites, only Manchester is adjacent to metropolitan areas. Fort Madison borders both Illinois and Missouri.

Program participation data suggest conflicting trends in the well-being of needy families with children. All seven counties saw a significant drop in the number of families on FIP rolls between 1993 and 1997. This finding might suggest that families are moving into jobs and improving their well-being. However, the number of K–12 students receiving free meals increased in all counties during the same period. This trend suggests that growing numbers of the families with school-age children are getting poorer. A summary of the population, employment, welfare program participation, and poverty characteristics of the seven counties is provided in Table 7.2.

The community case studies draw on 12–20 personal interviews with community leaders and two group vignettes conducted with front-line service providers in each of the study sites, all carried out in late 1997. The research protocol for the case studies was shared by the Urban Institute and was adapted from its ongoing national study, *Assessing the New Federalism*. Key informants included elected officials, representatives of local human service agencies and nonprofit organizations, health care providers, and employers. In addition, in-depth semi-structured interviews with five recipient families in each community have been conducted every six months over a three-year period. The 35 families were randomly selected from the FIP rolls and were first interviewed in late 1997. Due to attrition, 22 families remained in the study in late 1999. Teams of local extension staff who work in the targeted communities interviewed community informants and the FIP families. The multiple data sources and methods of analysis permitted a deeper understanding of the complexity and contextual diversity of welfare reform discussed in this section (Greene 2000).

Early reports from the project have identified that families in the study face a lack of many important resources that are essential for self-sufficiency: well-paying jobs for low-skilled workers, transportation, child care, health services, support networks, and the financial means to meet basic needs.  Community informants in all the study sites viewed transportation, child care, living-wage jobs, adequacy of emergency services, and a need for better interagency coordination as systemic barriers to meeting the needs of low-income families (see Fletcher et al. 1999; Litt et al. 2000).  Although the personal and systemic barriers facing families appear to be common, dimensions of the problems and effective strategies to address them are different for urban and rural communities.  One way of organizing our thinking about the differences in the dimensions of the challenge of moving from welfare to work is to apply Williamson's (1996) analogy between the concept of friction in mechanics and transaction costs in economic exchange:

> In mechanical systems we look for frictions: do the gears mesh, are the parts lubricated, is there needless slippage or other loss of energy?  The economic counterpart of friction is transaction cost: . . . are there . . . delays, breakdowns, and other malfunctions? Transaction cost analysis entails an examination of the comparative costs of planning, adapting, and monitoring task completion . . . (p. 58)

The differences in population density along the rural/urban continuum result in different accessibility and distance to services.  Rural welfare recipients encounter fewer community resources locally and services that are accessible on a less frequent basis (Table 7.3).  Rural residents moving from welfare to work find fewer job opportunities locally and must frequently travel long distances for employment.  Commuting is problematic because private vehicle ownership is clearly not the norm among the rural poor.  Rucker (1994) estimated that nearly 57 percent of the rural poor nationwide do not own a car.  A recent analysis in rural Lee County (which includes Fort Madison, one of our study sites) found that only one in four adult FIP recipients owned and registered a vehicle (Fletcher and Jensen 1999).  Although transportation is a ubiquitous problem for welfare families, effective solutions are likely to differ in rural and urban areas.  A pattern of differing access and distance to services is particularly notable with respect to jobs and the range of support services that facilitate work and family well-being: job training and education, health care, child care, and emergency services. Rural/urban dimensions of each of these issues and the "frictions" or transactions costs incurred by welfare recipients as they participate in

**Table 7.2 Population, Employment, Poverty, and Program Participation Statistics: Seven Iowa Counties**

| Variable | Linn | Marshall | Lee | Buena Vista | Delaware | Franklin | Ringgold |
|---|---|---|---|---|---|---|---|
| County population, 1997 (est.) | 181,704 | 38,789 | 38,654 | 19,565 | 18,449 | 10,874 | 5,337 |
| Change, 1990–97 (%) | 7.7 | 1.3 | -0.1 | -2 | 2.3 | -4.3 | -1.5 |
| Population of target community, 1996 (est.) | 113,482 | 25,321 | 11,613 | 8,880 | 5,398 | 4,030 | 1,694 |
| Minorities as % of K–12 students, 1997 | 8.1 | 11.6 | 7.4 | 16.3 | 1.7 | 7.3 | 0.8 |
| (# of minority students) | (2840) | (795) | (535) | (709) | (69) | (150) | (8) |
| Hispanics as % of K–12 students, 1997 | 1.4 | 8.2 | 2.4 | 9.4 | 0.5 | 6.9 | 0.2 |
| (# of Hispanics students) | (473) | (560) | (172) | (408) | (22) | (141) | (2) |
| Unemployed, 1997 (%) | 2.6 | 3.1 | 5.5 | 2.2 | 4.9 | 3.2 | 3 |
| Percent of total 1996 earnings in: | | | | | | | |
| Manufacturing | 26.3 | 34.8 | 38.7 | 22.8 | 21 | 16.7 | 8.9 |
| Services[a] | 27.1 | 17.4 | 15.9 | 15.8 | 11.2 | 14.5 | 18.8 |
| Median household income, 1993 ($) | 37,430 | 31,868 | 29,498 | 30,452 | 30,754 | 28,342 | 23,324 |
| Earnings per nonfarm job, 1997 ($) | 30,311 | 25,525 | 26,280 | 20,547 | 21,446 | 20,987 | 18,563 |
| % of all persons below poverty, 1995 | 7.8 | 9.5 | 11.6 | 9 | 10.9 | 9.6 | 15.9 |
| % of children below poverty, 1995 | 11.2 | 13.3 | 17 | 11.5 | 14.5 | 12.9 | 21.1 |
| % of pop. in FIP,[b] 1997 | 2.5 | 3.2 | 4.1 | 1.7 | 1.6 | 1.7 | 2.5 |
| Change in ave. monthly no. of FIP recipients, 1993–97 (%) | -22.9 | -25.7 | -23.7 | -22.3 | -25 | -23.8 | -15.5 |
| % of population receiving food stamps, 1997 | 4.9 | 6.9 | 7.6 | 4.3 | 3.8 | 4.7 | 8.2 |
| Change in no. receiving food stamps, 1993–97 | -17.7 | -11.6 | -20 | -12.1 | -30.2 | -20.2 | -18.1 |

| | | | | | | | |
|---|---|---|---|---|---|---|---|
| % of students w/free and reduced-price school meals, 1997–98 | 22.4 | 35.8 | 31.7 | 37.3 | 24.4 | 29 | 43.2 |
| Change in no. receiving free/reduced meals, 1992–93 to 1997–98 (%) | 6.1 | 33.9 | 31.3 | 40.7 | 3.6 | 13.5 | 5.6 |
| Difference in % of students receiving free/reduced-priced school meals (1997–98 minus 1992–93) | 0.1 | 7 | 8.3 | 6.8 | 1.9 | –2 | 0.9 |

[a] Excluding retail and wholesale trade; financial, insurance and real estate services.
[b] FIP = Family Investment Program.

**Table 7.3  Proximity of Services for Seven Iowa Communities**

| Service | Cedar Rapids (Linn) | Marshalltown (Marshall) | Fort Madison (Lee) | Storm Lake (Buena Vista) | Manchester (Delaware) | Hampton (Franklin) | Mount Ayr (Ringgold) |
|---|---|---|---|---|---|---|---|
| PROMISE JOBS/JTPA | * | * | * | | * | | |
| Community college | * | * | | * | | | |
| Other college | * | * | | * | * | | |
| Food pantry | * | * | * | * | * | * | * |
| Soup kitchen | * | * | | | | | |
| Shelter | | | | | | | |
| Adult males | * | * | * | | | | |
| Adult females | * | * | * | | | | |
| Children | * | * | | | | | |
| Youth | * | * | | | | | |
| Mental health | * | * | * | * | * | * | * |
| Drug/alcohol treatment | * | * | * | * | * | * | * |

NOTE: Names in parentheses in column heads are counties. An asterisk (*) indicates service located within the community itself.

the labor market are illustrated in the following section, in which the perspective of families and service providers are integrated.

## Job Opportunities

Access to jobs is a keystone of welfare reform and poverty reduction. With low unemployment rates, a business manager in Marshalltown described current economic conditions as a "window of opportunity" for individuals with limited skills and work experience. Community informants in every community reported wide availability of sales and service jobs paying $5–6 per hour. These jobs may provide the opportunity to gain work experience but are unlikely to lead to self-sufficiency or to offer opportunities for career advancement.

Members of the business and education communities in Cedar Rapids, the growing metropolitan city in the study, believe the local economy to be quite strong. Cedar Rapids does offer some telemarketing and manufacturing jobs that operate around the clock and pay better-than-average wages to dependable employees with minimal skills. In 1997, many companies were paying $7–8 per hour to attract entry-level workers, although a business representative acknowledged that these workers might have problems with child care and transportation because most are not "8 to 5" jobs. Several telemarketing firms in the city offer more attractive starting wages, although they need people who are available evenings and weekends, but they provide mostly part-time employment with no benefits. The existence of a fairly extensive city bus system coupled with a new van service (after city buses no longer run) to shuttle workers from some low-income neighborhoods to swing-shift jobs enhances welfare recipients' potential access to jobs in this community. As one Cedar Rapids mother describes the situation, however, the existence of bus service does not necessarily guarantee her access to the job:

> I could have had a job on the 15th [of the month] but I didn't have a vehicle. It takes about half an hour to 45 minutes just to get downtown on the bus. Then another 20 minutes after transferring to the appropriate bus. The buses don't even start out here until 6:15 in the morning. So how the heck can I get to work by 6:30?

Even if the city can continue to expand its mass transit system, families must cope with what one informant described as "a high cost of living . . . that depletes families' disposable income." A Cedar Rapids official assessed the progress of welfare reform in his community: "Child care, transportation, and a strong economy are needed to make welfare reform work; work has been the main focus but there has not been an emphasis on the support system."

Job opportunities within the six rural study sites vary considerably. Marshalltown, Storm Lake, and Hampton host food processing plants that operate multiple shifts. In general, there is a labor shortage in Marshalltown; businesses need both entry-level and technically skilled people. A major goal of the local economic development committee is to attract businesses to Marshalltown that offer higher salaries associated with non-entry-level jobs to increase the community wage base, which is currently in the $8–$9 per hour range. In 1997, the pork plant in Marshalltown offered starting wages of $7 per hour to unskilled workers "on the floor" under a "fast start" system in which the worker would plateau at $9.45 per hour by the end of two years. These jobs require physically demanding work and offer little scheduling flexibility to accommodate the needs of children. "For now there is certainly no lack of opportunity to work for people willing to put in an honest day's work," said a Storm Lake plant manager.

From one-third to one-half of the packing plant workforce in rural Iowa consists of immigrant workers, given that U.S. workers are reluctant to take these less-than-desirable jobs at such modest pay. The more or less steady supply (interrupted in one of the communities by a raid of illegal workers by the Immigration and Naturalization Service in August 1996) of immigrant workers has tended to keep wages from rising as much as one would expect in the tight labor situation of the past three or four years. Because of the demanding working conditions, lack of child care support, and lack of scheduling flexibility, only a few of the welfare recipients had previously worked in these plants, and none worked there during the period of our interviews.

In Hampton, despite high productivity in agriculture, various community informants cited a lack of well-paying jobs. A local business manager said that most jobs at his company are production-line work for which they require high school graduates able to "read, write, and follow directions." This manager reports that some welfare recipients turned down jobs offered them, saying they can "make more money on welfare." One former FIP recipient, the wife in a family with several children, put it somewhat differently: "There aren't enough good-paying jobs . . . You have to go to a bigger town. In order for people to make it any more, you have to be getting $12 to $16 per hour." Her husband added, "When I went through PROMISE JOBS . . . he [the PROMISE JOBS worker] said, 'Well, if you find a job, you might have to find a job with minimum wages.' I said, 'Hey, when you got family you can't even make it on minimum wages—that won't even pay for gas driving back and forth.' "

Mount Ayr, Fort Madison, Storm Lake, and Hampton are located in counties that are not adjacent to a metropolitan area, and according to the estimates in Table 7.2, have experienced population decline in the 1990s. All except Storm Lake have not shown much, if any, net job growth, which means that generally one must look outside the county for openings for "good" jobs—those that pay a living wage, provide benefits, and are pleasant to perform. Manchester, located in Delaware County, which is adjacent to metropolitan Dubuque and Cedar Rapids, also has a lot of out-commuting. In Manchester, the local Iowa Work-force Development office reports few openings for full-time jobs with benefits and wages capable of supporting a family. Job opportunities in Dubuque or Cedar Rapids require 80- to 90-mile daily commutes. These commuting jobs are often unavailable to women making the transition from welfare to work because travel may complicate child care arrangements and usually requires the worker to have a reliable vehicle.

There is a general perception among the rural welfare recipients in the study that there are no jobs in their communities that will pay them a living wage. "Good" jobs are in the "bigger towns" and that requires reliable, personal transportation. A Mount Ayr woman was asked about the job opportunities around there:

> There's not any—not for me anyway. I've applied at Blimpies, I've applied at Places, CGI, HyVee . . . I've even asked the neigh-borhood center if they needed help. They said, 'Not now.' I went out to Mount Ayr Products [a local factory] once. It's been a while. They weren't hiring; they were laying people off.

Many Mount Ayr residents travel to Osceola (46 miles away) and even Des Moines (85 miles away) for work because well-paying jobs in Ringgold County are hard to find, and few new jobs have been created. A local manager explained that typical jobs available for entry-level workers include nonskilled production, waiting tables, retail, clerical, and construction. A starting wage of $5.50 is common for such jobs, and salaries increase little, if any, over the years. Some persons get their first work experience in the nursing home, which is experiencing increased competition for workers from home health care. Small local manufacturing firms pay "higher" wages (between $6 and $7 per hour) for seasonal work involving occasional short weeks, layoffs, and over-time hours.

In Fort Madison, a workforce staff person stated that just about anyone could find a minimum wage job without benefits, but finding a "better-paying job with benefits" was more difficult. Local extension staff suggested that if persons "have the skills there's all sorts of jobs wanting." A community leader concurred, describing the county as "employee poor." Yet one mother in Fort Madison explained that it was a lack of local jobs that hinders her economic independence:

> You have to go to Burlington (40 miles) or Keokuk (20 miles away) to get a real good job any more. Even kids. High school kids are even going to those towns to get after-school jobs. [Question: *Do you think the community is doing anything to deal with these problems?*] No. Wal-Mart wanted to buy some property on the west end of town a couple of years ago. The city council wouldn't let them do it because they wouldn't be locally owned. They would have been Wal-Mart owned, and that's not a local thing. Everything in this town has to be locally owned for the city council to allow them into it . . . It would be nice if there were more businesses that weren't privately owned. A lot of businesses here are run just by their families. There isn't a job for anyone else to come in and get a job . . . Even some factories would do.

Community representatives may speak of an "employee" shortage in Fort Madison, but from the perspectives of welfare recipients, there is a "good job" shortage. Clearly, one's perspective on economic de-velopment is related to social location—and the opportunities in one's community.

## Support Services

### Job training and education

According to many of the welfare recipients in our study, the only way to "get ahead" is to improve job skills through education and train-ing. Iowa's PROMISE JOBS program offers a range of employment services and provides child care and transportation reimbursements for participants.  The PROMISE JOBS staff members work with individual welfare recipients to draft the Family Investment Agreement, an individualized plan for moving from welfare to self-sufficiency.  The extent to which job training services are co-located or well integrated with other human services varies considerably along the urban-rural continuum of our study sites.

Cedar Rapids has developed a strong collaborative approach to service delivery through neighborhood family resource centers and has worked closely with the local community college to provide job-training services at convenient locations throughout the city.  Consumers of these services acknowledge and appreciate the efforts to integrate services.  A FIP recipient in Cedar Rapids commented, "I didn't have to go out there [to the community college located on the edge of the city] and take a placement test. [College staff] came to PROMISE JOBS where we could take the placement test there."  Marshalltown's Workforce Development Center is one of the first in the state to institute the "one-stop shopping" concept, housing several employment-related services, including PROMISE JOBS and Job Training Partnership Act (JPTA) staff, under one roof.  The center is located near the community college that offers basic skills training and General Equivalency Diploma (GED) completion to FIP recipients.

For several reasons, Cedar Rapids and Marshalltown (the largest communities in the study) offer greater access to job training and education for welfare recipients compared with the smaller communities. These communities have taken steps to better integrate and coordinate employment services with the local community college.  The availability of a city bus system in both communities offers residents an option (albeit not always convenient) of mass transit rather than having to rely solely on personal vehicles to access job training and education.  A Cedar Rapids mother acknowledged the positive impact that the job training program has had on her ability to complete a two-year culinary arts degree at the local community college: "PROMISE JOBS has been helpful in making sure I get to school and [get] my monthly bus pass." Interestingly, she foresees the need to move in order to get a good job: "The Cedar Rapids job market is pretty good, but my instructor advises us . . . to [go] to a big city and work because that's where the most of the money is.  Most of the money for the restaurant business is not really here."

In contrast, local services for improving job skills and postsecondary education are much more limited in the five other communities. Although PROMISE JOBS staff members can be reached by telephone, they come to Storm Lake just one day per week and once every two weeks to Hampton; Mount Ayr residents must travel 35 miles to Creston to meet with PROMISE JOBS staff (Table 7.3). Four of the five smaller towns do not have community colleges; welfare recipients who need further training must rely on personal transportation to campuses that are from 20 to 40 miles away. Although the PROMISE JOBS program will reimburse recipients' transportation expenses (at 16¢ per mile) to training sites, families need access to reliable vehicles, and that rarely is the case. A Mount Ayr mother without transportation commented, "I'm working with JTPA right now. We're trying to figure out what I can do. Right now we can't do nothing without my car." A Storm Lake recipient sees distances to specialized training as a barrier to her career goal: "I'd like to take photography. I've called around and there's nowhere in Storm Lake or Cherokee [25 miles away] . . . possibly Fort Dodge [70 miles away], but it's so far away."

### Health care

Low-income residents of rural counties often experience difficulty with both availability of and access to adequate health care. Often the issue of availability is simply whether there are any physicians, mental health professionals, dentists, or family planning facilities at all. In rural towns, access involves whether anyone in the county is accepting Medicaid, how often the services are available, and, if there are no services, how far residents must travel to procure health services.

A community leader in Manchester said it succinctly: "Health care for low-income families is pretty nonexistent . . . [in this county]." He went on to say that because of dissatisfaction with Medicaid reimbursements, no dentist in the county was accepting new Medicaid patients. A welfare recipient in Marshalltown expressed her frustration with availability of dental care: "Why isn't our insurance any good? Why do we have to travel from town to town to see a specialist for a root canal? I have to take [my daughter] to Iowa City to have it done." Iowa City is 75 miles one way. Another Medicaid patient acknowledged the presence of services, but without a choice of providers.

"Delaware County is a pretty high-poverty county, so they didn't have very good medical care. There was one dentist we could choose from."

In Hampton, there are no local family planning services. A doctor from Iowa Falls, roughly 20 miles away, comes to town once a week to see uninsured pregnant women but was taking no new patients. Medicaid patients must go to Mason City, a 30-mile commute. Similarly, in rural Mount Ayr, there are no local family planning services; residents must seek help from a private physician or go to Planned Parenthood in Creston (35 miles away).

Even programs aimed at disease prevention and designed for low-income people are often only available in rural communities on a limited basis. One young mother, recently employed, described her experience with the Women, Infants, and Children (WIC) feeding program:

> I was on with [WIC] before, but my problem was that I had to take time off work to go see them. I can't afford to do that . . . It might be different, but the last time they were here, they were only here Friday mornings from 9:00 to 3:00. When you got there at 9:00 in the morning, you could have waited 45 minutes, because everybody else was there at 9:00. I can't afford to take the time off to go . . . It's an excellent program. It's fantastic. You can't go wrong with it. But I can't afford to take time off just to go.

For rural residents with special needs children, services are rarely available locally at any cost. This lack of availability is especially difficult for those with low incomes and unreliable transportation. The mother of an infant with multiple special needs in Manchester takes him to Cedar Rapids to physical therapy once a week, an hour there and an hour back. In addition, she takes him to a physician in Cedar Rapids for regular check-ups, and travels to Iowa City once every three months for consultations with a specialist. This same mother is looking for a job in town because her car is not sufficiently reliable for commuting to another town. Another informant drove 100 miles round-trip two times a week for two years to a speech pathologist for her son. She had to discontinue her visits because of vehicle problems.

For mental health care, many rural residents are required to travel to larger population centers for treatment. One informant traveled 60 miles round-trip to see a physician for depression. The travel necessitated his taking a day off work every other week for several months.

## Child care

Despite the notion expressed by one state official that "child care is the cornerstone of success in welfare reform," many low-income rural residents experience continuing problems in securing adequate and affordable care for their children while they are at work or are obtaining an education or training. Child care centers are a rarity in rural communities; most recipients rely on home day care providers or relatives to care for their children. Only 6 percent of the potentially eligible children (if eligibility was expanded to the federal maximum) receive child care subsidies in Iowa (Administration for Children and Families 1999). The lack of child care during second and third shift and a severe shortage of infant care is faced by both rural and urban families. As one rural mother put it,

> They have their own little group here . . . the day care providers that are registered all have their little group. They don't babysit past a certain time and they only babysit certain hours. Nobody will babysit on weekends. [Question: *So how do you deal with that? What do you do in your case?*] Find somebody that will. She's not registered. [Question: *How did you find her?*] A girl that works for ____. She takes her kids there and has had them for a year and really likes her.

However, rural families often face problems due solely to their more remote locations. In some small towns, there are no registered child care centers. One community informant in Hampton questioned the quality of nonlicensed providers because many lack formal training and take in more children than they should. But a recipient in Hampton seemed pleased with the unregistered provider she had for her daughter, even if there were certain inconveniences:

> [My daughter] was the youngest of 6 [children] per day–never more than that. My babysitter is fantastic with her—excellent with babies. I wouldn't trade her for the world . . . the only thing I'm not satisfied with is that the provider is taking too many days off. In the month of October, she will be taking 8 days out of 22 days off . . . it's more of an inconvenience for me trying to find a backup babysitter that will take her all 8 days. It's too hard on [my daughter] for her to go to one person for two days, then to go

someplace else, and the next week go someplace else. It's hard on her, plus you have to pay a little extra because they are considered a "drop in." It gets to be expensive and mind-wracking.

Availability of transportation to deliver children to providers is a common problem. One mother believed that what would really help her become more self-sufficient would be "if they had more care in the workplace so you could take your kids with you."

The cost of child care is another issue. As one Head Start staff person put it, "If you've got two children in child care and you're not making very much money, then child care is a big part of your income." When asked what would be of greatest benefit to her in helping her toward self-sufficiency, a FIP recipient in Storm Lake replied, "A day care that was affordable."

For rural children with special needs, local care may not be available at any cost. One mother of an autistic child travels 40 miles for respite care. She says, "They have got me on with [a local social service agency] . . . to have someone come in my home, but there's no one in our area. So they have to hire someone from our area to help me with respite in the home. Well, there's nobody for me. So I'm still driving to Mason City to take advantage of [respite care]."

### Emergency services

As is apparent from Table 7.3, emergency services such as shelters and soup kitchens are available only in larger towns. Even where services are available, however, they are often inadequate or are available on a very limited basis. A community informant in Marshalltown indicated the need to expand the capacity of a homeless shelter that now houses 15 people a night, but only during the months of November through May. "There are more homeless people in Marshalltown than we ever imagined," he stated. The shelter administrator would like to be able to stay open year round. In towns that have no homeless shelter, local police or the ministerial association often distribute vouchers for gas, food, or a night's lodging. In other areas, however, there are no local organizations that provide short-term shelter for the homeless.

All of the communities report available emergency food, but often on a limited basis. In Hampton, the pantry is open Tuesdays and Fridays from 10 a.m. until noon. All counties report limits on the amounts of food available and the number of times a year a recipient may actually receive groceries.

## Proximity and Access: The Rural/Urban Difference

Our analysis of seven community case studies in Iowa suggests that different effects of welfare reform policies hinge on differences in the proximity of jobs and access to support services. Urban centers offer more job opportunities and support a scale of auxiliary social services that cannot be matched in rural communities. Our data suggest that welfare recipients who live in or adjacent to urban areas have potential access to more jobs, and jobs that pay higher wages compared to recipients who live in remote rural communities. Capitalizing on proximal jobs requires access to reliable, affordable transportation, however. The feasibility of establishing cost-effective mass transit systems depends, in part, on population density and, therefore, is more likely to exist in urban areas. Families making the transition from welfare to work need an array of support services that may include job training, health care, child care, or a range of emergency services. Our interviews with welfare families and community informants suggest that increasing the accessibility and quality of these services will likely enhance family well-being and the ability of families to move toward self-sufficiency.

It is clear that welfare recipients in the more rural communities in our study have less access to support services compared with their urban counterparts. Some services (e.g., job training consultations, WIC clinics, or food pantries) are offered infrequently in rural communities—as little as once per week for limited hours—compared with daily office hours in urban areas. Other services (e.g., community college course offerings, homeless shelters, or registered infant care) simply do not exist in many rural communities. Whereas rural families with adequate resources often can overcome many of the constraints of rural communities, those who face the challenge of moving from welfare to work often find the distances to jobs and lack of support services to be serious barriers. Further research is needed to explore the extent to which both personal and systemic barriers are present among rural welfare recipients. Better information about the magnitude of these barriers and their influence on employment is critical as we face the reauthorization of the PRWORA and as states with sizable rural populations go forward with strategies to move families from welfare to work.

## RESEARCH AND POLICY IMPLICATIONS

A strong economy with record low unemployment and a tight labor market suggests that Iowa is in a good position to move welfare families off the FIP rolls and into jobs. If the goal of welfare reform extends beyond the reduction of welfare dependency to a reduction in poverty and an improvement in family well-being, findings from current research have implications for a new research and policy agenda. There is a need to explore ways to improve the well-being of those who have moved from welfare to work, to reduce barriers and the costs associated with obtaining and retaining jobs, and to explore alternatives for those who are unable to find work. Perhaps the most challenging research and policy questions relate to improving service delivery in rural communities. Each of these issues is briefly discussed below.

The drop in the FIP caseload suggests that, under current economic conditions, many recipients are moving into the labor force. Evidence from our case studies suggests, however, that those who are working frequently receive low wages and no benefits. The average earnings of Iowa's welfare recipients were $9,176 per year, according to data submitted by the state to the U.S. Department of Health and Human Services. This suggests that many welfare leavers had only intermittent work or part-time work (Tweedie, Reichert, and O'Connor 1999). If, indeed, the state does not want to "move people from the FIP rolls to working poor status," there is a need to address policies that make work pay. For FIP recipients who have jobs, but because of low wages or limited work hours are unable to earn enough to become self-sufficient, policies that subsidize wages should be considered. A critical question is the extent to which there should be urban-rural differentials in these subsidies. Clearly uniform subsidies, whether administered on the state or federal level, are simple to administer. Whether they are "fair" is another matter. If thresholds for such subsidies are to reflect some predetermined level of self-sufficiency (i.e., at what income level is one "needy" and eligible for the subsidy?), there is a need to develop a better understanding of both basic living costs and employment costs in rural and urban areas.  To date, there is no strong scientific basis for arguing for (or against) such geographic cost-of-living variations (see Citro and Michael 1995, p. 61).  Similarly, the qualitative data from service providers and welfare recipients in seven Iowa communities suggest that there may be different levels of costs associated with managing the transactions inherent in labor force participation along the rural-urban continuum.  If this is the case, policy adjustments that can offset higher transaction costs faced by some welfare recipients should be considered.  For example, individuals who face long commutes to work or job training might have commuting time counted in the calculation of work requirements.

At the federal level, further expansion of the Earned Income Tax Credit would directly benefit welfare families who have moved into low-paying jobs.  At the state level, wage subsidies could take the form of expanded and refundable state earned income tax credits, as well as an expansion of the Child Health Insurance Program (CHIP), or vouchers for child care and transportation.

There are recipients who remain on the welfare rolls because of a set of barriers to employment.  We know more about the nature of these barriers among urban recipients (see Danziger in this volume).  Quality, affordable child care is an ongoing challenge, particularly for parents who are offered entry-level jobs at nontraditional hours.  Many struggle to find affordable, reliable transportation.  At the community level, systemwide efforts to expand quality, affordable child care and transportation could be effective strategies that would benefit a broad range of families and workers.  How to make these services sustainable in rural communities is not well understood.

In-depth interviews with FIP families suggest that, despite low unemployment rates, some individuals cannot obtain jobs.  Further research is needed to understand the dimensions of the barriers facing those who remain on the welfare rolls, but it seems clear that there are some who simply cannot get a job under current conditions, and there will be more of these individuals when the economy falters.  Better assessments are needed of physical and mental health conditions that limit the employability of some welfare recipients.  Little attention has been given to devising a mechanism for providing "jobs of last resort" (see Ellwood 1988; Sherwood 1999). Small-scale demonstration sites in both rural and urban areas could provide very useful information about how to foster work skills among the difficult-to-employ and how to establish an appropriate scale for the investment required in such projects.

Finally, findings from our study have implications for service delivery in rural communities. Exploring ways to remove the disadvantages inherent in the set of support services currently available in rural communities will not be easy. Although some of the rural communities in our study had established ways to exchange information among service providers with a goal of achieving greater coordination, none had taken the next step of planning for a seamless system. Clearly, eliminating policies that create barriers to pooled funding and service integration is one step. High quality, accessible services—ranging from job training to mental health services to basic social services—along with transportation to get there, could enhance the well-being of rural welfare recipients and facilitate their transition from welfare to work.

# Notes

Portions of this chapter are drawn from a baseline report of the "Family Well-Being and Welfare Reform in Iowa" project (Fletcher et al. 1999). This study was conducted under the auspices of Iowa State University Extension and the Center for Family Policy, College of Family and Consumer Sciences. The authors acknowledge the assistance of graduate assistants Michelle Overstreet, now at Oklahoma State University; Ann M. Perkins and Seongyeon Auh, graduate students, Department of Human Development and Family Studies, and Hugh Hansen, former graduate assistant in the Department of Sociology, all at Iowa State University. The research would not have been possible without the contributions of eight faculty who carried out the field work for the state case study and 45 extension field staff members who conducted interviews in the seven communities. We acknowledge the Iowa Department of Human Services for providing the list of Family Investment Program recipients from which participants in the welfare-recipient study were selected.

1.  A metropolitan area must have a central city of at least 50,000 population. Based on commuting patterns and county boundaries, smaller places and open countryside can be included within a Standard Metropolitan Area (SMA). The official census definition of rural, which was devised when the bulk of the population lived outside major cities, is open country and villages of less than 2,500 population. As the society has urbanized that definition has become less and less relevant.

# References

Administration for Children and Families. 1999. *Access to Child Care for Low-Income Working Families.* U.S. Department of Health and Human Services. Available at <http://www.acf.dhhs.gov/programs/ccb/reports/ccreport.htm>.

Allen, J.C., and D.A. Dillman. 1994. *Against All Odds: Rural Community in the Information Age.* Boulder, Colorado: Westview Press.

Besser, T. 1998. "Employment in Small Towns." *Rural Development Perspectives* 13(2): 31–39.

Bureau of the Census. 1998. "Estimates of the Population by States (ST-97-3)." Available at <http://www.census.gov/population/estimates/state/ST9097T1.txt>.

Bureau of the Census. 1998. "Regional Accounts Data," Table 4. Bureau of Economic Analysis. Available at <http://www.bea.doc.gov/bea/dr/spitbl-d.htm>.

Burton, L., A.J. Cherlin, J. Francis, R. Jarrett, J. Quane, C. Williams, and N.M. Cook. 1998. *What Welfare Recipients and the Fathers of Their Children Are Saying about Welfare Reform.* Baltimore, Maryland: Johns Hopkins University, June.

Citro, C.F., and R.T. Michael. 1995. *Measuring Poverty: A New Approach.* Washington, D.C.: National Academy Press.

Eathington, L., D. Swenson, and D. Otto. 2000. *Nonfarm Employment Change in Iowa from 1987 to 1997.* Available at <http://www.econ.iastate.edu/outreach/community/menu.asp?code=3C>.

Ellwood, D.T. 1988. *Poor Support: Poverty in the American Family.* New York: Basic Books.

Fitchen, J.M. 1991. *Endangered Spaces, Enduring Places: Change, Identity, and Survival in Rural America.* Boulder, Colorado: Westview Press.

Fletcher, C.N., B.J. Gaddis, J. Flora, H.B. Hansen, K. Shirer, M. Winter, J. Litt, N. Norman, and C. Betterley. 1999. *Family Well-Being and Welfare Reform in Iowa: A Study of Income Support, Health, and Social Policies for Low-Income Families in Iowa.* Ames: Iowa State University Extension.

Fletcher, C.N., and H.H. Jensen. 1999. *Iowa Rural Welfare to Work Strategies Project: Interim Report to the Iowa Department of Human Services.* Iowa State University.

Flora, C., J.L. Flora, J.D. Spears, and L.E. Swanson. 1992. *Rural Communities: Legacy and Change.* Boulder, Colorado: Westview Press.

Goudy, W., and S.C. Burke. 1996. *Iowa's Counties: Selected Population Trends, Vital Statistics, and Socioeconomic Data..* Ames: Iowa State University, Department of Sociology.

Goudy, W., S.C. Burke, and M. Hanson.  1999.  *Iowa's Counties: Selected Population Trends, Vital Statistics, and Socioeconomic Data.*  Ames: Iowa State University, Department of Sociology.

Greene, J.C.  2000.  "Integrating Multiple Methods to Better Understand Welfare Reform."  *Poverty Research News* 4(1): 13–15.

Litt, J., B.J. Gaddis, C.N. Fletcher, and M. Winter.  2000.  "Leaving Welfare: Independence or Continued Vulnerability?"  *Journal of Consumer Affairs* 34(1): 82–96.

Parker, T.  1997.  "Multiple Jobholding among Rural Workers."  Paper presented at the annual meeting of the Rural Sociological Society, Toronto, Canada.

Quint, J., K. Edin, M.L. Buck, B. Fink, Y.C. Padilla, O. Simmons-Hewitt, and M.E. Valmont.  1999.  *Big Cities and Welfare Reform: Early Implementation and Ethnographic Findings from the Project on Devolution and Urban Change.*  New York: Manpower Demonstration Research Corporation.  Available at <http://www.mdrc.org/Reports99/UrbanChange/UC-ExecSum.html>.

Rucker, G.  1994.  *Status Report on Public Transportation in Rural America.*  Washington, D.C.: Department of Transportation, Federal Transit Administration, Rural Transit Assistance Program.  Available at <http://www.fta.dot.gov/library/program/rurlstat/rurlstat.html>.

Ryan, W.  1972.  *Blaming the Victim.*  New York: Vintage Books.

Sherwood, K.E.  1999.  *Designing and Administering a Wage-Paying Community Service Employment Program under TANF.*  New York: Manpower Demonstration Research Corporation.  Available at <http://www.mdrc.org/Reports99/CSE-TANF-wkgppr/CSE-TANF-wrkppr.html#>.

Tönnies, F.  1963.  *Community and Society.*  C.P. Loomis, trans. and ed.  New York: Harper and Row.  (Original work published in 1887.)

Tweedie, J., D. Reichert, and M. O'Connor.  1999.  "Tracking Recipients after They Leave Welfare."  Washington, D.C.: National Conference of State Legislatures.  Available at <http://www.ncsl.org/statefed/welfare/leavers.htm>.

U.S. Department of Commerce.  1997.  *Statistical Abstract of the United States, 1997.*  Washington, D.C.: U.S. Government Printing Office, p. 401.

Vidich, A.J., and J. Bensman.  1968.  *Small Town in Mass Society.*  Rev. ed.  Princeton, New Jersey: Princeton University Press.

Williamson, O.E.  1975.  *Markets and Hierarchies.*  New York: Free Press.

———.  1996.  *The Mechanisms of Governance.*  New York: Oxford Press.

# 8

# Where All the Counties Are Above Average

## Human Service Agency Directors' Perspectives on Welfare Reform

Ann Tickamyer, Julie White, Barry Tadlock, and Debra Henderson
*Ohio University*

When asked to rate their counties in progress toward welfare reform, the directors of human service agencies in Appalachian Ohio almost uniformly describe their county as "above average." This echo of the fabled Lake Wobegon is from agency administrators in counties in a remote rural region characterized by high poverty and unemployment rates and low levels of economic and infrastructure development, an area largely bypassed by the economic growth of the last decade of the 20th century. How can we explain the nearly universal optimism about the impact of welfare reform and its prospects expressed by these bureaucrats, who are most responsible for its design and implementation? This question appears especially puzzling for a region that has seen few real benefits from economic expansion and that, by all objective indicators, remains desperately poor and underdeveloped.

We examine the views of the 29 directors of human service agencies in the rural Appalachian counties of southeastern Ohio. The directors of these agencies are the principal agents of welfare reform, the officials who are charged with the design and implementation of the new policies, and the individuals who ultimately will be held responsible for its success or failure at the local level. We contrast their perspectives with that of the ideology and policy climate that drove the reorganization of the welfare system and with the perspectives of the clients who are the focus of the new policies. This research is part of a larger multimethod, multiyear, multigroup study of the impact of welfare reform in poor rural communities.  The results of this component show that despite realistic assessment of the numerous barriers to success in welfare-to-work programs, the reorganization of the way welfare is administered has resulted in a largely positive, often enthusiastic, endorsement.

## BACKGROUND PERSPECTIVES

### Elite Views of Welfare Reform

Current welfare policies are a legacy of the conservative attack on the liberal welfare state that gained momentum in the Reagan era and subsequently became entrenched in political discourse by the beginning of the 1990s.  Although there had been a long history of elite dissensus (Teles 1998), by the time of the Clinton administration, welfare reform had became a bipartisan preoccupation, with only minor variation in the types of changes advocated across the political parties.  The Clinton administration policy advisors found common ground with a new Republican congressional majority to drastically alter the parameters of the safety net.  The result was the Personal Responsibility and Work Opportunity Reconciliation Act of 1996 (PRWORA), the welfare reform bill whose purpose was "to end welfare as we know it."

This legislation did, in fact, put an end to long-standing entitlement programs that guaranteed qualified recipients access to public assistance.  Most notably, it marked the end of the primary program of cash assistance, Aid to Families with Dependent Children (AFDC), and substituted the more circumscribed Temporary Assistance for Needy Families (TANF).  The latter's purpose was seen as temporary, limited, and geared toward moving recipients toward self-sufficiency through formal employment.  The legislation gave the states great flexibility in designing and implementing their own welfare programs, but a primary parameter was a 60-month lifetime maximum for receiving assistance.  Many states, including Ohio, designed programs that placed far lower limits on eligibility, usually restricting it to two or three years.

The route to creating political consensus on the need for welfare reform can be traced in the debates about causes, consequences, and remedies for poverty that emerged from the perceived failure of War on Poverty programs in the decades following their expansion. Individual incapacity, cultural deviance, or structural barriers were each identified and hotly defended as the primary source of poverty and thus the most appropriate target for public policy (Epstein 1997; Katz 1989, 1996; Schram 1995; Teles 1998). Foremost among the issues that figured prominently in these debates was welfare dependency and its sources (Gordon 1990; Handler and Hasenfeld 1997). Increasingly, the welfare system was redefined as the cause of poverty and dependency rather than its remedy.

The most influential of these attacks came from the right in a "war on welfare" that reversed the logic of the War on Poverty by inverting the causal link between poverty and welfare. While liberal analysis saw welfare programs as a necessary response to complex social problems, conservative analysts argued that the existence of welfare itself created, sustained, and deepened poverty by providing disincentives to work and to traditional nuclear family formation. This, in turn, created a rational calculus for dependency and antisocial behaviors, such as nonmarital childbearing (Gilder 1981; Murray 1984). These arguments were incorporated into the *Contract with America* (Gingrich 1994, p. 67) to form a centerpiece in the drive to gain Republican control of Congress and a blueprint for the campaign and future legislation.

The charge of dependency was not limited to conservative analysis. Increasingly, researchers and policy analysts with liberal identification also adopted welfare dependency as the principal problem of the welfare system. For example, Mary Jo Bane and David Ellwood (1994)— the primary architects of Clinton administration welfare policy—conflate poverty and dependency; they accept the conservative diagnosis of the problem but substitute government programs to make work pay for the free market and laissez-faire approaches advocated by the right (Epstein 1997). Even from the opposite end of the political spectrum, feminist theorists also found fault with the welfare system for cultivating dependency among its recipients, although their diagnosis differed markedly in the forms and sources of the problem. They were particularly vocal in arguing that the welfare system creates a system of public patriarchy that substitutes impersonal, public control of women by the state for the more direct private control of family and male kin

(Abramovitz 1988; Brown 1981; Fraser 1990; Tickamyer 1995–1996). In other words, welfare bureaucracies position clients in the role of dependent (Ferguson 1984, p. 45).

## Models of Public Policy: Carrot and Stick

The common thread that unites the different approaches is a model of human behavior that assumes individual rationality as the basic premise. Programs are criticized for their failure to provide appropriate incentives for valued behavior (labor force participation, traditional family formation, avoidance of substance abuse) or sanctions for deviance from mainstream norms and values. Thus, a conservative analyst such as Charles Murray (1984) pointed to the "moral hazards" of welfare as the inducement for dependency. *The Contract with America* states that "incentives affect behavior . . . It's time to change the incentives and make responsible parenthood the norm and not the exception" (Gingrich 1994, p. 75). The claim that behavior is a product of a simple benefit calculation undergirds liberal prescriptions as well. Bane and Ellwood (1994) adopted a rational choice model that makes welfare more desirable than work when work doesn't pay. The individual in both approaches is a rational actor, calculating how to maximize opportunity, even in a system that supplies limited options. If the incentives are perverse, it is only reasonable that a rational actor will act accordingly.

This assumption of individual, economic rationality increasingly was reflected in the criticisms of existing welfare provision and in the specifics of reform proposals. Although by no means the only assumption and value embedded in these policies (others included the value of free market mechanisms and traditional patriarchal family forms, reliance on private rather than public sectors, and distrust of centralized government intervention), all politically viable welfare reform proposals called for changes that entailed a system of rewards for work and self-sufficiency and punishment for dependency and deviance. Whether emphasizing the carrot of making work pay and providing programs to enhance employability or the stick of time limits and sanctions for failure to adhere to social and program rules, norms, and values, reform policies purported to embody a commitment to a behavioral model that focused on individual rationality and utility maximization (Tickamyer et al. 2000).

In the debates over welfare reform, discussion of structural impediments and barriers was minimal. Issues that had previously loomed large in liberal analysis, such as discrimination, lack of access to education, jobs, or opportunity, formed little part of the discussion and were generally seen as secondary to issues of motivation and dependency. In other words, in the development of an elite consensus over the shape of welfare reform, structural analysis was discarded in favor of an individualized approach that emphasized character issues and individual choice. The only structural barrier that was widely acknowledged was the institutionalized welfare system itself. Thus, it should not be surprising that, in this environment, consideration of spatial variation in sources and consequences of poverty, welfare provisions, and the impact of reform efforts was almost completely missing. Poverty and welfare dependency are typically viewed as urban problems and analyzed in a national context. Despite widespread rural poverty, and unique barriers to successful implementation of welfare reform, rural issues take back seat in research and policy analysis.

**Devolution and Barriers to Rural Welfare Reform**

Although regional differences were largely ignored in policy debates, devolution, the other key feature of reform, highlights such differences. Shifting responsibility for welfare reform programs from federal to state and local jurisdictions was promoted as a means to overcome the "one size fits all" federal policy. This policy, it was argued, failed to recognize variation in social, political, and economic circumstances and prevented creative experimentation and program innovation. At least in theory, devolution from the federal to the state level provides an opportunity to design policies and programs tailored to the needs and capacities of local areas and that emphasize democratic input and local control and responsibility. In practice, there is as yet little evidence that specifically rural problems and needs have received much sustained attention from either the federal or state governments. This is particularly important given that local jurisdictions vary in their capacity to implement welfare reform, and that devolution puts great strain on local capacity, requiring poor rural areas with limited resources to design and implement programs to meet state and federal mandates that do not recognize unique rural problems.

Among these problems are severe deficits in resources, employment opportunities, infrastructure, social and human capital, leadership, and political influence at more central levels of government. The Appalachian Regional Commission (ARC) points out that rural economies face many obstacles compared with urban economies in their potential for creating job opportunities for welfare recipients. Rural communities lack the advantages of metropolitan areas that can attract new investment; rural areas cannot achieve the same economies of scale in delivering social services for education and training, child care and transportation; and they generally lack access to capital and credit for job creation. Rural areas also have significant numbers of "working poor"—people who are employed, but are working part-time or in low-wage jobs that provide few, if any, benefits. The contrast between urban and rural is always stark in these respects, but particularly in light of the economy of the 1990s, in which many urban areas achieved historically low unemployment rates. It is therefore important to call attention to the problems of infrastructure and unemployment that still define much of the rural United States.

As a consequence of these structural features of the economy, rural residents often face an underdeveloped infrastructure of support for employment, even when there are jobs. Everything from the difficulty of travel in these areas to the absence of child care can be included as obstacles to employment. In light of this, we can expect that the impact of welfare reform, and specifically of welfare-to-work programs will be very different in rural and urban areas. Similarly, the needs of welfare-to-work participants will also differ, as will the capacities of human service agencies to manage welfare reform.

## THE SETTING AND THE STUDY:
## WELFARE REFORM IN APPALACHIAN OHIO

Data for this study are drawn primarily from in-depth, semistructured interviews with the 29 directors of Departments of Human Services (DHS) in Appalachian Ohio. Interviews were conducted in spring 1999, halfway into the 36-month eligibility window for Ohio recipients of cash assistance.[1] The research was designed to provide qualitative data from each of the participating groups at the beginning of reform and after initial eligibility expires in order to discover the subjective meaning of these changes from both a bottom-up and a top-down perspective, rather than imputing or imposing them from above (Reinharz 1992; Schram 1995). We also draw on results from an analysis of focus groups of program participants in four counties selected for more intensive study. Details of the design of this component of the study and its results are reported more extensively in Tickamyer et al. (2000). The contrast between the differing perspectives of actors with different levels of power and responsibility are a central focus of this chapter.

Ohio makes a particularly interesting arena for studying welfare reform because devolution was taken one step further, from the state to the local level. Under a plan called Ohio Works First (OWF), the state adopted a 36-month lifetime limit for assistance and stringent work requirements for program participants. Responsibility for specific program design and implementation was devolved to the counties. County DHS directors are charged with applying reform policies in their communities and have a significant amount of authority, latitude, and flexibility in how they accomplish this task. Their agencies are also subject to sanctions if their counties are unable to meet state-imposed goals when eligibility limits expire.

Counties vary in the types of measures they have adopted, but even more in their capacity to meet the requirements of reform measures. Although most counties in the region share high levels of poverty, unemployment, and remoteness from urban centers, there is a substantial amount of variation in these measures of economic activity, and even more in less tangible factors such as sources of local social and human capital, economic development initiatives, and access to training and educational resources. Table 8.1 shows the poverty, unemployment, and median household income for the 29-county area, using the most recently available statistics at the time of data collection.

The larger study from which this chapter is drawn focuses on four "showcase" counties selected to represent areas that reflect different levels of capacity to manage welfare reform, given both the economic

**Table 8.1  Poverty, Unemployment, and Median Household Income in Appalachian Ohio, by County**

| County | % Below poverty 1995 | Unemployment rate (%), Feb. 2000 | 1995 Median household income ($) |
|---|---|---|---|
| Adams | 20.3 | 12.8 | 22,529 |
| Athens | 20.1 | 6.5 | 26,020 |
| Belmont | 15.7 | 5.9 | 26,337 |
| Brown | 12.1 | 7.7 | 31,324 |
| Carroll | 10.9 | 6.2 | 32,245 |
| Clermont | 7.1 | 4.6 | 40,689 |
| Columbiana | 14.0 | 6.3 | 30,139 |
| Coshocton | 11.9 | 7.7 | 29,308 |
| Gallia | 18.9 | 10.3 | 27,426 |
| Guernsey | 15.9 | 10.0 | 26,077 |
| Harrison | 15.9 | 8.0 | 24,444 |
| Highland | 12.9 | 5.7 | 27,201 |
| Hocking | 13.0 | 11.1 | 28,865 |
| Holmes | 10.6 | 3.3 | 31,786 |
| Jackson | 17.5 | 8.3 | 25,050 |
| Jefferson | 15.5 | 6.4 | 27,538 |
| Lawrence | 19.9 | 7.1 | 24,818 |
| Meigs | 21.4 | 14.9 | 23,558 |
| Monroe | 17.4 | 11.8 | 25,926 |
| Morgan | 15.7 | 18.3 | 26,458 |
| Muskingum | 14.2 | 8.6 | 29,079 |
| Noble | 14.5 | 12.1 | 27,190 |
| Perry | 16.0 | 10.2 | 26,899 |
| Pike | 19.5 | 11.4 | 26,814 |
| Ross | 15.1 | 6.1 | 30,750 |
| Scioto | 21.4 | 10.5 | 24,219 |
| Tuscarawas | 10.6 | 6.6 | 30,564 |
| Vinton | 19.1 | 17.1 | 24,530 |
| Washington | 12.3 | 6.7 | 31,127 |
| Total | 15.5 | 9.0 | 27,893 |

conditions in the county and less tangible resources such as sources of human and social capital available for county officials and agency personnel. In this chapter, however, we analyze the interviews conducted with all 29 of the DHS directors. With the exception of the four counties selected for closer scrutiny in the case study, the interviews were conducted by telephone by members of the project team and student assistants. In the four showcase counties, face-to-face interviews were conducted by the principal investigator. Interviews were tape recorded with permission of the DHS directors. Early in the research, equipment failure resulted in several cases without usable tapes. In each instance, however, there were at least two persons present during the session, each of whom wrote extensive notes almost immediately following the interview.

As public officials, DHS directors are not subject to the same levels of protection of anonymity and confidentiality required and desired for other populations in this study, but in requesting cooperation, we indicated that we would make every effort to report results in a manner that would focus on larger aggregate trends rather than on identifiable individuals. In general, directors were eager to assist in the project and to discuss their views. In a number of cases, DHS directors invited other staff to be present. Interviews lasted for an hour, on average. Interviews were professionally transcribed and checked against the audio tapes. Analysis is conducted via the use of NUD*IST, a qualitative data analysis program and by standard inductive approaches.

## FINDINGS: VARIATIONS ON A POSITIVE THEME

On first examination, the views of the DHS directors appear to vary widely; closer inspection reveals more similarity than difference, however. In particular, DHS directors express positive views about welfare reform in general and in their communities in particular. Typical views included a favorable overall attitude about the purpose and goals of welfare reform, but not necessarily its outcomes. There was also widespread acknowledgment of the real problems facing both program participants and their human service agencies. These views combine two sets of explanations that are often characterized as contradictory in the literature, but in this case represent a complex and multilayered understanding of the realities of poverty and welfare in their communities: they attributed blame to individuals, which often reflected "culture of poverty"[2] explanations, and they also recognized the significant structural barriers particularly to poor rural counties and the region. Finally, they shared mixed views of the organizational mandates of welfare reform and the implications for their agencies, with general enthusiasm reserved for potential and actual flexibility in program design and implementation.

We examine each of these in detail and compare these views with those expressed by program participants. Not surprisingly, we find a very different orientation among the two groups. We conclude with an overview of how top and bottom perspectives provide different windows on the prospects for successful welfare reform policy.

## Attitudes about Welfare Reform

The DHS directors generally expressed positive views about welfare reform. In the 29 counties, only one director could be classified as unsupportive, and it might be argued that this judgment is more a reflection of political views that favor a more drastic curtailment of welfare than of disapproval of reform efforts per se. This individual is very much alone in both a strong expression of partisan ideology and in failure to express support for reform. Another seven directors (24 percent) could be classified as expressing some degree of skepticism about reform, but this was the dominant opinion for only two of these officials. The other five combined skepticism with general support. Support was strong and unconditional among the remaining directors.

Typical comments about the positive aspects of welfare reform include large drops in caseloads; the opportunity to encourage a positive work ethic, increase in self-esteem, and independence among recipients; reduction in public burden or responsibility and expense; the end of what they termed "generational poverty"; and the opportunity to generate public support for public assistance given that welfare is no longer seen as an inducement to sloth and dependency in public opinion. The idea that public opinion is changing looms large in many of the directors' assessments:

I think there's a general perception, "[H]ey, you guys are finally doing something right down there." You know, I think people want to see the quid pro quo. People are employable. That we're getting ourselves and them off our butts and doing something about it. So yeah, I think there's generally a positive impact from the community.

I think the American people . . . after all the bad publicity . . . [have a] very bad conception that all they do is stay at home and make more babies . . . If you look at the facts . . . you know that doesn't hold true, but this whole vision . . . of our welfare population . . . became a political hot potato and obviously something had to be done and . . . they've come up with a workable solution . . .

Negative comments mainly take the form of skepticism about the ultimate success of the efforts and the political will of policymakers whose support is necessary.

So what can happen—worse-case scenario—recession comes along, our rolls go up, our money has been depleted or taken away for education reform or other things, then, worse-case scenario, welfare reform has failed . . . When it's all said and done, if all those worse-case scenario factors would come into play, we could be in the same position we were three years ago.

There was no apparent pattern in the degree of support among directors. The only overtly oppositional view was expressed by a director from one of the better-off counties. The seven skeptics represented some of the poorest and some of the more affluent counties. Similarly, directors' backgrounds seem to matter little. In part, this reflects lack of variation in this population. Although their education varies from little more than a high school diploma to several with graduate work or degrees, in other respects they seem more similar than different. They are usually from the region and are long-time, often life-long, residents of their communities. They have worked in this or similar agencies for many years and have numerous local attachments that give them deep roots and civic prominence. They are also white and, unlike their employees, predominantly male. In general, this group of officials is locally oriented and somewhat insulated from experience beyond their counties and the state of Ohio.

This combination of local boosterism and insularity was highly evident in their response to the question of how their county is doing compared with others, resulting in the broad assessment of "above average," regardless of where their county stands on objective measures. Ohio also is seen as doing better than other states. These views are widely held, despite a realistic assessment of the problems that face their communities, agencies, and clients.

## Problems of Welfare Reform

Favorable views about welfare reform do not preclude candid assessment of the problems facing both recipients and their agencies. Themes that emerge from their evaluations range across a broad array of practical problems, including deficits in both individual characteristics and local opportunity structure. The former include numerous attitude and character issues attributed to recipients, such as lack of work ethic, lack of interest in education, substance abuse, domestic violence, and passive acceptance of "generational poverty."

> One of the challenges that we have with the hard-to-serve ones which we currently have is basic skills such as personal hygiene, working your full eight hours each day. We've had people just walk off the job without telling the supervisor where they're going or not reporting to work in the morning.

Structural issues that were widely and repeatedly mentioned include inadequate transportation, child care, health care, poor educational facilities, and a general lack of infrastructure and economic development. The problems that emerge with greatest frequency are a recognition of the serious transportation problems facing even the most dedicated welfare-to-work participants and concerns about the quantity and quality of jobs, especially if the economy were to falter.

> The problem now is do we have enough jobs? Is the economy gonna be strong? Will it weaken or will it be [sic], if it does and we go back down and lose a step or two because never in the history has the country been in better shape.

These concerns are mentioned often both as stand-alone issues and as particular vulnerabilities of rural location, political isolation, and regional development issues.

> This is a region in the state that needs economic development . . .
> They need health care.  They need roads . . . I think we're one of
> the few counties that does not have a four-lane highway . . . I
> don't think they really address the needs of the Appalachian area
> when they come up with these policies . . .

These views mirror the larger policy and academic debates about individual, cultural, and structural approaches to explaining poverty and welfare use, except that they are not held as alternative views or "moral practices" (Hasenfeld 2000) but are held concurrently.  Recipients are blamed for lacking a work ethic, being "generationally" dependent on welfare, suffering personal deficits in motivation and education, and being victim and perpetrator of a variety of abuses from substance abuse to domestic violence.  At the same time, directors are quick to recognize strengths in their clients that surface in the face of structural adversity, including lack of jobs and all the support services necessary to maintain steady employment, from lack of transportation to lack of teeth.  Virtually all variations on these themes can be found in these interviews, most often simultaneously by the same individuals. In other words, the same director will blame Appalachian culture both for promoting and overcoming poverty and adversity, criticize recipients for their personal problems and simultaneously acknowledge structural barriers. These are not seen as either/or phenomena but rather are rolled into sometimes contradictory, generally more complex, multilayered views, as the comments below reveal.

> They are facing many barriers be it education, drug or alcohol
> abuse and it is quite costly to get 'em to the point where they are
> . . . employable.  One thing is the local job market.  What we're
> looking at, I really hate to say it, but what we're looking is trans-
> porting our people [out] of the county.

> And so we've got these essentially, I don't want to say dysfunc-
> tional, but sort of aberrant family patterns that have emerged, and
> if we're gonna get anywhere with that, then we need to get to some
> of the root causes . . . We got the rural cultural orientation that we
> have to do there, and I think that's gonna take a real concerted ef-
> fort to get it . . .

> I think willingness to work has a lot do with opportunity, and I
> think personal responsibility, I mean I think in general, . . . Ameri-

ca's, you know, sort of evolving this, "I don't want to take responsibility for myself, you caused my problem." I don't think that's something that just goes along with poor people, so that could be a social problem that we face in the broader scale . . . I don't think we had a real work ethic problem with a lot people. I think what we did, I mean, surviving is work when you're poor. Some of the most industrious people I've ever met in my life have been on public assistance or SSI, but they were very industrious about keeping themselves and their family alive. They just didn't get paid or recognize that as work.

I just know that in this particular part of the country, in Appalachia, I know there's been a real sense of folks taking care of one another, and I don't know about the extended family anymore.

When DHS directors' views are compared with those of the recipients they serve, there is a large discrepancy in the relative seriousness of and frequency that certain problems are mentioned. For example, child care is critical in the minds of recipients (Tickamyer et al. 2000) but is seen as much less important by DHS directors. Although directors mention child care issues, they are more likely to think that this problem is relatively easily solved as they increase efforts to train and certify local child care providers. Issues of quality and access to child care are mentioned repeatedly by recipients but dismissed by most directors or seen as exaggerations or rationalizations of compliance failure.

The use of sanctions ranks low on DHS director horizons; they perceive that they are used judiciously and only after following elaborate rules that guide their application. Sanctions, however, loom large for recipients, who are vocal in their resentment of a sanction system that seems irrational, capricious, and personal. Similarly, while both worry about the lack of jobs that pay a living wage, recipients are more focused on managing what they see as competing responsibilities of caring for children and other dependents than on employment. Directors dismiss these concerns as either failures to develop a realistic work ethic or cultural aberrations associated with class and region.

As a corollary, directors are much more concerned about immediate and long-term prospects of employment for welfare recipients than the recipients themselves; recipients want to work but are more likely to worry about the necessary tradeoffs, such as their families' safety. In some cases, they have traded jobs in urban areas for their child's security in smaller rural communities. Directors worry about the economy; recipients darkly predict dire consequences for law and order, child custody, and their own fates should a recession occur (Tickamyer et al. 2000). A couple of directors echo recipient predictions of social problems and unrest in the event of economic downturn, but these are the exceptions, and even among these, concerns focus more on problems for administrators (security of the agency and increased caseloads for agencies and courts) rather than recipients. Only transportation problems are accorded equal levels of concern by both groups.

## The Bottom 20 Percent

The means by which directors reconcile their seemingly contradictory views appear to be through making sharp distinctions among the clients that they serve. Teles (1998, pp. 183–184) divides the welfare universe into five groups: "those receiving aid while working off the books; those eligible for aid but not receiving it; those who are 'job ready' and using welfare on a very temporary basis; those with poor work histories but capable of training for low-wage jobs; and those who are dysfunctional for physical, mental, psychological, or emotional reasons." Welfare-to-work programs can have a substantial impact on members of the first three groups, providing means to find employment under current economic conditions. It is only the last two groups that require massive effort and investment of time and resources, with little prospect of success in a purely market economy.

Although few DHS directors apply such fine distinctions to their clients, they de facto adopt this view in their assessment of welfare reform prospects. Their analysis tends to distinguish program participants into those who really only need some form of temporary assistance—whether it is job training, transportation, or health care assistance—and a smaller group of more problem-prone individuals who have serious physical, mental, or family barriers to finding and keeping jobs. As one director elaborates,

> [A]nd some of those are just, you know, just had bad luck and are ready and . . . need assistance, and we try to assist them into getting them jobs and so forth. But there are those ones who . . . just

> don't want to work . . . Mama and dad didn't do it and so I'm not
> going to do it. It's habit that they have formed in their . . .
> lifestyles.

Similarly,

> So, I think because some of the people, especially the few that we
> have left on are kind of generational welfare and that's exactly the
> people we have left on pretty much, people that their parents were
> on and . . . the system's always been there for 'em and now we're
> saying you need to become self-sufficient, you need to work and
> we'll give you the supporting services. It's not a message that
> some of these people want to hear.

> We're always going to have that group . . . the 20 percent that just
> aren't going to be successful . . .

By law, 20 percent of the welfare population can be exempted from
federal and state mandates that the majority of welfare recipients leave
the rolls by the end of the 36-month eligibility period, backed up with
the threat of sanctions if this quota is not met. This analysis has the effect of diminishing the significance of real structural barriers and ele-
vating an explanation that stresses the importance of individual failure
as the ultimate source of problems. This has the somewhat paradoxical
effect of providing issues that directors feel more able to influence and,
simultaneously, a built-in excuse for failure if their best efforts do not
work. Even directors who are most aware of the lack of living-wage
jobs, the poor prospects for economic development, and the failures of
infrastructure and institution-building in their communities resort to a
moral analysis that emphasizes the individual's personal problems by
differentiating between the potentially successful versus the bottom 20
percent.

### "Lead Them by the Hand"

In many cases, the focus on individuals is expressed in highly paternalistic images that reflect concern with the depth of problems that
remain in the welfare population. One director states,

> [I]t's just the folks that we're dealing with now, many, many barri-
> ers. They don't know how to get out of it themselves so you have
> to lead them by the hand to get through these issues and work

them one at a time . . . it's almost like taking a small child and trying to teach it how to walk or talk . . .

The analogy to rearing children was elaborated by another director:

> This kind of intervention we've seen over and over again if you
> have the patience and the understanding . . . it's kind of like rais-
> ing your children. I don't mean to be derogatory about that, but
> you don't just tell your children to do this and they do it right from
> that point, that's constantly overseeing them and reminding them
> and encouraging them . . .

Others provide elaborate anecdotes that illustrate the same perspective. Rather than invoking the simplified rational choice model favored
by policymakers, directors adopt an alternative model that accepts the
premise of requiring personal responsibility on the part of recipients,
while believing in the necessity of significant interventions before such
responsibility can be expected. Their view leads them to assume responsibility for intensive intervention to manage clients who are not
fully able to take responsibility for themselves.

## Organizational Changes

The key to DHS directors' views lies more in their response to organizational changes and mandates of welfare reform than in their assessment of prospects for success or failure among clients and program
participants. Perhaps not surprisingly for administrators of large agencies (which vary from fewer than 50 employees to close to 200), their
concerns are much more focused on how welfare reform is organized,
managed, and implemented than on the clientele that it serves. Both in
spontaneous remarks and in response to interview questions, directors
were most likely to raise issues that affect their organizations, their
jobs, and their resources.

A consistent theme is the changing nature of the tasks confronting
the agencies and their personnel:

> We need to go far beyond simply determine eligibility and, and sit-
> ting down and taking re-applications from the individuals.

> [W]e went from an agency that gave services based on income el-
> igibility to helping people become self-sufficient through other
> means. So it was like a total change for not only our recipients but
> for our staff, too.

> [Y]ou know, you're more of a social worker now and you don't really focus so much on getting a person a check . . . but you're doing a lot of this other hand-holding and mentoring with the people.

## Flexibility

Although numerous sources of satisfaction and dissatisfaction were mentioned by directors, the strongest and most consistent theme running through the interviews was the idea that welfare reform provides increased flexibility for them and their agencies. This was expressed in a variety of ways, from describing particular program innovations that they had implemented to larger philosophical statements about the changing nature of the agencies, the new ways they would have to serve clients, and the new populations they might serve. Directors praised the end of a "cookie cutter approach" and were particularly enthusiastic about the reduction of rule-oriented procedures.

> We went from a system that was so totally irrational, it was a system of dotting i's and crossing t's and filling out forms without any real regard to what the end game was, what we really wanted to accomplish, and that was to help people become independent.

> [W]hat I think welfare reform was all about [is] when we started talking about devolving and bringing the programs back to the local level and letting the local communities be responsible to identify what the needs are and how we go about addressing those needs. One of the greatest barriers before welfare reform, and one of the greatest reasons that I think brought us to the need to reform welfare, was what I call mid-level bureaucracy. You know, you have the federal bureaucracy or national bureaucracy, and you have the state-level bureaucracy, and then you have the local bureaucracy, who actually implements or administering the program. In the past, we had 75,000 paragraphs of rules and regulations and interpretations, and these things always came out of that mid-level . . .

Flexibility brings its own problems, however:

> But, my biggest problem is . . . I know that there's all these things out there that all these counties are doing, and you know the county flexibility is great, but trying to keep up with what everybody else is doing . . . and what's working for them.

## Funds

Flexibility also went hand in hand with increased resources and greater ability to spend money when deemed necessary, especially to find the funds to create new programs and approaches.

> For probably the first time in the nine years that I've been here . . . we have the adequate funding to do what we need.

> We went from never being able to spend money on much anything . . . so now they're saying spend all you want, if you need more call us, we'll get it to ya . . . I think that's the hardest thing for me. I still want to pinch pennies and I don't need to anymore.

> [T]his year we chose to have consolidated allocations . . . and we'll choose what meets the needs of our community best and we'll spend the money which every way we feel we need to rather than having this little tiny pots of money everywhere and having to meet the criteria to each one that's attached to each one of those pots.

Somewhat to our surprise, with one or two exceptions, directors stated that amount of money was no problem, even though they generally pointed out that the reform effort and the mandate to move recipients into employment was more expensive in both the short and long run.

> [I]f the taxpayer actually knew what we were trying to do . . . they would be appalled at the . . . actual expense . . . versus just leaving clients sit on public assistance.

Using the money was sometimes seen as problematic, however.

> I guess the big problem we've had here is cash flow because we have to spend the money before we get the money.

## Sanctions

It is in this area, sanctions, that the most interesting parallels can be found between DHS directors and program participants. In particular, directors express some of the same fears of sanctions as recipients, but directors' fears center on the apparent irrationality of sanctions. Thus, directors worry about meeting state numerical goals or quotas or the economic sanctions that will result if they are unable to meet expectations, and they often view the state as an irrationally organized, or disorganized, bureaucracy that they must successfully negotiate in order to run their own agencies.

> [T]he drawback is . . . the sanctions. What if we can't meet all these participation rates or all the requirements that we have to. Any sort of a sanction against a small county like mine would basically bankrupt us.

> [A]nd of course if you don't meet the goal as a state, you get sanctioned from the federal government, which amounts to having money withdrawn, and the state, of course, would turn around and probably—this hasn't happened yet—but probably what they'll do is they'll look for counties who a have low—lower than 90 percent—participation rate and spread the sanction across those counties . . . And, you know, we're kind of at a disadvantage down here 'cause I think our last unemployment figure was 11 percent.

The difference is that the directors understand the sanction system and what they must do to avoid them. Recipients do not, a circumstance that is understood by only a very few directors:

> I see that the clients don't really understand fully the impact of time limits, nor do they really fully understand the fact that they need to take responsibility for the position that they're in at this point and time, and they end up wanting to blame the, you know, the agencies or the systems for why they are being punished or sanctioned.

## CONCLUSION: IT TAKES A COMMUNITY

Directors of human service agencies responsible for implementing welfare reform share the values that drove the reform effort, but they do not fully subscribe to the underlying behavioral model. Rather, they substitute an interventionist and paternalistic approach that emphasizes the need for their services. Like both the elites who created the policy and the recipients whose lives are its ultimate test, they accept the values of work, personal responsibility, and family values. They agree with the impulse that carried reform legislation to its successful passage. They endorse the idea that the old system was broken. However, their analyses of the reasons for failure are more complex and, hence, so are their views on the prospects for success. They generally reject simple, polarized models of individual responsibility versus structural impediments. They are well aware of many of the barriers their clients face, and they are often deeply pessimistic about long-range prospects given their rural location, lack of jobs, lack of infrastructure, and lack of political interest on the part of policymakers to address these issues.

This knowledge is contradicted by their actions, however, which are oriented toward fixing the individual problems that clients face. Directors are all too aware that they are dealing with a larger structural issue, endemic to the region, but it is beyond their power to do anything at this level. Thus, they are constrained to addressing even large-scale structural problems on an individual basis, case by case. For example, the large and pervasive problem of transportation that affects virtually every county and most program participants can only be addressed by band-aid interventions of small loans for vehicle purchase or repair, or by providing temporary or emergency taxi and shuttle services. Interventions are designed to make participants "work ready." Much of it is focused on instilling work discipline, from knowing how to get up on time to proper dress and hygiene. In the worst case, the most that the agency can do is threaten and sanction with little backup assistance. Directors' hands are tied in this respect. They can institute individual interventions more so than structural changes.

Perhaps because of their awareness of the real restrictions on their ability to make meaningful changes at a structural level, or perhaps because they are administrators whose interest centers on the operation of their organizations, they reserve their greatest enthusiasm for the expanded opportunities and material benefits that have accrued to their organizations as the result of reform. They particularly relish the increased flexibility, autonomy, and material resources. They appreciate the loosening of bureaucratic rules, and it may be argued that the greatest benefit they perceive is a reduction in state paternalism governing their operation. In bringing devolution to the counties, the state has given them a freer environment to design programs and use resources in a manner that seems meaningful to the directors.

Ironically, at the same time that directors have experienced expanded authority and autonomy, the same cannot be said of program participants.  Directors appear unaware that the same oppressive bureaucratic structures, rules, regulations, and red tape that they resent are, in the opinion of program participants, applied with increasing pressure and lack of clear purpose.  Program participants lack understanding of the parameters of welfare reform and particularly fail to see the logic of sanctions (Tickamyer et al. 2000).  They perceive these as capricious and irrational obstacles in much the same way that overly regulated, overly rule-oriented bureaucratic policies appear to the directors.  The larger policy calls on recipients to take responsibility for their lives, to move away from a system of dependency to one of self-sufficiency, yet programs are designed in a highly paternalistic fashion, and the general assumption is that clients are incapable of making judgments or decisions for themselves; instead, interventions must be designed to "lead them by the hand."  Although agencies will work intensively with clients to deal with their problems, it does not occur to directors to solicit participant views or to include them in planning efforts for designing and implementing reform programs.

Interestingly enough, many directors do recognize that successful welfare reform must be a community-wide effort.  They discuss the responsibilities of county officials, local employers, and the public at large.  They speak proudly of mobilizing their communities in the planning process in the first stage of their efforts.  They know there are few quick fixes, and although they are optimistic and appreciative of some of the aspects of welfare reform, they are realistic enough to know that the larger issues take a community effort, at the very least.

> What's gonna be the solution to their problem a year from now when cash benefits go away? . . . I guess I'd like to see a little more fire in the belly and aggressiveness out in the community, and I'm trying to instigate that . . . I think that just increasing the awareness of the public that this is a long-term problem, not a little three-year fix, and we all got to pull together to get something done about it . . . It really does take a community strategy to take care of each other . . .

What they have yet to fully incorporate into their thinking is that recipients are part of the community, and their input and cooperation are also required.

# Notes

This research was supported by grants from the Joyce Foundation, the National Research Initiative of the U.S. Department of Agriculture, and Ohio University. We are grateful for the assistance of all parties involved in this research. All opinions expressed are our own.

1. The interviews are one phase of a multiyear, case comparative study of devolution and welfare reform in poor rural counties of Appalachian Ohio. In subsequent developments, the agencies reported in this research have been reorganized and renamed to include job and family services. Other components of the study include existing statistics and primary data collection from focus groups, surveys, and in-depth interviews with employers, human service agency personnel, and local decision-makers.
2. Greatly simplified, the culture of poverty assumes that the poor become purveyors of deviant values, attitudes, and behaviors that perpetuate their poverty. This "culture of poverty" differs from the mainstream and is transmitted intergenerationally.

# References

Abramovitz, M. 1988. *Regulating the Lives of Women: Social Welfare Policy from Colonial Times to the Present*. Boston: South End Press.

Bane, M., and D. Ellwood. 1994. *Welfare Realities: From Rhetoric to Reform*. Cambridge: Harvard University Press.

Brown, C. 1981. "Mothers, Fathers and Children: From Private to Public Patriarchy." In *Women and Revolution*, Lydia Sargent, ed. Boston: South End Press, pp. 239–267.

Epstein, W. 1997. *Welfare in America: How Social Science Fails the Poor*. Madison: University of Wisconsin Press.

Ferguson, K. 1984. *The Feminist Case against Bureaucracy*. Philadelphia: Temple University Press.

Fraser, N. 1990. "Struggle Over Needs: Outline of a Socialist-Feminist Critical Theory of Late-Capitalist Political Culture." In *Women, the State, and Welfare*, L. Gordon, ed. Madison: University of Wisconsin Press, pp. 199–225.

Gilder, G. 1981. *Wealth and Poverty*. New York: Basic Books.

Gingrich, N. 1994. *Contract with America*. New York: Republican National Committee.

Gordon, L., ed. 1990. *Women, the State and Welfare*. Madison: University of Wisconsin Press.

Handler, J., and Y. Hasenfeld. 1997. *We the Poor People: Work, Poverty, and Welfare*. New Haven and London: Yale University Press.

Hasenfeld, Y. 2000. "Organizational Forms as Moral Practices: The Case of the Welfare Department." *Social Service Review* 74(3): 329–351.

Katz, M. 1989. *The Undeserving Poor: From the War on Poverty to the War on Welfare*. New York: Pantheon Books.

———. 1996. *In the Shadow of the Poorhouse: A Social History of Welfare in America*. Rev. ed. New York: Basic Books.

Murray, C. 1984. *Losing Ground: American Social Policy, 1950–1980*. New York: Basic Books.

Reinharz, S. 1992. *Feminist Methods in Social Research*. New York: Oxford University Press.

Schram, S. 1995. *Words of Welfare: The Poverty of Social Science and the Social Science of Poverty*. Minneapolis: University of Minnesota Press.

Teles, S. 1998. *Whose Welfare? AFDC and Elite Politics*. Lawrence: University Press of Kansas.

Tickamyer, A. 1995–1996. "Public Policy and Private Lives: Social and Spatial Dimensions of Women's Poverty and Welfare Policy in the United States. *Kentucky Law Journal*, 84(4): 721–744.

Tickamyer, A., D. Henderson, J. White, and B. Tadlock. 2000. "Voices of Welfare Reform: Bureaucratic Rationality versus the Perceptions of Welfare Participants." *Affilia* 15(Summer): 171–190.

# Part 3

# Employment and Family Well-Being under Welfare Reform

# 9
# The Impact of Welfare Policy on the Employment of Single Mothers Living in Rural and Urban Areas

Signe-Mary McKernan, Robert Lerman,*
Nancy Pindus, and Jesse Valente
*The Urban Institute*
and
*American University*

Moving recipients off welfare rolls and into employment was one of the primary goals of the Personal Responsibility and Work Opportunity Reconciliation Act (PRWORA) of 1996.[1] Early evidence indicates that since PRWORA was enacted, caseloads, unemployment rates for the working-age poor, and child poverty rates have all declined, but—as this volume addresses—perhaps not uniformly across all regions of the United States. Evidence from selected studies suggests that nonmetropolitan (nonmetro) areas are faring worse than metropolitan (metro) areas in responding to changes in the welfare system (Bosley and Mills 1999; Rural Policy Research Institute 1999). So far, however, the case for a weaker response in nonmetro areas is far from clear. This chapter presents new evidence on area differences in the ability to achieve a major goal of PRWORA, i.e., expanding employment among potential welfare recipients. This issue is of considerable importance to nonmetro areas, given that 20 percent of working-age welfare recipients live in nonmetro areas and the special hardships observed in nonmetro areas may indicate the need to adjust policy to deal with area differences.[2]

Because single mothers and their families are the primary beneficiaries of cash welfare, we focus on differences between nonmetro and metro areas in the employment trends of single mothers. Specifically, we look at changes in employment among single mothers between the period 11 months prior to PRWORA and 3 years later. To avoid attributing gains in employment to a healthy economy, we focus on the extra gains achieved by single mothers beyond those achieved by a comparison group. Because welfare policy changes affected single parents but not the comparison group, the different gains experienced by single mothers represent one estimate of the effects of several policy changes. The shift from the Aid to Families with Dependent Children (AFDC) program to the Temporary Assistance for Needy Families (TANF) program was not the only change in welfare policy that began in 1996. The expansion of the Earned Income Tax Credit (EITC) passed in 1993 but only became fully operational for the 1996 tax year. Increases in the availability of subsidized child care and health insurance improved the work incentives among single mothers after 1996. Our estimates thus link changes in employment among single mothers to changes in several social policies, not simply the dramatic transformation of the cash assistance program for families with children.

The chapter uses field research in 12 selected rural areas and monthly data from the nationally representative Current Population Survey (CPS) to analyze the relationship between nonmetro and metro locations, changing welfare policies, and the employment of single mothers. To add to the rapidly growing quantitative welfare reform literature, we focus on the effects of welfare changes on employment rather than on caseloads.[3] We also use a "difference-in-difference" approach. The basic idea is to assess what took place during the first few years after the passage of TANF by comparing changes in employment of welfare-eligible single mothers with employment changes of a comparison group not eligible for welfare. This approach departs from the common method of focusing on deviations from time trends, which measures the trend of employment and looks for changes from that trend around the time of welfare reform. Finally, we use monthly rather than annual data, and we analyze the different effects of welfare changes in nonmetro and metro areas.

PRWORA increased the focus on work by imposing a five-year lifetime limit on receiving federal welfare benefits (and permitting states to impose even shorter time limits), penalizing states that have too few recipients in work activities, and requiring recipients to participate in work activities within two years of receiving benefits. Within this framework, states have considerable flexibility in designing and operating their welfare programs.

PRWORA became law in August 1996 and by October 1997, all state TANF plans had been approved. Although variation in state welfare policies was already under way by the mid 1990s under federal waivers, our focus is on the post-PRWORA period. By 1998–1999, state TANF programs were fully implemented and were using the flexibility provided first through waivers, and then under TANF, in setting eligibility and benefits, time limits, work participation requirements, and other aspects of personal responsibility, including school attendance, immunization compliance for children, and family caps (that is, no increase in benefits for children conceived while the mother is receiving cash assistance).[4] Beyond rules for cash assistance programs, PRWORA provides states with flexibility in funding and administering other services that support working parents, including child care assistance programs (Long et al. 1998) and transportation services to support welfare reform's employment goals (Nightingale 1997).

Employment rates of single mothers might differ between nonmetro and metro areas because of differences in economic growth, job availability, wage levels, public transportation, and access to child care. Geographic dispersion of the nonmetro poor may limit their access to social services that could help overcome barriers to getting and keeping jobs (Deavers, Hoppe, and Ross 1996; Rural Policy Research Institute 1999). Differences in work incentives could also lead to different employment rates of single mothers in nonmetro and metro areas. Recent work by Lerman, Duke, and Valente (1999) found slightly greater financial incentives to work in nonmetro areas than in metro areas. Welfare benefits are generally lower in nonmetro areas while the federal EITC and Food Stamp program benefits are the same throughout the country. Because welfare benefits decline nearly a dollar for each dollar of earnings, going to work means giving up more cash welfare benefits in metro than in nonmetro areas in exchange for the same amount of earnings, food stamps, and EITC payments. As a result, the net gain from working at the minimum wage or another low wage will be generally higher in nonmetro areas than in metro areas. Moreover, among those working at the minimum wage, nonmetro residents will reach higher incomes relative to the average than metro residents because average incomes are lower in nonmetro areas.

The effects of welfare policy changes on employment may differ as well.  Vehicle asset limits (limits on the value of a vehicle that an individual can own and still be eligible for welfare) may impose greater restrictions on nonmetro residents, who require reliable automobiles for long commutes to work.  The lack of public transportation or reliable private transportation may serve as a disincentive to employment or may restrict individuals to low-paying jobs close to home.  Finding employment in some nonmetro areas may take longer because there are a limited number of available jobs; consequently, clients may risk losing benefits if they exceed time limits.  Work activity requirements in areas of limited employment opportunities may be filled by part-time employment, community service, or skills training.  These activities could lead to full-time employment, but higher unemployment may make such transitions less likely in nonmetro areas.  Bosley and Mills (1999) found that nonmetro southwest Virginia has higher rates of unemployment and lower rates of female labor participation than metropolitan northern Virginia.

This chapter looks at the effects of welfare policy changes from two perspectives.  We begin with reports from field studies on the operation of welfare programs in 12 selected nonmetropolitan areas.  Although we find important program and environmental barriers to employment for welfare recipients in these areas, the distinction between nonmetro and metro areas is not as stark as anticipated.  In light of extensive field work in metropolitan areas conducted as part of the Urban Institute project "Assessing the New Federalism,"[5] we find that many of the issues faced by these rural communities are similar to those faced by any poor community trying to serve its neediest citizens.  Nevertheless, remote locations, sparse population, and limited economic development do appear to exacerbate the problems of the poorest rural communities visited (Pindus 2000).  We then develop estimates of the gains in employment induced by welfare policy and explain how these gains vary between metro and nonmetro areas in the nation as a whole.  The next sections describe the empirical models, data, and the empirical results.  Our conclusions are sanguine for nonmetro areas.  Neither the site visit evidence nor the national data indicate that welfare policy is leading to worse outcomes for single mothers in nonmetro than in metro areas.

# HOW WELFARE REFORM AFFECTS NONMETROPOLITAN AND METROPOLITAN AREAS

Site visits were held in 12 localities in Arkansas, California, Maine, and Alabama to examine the implementation of program rules in several, distinctive local settings. The sites selected varied by economic, geographic, and demographic characteristics, the TANF benefit level, the unemployment rate, the percentage of families in poverty, the number of TANF recipients, the AFDC/TANF caseload change between 1993 and 1998, the percentage of the state's population that was foreign born, and transfer payments as a percentage of total personal income. State TANF policies, including the strictness of work activity requirements, sanctions, time limits, and exemptions, varied widely among states.

We intentionally oversampled the South because more rural TANF and food stamp recipients lived there. The 12 sites included counties adjacent to large metropolitan areas and counties much more isolated. Unemployment rates in the selected counties ranged from 5.1 percent to 25.7 percent in 1998. The counties relied on a variety of industries, from farming to government, services, and manufacturing. Four of the selected counties had an African-American population of more than 40 percent, and two of the counties included a substantial proportion of Hispanics.[6]

At the two-day site visits, we interviewed welfare staff (including the county welfare director, case managers, eligibility workers, and supervisors of welfare, food stamps, and work-related programs for welfare recipients), employment and training service providers, child care referral agency staff, emergency service providers such as food banks and shelters, and providers of substance abuse treatment, mental health, and transportation. We also met with community representatives in those local areas with coalitions working on welfare reform.

In most counties, low-wage jobs were readily available, but a few counties not adjacent to metro areas were experiencing quite high unemployment. Employment in some counties is highly dependent on a few firms or industries and thus subject to considerable fluctuations. Service and retail trade jobs are most accessible, but the pay is low. In fact, low pay is widespread across many types of jobs.

The most serious barriers to jobs facing welfare recipients, according to most respondents, were inadequate transportation and limited access to employment services.  Given the lack of public transportation, car ownership is important, but many lack the resources to maintain a car in operating condition.  The long distances in nonmetro areas meant that transportation problems limited access not only to employment, but also to child care, health care, and other services (Rural Policy Research Institute 1999).  At the same time, several sites have tried to limit the transportation barriers by establishing van pools, providing assistance for car repairs, having caseworkers drive clients to service providers, and expanding county-operated bus routes.  The transportation problem could influence work outcomes indirectly to the extent that it limits the implementation of work requirements.  Although most counties continue to enforce rigorous work rules, some relax the provisions in cases where transportation is unavailable.

The special importance of car ownership in rural areas increases the possible negative impact of asset limits in the food stamp and other programs.  Under PRWORA, states have the flexibility to set their own asset rules for TANF eligibility.  However, for the time period of this study, all states were subject to the $4,650 vehicle limit for food stamp eligibility for non-TANF food stamp applicants.[7]  Officials identified these limits as problems in a few counties.  The effect on work, however, is uncertain.  In some cases, recipients may be deterred from having an adequate car because it would disqualify them from food benefits.  In others, working people with cars worth more than the asset limit may simply forego food stamps.

Many of the barriers cited in general studies of welfare populations surfaced in our rural interviews (Clark et al. 1998; Geen et al. 1998; Pindus et al. 1998; Pindus 2000).  Respondents commonly cited a lack of affordable housing and a limited availability of mental health, substance abuse treatment, domestic violence, and emergency food and shelter services in nonmetro communities.  However, it is unclear that these problems were more severe in rural areas.

Although labor market conditions varied across the sites visited, employment opportunities, especially for women, were dominated by minimum wage, service industry jobs with little opportunity for advancement.  Contrary to traditional views, most rural local economies were not heavily dependent on agriculture, and seasonal employment was important in only one or two local sites. However, many employment positions were part-time or intermittent. Not surprisingly, counties adjacent to metropolitan areas had better job opportunities than nonadjacent counties. Particularly in the rural South, low education is a substantial barrier to employment.

The availability, duration, and ease of access to transitional benefits are important factors in employment decisions and the move toward self-sufficiency. Especially in the South, where income eligibility levels are low, many families are no longer eligible for TANF once employed. In these states, respondents pointed to the ease of accessing transitional Medicaid benefits and subsidized child care as important factors for remaining off welfare. Alabama, Arkansas, and Maine provide one year of transitional child care. Reports from these states indicate that people were returning to TANF after one year in order to obtain additional child care benefits. California provides two years of transitional child care. Respondents do not see the lack of available child care as a particularly important barrier so long as subsidies are available. Most but not all rural counties in the sample have licensed centers. Gaps in supply exist, but there is no indication they are more serious than in urban areas.

The site visits revealed differences in state and local practices regarding the ease of accessing transitional benefits. In some sites, when a client left cash assistance, her or his case was automatically transferred to a caseworker who handled transitional benefits; in other sites, the client had to take the initiative to apply for transitional benefits. The timing and method (e.g., in-person interview, mail-in form) for recertification varied as well in ways that may affect access.

Most of the jobs obtained by welfare recipients did not provide health insurance or other benefits. The information reported was consistent with the predominance, in rural areas, of small employers who are less likely to provide health care insurance (Rural Policy Research Institute 1999). Transitional Medicaid or other subsidized health insurance is expected to have a positive impact on work decisions (Meyer and Rosenbaum 2000).

In summary, the site visits identified inadequate transportation, limited employment services, weak labor markets, low education levels, and shortfalls in transitional benefits as problems in rural areas. Whether these obstacles to employment are more severe or exert a larger impact in nonmetro than in metro areas requires further study. The next section provides two approaches to testing for larger obstacles to employment in nonmetro areas.

## EMPIRICAL METHOD

Our primary empirical approach uses difference estimators to measure the effect of TANF on the employment of single mothers and to measure how this effect differs in nonmetropolitan and metropolitan areas.[8] Difference estimators provide a simple, powerful, and intuitive tool for evaluation analysis. They enable us to measure the effect of TANF by using simple differences to answer questions. What is the difference in employment since TANF? (In other words, after subtracting the average pre-TANF employment level from the average post-TANF employment level, do we find employment has changed? Is employment higher after TANF than it was before TANF?) Is the difference in employment since TANF greater in nonmetro or metro areas? To explore the role that dissimilar demographic and economic factors in nonmetro and metro areas play in any differences we find, we also use regression analyses to estimate the effect of TANF while controlling for these factors.

We use three levels of comparisons to draw conclusions about welfare reform independent from the thriving economy evident since welfare reform. We compare employment in nonmetropolitan areas relative to metropolitan areas, employment before and after TANF, and employment for potentially welfare-eligible single mothers relative to welfare-ineligible single women without children under the age of 18. Under varying assumptions, simple difference estimators provide us with a consistent estimate of the relationship between TANF and living in a nonmetro area.

### Difference Estimator

We first obtain the difference across areas in post-TANF employment by subtracting average post-TANF metro employment from average post-TANF nonmetro employment. This difference is only an appropriate measure of area differences in TANF's impact on employment under the following two conditions. First, the pre-TANF employment level must be the same in nonmetro and metro areas. If pre-TANF employment differed between areas, then any difference in the post-TANF employment level could be due to these preexisting differences. Second, the growth in employment in nonmetro and metro areas would have to have been the same in the absence of TANF. If employment was growing over time at a faster rate in metro areas than in nonmetro areas (or vice versa) in the absence of welfare reform, then the difference estimator would wrongly attribute gains to TANF that are actually due to the faster general employment growth. Because these conditions probably do not apply, we turn to a more complicated difference estimator.

### Difference-in-difference estimator

The derivation of this estimator involves calculating the change in employment of single mothers in nonmetro areas between pre-TANF and post-TANF periods, the comparable change in employment in metro areas, and then the difference in these two changes. This nonmetro/metro difference in the change in employment is the difference-in-difference estimator. It controls for initial area differences in pre-TANF employment rates. The estimator also takes account of greater initial difficulties in being an employed mother in nonmetro versus metro areas that are not attributable to TANF, given that it essentially subtracts any initial advantage or disadvantage of one area over another in the employment of single mothers. However, this difference-in-difference estimator is still only appropriate if the employment growth rates for metro and nonmetro areas would be the same in the absence of TANF. Subtracting one more difference from our estimator controls for differing employment growth rates in nonmetro and metro areas.

### Difference-in-difference-in-difference estimator

We extend our difference-in-difference estimator to allow employment growth rates to differ by comparing the pre-TANF to post-TANF employment growth of single mothers, which is our treatment group, with that of a comparison group that should experience a similar growth rate but not be affected by welfare reform, in this case, single females without children under age 18. We use this latter group to control for the general growth in employment for single females because family status is likely to be unimportant to the general time trend of employment for these women; the trends of single females with and without children are comparable. However, family status is important for welfare law and related social policies; single females with children under age 18 may be eligible, but single females without children under age 18 are ineligible. Thus, TANF should affect the employment probability of single females with children under 18, but not those without children.[9]

One might ask, are single women without children a good comparison group for single females with children? *A priori,* the answer is yes. There is little reason to expect that the growth rate of employment differs for these two groups. Empirical evidence presented in Figure 9.1 indicates that single females without children are a good comparison group. The pre-TANF employment trends for the two groups are relatively similar, although it is important to note the levels of employment between the two groups need not be similar. The difference-in-difference-in-difference estimator assumes similar employment growth rates for single females with and without children under age 18, but does not assume similar levels of employment for the two groups. Different levels of employment for the two groups are differenced (subtracted) away; they no longer matter because this estimator compares *changes* in the levels of employment, not the levels of employment.

A potential concern arises from using single females without children under 18 as a comparison group if fertility decisions are affected by welfare policy changes. If so, then TANF could affect whether some females end up in the treatment group or the comparison group and potentially the employment probability of the comparison group. As a result, the difference-in-difference-in-difference model would understate the effect of welfare on the employment of single mothers by subtracting its effect on potential single mothers. Because the evidence on the effects of welfare on fertility shows only insignificant or small significant effects, we expect any bias to be small or insignificant.[10]

By comparing pre-TANF and post-TANF differences in employment rates for single women with children under age 18 (who may be eligible for welfare) and single women without children under the age of 18 (who are ineligible for welfare), we can control for differences in

**Figure 9.1  Average Employment Trends of Single Females with and without Children under Age 18**

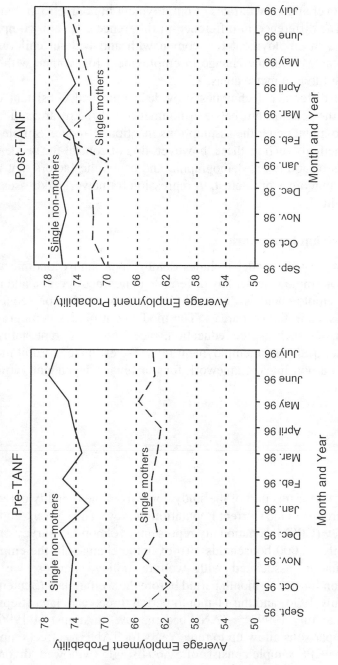

NOTE: All averages are multiplied by 100. The weighted sample of 59,604 single females age 19–45 is from the Current Population Survey group data for the 22 months of 9/95 to 7/96 (pre-TANF) and 9/98 to 7/99 (post-TANF).

SOURCE: McKernan et al. 2000.

both the level and growth rates of employment in nonmetro and metro areas.[11] The difference-in-difference-in-difference estimator compares the change in employment for women with and without children in nonmetro areas with the change in employment for women with and without children in metro areas.

These difference techniques provide simple and consistent estimates of the relationship between nonmetro and metro areas, TANF, and employment under the assumptions mentioned above. Simple difference methods such as these, however, do not control for or identify the effects of additional demographic and economic factors that may affect our outcomes of interest. A regression framework addresses this shortcoming.

### Regression framework

Our regression model includes demographic and economic variables to determine whether any difference in nonmetropolitan and metropolitan employment is due to different demographic or economic characteristics in the two areas. The model controls for demographic characteristics such as age, education, race, and immigrant status, as well as the local area unemployment rate. We estimate a probit model to provide a non-linear framework for our binary dependent variable, employment.

### DATA

The data for this part of the study come from the monthly outgoing rotation groups in the Current Population Survey. The Current Population Survey (CPS) is a nationally representative monthly survey of approximately 50,000 households. To examine changes in the employment situation associated with welfare policy changes, we use information for the 11-month period before the welfare law (September 1995 to July 1996) and the 11-month period three years later (September 1998 to July 1999).[12] TANF became law in August of 1996, so these comparisons allow up to three years for TANF to affect employment. The CPS sample consists of 59,604 single (widowed, divorced, separated, or never married) females living in nonmetropolitan and metropolitan areas.

Employment is the primary variable of interest. As defined in the monthly CPS data, an individual is either employed (if working for pay for at least one hour) or non-employed (all other cases) during the survey week.[13] The census definition of *metropolitan* is an area with a large core population (such as a city with a population of 50,000 or more) and adjacent communities with a high degree of social and economic integration with the core (U.S. Census 2000).[14] People living elsewhere reside in nonmetropolitan areas. A narrower definition would probably represent the concept of rural areas better than the nonmetro area grouping, but no such definition is available in the public-use CPS data. We separate single females into mothers with at least one child under 18 and other single females and distinguish between the pre- and postwelfare change. In multivariate analyses, we control for the following characteristics: age, age squared, and indicators for race or ethnicity, education level completed, and non-U.S. citizenship.

To obtain monthly average measures of unemployment rates in each type of area (central city, balance MSA, nonmetro, not identified), we tabulate two measures, based on information from all rotations of the CPS monthly data for our 22-month period of interest. The first measure excludes single females from the weighted mean calculation in order to avoid including members of our study population in our independent measure of the unemployment rate. The second measure includes all respondents age 16 and over in the weighted mean calculation. Our results are not sensitive to the measure used.

## EMPIRICAL RESULTS

In the three years since TANF, labor market and welfare indicators all show gains nationally (Table 9.1). The employment–population ratio (hereafter called *employment rate*) increased 1.4 percentage points, the unemployment rate fell 1.2 percentage points, and welfare caseloads fell 43 percent. Nonmetropolitan and metropolitan areas both shared in the national improvement. However, nonmetro areas were not doing as well prior to reform and saw less of an improvement after

**Table 9.1 Employment, Unemployment, and Welfare Caseloads**

| Time period | Employment/ population ratio[a,b] (%) | Unemployment rate[b] (%) | No. of welfare caseloads[c] (AFDC/TANF) |
|---|---|---|---|
| Pre-TANF, 9/95–7/96 | | | 4,415,000 |
| National | 62.9 | 5.6 | |
| Nonmetro | 61.3 | 5.9 | |
| Metro | 64.6 | 5.4 | |
| Post-TANF, 9/98–7/99 | | | 2,536,000 |
| National | 64.3 | 4.4 | |
| Nonmetro | 61.9 | 4.8 | |
| Metro | 66.1 | 4.2 | |
| Difference, post-TANF – pre-TANF (pct. pt.) | | | 1,879,000 (–43%) |
| National | 1.4 | –1.2 | |
| Nonmetro | 0.5 | –1.1 | |
| Metro | 1.4 | –1.1 | |

[a] Also called "employment rate" in text.
[b] Weighted employment and unemployment means calculated from all rotations of the Current Population Survey for the specified period.
[c] Welfare family caseloads for August 1996 (pre TANF) and June 1999 (post TANF) as measured by the U.S. Department of Health and Human Services Administration for Children and Families (1999).
SOURCE: McKernan et al. 2000.

reform.   Pre-TANF employment rates were lower in nonmetro areas (61.3 percent) than metro areas (64.6 percent) and improved less over the three-year period (0.5 percentage points nonmetro, 1.4 percentage points metro).   Similarly, pre-TANF unemployment rates were higher in nonmetro areas (5.9 percent nonmetro, 5.4 percent metro), although the improvement was similar (1.1 percentage points for nonmetro and metro areas, respectively).

## Difference Estimators

The difference estimators provide a measure of the effects of TANF on employment and how any effects differ between nonmetro and metro areas.  The first results are for all single females age 19–45.  The next set of findings shows patterns for less- and more-educated single mothers and for white, Hispanic, and African-American single mothers.

### All single females, ages 19–45

During the pre-TANF period, single mothers with children under age 18 had identical employment rates in nonmetro and metro areas (Table 9.2).  Single mothers in nonmetro areas experienced increases in employment rates of 8 percentage points, from the pre-TANF level of 64 percent to the post-TANF level of 72 percent.  This jump in employment is high in percentage terms and in relation to the experience of other groups.  To test whether these gains came mainly from the economy or from the social policy changes culminating with TANF, we compare the employment gains of single mothers with those of our comparison group, single women in the same age group but without children. Note that the employment rate of the welfare-ineligible women started at 71 percent, a rate much higher than the initial rate for single mothers.[15]   However, single women without children experienced no significant increase in jobholding; employment remained close to 71 percent in the post-TANF period.  Thus, TANF and other social policies appear to have raised the employment of single mothers relative to that of their ineligible counterparts in nonmetro areas.  A summary estimate of this effect appears in the final row in the first data column.  It subtracts the comparison group's gain in employment from the increase experienced

**Table 9.2  Differences in Average Employment Probabilities
of Single Females**

| Category | Nonmetro | Metro | Nonmetro minus metro (pct. pt.) |
|---|---|---|---|
| Mothers with children age <18 (C=1) | | | |
| Pre-TANF level, 9/95–7/96 (%) | 63.9** | 63.7** | +0.2 |
| Post-TANF level, 9/98–7/99 (%) | 71.5** | 73.1** | –1.5[a] |
| Difference, Post/pre-TANF (pct. pt.) | +7.6** | +9.4** | **–1.8** |
| Females without children age <18 (C=0) | | | |
| Pre-TANF level, 9/95–7/96 (%) | 70.7** | 75.6** | –5.0** |
| Post-TANF level, 9/98–7/99 (%) | 71.7** | 76.3** | –4.7** |
| Difference, Post/pre-TANF (pct. pt.) | +1.0 | +0.7 | +0.3 |
| Females with and without children age <18 | | | |
| Difference-in-difference (pct. pt.) | +6.7** | +8.7** | **–2.1** |
| (post-TANF – pre-TANF I C=1) – | | | |
| (post-TANF – pre-TANF I C=0) | | | |

NOTE: Weighted sample of 59,604 single females age 19 to 45 is from the Current
Population Survey outgoing rotation group data for the 22 months 9/95–7/96 (pre-
TANF) and 9/98–7/99 (post-TANF). All averages are multiplied by 100. ** = Statistical significance at the 0.05 level.
[a] Bold values are estimates of the differential effect of TANF between metro and nonmetro areas.
SOURCE: McKernan et al. 2000.

by single mothers.  Because single women without children saw little
or no growth in employment, the policy effect on single mothers in
nonmetro areas remains large, at over 6 percentage points.

How do these gains compare with gains in metro areas? As the second data column shows, single mothers in metro areas achieved large
and significant employment gains (9 percentage points, or 15 percent)
between the pre- and post-TANF periods, while no significant difference over this time took place for the comparison group. Thus, the net
social policy effect in metro areas remains at 9 percentage points.

Estimates of the differential effect of TANF between nonmetro and
metro areas appear (in bold) in the third data column of Table 9.2.  Our
first difference estimator measures the simple difference between the

post-TANF employment rate in nonmetropolitan and metropolitan areas (by subtracting the post-TANF metro employment level [73.1 percent] from the post-TANF nonmetro employment level [71.5 percent]) and is shown in the second row in data column 3. Although nonmetro areas had lower post-TANF employment levels than did metro areas, the difference was only 1.5 percentage points and was not statistically different from zero. However, as explained in our description of the empirical method, this simple difference estimator is only appropriate if the pre-TANF employment level was the same in nonmetro and metro areas (among other conditions).

The second and third estimators find slightly larger, but still statistically insignificant, effects. The second estimator, difference-in-difference, compares differences in pre- and post-TANF employment in nonmetro (7.6 percentage points) and metro (9.4 percentage points) areas by subtracting the metro difference from the nonmetro difference (7.6 minus 9.4). The difference-in-difference estimator finds that the social policy effect was −1.8 percentage points, or 19 percent smaller in nonmetro areas than in metro areas. This method controls for differences in initial employment rates, but does not control for differential changes in the economies of metro and nonmetro areas that might have affected employment growth in the absence of TANF and other social policies.

The third estimator, difference-in-difference-in-difference, controls for area economic growth by subtracting each area's employment gains for our comparison group—single women without children under age 18 who are ineligible for welfare—from each area's employment gains of single mothers. Because there was little difference in pre- and post-TANF employment for the comparison group, the third estimator yields results similar to the second, with TANF and other social policies exerting a 2 percentage point (or 24 percent) smaller effect in nonmetro areas than in metro areas, though the difference is not statistically significant.

Overall, the results presented in Table 9.2 suggest that TANF and other social policies increased the employment of single mothers by 7 to 9 percentage points in nonmetro and metro areas. The increase may have been slightly smaller in nonmetro areas than in metro areas, but the measured gap is not large enough to declare a clear difference between the two areas.

## Less-educated and more-educated single females

How should the effects of TANF and related policies vary by education? On one hand, the social policy impact on single-parent employment should be greater among less-educated women (less than a high school degree) because they are more disadvantaged and more likely to be on welfare and thus affected by welfare policies, such as work requirements. On the other hand, social policies could have a smaller effect on the employment of less-educated women because these women are the least skilled and, therefore, have fewer ways of responding to the various incentives and pressures to work. It is important to note that, contrary to popular opinion, a significant proportion (ranging from 9 percent to 26 percent) of welfare recipients have higher levels of education (i.e., more than a high school education).[16]

The differing social policy effect between nonmetro and metro areas may also differ for less- and more-educated single mothers. For example, if there are fewer low-skilled and more high-skilled jobs available in nonmetro areas than in metro areas, then we would expect TANF and other policies to have a smaller effect on the less educated and a larger effect on the more educated in nonmetro areas. The results presented in Table 9.2 may mask these differences by aggregating the averages for less- and more-educated mothers. In this analysis, we distinguish between two groups: women with a high school education or less (less educated) and women with more than a high school education (more educated).

The patterns of social policy effects are complex, as shown in Table 9.3. Note that the rows are similar to those of Table 9.2; data columns 1 to 3 relate to the less educated and data columns 4 to 6 relate to the more educated. Both before and after TANF, employment levels are much higher for the more educated than for the less educated. For example, prior to TANF, the nonmetro employment rate for those with a high school degree or less was 58 percent, well below the 73 percent rate for those with more than a high school degree. The 15 percentage point disparity remains in the post-TANF period. The disparity is even larger in metro areas, where it starts at 24 percentage points prior to TANF and falls to 20 percentage points afterwards.

Despite initial differences in job-holding by education, changes in employment rates are similar among less- and more-educated single

**Table 9.3  Differences in Average Employment Probabilities of Single Females, by Education**

| Category | Education ≤ high school | | | Education > high school | | |
|---|---|---|---|---|---|---|
| | Nonmetro | Metro | Nonmetro minus metro (pct. pt.) | Nonmetro | Metro | Nonmetro minus metro (pct. pt.) |
| Mothers with children age <18 (C=1) | | | | | | |
| Pre-TANF level, 9/95–7/96 (%) | 58.5** | 53.7** | +4.8** | 73.1** | 77.4** | −4.3** |
| Post-TANF level, 9/98–7/99 (%) | 65.4** | 64.7** | +0.7 | 81.1** | 84.3** | −3.2* |
| Difference, post-TANF – pre-TANF (pct. pt.) | +6.9** | +10.9** | −4.0 | +8.0** | +6.9** | +1.0 |
| Females without children age <18 (C=0) | | | | | | |
| Pre-TANF level, 9/95–7/96 (%) | 62.6** | 66.2** | −3.6** | 78.3** | 80.6** | −2.3* |
| Post-TANF level, 9/98–7/99 (%) | 65.7** | 69.1** | −3.4** | 76.9** | 80.1** | −3.3** |
| Difference, post-TANF – pre TANF (pct. pt.) | +3.1 | +2.9** | +0.3 | −1.4 | −0.4 | −0.9 |
| Females with and without children age <18 | | | | | | |
| Difference-in-difference (pct. pt.) (post-TANF – pre-TANF | C=1) – (post-TANF – pre-TANF | C=0) | +3.8 | +8.1** | −4.3 | +9.3** | +7.4** | +2.0 |

NOTE: Weighted sample of 59,604 single females age 19 to 45 is from the Current Population Survey outgoing rotation group data for the 22 months 9/95–7/96 (pre-TANF) and 9/98–7/99 (post-TANF). All averages are multiplied by 100.  ** = significance at the 0.05 level; * = significance at the 0.10 level.
SOURCE: McKernan et al. 2000.

mothers. Gains between pre- and post-TANF periods ranged from about 7 to nearly 11 percentage points. Estimates of single-mother employment gains net of any increased employment among single women without children appear in the "Difference-in-difference" row. The effects ranged from 4 to 8 percentage points for less-educated mothers and from 7 to 9 percentage points for more-educated mothers.[17] The finding of such a large and significant social policy effect on the employment of more-educated, single mothers suggests that these women may not serve as a valid comparison group for measuring the effects of TANF as suggested by some authors (Schoeni and Blank 2000).

The size of the impacts by education varied between nonmetropolitan and metropolitan areas. Within nonmetro areas, TANF and other social policies had a 6 percentage point smaller effect on the employment of less-educated mothers than on that of more-educated mothers (Table 9.3, data columns 1 and 4, difference-in-difference row; difference significant at the 10 percent level [not shown in table]). Within metro areas, social policies had a similar 7–8 percentage point effect on both less-educated mothers and more-educated mothers (columns 2 and 5).

The difference-in-difference row estimates of area differences in net social policy effects reveal differences by education. The social policy effect on employment of less-educated, single mothers shows up as 4 points smaller in nonmetro areas than in metro areas (column 3), although this difference is not statistically different from zero at the 10 percent confidence level. Prior to TANF, less-educated, nonmetro, single mothers were more likely to be employed than their metro counterparts (58 percent nonmetro, 54 percent metro). Post-TANF, the nonmetro and metro levels of employment are similar (65 percent nonmetro and metro). Any greater employment gains in metro areas only served to leave low-education, metro, single mothers with the same level of employment as their nonmetro counterparts. In contrast to the smaller social policy effect in nonmetro areas on less-educated women, the measured impact is a two percentage point larger effect in nonmetro areas among more-educated women.[18]

## White, Hispanic, and African-American single mothers

Table 9.4 presents the difference analysis separately for whites, Hispanics, and African Americans. We might expect different effects

**Table 9.4 Differences in Average Employment Probabilities of Single Females by Race/Ethnicity**

| Category | White | | | Hispanic | | | African American | | |
|---|---|---|---|---|---|---|---|---|---|
| | Nonmetro | Metro | Nonmetro – metro difference (pct. pt.) | Nonmetro | Metro | Nonmetro – metro difference (pct. pt.) | Nonmetro | Metro | Nonmetro – metro difference (pct. pt.) |
| **Mothers with children age < 18 (C=1)** | | | | | | | | | |
| Pre-TANF level: 9/95–7/96 (%) | 68.0** | 72.5** | −4.4** | 60.1** | 51.6** | +8.5 | 54.5** | 58.3** | −3.8 |
| Post-TANF level: 9/98–7/99 (%) | 76.1** | 79.7** | −3.6** | 53.5** | 64.1** | −10.6* | 66.6** | 69.4** | −2.8 |
| Difference, post – pre-TANF (pct. pt.) | +8.1** | +7.2** | +0.8 | −6.6 | +12.4** | −19.0** | +12.1** | +11.1** | +1.0 |
| **Females without children age < 18 (C=0)** | | | | | | | | | |
| Pre-TANF level: 9/95–7/96 (%) | 72.9** | 79.5** | −6.7** | 66.3** | 66.1** | +0.3 | 58.8** | 67.5** | −8.8** |
| Post-TANF level: 9/98–7/99 (%) | 75.0** | 79.9** | −5.0** | 58.3** | 69.6** | −11.3 | 61.7** | 69.4** | −7.7** |
| Difference, post – pre-TANF (pct. pt.) | +2.1 | +0.4 | +1.7 | −8.0 | +3.5* | −11.5 | +2.9 | +1.9 | +1.1 |
| **Females with and without children age < 18** | | | | | | | | | |
| Difference-in-difference (pct. pt.) (post – pre-TANF | C=1) – (post – pre-TANF | C=0) | +6.0** | +6.8** | −0.9 | +1.4 | +8.9** | −7.5 | +9.2 | +9.2** | 0.0 |

NOTE: Weighted sample of 59,604 single females age 19 to 45 is from the Current Population Survey outgoing rotation group data for the 22 months 9/95–7/96 (pre-TANF) and 9/98–7/99 (post-TANF). All averages are multiplied by 100. ** = statistical significance at the 0.05 level; * = statistical significance at the 0.10 level.
SOURCE: McKernan et al. 2000.

if, for example, minority groups face additional barriers (such as language or discrimination) to employment. The last row of the table (difference-in-difference) shows that TANF and other social policies increased employment by a range of 6–10 percentage points for all but the nonmetro Hispanic group, who seem to have experienced essentially no employment gains at all. The higher jump in employment among African-American single mothers is particularly noteworthy. These mothers raised their employment by 12 percentage points in nonmetro areas and 11 points in metro areas. Even after subtracting the approximate 2 percentage point gains for single, African-American women without children, the social policy effects on African-American single parents are about 9 percentage points in both nonmetro and metro areas, well above the 6-point gains for white single mothers. Moreover, the size of the African-American gains are especially dramatic given their lower employment levels in the pre-TANF period.

Hispanics are the only group showing virtually no increases in employment in nonmetro areas. Given the 9 percentage point increase in Hispanic employment in metro areas, social policies apparently exerted an 8 percentage point smaller effect on Hispanic employment in nonmetro areas than in metro areas, although this difference is not significant at the 10 percent confidence level.

Why should TANF affect nonmetropolitan Hispanics differently? Our site visit findings suggest that English language resources are not as readily available in some nonmetro areas, making it more difficult for nonmetro Hispanics to obtain the English language skills necessary for employment in some positions. Many Hispanics are thus limited to entry-level service jobs such as hotel housekeeper. If there are fewer such jobs in nonmetro areas and most less-educated women work, there may be fewer job opportunities for Hispanics. This situation may be exacerbated by the fact that nonmetro areas have smaller Hispanic communities, which means a smaller network to help find or provide employment.

All together, our results indicate that TANF increased the probability of employment for welfare-eligible single mothers (those with children under age 18) by 7–9 percentage points in nonmetro and metro areas. This increase was shared by less- and more-educated single mothers, and by white, metro Hispanic, and African-American single mothers.

**Regression Model**

To explore whether TANF's effects in nonmetro and metro areas are due to dissimilar demographic or economic characteristics, we estimated an employment equation that controls for these characteristics. The results yielded social policy effects similar to those revealed in the simple comparisons. The coefficients from the regressions (not shown) indicate that TANF and other social policies increased employment by 9 percentage points for metro single mothers, 2 percentage points more than for nonmetro single mothers, although the difference is not statistically significant at the 10 percent level. According to the regressions, single females with no children under age 18 experienced no statistically significant change in employment in metro and nonmetro areas.

To incorporate a nonlinear framework for our 0-to-1 dependent variable (employment), we estimate a set of probit models (estimates are available on request to the authors). The results from this estimation were very similar in magnitude to earlier findings, even after we control for a variety of individual and area characteristics. For example, we incorporate a measure of the individual's age, education, whether she was a U.S. citizen, and area unemployment rates. Still, we find no significant difference between the effects of social policies in nonmetro and metro areas.

Although controlling for individual and area characteristics does not alter our estimates of social policy in nonmetro and metro areas, these variables yielded interesting, although not surprising, findings. First, older single females were more likely to be employed than younger single females. Second, all racial and ethnic groups were less likely to be employed than whites. Third, each successive education degree increased the probability of employment. Fourth, single females who are not U.S. citizens were less likely to be employed than females who are U.S. citizens. Finally, adding the monthly unemployment rate—an important determinant of labor market conditions—exerted little effect on the magnitude or significance of our estimates of policy impacts.

## CONCLUSION

Based on traditional views about nonmetropolitan areas, past evidence, and site visits, one might expect that work-oriented welfare reforms would be much harder to implement and yield worse outcomes in nonmetropolitan areas than in metropolitan areas. Low population density appears to make travel and connections with services and employment difficult in nonmetropolitan areas. Indeed, Bosley and Mills (1999) found worse employment outcomes in nonmetropolitan areas for a small sample of females in Virginia. In contrast, Lerman, Duke, and Valente (1999) found greater work incentives in nonmetropolitan areas than in metropolitan areas.

Contrary to expectations, we find that the employment level of single mothers was similar in nonmetropolitan and metropolitan areas prior to TANF and gained almost as much in nonmetropolitan areas as in metropolitan areas after TANF. We find no strong evidence that TANF and other social policies affected the employment of single mothers differently in nonmetro and metro areas. Within the group of single mothers, we find some differences by education. Despite the higher unemployment rate in nonmetropolitan areas, less educated, single mothers are more likely than their metropolitan counterparts to have worked prior to TANF. Although metropolitan areas have since caught up, there are gains in nonmetro areas as well. On the other hand, the level of employment for more educated, nonmetro, single mothers falls slightly short of their metropolitan counterparts. However, the level is high in both areas, and the nonmetropolitan gains are as solid as the metropolitan gains. Apparently, the obstacles to employment are not so severe that they prevent nonmetropolitan areas from effectively implementing welfare-oriented policies.

Our results are consistent with those of Danziger (in this volume)—who finds that patterns of work effort, welfare receipt, and the poverty rate are "strikingly similar regardless of place of residence" (p. 31)—and those of Lichter and Jensen (in this volume)—who find "for the most part, recent trends in rural poverty, earnings, and welfare receipt have followed national patterns" (p. 103). Our national-level results are less consistent, although also less comparable, with Gennetian, Redcross, and Miller's (in this volume, p. 287) state-specific results. Similar to our results, they find that Minnesota's welfare reform increased employment in both rural and urban areas. Unlike our results, they find a significant difference in the employment increases between areas; the rural area increases faded over time and fell behind the urban area increases. Surprisingly, much of this difference in Minnesota welfare reform's effects in rural and urban counties could be explained by the fact that rural Minnesota welfare recipients were better prepared to enter the workforce, reported fewer child care barriers, and were more likely to have been previously married than their urban counterparts.

Considered together with Lerman, Duke, and Valente (1999), our empirical findings suggest that the obstacles to employment do not yield poorer outcomes in nonmetro areas than in metro areas. Nonmetro areas are becoming more diverse, and low-wage service economies are relevant for both nonmetro and metro areas. Similar to metro areas, the growth of the nonmetro service economy has reinforced the mass entry of women into the formal labor market (see Gibbs, in this volume, for a discussion of this trend). As Gibbs concludes, "rural labor markets may be better positioned for welfare reform than is often assumed because rural and urban job structures appear to be converging" (p. 70).

Yet how do we reconcile the empirical findings with the inadequate transportation, limited employment services, low education levels, and shortfalls in transitional benefits identified as problems in our site visits? Although we found a variety of barriers facing single mothers, jobs appeared readily available in most of the rural sites. Perhaps, the most serious rural problems reflect only pockets of poverty or a limited number of nonmetro areas. As Howell reports in this volume, local nonmetro labor markets vary widely in their ability to create jobs for TANF recipients. Our rural sites may not characterize most nonmetro areas, just as pockets of poverty in metropolitan areas do not define all metro areas.

This chapter analyzes only the gains in employment of single mothers, not their gains in earnings. Although women in nonmetro areas may be as likely to be employed, they may be employed in lower paying or more part-time jobs. Additional research is needed to examine whether nonmetro areas do as well as metro areas in raising the earnings of single mothers.

# Notes

The research reported in this chapter was supported by the U.S. Department of Agriculture's Economic Research Service, Food Assistance and Nutrition Research Program. The chapter draws on a more technical paper by the authors titled "Metropolitan and Nonmetropolitan Locations, Changing Welfare Policies, and the Employment of Single Mothers," (working paper no. 192, Joint Center for Poverty Research, Chicago, 2000). The authors thank Amy-Ellen Duke for input to the chapter, Lorna M. Aldrich, Harry J. Holzer, Caroline Ratcliffe, and Douglas Wissoker for comments and advice, Fay Schwartz and Ludovick Shirima for research assistance, and Joyce Morton and Greg Welland for programming and data assistance. Contact information: smckerna@ui.urban.org; phone: (202) 261-5330.

1. PRWORA replaced the federal program Aid to Families with Dependent Children (AFDC) with Temporary Assistance for Needy Families (TANF), which provides block grants to states that can be used for cash assistance, child care, and other services that support the goals of welfare reform.
2. March 1998 Current Population Survey.
3. Important contributions to the welfare reform literature have been made by Grogger (2000), Meyer and Rosenbaum (2000), Moffitt (1999), Schoeni and Blank (2000), Wallace and Blank (1999), and Ziliak et al. (2000), among others.
4. Gallagher et al. (1998) provides detailed information on state TANF decisions as of October 1997.
5. See for example, Clark et al. (1998), Geen et al. (1998), and Pindus et al. (1998).
6. Pindus (2000) provides detailed descriptions of the sites and site visit findings.
7. New Food Stamp program regulations, approved in November 2000, exempt all cars with an equity value less than $1,500 and, for cars above this value, exempt one car per adult in the household plus any car used by a teenager to drive to work or to school.
8. See McKernan et al. (2000) for a more technical description of the empirical method.
9. Welfare reform could affect employment of single females without children if it affects the entire labor market for low-skilled workers. It might be that welfare recipients entering the labor force take low-skill jobs and increase unemployment for other low-skilled workers. However, this scenario is unlikely. Lerman, Loprest, and Ratcliffe (1999, p. 6) projected that, on average, metropolitan areas "will experience decreases in unemployment, even with the entry of welfare recipients into the labor force, largely because of growth in low-skill employment."
10. Alternative methods used to control for employment trends have other shortcomings. One approach is to capture trends with year fixed effects and an interaction between a time trend and state variable. However, this approach assumes linear employment trends and requires a longer time period of data.
11. The difference models are based in part on similar models described by Card and Sullivan (1988) and Moffitt (1991).

12. August 1995 and August 1998 were dropped from the data because geographic variables necessary to identify nonmetro and metro areas were not available in the August 1995 CPS data.

13. Of the non-employed, some are counted as officially unemployed because they are available for work and actively seeking a job, while others are outside the labor force.

14. 157 respondents lived in areas that were geographically classified as "not identified" in the CPS. We dropped these respondents from the analysis.

15. A higher pre-TANF level of employment for our comparison group does not pose a problem for our difference estimator. Although our estimator assumes similar trends in employment for single females with and without children, it does not assume similar levels of employment; the levels are differenced away.

16. A significant proportion of more educated welfare recipients are reported from both national-level and state-level data. At the national level, the U.S. Department of Health and Human Services (1995) reported that 9 percent of mothers receiving AFDC in 1995 had more than a high school degree (though the education level was unknown for 43 percent of the sample); Ratcliffe (2000) found that 26 percent of single mothers who received TANF in 1997 had more than a high school education; Loprest (1999) reported that 33 percent of former welfare recipients had more than a high school education; and Pavetti (1995) reported that 53 percent of all first-time AFDC recipients had at least 12 years of education. Using state administrative data, Howell (2000) found that 14 percent of 1996 TANF recipients in Mississippi had more than a high school degree and that a significant number of recipients held college degrees. Howell discusses related findings in this volume (p. 313).

17. Due to the large standard error on this estimate for less-educated women, we cannot reject the hypothesis that the 4 percentage point effect of TANF on low-education single mothers in nonmetro areas is zero. However, we also cannot reject the hypothesis that the 4 percentage point effect in nonmetro areas is the same as the 8 percentage point effect in metro areas.

18. Although neither difference is statistically different from zero at the 10 percent confidence level, the two differences are statistically different from one another at the 10 percent confidence level.

# References

Bosley, Sarah, and Bradford Mills. 1999. *How Welfare Reform Impacts Nonmetropolitan and Metropolitan Counties in Virginia.* Virginia Tech Rural Economic Analysis Program, available at <http://www.reap.vt.edu/reap/publications/reports/r46.pdf>, March 2000.

Bureau of the Census. 2000. *Revised Standards for Defining Metropolitan Areas in the 1990s.* Accessed at <http://www.census.gov/population/www/estimates/mastand.html>, June 2000.

Card, David, and Daniel Sullivan. 1988. "Measuring the Effect of Subsidized Training Programs on Movements in and out of Employment." *Econometrica* 56(3): 497–530.

Clark, Sandra J., Sharon K. Long, Krista Olson, and Caroline Ratcliffe. 1998. *Income Support and Social Services for Low Income People in Alabama.* Washington, D.C.: The Urban Institute, Assessing the New Federalism Project.

Deavers, Kenneth, Robert Hoppe, and Peggy Ross. 1996. "Public Policy and Rural Poverty: A View from the 1980s." *Policy Studies Journal* 15(2): 291–309.

Economic Research Service. 2000. *Rural Labor Market Indicators.* Available at <http://www.econ.ag.gov/reofong/rural/labor/index.htm> on March 23, 2000.

Gallagher, L. Jerome, Megan Gallagher, Kevin Perese, Susan Schreiber, Keith Watson. 1998. *One Year after Federal Welfare Reform: A Description of State TANF Decisions as of October 1997.* Occasional Paper Number 6, The Urban Institute, Washington, D.C.

Geen, Rob, Wendy Zimmermann, Toby Douglas, Sheila Zedlewski, and Shelley Waters. 1998. *Income Support and Social Services for Low Income People in California.* Washington, D.C.: The Urban Institute, Assessing the New Federalism Project.

Grogger, Jeff. 2000. "Time Limits and Welfare Use." Unpublished manuscript, Department of Policy Studies, University of California, Los Angeles, and National Bureau of Economic Research, February 23.

Howell, Frank M. 2000. "Prospects for 'Job-Matching' in the Welfare-to-Work Transition: Labor Market Capacity for Sustaining the Absorption of Mississippi's TANF Recipients." Paper presented at Rural Dimensions of Welfare Reform: A Research Conference on Poverty, Welfare and Food Assistance. Washington, D.C., May 4–5.

Lerman, Robert I., Amy-Ellen Duke, and Jesse Valente. 1999. "Do Income Support Levels and Work Incentives Differ between Rural and Urban Areas?" Paper prepared for the Economic Research Service, Food Assistance and Nutrition Research Program, by the Urban Institute, Washington, D.C.

Lerman, Robert I., Pamela Loprest, and Caroline Ratcliffe. 1999. *How Well Can Urban Labor Markets Absorb Welfare Recipients? Assessing the New Federalism.* Policy Brief A-33. Washington, D.C.: The Urban Institute.

Long, Sharon K., Robin Kurka, Shelley Waters, and Gretchen Kirby. 1998. *Child Care Assistance under Welfare Reform: Early Responses by the States.* Occasional paper no. 13, The Urban Institute, Washington, D.C.

Loprest, Pamela. 1999. *Families Who Left Welfare: Who Are They and How*

*Are They Doing?* Discussion paper 99-02, The Urban Institute, Washington, D.C.:

Meyer, Bruce D., and Dan T. Rosenbaum. 2000. *Making Single Mothers Work: Recent Tax and Welfare Policy and Its Effects.* Working paper no. 7491, National Bureau of Economic Research, Cambridge, Massachusetts.

McKernan, Signe-Mary, Robert Lerman, Nancy Pindus, and Jesse Valente. 2000. "Metropolitan and Nonmetropolitan Locations, Changing Welfare Policies, and the Employment of Single Mothers." Unpublished manuscript, The Urban Institute, Washington, D.C., August.

Moffitt, Robert. 1991. Program evaluation with nonexperimental data. *Evaluation Review* 15(3): 291–314.

———. 1999. "The Effect of Pre-PRWORA Waivers on AFDC Caseloads and Female Earnings, Income, and Labor Force Behavior." Unpublished manuscript, Johns Hopkins University, May.

Nightingale, Demetra Smith. 1997. *Transportation Issues in Welfare Reform: Background Information.* The Urban Institute, Washington, D.C.

Pavetti, L. 1995. "Questions and Answers on Welfare Dynamics." Paper presented at a research meeting on welfare dynamics, The Urban Institute, Washington, D.C., September 11, 1995. As cited in the *1998 Greenbook*, Section 7, 553. accessed at <http://www.access.gpo.gov/congress/wm001.html>, June 2000.

Pindus, Nancy. 2000. "Implementing Welfare Reform in Rural Communities." Draft paper prepared for the Economic Research Service, Food Assistance and Nutrition Research Program by the Urban Institute, Washington, D.C.

Pindus, Nancy, Randy Capps, Jerome Gallagher, Linda Giannarelli, Milda Saunders, and Robin Smith. 1998. *Income Support and Social Services for Low-Income People in Texas.* The Urban Institute, Washington, D.C., January.

Ratcliffe, Caroline. 2000. Unpublished tabulation from the 1997 National Survey of America's Families (NSAF).

Rural Policy Research Institute. 1999. *Rural America and Welfare Reform: An Overview Assessment.* Accessed at <http://www.rupri.org/pubs/archive/old/welfare/p99-3/index.html>, March 2000.

Schoeni, Robert F., and Rebecca M. Blank. 2000. "The Effects of Welfare Reform and Welfare Waivers on Employment, Income, Poverty, and Family Structure." Unpublished manuscript, RAND Corporation and the School of Public Policy, University of Michigan, February.

U.S. Department of Health and Human Services. 1995. "Table 7-19–AFDC Characteristics, Selected Years 1969–95." As cited in the *1998 Greenbook*,

Section 7, 440; accessed at <http://www.access.gpo.gov/congress/wm001. html>, June 2000.

U.S. Department of Health and Human Services. 1999. "Change in Welfare Caseloads Since Enactment of New Welfare Law." Accessed at <http:// www.acf.dhhs.gov/programs/opre/particip/fy98/pr98t1.htm>, March 2000.

Wallace, Geoffrey, and Rebecca M. Blank. 1999. "What Goes Up Must Come Down? Explaining Recent Changes in Public Assistance Caseloads." In *Economic Conditions and Welfare Reform*, Sheldon H. Danziger, ed. Kalamazoo, Michigan: W.E. Upjohn Institute for Employment Research, pp. 49–89.

Ziliak, James P., David N. Figlio, Elizabeth E. Davis, and Laura S. Connolly. 2000. "Accounting for the Decline in AFDC Caseloads." *Journal of Human Resources* 35(3): 570–585.

# 10
# Welfare Reform in Rural Minnesota
## Experimental Findings from the Minnesota Family Investment Program

Lisa A. Gennetian, Cindy Redcross, and Cynthia Miller
*Manpower Demonstration Research Corporation*

Although issues of poverty affect families and children in both urban and rural areas of the United States, the plight of the urban poor rings nearer for many researchers and caseworkers. In fact, child and adult poverty rates vary considerably across regions; they are highest in highly urban areas (central cities) and in nonmetropolitan areas and lowest in the suburbs. A number of trends in the 1990s—declining welfare caseloads, increased labor force participation among the poor, and lessening child poverty—also varied substantially across regions (Rural Policy Research Institute 1999). Unlike patterns in urban areas, caseload declines in rural areas have not run parallel with increases in employment or reductions in poverty. These trends in part reflect the unique challenges that the poor and welfare recipients face in rural areas. The most prominent are access to child care and transportation and the availability and quality of employment opportunities.

Despite these regional differences, the landmark 1996 welfare reform legislation (the Personal Responsibility and Work Opportunity Reconciliation Act, or PRWORA) treats eligibility and mandates for welfare assistance in rural and urban areas alike. The effects of this legislation on rural, compared with urban, regions are not well understood and are relatively understudied. Fortunately, prior to the passage of PRWORA, several states were granted federal waivers to implement and test innovative welfare reform policies. Using two years of follow-up data, we examine the effects on employment and earnings among rural, long-term recipients participating in one such experimental wel-

287

fare waiver evaluation—the Minnesota Family Investment Program (MFIP). The MFIP evaluation included welfare recipients who resided in both urban and rural counties, allowing a comparison of its effects across a diverse cross-section of counties. MFIP was first implemented on a field trial basis in April 1994 in three urban counties of Hennepin (Minneapolis), Anoka, and Dakota, and four rural counties, Mille Lacs, Morrison, Sherburne, and Todd.

Recent findings show that MFIP had a range of positive effects on long-term recipients, increasing parents' employment, earnings, and income and improving their children's behavior and school performance (Miller et al. 2000; Gennetian and Miller 2000). The findings also show, however, that MFIP's effects for long-term recipients differed somewhat for those in urban and rural counties. In contrast to the large and lasting employment and earnings increases in urban counties, average employment increases by the second year of follow-up were much smaller for recipients in rural counties. In addition, MFIP did not significantly increase rural recipients' average earnings.

This chapter examines MFIP's impact in rural and urban areas in more detail and attempts to explain why the impacts were smaller in rural counties. The research makes several contributions. First, it adds to emerging findings about the effects of welfare reform interventions on single-parent families who are long-term welfare recipients. Second, the MFIP data provide a unique opportunity to examine the effects of an identical intervention in two very different contexts—rural and urban areas. Third, the wealth of detailed information about economic and demographic characteristics and behavior allow an in-depth analysis of why or how welfare reform interventions such as MFIP might have different effects for urban and rural recipients. Finally, perhaps unlike many other experimental evaluations, these findings can inform current state policy because the current statewide version of MFIP is very similar to the program implemented for the evaluation.

We find that rural recipient families differ from urban recipient families both in terms of their demographic characteristics and in their work experience and attitudes or perceptions about welfare and work. In particular, compared with urban recipients, more rural recipients are white, more have been previously married, and more have recent work experience prior to entering the evaluation. Moreover, compared with urban recipients, rural recipients are more likely to report a sense of stigma associated with receiving welfare. These differences in observable characteristics, particularly prior marital status and work experience, can explain a substantial part of the difference in effects for three of the rural counties. However, we also find that MFIP's most negative effects were confined to one particular rural county and that differences in observable characteristics explain very little of the difference in this county. The differences in MFIP's effects in this one county may be due to aspects of the local economy that were unique to this county or to unobservable differences between these recipients and recipients in other counties. Nonetheless, the results highlight the role that regional differences should play in formulating welfare and employment policies.

## THE MFIP MODEL AND EVALUATION

### MFIP Model

MFIP integrated several programs in the Minnesota welfare system. These included Aid to Families with Dependent Children (AFDC), the core of the traditional system, and STRIDE, the state's employment and training program for AFDC recipients,[1] which operated on a voluntary basis for certain targeted groups. It also included the state-run Family General Assistance program,[2] which allowed some low-income families to qualify for welfare who would not qualify under AFDC. MFIP also included the federally funded Food Stamp program, which provided assistance in the form of coupons to be spent on food.[3] MFIP did not replace or change Medicaid, the federal-state health program serving low-income families, which is available equally to recipients of MFIP and AFDC.

MFIP differed from the AFDC system in three fundamental ways. First, MFIP made work pay for families receiving welfare. This was accomplished primarily by decreasing the extent to which families' welfare grants were reduced when they went to work. For a family on AFDC, some earnings were disregarded when benefit amounts were calculated, but benefits were still reduced substantially for each dollar of earnings. Under MFIP, much more of a family's earnings were disregarded when determining benefit levels. MFIP's more generous disregard ensured that working always resulted in more income than not working. For example, in 1994 a single parent with two children who had no income from work received the same $769 in monthly welfare benefits under MFIP or the AFDC system. If she worked 20 hours per week at $6 per hour, her grant was reduced by $237 less under MFIP than it would have been under AFDC. This raised the reward for working—the difference in total income between working and not working—from $255 to $492, or a 93 percent increase.

MFIP child care payments also encouraged work because MFIP paid child care expenses directly to the provider, leaving recipients with no up-front costs. AFDC recipients, in contrast, had to pay for child care up-front, and those costs could be subtracted from their income when their AFDC grant was calculated. Although AFDC recipients were eventually reimbursed for child care expenses, this process could take up to two months.

The second way MFIP varied from AFDC was that MFIP required long-term public assistance recipients to participate in employment and training services. Under MFIP, single parents who had received public assistance for 24 of the prior 36 months were required to participate in employment and training activities in order to continue receiving their full grants. Individuals were exempt from participating if they had a child under the age of 1, if they had other "good cause" reasons, or if they were working at least 30 hours per week.

For single-parent families, MFIP's employment and training services were a substitute for those provided under AFDC through the STRIDE program. MFIP differed from STRIDE in two significant ways: STRIDE was essentially a voluntary program and had a strong focus on education and training, whereas MFIP was mandatory for long-term recipients and placed greater emphasis on rapid entry into employment.

Finally, MFIP consolidated benefits and streamlined public assistance rules and procedures. MFIP combined the benefits of AFDC, Family General Assistance, and food stamps into a single program; therefore, families on MFIP encounter a single set of rules and procedures. In addition, recipients received food stamp benefits as part of their cash assistance grant instead of separately as coupons (as they did under the AFDC system).

Minnesota implemented a revised version of MFIP in January 1998 in response to new flexibility under federal Temporary Assistance for Needy Families (TANF) rules.  The many similarities between the original MFIP program and statewide MFIP make the evaluation results a good starting point for predicting the likely results of statewide MFIP, even though the changes in the program make it difficult to make such predictions with accuracy.  The biggest policy changes in the new program are aimed at reducing costs and increasing the urgency of the employment message.  These include the five-year time limit, the reduced basic grant, the reduced earnings threshold for leaving welfare, the more immediate participation mandate, tighter sanctions, and the increased orientation toward full-time work.

The statewide program may exhibit other strengths and weaknesses relative to the field trials, which is true of many programs that move from an experiment to a wider application.  On the one hand, the results presented here may be more favorable than would be the case in a statewide program because each county in the statewide program will probably receive less intensive "hand-holding" by state staff than was true in the field trials.  Also, staff may be less enthusiastic than the staff in counties that volunteered to participate in the field trials.  In addition, as more welfare recipients are subject to work requirements, any employment effects that resulted from "jumping the queue" of employment over other workers may be more difficult to achieve as more workers become subject to the same requirements.  On the other hand, the new program has the advantage of potential "community effects," or change in community norms that will occur now that MFIP is saturating the entire state caseload rather than affecting just a subset of families within particular counties.

## The MFIP Evaluation

The MFIP field trials began in 1994 and included single-parent and two-parent families in seven urban and rural counties in central Minnesota.[4]  Random assignment began in April 1994 and concluded in March 1996, after a total of 14,639 families had entered the research sample.  Welfare recipients already on the AFDC caseload were randomly assigned when they reapplied for assistance.  At this time, single-parent families in urban and rural counties could be assigned to one of two research groups—the MFIP group or the AFDC group.[5] All single-parent families assigned to the MFIP group received the full MFIP program. This included MFIP's benefit structure, its financial incentives, and, once they had received public assistance for 24 of the prior 36 months, the requirement to participate in MFIP's employment and training services. Single-parent families assigned to the AFDC group were eligible for the benefits and services offered by Minnesota's AFDC system. They were subject to the financial rules of the AFDC and Food Stamp programs,[6] and, if in a STRIDE target group, they were eligible to volunteer for STRIDE services.

## DATA AND DESCRIPTIVE CHARACTERISTICS

There are two main samples in the MFIP evaluation—the full evaluation sample and a smaller survey sample that was interviewed three years after random assignment. Administrative data are available for two-and-one-half years after random assignment for the full evaluation sample. The administrative data include public assistance benefit records provided by Minnesota's Department of Human Services and unemployment insurance records provided by Minnesota's Department of Economic Security. These data are used to construct average quarterly measures of employment, earnings, and welfare receipt. A client survey was administered approximately three years after random assignment, collecting information about the characteristics of employment, family structure, and a number of other measures of family well-being.

As noted, we focus here on long-term recipients, defined as single-parent families that have received welfare for 24 months or more at the time of random assignment. The primary reason for defining long-term recipients in this way is because these families were required to participate in employment services if they did not already work at least 30 hours per week. The sample used here includes 2,373 single-parent recipient families—1,780 urban and 593 rural—for which administrative data are available, and 976 single-parent recipient families—724 urban and 252 rural—with survey data.[7]

Table 10.1 presents descriptive characteristics by area of residence

**Table 10.1  Selected County and Single-Parent-Family Characteristics in Rural and Urban Counties**

| Characteristic | Urban | Rural | Total sample |
|---|---|---|---|
| Demographic | | | |
| Race/ethnicity (%) | | | |
| White, non-Hispanic | 43.4 | 92.3 | 55.7* |
| Black, non-Hispanic | 41.9 | 0.7 | 31.6 |
| Hispanic | 2.1 | 0.3 | 1.7 |
| Native American/Alaskan/Asian | 12.6 | 6.7 | 11.1 |
| Average age (yr.) | 30.1 | 31.5 | 30.8 |
| Family structure (%) | | | |
| Never married | 68.4 | 44.6 | 62.5* |
| Youngest child under 6, or client pregnant at the time of random assignment | 65.5 | 60.6 | 64.3* |
| Labor force status (%) | | | |
| Worked full-time for 6 months or more for one employer | 51.4 | 64.0 | 54.5* |
| Any earnings in past 12 months | 15.0 | 21.1 | 16.5 |
| High school diploma or GED | 66.9 | 71.7 | 68.1* |
| Received AFDC for 5 years or more | 55.9 | 45.7 | 53.3* |
| Lives in public/subsidized housing | 43.4 | 37.3 | 41.8* |
| Currently enrolled in education or training | 22.7 | 24.8 | 23.2 |
| Average unemployment rate, 1997[a] (%) | 2.3 | 6.3 | 4.3 |
| Employment by industry, 1990[a] (%) | | | |
| Agriculture | 1.0 | 10.9 | 6.0 |
| Manufacturing | 20.5 | 20.3 | 20.4 |
| Wholesale/retail trade | 22.8 | 19.4 | 21.1 |
| All other | 55.7 | 49.4 | 52.6 |
| Sample size (total = 2,373) | 1,780 | 593 | 2,373 |

NOTE: The sample includes AFDC and MFIP group members who were randomly assigned from April 1, 1994, to March 31, 1996. An asterisk (*) denotes that the differences between urban and rural counties on this characteristic are statistically significant at the 10% level. The box in the ethnicity category indicates the overall significance of ethnicity.

[a] Calculated using data from the City and County Data Book, and the 1990 Census, "USA Counties." These data were calculated using unweighted averages of the relevant county statistics. The differences in these characteristics were not tested for statistical significance.

SOURCE: MDRC calculations using data from the Background Information Form (BIF).

for single-parent recipients.[8] The data used to calculate these descriptive characteristics come from a baseline information form that each parent completed at the time of random assignment. The majority of the sample was white, most were never married, most had some work experience, and over half had been on welfare for five or more years when they entered the evaluation.[9] The MFIP evaluation sample, as a whole, looks quite similar to the Minnesota caseload in 1994, with the exception that a slightly lower proportion of the evaluation sample was white. However, a depiction of the national welfare caseload in 1994 shows that the MFIP sample, compared with recipients in other states, had a higher proportion of white families and a lower proportion of Hispanic families, and recipients had higher levels of education (U.S. House of Representatives 1996).

Urban and rural single-parent recipients were different in a number of ways. (Significant differences are indicated by an asterisk in Table 10.1.) Approximately 81 percent of the urban recipients lived in Hennepin County, which includes Minneapolis (data not shown); 43 percent were white, and 68 percent were never married. In contrast, 92 percent of the rural recipients were white and 45 percent were never married. Parents in rural counties appear better prepared to enter the workforce; 64 percent had worked full-time at some point, and 21 percent had worked in the year prior to random assignment, whereas about 15 percent of urban recipients had recent work experience. Recipients in rural counties were also more likely than urban recipients to have completed some kind of secondary education. For example, rural recipients were 5 percentage points more likely than urban recipients to have a high school diploma. Local environments also differed. The rural areas had higher unemployment rates in 1997 and relatively more employment in the agricultural sector.

Table 10.2 presents information about recipients' attitudes and opinions on work and welfare based on data from a Private Opinion Survey administered at the time of random assignment. Although a large majority of the sample reports a preference to work part-time or full-time (not shown), a majority also report at least one barrier to part-time employment, including child care, transportation, and health and emotional problems. Many respondents report being ashamed of being on welfare and that people looked down on them for being on welfare, yet most still believe that welfare provided better income than work.

**Table 10.2  Selected Attitudes and Opinions of Single-Parent Sample Members in Urban and Rural Counties (%)**

| Characteristic | Urban | Rural | Total sample |
|---|---|---|---|
| Client-reported barriers to employment (among those not currently employed, those who agreed or agreed a lot that they could not work part-time[a] right now for the following reasons) | | | |
| No way to get there every day | 45.9 | 39.6 | 44.2* |
| Cannot arrange for child care | 53.8 | 37.8 | 49.6* |
| A health or emotional problem, or a family member with a health or emotional problem | 26.2 | 29.9 | 27.2 |
| Too many family problems | 25.2 | 23.1 | 24.6 |
| Already have too much to do during the day | 23.1 | 25.8 | 23.8 |
| Any of the above five reasons | 79.5 | 74.0 | 78.0* |
| Client-reported attitudes toward welfare (those who agreed or agreed a lot with the following statements) | | | |
| I feel that people look down on me for being on welfare | 63.3 | 75.1 | 66.5* |
| I am ashamed to admit to people that I am on welfare | 54.1 | 67.8 | 57.7* |
| Right now, being on welfare provides for my family better than I could by working | 58.8 | 68.9 | 61.5* |
| I think it is better for my family that I stay on welfare than work at a job | 17.7 | 22.2 | 18.9* |
| Client-reported social support network (those who agreed or agreed a lot with the following statements) | | | |
| Among my family, friends, and neighbors, I am one of the only people who is on welfare | 34.4 | 42.1 | 36.4* |
| When I have trouble or need help, I have someone to talk to | 75.0 | 83.1 | 77.2* |
| Client-reported sense of efficacy (those who agreed or agreed a lot with the following statements) | | | |
| I have little control over the things that happen to me | 21.5 | 19.5 | 20.9 |
| I often feel angry that people like me never have a chance to succeed | 49.4 | 46.9 | 48.8 |

**Table 10.2  (Continued)**

| Characteristic | Urban | Rural | Total sample |
|---|---|---|---|
| Sometimes I feel that I'm being pushed around in life | 42.2 | 51.2 | 44.6* |
| There is little I can do to change many of the important things in my life | 33.4 | 30.8 | 32.7 |
| All of the above | 7.9 | 9.5 | 8.4 |
| None of the above | 28.5 | 27.0 | 28.1 |
| Sample size (total = 2,373) | 1,780 | 593 | 2,373 |

NOTE: The sample includes AFDC and MFIP group members who were randomly assigned from April 1, 1994, to March 31, 1996. Twenty-seven percent of single-parent sample members did not fill out a Private Opinion Survey because the survey began in the second month after the start of random assignment. An asterisk (*) denotes that the differences between urban and rural counties on this measure are statistically significant at the 10% level.
[a] Part-time is defined as a minimum of 10 hours per week and less than 40 hours per week.

These attitudes and perceptions differ considerably among urban and rural recipients. It is particularly striking that, compared with urban recipients, rural recipients are much more likely to perceive stigma associated with welfare; that is, they are ashamed to admit being on welfare. Yet, at the same time, those in rural counties were more likely to agree that welfare provides a better alternative than work. The other striking difference is that rural recipients were less likely than urban recipients to report a barrier to part-time work. In particular, rural recipients were more than 6 percentage points less likely to report transportation as a barrier to part-time employment and 16 percentage points less likely to report child care as a barrier. Shelton et al. (in this volume, p. 345) also found that urban recipients report child care as a barrier to work more often than rural recipients.

## EXPECTED EFFECTS AND BASIC EMPIRICAL ESTIMATION

### Expected Effects

Both of MFIP's primary components—enhanced financial incentives and mandatory employment-focused activities—should affect parents' employment decisions, although not always in the same way. When thinking about their effects, it is helpful to consider what parents would have done in the absence of the program. As an extreme example, if all people receiving welfare in Minnesota typically went to work soon after they started receiving benefits, the program would have no effect on employment rates. In reality, however, some parents return to work quickly, some after several months, and others do not work.

The mandatory employment and training activities were purposefully targeted to parents who had remained on welfare for a long period without working, or parents who would not have worked in the absence of MFIP. By requiring that they participate in case management and employment activities if not employed at least 30 hours per week, the mandates should increase full-time employment. By increasing full-time employment, the mandates should decrease welfare receipt. The mandates will have little effect on people who would have worked full-time anyway.

Financial incentives have somewhat different expected effects. A single parent can obtain a higher total income under MFIP than AFDC if she works either part-time or full-time. For parents who would not have worked under AFDC, MFIP should increase their incentive to find a job. MFIP's incentives were relatively more generous for part-time work. Thus, parents who go to work may be more likely to take a part-time than a full-time job.

Some parents, however, would have returned to work in the absence of MFIP. Providing them with more generous benefits will not affect their decision about getting a job, but it may affect the intensity of their work effort. Consider a parent working 30 hours per week. MFIP provides her with higher benefits than she could have obtained under AFDC and, therefore, higher total income. If she cut back her work hours, substituting welfare benefits for earnings, she could receive the same total income as she would have received under AFDC but with less work. Note that she will not be encouraged to leave her job because MFIP's more generous benefits are only provided to parents who work. In contrast, because she can keep more of her benefits under MFIP compared with AFDC, as her earnings rise, she may be encouraged to increase her earnings further by increasing the number of hours worked. Thus, for parents who would have worked in the absence of MFIP, its incentives may either increase or decrease work intensity, depending on which of these two effects dominates.

For those who would not have worked in the absence of MFIP, the incentives should increase employment. MFIP may produce large increases in part-time employment, however, because its incentives are more generous for part-time work. The incentives should also increase welfare receipt, at least in the short term, given that they allow families that earn more to still receive some benefits.

How do we expect MFIP's effects to differ in urban and rural counties given the differences in characteristics previously noted? On the one hand, because rural recipients have more recent work experience and more of a sense of welfare stigma, they generally may be more likely to go to work in the absence of MFIP. In this case, we would expect MFIP to have less of an effect on their employment and earnings compared with urban recipients. On the other hand, MFIP's participation requirements may be more effective for a group of welfare recipients who are better prepared to work, such as the rural recipients, and, in this case, MFIP may have a more positive effect on rural recipients compared with urban recipients.

**Basic Empirical Estimation**

To evaluate the effects of MFIP relative to the AFDC system, recipients were randomly assigned to either the AFDC system or the MFIP system. Random assignment provides a powerful tool for estimating program effects. Because sample members were assigned randomly in a lottery-like process, the characteristics of individuals in each research group should not differ systematically at the time of random assignment, known as "baseline." Therefore, any significant differences in outcomes between these research groups can be attributed to the program, and a comparison of the outcomes for families assigned to each group provides a reliable estimate of MFIP's impact.[10]  Because changes in employment and earnings somewhat mirror changes in the receipt of welfare or the amount of welfare payments, the focus of this study is on earnings and employment rather than welfare receipt or payments.  A unique feature of the MFIP evaluation is that both rural and urban counties were included in the evaluation.  To assess whether MFIP's effects differed by region, the impact was estimated separately for recipients in urban counties and rural counties.

## IMPACTS IN RURAL AND URBAN COUNTIES

Figure 10.1 presents MFIP's impact on quarterly employment and earnings for two years after random assignment.  The results are based on administrative data on employment from unemployment insurance records.  Average quarterly employment rates for the MFIP and AFDC groups in the urban counties (left panel of Figure 10.1) both increased steadily over the follow-up period.  Rates for the MFIP group, however, increased at a faster rate than their AFDC counterparts.  In quarter five, for example, 49.6 percent of the MFIP group was employed compared with 33.1 percent of the AFDC group.  MFIP increased employment an average of 13–14 percentage points per quarter throughout the two-year follow-up.

MFIP's effects on earnings in urban areas are similar to its effects on employment.  Both groups see an increase in average earnings throughout the follow-up period, and the increase is larger and faster for members of the MFIP group.  These results persisted throughout the follow-up period.

MFIP's effects on earnings and employment in the rural counties (right panel, Figure 10.1) show that, as with urban counties, average employment and earnings for the MFIP and AFDC groups increased throughout the follow-up period.  However, average employment rates increased faster for the MFIP group in earlier quarters.  In later quarters (corresponding to the second year of follow-up), the difference in employment rates for the AFDC and MFIP groups decreased somewhat, and the AFDC group began to catch up with the MFIP group.  Average employment rates for the MFIP group were nearly 12 percentage points

**Figure 10.1  Quarterly Employment and Earnings for Long-Term Recipients in Urban and Rural Counties**

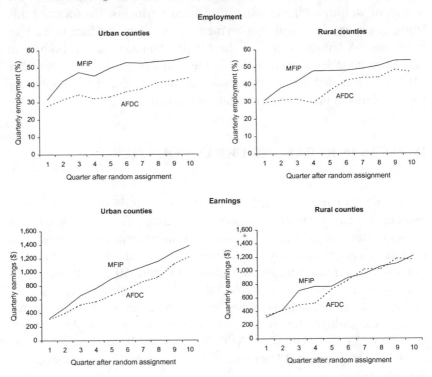

SOURCE: MDRC calculations using data from Minnesota's unemployment insurance (UI) earnings records.

higher than the AFDC group in the first five quarters.  By quarter six, the difference in employment rates between the MFIP and AFDC group was only 6 percentage points and no longer significant.

The effects of MFIP on average earnings follow a similar pattern. In fact, in later quarters, the MFIP group had lower earnings on average than the AFDC group despite having somewhat higher employment rates (Figure 10.1, bottom right panel).  Positive effects on employment rates without positive effects on earnings suggests that some parents in the MFIP group who would have worked anyway reduced their hours worked.  As noted earlier, this is one of the potential effects of en-

hanced financial incentives. Although not shown, MFIP increased income (measured from welfare and earnings) for recipients in urban and
rural counties. However, income increases for urban recipients were
both from more earnings and more welfare income, whereas income increases for rural recipients derived primarily from more welfare income. MFIP's effects on annual employment and welfare receipt are
presented in Table 10.3. The types of jobs rural recipients obtained
were also somewhat different from those of their urban counterparts
(Table 10.4). Although there are some differences in impacts, the data
highlight differences in the types of jobs recipients secure in rural and
urban areas. A comparison of the two AFDC groups, for example,
shows that although more rural recipients reported working during the
period, more of them were working part-time. In addition, their wages
were lower on average—a higher fraction of rural workers earned
$5–$7 per hour.

Looking in more detail at the effects in the rural counties, Figure
10.2 presents MFIP's impacts on earnings for each individual rural
county, using administrative records data for the full sample. Because
the sample sizes for each individual county are fairly small, none of the
effects are statistically significant. Nonetheless, the figure shows that
the impacts are smaller in the rural counties when grouped together
largely because of MFIP's negative effects in Sherburne County. The
pattern in Sherburne County indicates that, in the first five quarters,
MFIP increased earnings, but in quarter six, the pattern changes, and
MFIP actually lowered earnings in later quarters. MFIP's effects in
Sherburne County, however, do not explain the entire story. The effects
in the other three rural counties are also, on average, smaller than those
in the urban counties.

Part of the explanation for the different impacts in Sherburne
County may be that employment and earnings were very high for the
AFDC group; although not shown, 55 percent of the AFDC group
worked in each quarter, compared with only 33 percent to 43 percent in
the other counties. Programs typically have a more difficult time increasing employment when so many of the participants would have
worked anyway. Also, as mentioned earlier, MFIP's financial incentives might reduce earnings on average for recipients who would have
worked anyway by causing some of them to cut back on their work

**Table 10.3  Summary of MFIP's Impacts on Employment and Welfare for Single-Parent, Long-Term Recipients in Urban and Rural Counties**

| Outcome | Urban counties | | | Rural counties | | |
|---|---|---|---|---|---|---|
| | MFIP | AFDC | Impact (difference) | MFIP | AFDC | Impact (difference) |
| Employment and earnings | | | | | | |
| Average quarterly employment (%) | | | | | | |
| Year 1 | 46.0 | 32.8 | 13.3*** | 43.8 | 32.0 | 11.8*** |
| Year 2 | 53.2 | 39.3 | 13.9*** | 50.3 | 44.5 | 5.8* |
| Average quarterly earnings ($) | | | | | | |
| Year 1 | 699 | 537 | 163*** | 665 | 536 | 128 |
| Year 2 | 1,129 | 913 | 216*** | 1,002 | 1,019 | –17 |
| Welfare receipt[a] | | | | | | |
| Average quarterly receipt rate (%) | | | | | | |
| Year 1 | 92.4 | 90.7 | 1.7* | 92.8 | 87.6 | 5.2** |
| Year 2 | 81.0 | 75.7 | 5.3*** | 81.9 | 69.5 | 12.4*** |
| Average quarterly benefit ($) | | | | | | |
| Year 1 | 1,964 | 1,810 | 154*** | 1,915 | 1,646 | 269*** |
| Year 2 | 1,627 | 1,484 | 143*** | 1,583 | 1,192 | 391*** |
| Sample size (total = 2,373) | 846 | 934 | | 295 | 298 | |

NOTE: The sample includes members randomly assigned from April 1, 1994, to March 31, 1996, excluding the small percentage who were receiving or applying only for food stamps at random assignment. A two-tailed t-test is applied to regression-adjusted impact estimates. Statistical significance levels are indicated as *** = 1%; ** = 5%; * = 10%.

[a] Welfare receipt is defined as receipt of either food stamp coupons or cash benefits from AFDC, Family General Assistance, or MFIP. Average welfare benefits are the sum of benefits from any of these sources.

SOURCE: MDRC calculations using data from Minnesota's unemployment insurance (UI) earnings records and public assistance benefit records.

hours. This type of effect was found in the urban counties for recent applicants and for a subgroup of long-term recipients with recent work experience (see Miller et al. 2000).

Further analysis showed that Sherburne County differed from the other rural counties in a number of ways, one being its lower unemployment rate. Although all of the rural counties are concentrated in the eastern part of the state, Sherburne County is closest to the urban areas, bordering Anoka County. In general, rural counties that were close to urban areas may have experienced faster job growth during the early 1990s than more remote rural areas (Conoway 1998). In a separate chapter in this volume, McKernan et al. (p. 257) also found that among rural counties, employment opportunities were better if the county was adjacent to a metropolitan area. Recipients in Sherburne County also differed in many ways from recipients in the other three rural counties. Although the data are not shown, Sherburne County recipients were somewhat younger on average, were more likely to be white, and were more likely to have children under age 6 when they entered the study.

In terms of employment prospects, recipients in Sherburne County were more likely than other rural recipients to have had recent work experience and more had obtained a high school diploma or a higher degree. They were also much more likely to have been enrolled in education or training (primarily vocational education and skills training) at the time of random assignment. All of these differences are consistent with the fact that the AFDC group in Sherburne County had much higher employment rates and average earnings than the AFDC groups in the other three counties (Figure 10.2). Recipients in Sherburne County were also more likely to perceive stigma associated with welfare compared with their rural counterparts, and they were more likely to report transportation and child care as barriers to employment.

In summary, MFIP increased employment in both urban and rural counties. However, in contrast to the large and lasting employment increases in urban counties, MFIP's effects faded considerably by the second year in the rural areas. Much of the difference for the rural counties is driven by MFIP's effects in Sherburne County. However, MFIP's effects in the other three counties are still, on average, smaller than in the urban counties.

Table 10.4  MFIP's Impact on Household Composition, Marital Status, and Characteristic of Current or Most Recent Job for Long-Term Recipients in Rural and Urban Counties

| Outcome | Urban counties | | | Rural counties | | |
|---|---|---|---|---|---|---|
| | MFIP | AFDC | Impact (difference) | MFIP | AFDC | Impact (difference) |
| For most recent or current job (%) | | | | | | |
| Worked since random assignment | 85.2 | 73.7 | 11.6*** | 86.7 | 82.2 | 4.5 |
| Part-time (less than 30 hr.) | 22.3 | 18.1 | 4.2 | 28.4 | 24.4 | 4.0 |
| Full-time (more than 30 hr.) | 62.8 | 54.8 | 8.0** | 58.3 | 57.8 | 0.5 |
| Wage rate | | | | | | |
| Less than $5 | 5.3 | 6.6 | -1.4 | 7.5 | 7.1 | 0.4 |
| $5 to $6.99 | 22.2 | 17.5 | 4.7 | 32.6 | 33.6 | -1.0 |
| $7 to $8.99 | 32.8 | 25.9 | 6.9** | 31.2 | 24.5 | 6.7 |
| $9 or above | 23.5 | 21.5 | 2.0 | 13.0 | 14.9 | -1.9 |
| Health benefits | 42.2 | 33.6 | 8.6** | 31.2 | 34.3 | -3.1 |
| No health benefits | 42.4 | 39.7 | 2.7 | 53.9 | 46.8 | 7.1 |
| Household composition | | | | | | |
| Size of household | 3.7 | 3.7 | 0.0 | 3.9 | 3.8 | 0.1 |
| Living with related adults (%) | 10.7 | 13.3 | -2.7 | 7.8 | 7.7 | 0.2 |
| Living with unrelated adults (%) | 5.5 | 7.4 | -1.9 | 17.4 | 21.7 | -4.4 |

| | | | | | | |
|---|---|---|---|---|---|---|
| Marital status (%) | | | | | | |
| Currently married | 8.6 | 5.8 | 2.8 | 23.4 | 15.6 | 7.9 |
| Divorced/separated | 27.1 | 29.0 | -2.0 | 28.3 | 32.8 | -4.6 |
| Never married | 47.3 | 49.3 | -2.0 | 26.0 | 27.7 | -1.7 |
| Currently cohabiting | 15.3 | 14.8 | 0.6 | 20.2 | 22.8 | -2.6 |
| Currently married or living with partner | 23.9 | 20.8 | 3.2 | 43.6 | 38.4 | 5.3 |
| Household sources of income (%) | | | | | | |
| Respondent earnings | 54.6 | 52.8 | 1.8 | 72.2 | 60.8 | 11.4* |
| Other household earnings | 24.3 | 28.8 | -4.5 | 46.9 | 46.0 | 0.9 |
| Child support | 14.5 | 19.3 | -4.8* | 32.4 | 31.9 | 0.4 |
| Public assistance | 65.1 | 59.7 | 5.4 | 51.0 | 51.9 | -0.8 |
| Other | 19.1 | 19.1 | -0.1 | 16.5 | 21.5 | -4.9 |
| Sample size (total = 976) | 372 | 352 | | 116 | 136 | |

NOTE: The sample includes members randomly assigned from April 1, 1994, to March 31, 1996, excluding the small percentage who were receiving or applying only for food stamps at random assignment. A two-tailed t-test is applied to regression-adjusted impact estimates. Statistical significance levels are indicated as *** = 1 percent; ** = 5 percent; * = 10 percent.

SOURCE: MDRC calculations using data from Minnesota's unemployment insurance (UI) earnings records and public assistance benefit records and the 36-month survey.

**Figure 10.2  Quarterly Earnings for Long-Term Recipients
in Rural Counties**

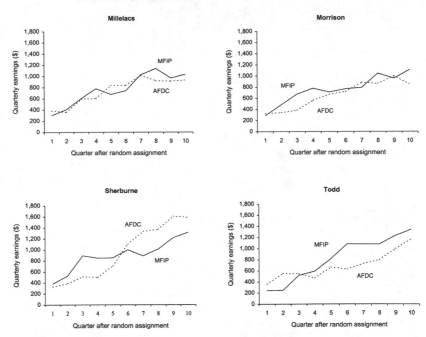

SOURCE: MDRC calculations using data from Minnesota's unemployment insurance
(UI) earnings records.

## DISCUSSION

There are a number of possible reasons why the effects of MFIP
differed in rural and urban counties.  First, the recipients themselves
may differ in ways that are related to how they are affected by the program.  As previously discussed, urban and rural recipients differ across
a range of demographic characteristics and thus may have been affected by the program differently.  It is easy to imagine, for example, that
MFIP might have smaller effects on recipients who had recent work experience, given that many would probably have worked in the absence

of the program.  If rural recipients, on average, were more employable than their urban counterparts, MFIP might have smaller effects in rural areas.  Further statistical analysis showed that, for the three rural counties (excluding Sherburne County), marital status, prior work experience, and child care problems explain much of the difference in MFIP's effects in rural and urban counties.

It is easy to understand why the program's effects might differ by prior employment status, given that employment effects are likely to be smaller among those who would have worked anyway.  But why would its effects vary by prior marital status?  One hypothesis is that rural recipients who are more likely to have been previously married may also be more likely to receive child support income.  This, in turn, may allow them to rely less on their own earnings.  For example, previously married, rural welfare recipients may be more likely than their urban counterparts to cut back on work both because they have the safety net of MFIP's additional benefits and because they receive child support income.  Table 10.4 offers some support for this hypothesis.  Rural recipients in both the MFIP and control groups are nearly twice as likely to receive child support income in the month prior to the survey compared with urban recipients.

An alternative hypothesis is that prior marital status is a good predictor of the likelihood of remarriage or cohabitation during the follow-up period, which, in turn, may affect individual work effort.  Although not shown, the survey data revealed that previously married women were more likely than never-married women to be formally married by the end of the third year, but they were not more likely to be cohabiting (either formally married or living with a partner), with the exception of Sherburne County.  In addition, recipients in rural areas were more likely to be married or coupled than urban recipients, regardless of their prior marital status.

Another possible reason for the different effects is that MFIP may have affected other aspects of family life differently in urban and rural areas, which, in turn, led to different effects on employment and earnings.  The survey data allowed us to estimate program effects on a range of other outcomes, such as household composition and marital status.  MFIP's effects on these selected outcomes for both regions are shown in Table 10.4.  In general, the impact was similar in urban and rural counties. For example, MFIP generally had no effect on household composition or sources of household income for recipients in both urban and rural counties, except that rural recipients were more likely to report some earnings in the month prior to the survey. This finding is somewhat inconsistent with employment effects (shown in Figure 10.1) found from administrative records data. However, although MFIP's effects on marital status were not significant for urban and rural recipients, a larger proportion of rural recipients were married at 36 months compared with urban recipients.

MFIP might have had different effects on women who cohabited or married after random assignment given that they would have less of a need to work. (Note that MFIP's participation mandates require that only one parent work or participate in services, and either parent can fill this requirement.) In fact, for two-parent families, MFIP did not affect the likelihood that at least one parent was employed, but it did decrease the likelihood that both parents worked; in other words, at least one parent cut back his or her work effort (Miller et al. 2000). Furthermore, results from the Negative Income Tax experiments and, more recently, from research on the Earned Income Tax Credit show that married women reduced their labor supply more, relative to single women, in response to extra financial benefits (Munnell 1986; Eissa and Hoynes 1998). Nonexperimental analysis does suggest that MFIP had larger employment effects for women who were not married or cohabiting at the time of the survey compared with those who were.

Finally, the differences in program effects across the two areas may arise from differences in the local environments. It is not always clear how the local economy might affect a program's impact, but perhaps jobs were more readily available to recipients in urban counties, or perhaps the types of jobs available in rural and urban areas differed. Further analysis provided some evidence that the local economy alone cannot explain the differences in MFIP's effects. If the local economy were the primary explanation, then we would expect that most subgroups of the population in rural counties would be equally affected by MFIP. Instead, we found that MFIP had very different effects on different groups of individuals in rural counties, the most striking being those defined by prior marital status.

# CONCLUSION

Unlike patterns in urban areas, caseload declines in rural areas have not corresponded with increases in employment or reductions in poverty. Furthermore, the effects of the 1996 welfare reform legislation in rural versus urban regions are not well understood. Our study sought to inform the gap in this research about the role of regional differences in welfare policy. In contrast to the large and lasting effects on employment and earnings in urban counties, the Minnesota Family Investment Program's effects on employment faded considerably in the rural counties by the second year. Moreover, the program's effects became negative in the second year in one of the rural counties.

We raised several hypotheses to explain this pattern of impacts. Some of them were able to be tested with these data and some were not. One hypothesis was that rural recipients differ from their urban counterparts. The evaluation data show that rural recipient families differ from their urban counterparts both in terms of demographic characteristics and in their work experience and attitudes or perceptions about welfare and work. In particular, compared with urban recipients, more of the rural recipients are white, had been previously married, and appeared better prepared to enter the workforce. Moreover, rural recipients were more likely to report a sense of stigma associated with receiving welfare.

We find that differences in observable characteristics, particularly prior marital status and work experience, can explain much of MFIP's different effects in three of the rural counties. However, these factors explain little of the difference in the one remaining rural county. The different effects in this county may be due to the local economy, or other aspects particular to that county, or to unobservable differences in characteristics between its recipients and other recipients. The findings in this chapter provide evidence that regional differences play an important role in mediating the effects of welfare and antipoverty policies on the employment behavior of welfare recipients, and lend support to recent efforts to consider regional differences when formulating these policies. The current statewide version of MFIP is one example of such an effort, as counties, rather than the state, are allowed to determine the length of welfare receipt prior to imposing participation requirements.

# Notes

Corresponding author, Lisa Gennetian, MDRC, 16 East 34th Street, New York, New York, 10016; lisa_gennetian@mdrc.org. This research was supported by funding from the Minnesota Department of Human Services, the Ford Foundation, the U.S. Department of Health and Human Services, the U.S. Department of Agriculture, the Charles Stewart Mott Foundation, the Annie E. Casey Foundation, the McKnight Foundation, and the Northwest Area Foundation. Many thanks for helpful comments from Joel Kvamme, Greg Duncan, Kathy Edin, Virginia Knox, and Bo Beaulieu.

1.  STRIDE was operated with funding from the Job Opportunities and Basic Skills Training (JOBS) program, which was established by the Family Support Act of 1988 and designed to move people from welfare to work through education, training, and work experience.
2.  The FGA program was designed to allow certain types of families to receive cash assistance who did not qualify for AFDC. In particular, some two-parent families who did not qualify for AFDC due to the stringent work history requirements or the 100 hour per month restriction on working in the AFDC-UP program could reapply and qualify for the FGA program. Benefit levels for families that qualified for the FGA program were the same as in AFDC.
3.  Throughout this paper, the terms "welfare" and "public assistance" are used to present the range of benefits that are provided in either the MFIP or AFDC systems, including MFIP, AFDC, FGA, and Food Stamps.
4.  The three urban counties included Hennepin (Minneapolis), Anoka, and Dakota. The four rural counties included Mille Lacs, Morrison, Sherburne, and Todd.
5.  In urban counties, single-parent families could also be randomly assigned to The MFIP Incentives Only group. These families were not required to participate in employment related services. In Hennepin County (Minneapolis) only, some families were also randomly assigned to a fourth group, an AFDC/No Services group. This group continued to receive assistance under the AFDC system but was not eligible to receive STRIDE services, to allow an evaluation of the STRIDE program compared to providing no employment and training services.
6.  A small proportion of the AFDC group received cash assistance from the FGA program instead of AFDC.
7.  The survey sample is representative of the full administrative records sample. Non-response analyses also indicate that random assignment worked; baseline characteristics of experimental group members are similar to the characteristics of control group members (see Miller et al. 2000).
8.  The sample sizes do not reflect the composition of the caseload in the seven counties, because only a fraction of the caseload in the three urban counties was in-

cluded in the evaluation.  In the rural counties, in contrast, the entire caseload was randomly assigned to either the MFIP or AFDC research groups.

9.   Over 95 percent of the sample is female.

10.   All impacts are tested for statistical significance. Only those impacts that are statistically significant using a two-tailed $t$-test at the 10 percent level are deemed program impacts.  Significance tests are based on the fact that some estimated impacts, or differences between the groups, may arise solely by chance or random variation.  Impacts that are statistically significant can be thought of, with a reasonable degree of confidence, as representing a true difference between the groups, rather than a difference arising by chance.

# References

Conoway, C.   1998.   "From Uncertainty to Optimism: Minnesota's Rural Workforce in the 1990's."  *Minnesota Economic Trends*.  Department of Economic Security, Research and Statistics Office, St. Paul, Minnesota.

Eissa, N., and H. Hoynes.  1998.  "The Earned Income Tax Credit and the Labor Supply of Married Couples."  Unpublished manuscript, Department of Economics, University of California, Berkeley.

Gennetian, Lisa, and Cynthia Miller.  2000.  *Reforming Welfare and Rewarding Work:  Final Report on the Minnesota Family Investment Program. Volume 2: Effects on Children*.  New York: Manpower Demonstration Research Corporation.

Miller, Cynthia, Virginia Knox, Lisa Gennetian, J.A. Hunter, M. Dodoo, and Cindy Redcross.  2000.  *Reforming Welfare and Rewarding Work: Final Report on the Minnesota Family Investment Program.  Volume 1: Effects on Adults*.  New York: Manpower Demonstration Research Corporation.

Munnell, A.H.   1986.  *Lessons from the Income Maintenance Experiments: Proceedings of a Conference Held in September 1986*.  Boston: Federal Reserve Bank of Boston and Washington, D.C.: The Brookings Institution.

Rural Policy Research Institute.   1999.  *Rural America and Welfare Reform: An Overview Assessment*.  Available at <http://www.rupri.org/pubs/archive/old/welfare/p99-3/index.html>, accessed April 2000.

U.S. House of Representatives, Committee on Ways and Means.  1996.  *1996 Green Book: Background Material and Data on Programs within the Jurisdiction of the Committee on Ways and Means*.  Washington, D.C.: U.S. Government Printing Office.

# 11
# Will Attainable Jobs Be Available for TANF Recipients in Local Labor Markets?

## Evidence from Mississippi on Prospects for "Job-Skill Matching" of TANF Adults

Frank M. Howell
*Mississippi State University*

One of the keys of the Personal Responsibility and Work Opportunity Reconciliation Act (PRWORA) is the welfare-to-work transition provision, which institutes a maximum 60-month "lifetime" benefit window for recipients of Temporary Assistance for Needy Families (TANF) and requires them to find paid employment somewhere in the extant labor force. In many ways, this welfare-to-work transition constitutes the most important element of the welfare reform initiative because it reflects the most tenuous element of the "social contract" set by Congress in legitimating the PRWORA. This chapter examines what is most likely to happen to TANF recipients in Mississippi as they negotiate this legal mandate. As I show below, there is a significant spatial unevenness in the prospects for TANF beneficiaries to compete for paying jobs in their local labor market areas. I match the educational credentials of the 1996 cohort of TANF recipients in Mississippi to the types of new jobs projected to materialize across the state during a five-year window, from 1997–2002, as a means of discerning these prospects. I then compare these results by labor market areas. The results identify substantial variation in job prospects, with some rural labor markets holding little promise for those moving off of welfare to successfully compete for new jobs, while other labor markets appear positioned to fare much better.

A large proportion of the Mississippi population falls beneath the official poverty line. Estimates based on an experimental model by the U.S. Bureau of the Census show that, in 1993, almost one-fourth (24.6 percent) of the Mississippi population lived in poverty (Howell 1997a). With the exception of Louisiana (23.9 percent), Mississippi's poverty rate was substantially higher than surrounding states in the region. With the economic progress of the 1990s, this figure had declined by 1997 (to 18.1 percent) but remains only slightly ahead of Louisiana (18.3 percent) (Bureau of the Census 2000). Mississippi also has a higher proportion of working-age adults (ages 16–64) with work-related disabilities than other states in the region (Howell 1997b). Thus, Mississippi suffers greatly by comparison to its neighboring states in terms of the share of its population that is poor and that has physical disabilities that inhibit them from holding steady employment. What we know very little about is the capacity of local labor markets in Mississippi to "absorb" persons who are scheduled to move from welfare programs to active paid employment (Howell 1997c).

## PURPOSE OF THE STUDY

I examine two key aspects of the transition to work under the provisions of welfare reform legislation in Mississippi—the ability of labor markets to absorb TANF recipients and the availability of child care. I then relate these to the rural-urban continuum as measured through the USDA's urban influence classification for Mississippi counties (Ghelfi and Parker 1997).

I estimate the prospects for local labor markets to "absorb" the 1996 cohort of TANF recipients by "matching" their current educational credentials with the projected job growth in fields that require only minimum educational levels. The period examined (1997–2002) corresponds with the 60-month lifetime limit for receiving TANF under welfare reform. This effort builds on my previous work (Howell 1997c) that documented dramatic regional variation in the crude "absorption capacity" of Mississippi labor markets to handle this cohort of TANF recipients without regard to their educational credentials. I identify licensed child care facilities in each county within the labor market area and their spatial distribution to ascertain the relative availability of these services for TANF recipients.


## BACKGROUND


There is a growing recognition that the welfare-to-work transition is pivotal to the success of welfare reform, and also that it is fraught with barriers impeding successful employment by those on the welfare rolls (Danziger, in this volume, p. 25). Although the concern over what drives public assistance caseloads and, specifically, how the economy shapes or determines them, is an important avenue of inquiry (see, e.g., Blank 1997a, b; Blank and Ruggles 1996; Congressional Budget Office 1993; Kuhn, LeBlanc, and Gundersen 1997; Martini and Wiseman 1997; Ziliak et al. 1997), an important issue is the extent to which TANF beneficiaries who are scheduled to leave the program have likely job prospects in their local labor market. The so-called capacity of local labor markets to successfully absorb former TANF recipients is perhaps the pivotal issue in the 1996 welfare reform legislation as attention now turns to what happens to the TANF population that has left the welfare rolls (Lichter and Jensen, in this volume, p. 77).

A few research studies lend insight into both the employment prospects for TANF beneficiaries and the local economy's effect on caseloads. Unfortunately, most of these studies focus on urban settings and give short shrift to rural America's labor markets (for exceptions, see Gennetian, Redcross, and Miller, in this volume, p. 287; McKernan et al., in this volume, p. 257; and Lichter and Jensen). I briefly review some of these broader efforts.

Work by Leete and colleagues is particularly insightful in that they articulate many of the theoretical and practical issues surrounding the capacity for local labor markets in Cleveland, Ohio, to accommodate individuals receiving TANF benefits (Leete and Bania 1996). In evaluating the demand for jobs created by almost 20,000 former Aid to Families with Dependent Children (AFDC) recipients entering the labor market in the Cleveland-Akron metropolitan area, the authors find that the area must double or triple the number of low-skilled job openings over the next year to accommodate those scheduled to leave the cash assistance program.  It is important to note that this study is distinctly urban in its focus, and the results may not be generalizable to rural, nonmetropolitan areas of the United States.

In a separate analysis of the same study area, Leete, Bania, and Coulton (1998) examined the degree of spatial "mismatch" between job openings and beneficiaries.  Their key findings were that cash assistance (then AFDC) recipients were highly concentrated in inner-city locations and geographically isolated from prospective jobs.  Supporting the "spatial mismatch" hypothesis, most of the projected low-skill job growth is likely to be in the suburban fringes of the metropolitan area.  Moreover, most of those suburban jobs are inaccessible to recipients via public transportation because only 8–15 percent of these jobs are within the 20-minute commute time used to define "accessible" jobs.

In an earlier study (Howell 1997c), I focused on the capacity of local labor markets in Mississippi to absorb persons who are scheduled to leave TANF.  This approach differs considerably from that used by Leete and colleagues in Cleveland in several important ways, including the use of both rural and metropolitan labor market definitions as well as projections of all types of jobs (i.e., total employment) rather than just low-skill jobs.  I created an "absorption index" of the local labor market's capacity to incorporate AFDC recipients into the paid labor force, spread over a three-year transition period and then recalculated for labor market areas (LMAs) in Mississippi.  The labor market area index better reflects the local area's ability to generate jobs to match the requirements of the new welfare program.  Briefly, these results showed great regional variability in the likelihood for job growth that will match the welfare-to-work transition introduced by PRWORA.

This exploration of the capacity of Mississippi's labor markets to generate new jobs was, indeed, exploratory.  It used projected employment that, although historically quite accurate, may not prove so over the period considered.  The method is "optimistic" in the sense that it only examines the crude ratio of one year of AFDC recipients to projections of total employment growth, without matching job requirements to persons seeking employment.  It also assumes that welfare recipients will search for jobs only within their current labor market area.  Moreover, the total employment projection used in Howell (1997c) makes one additional crucial assumption: that all TANF beneficiaries will compete equally for any and all job growth, both with each other and with non-welfare job-seekers. This simplifying assumption, of course, is not very realistic. There is a need to match the educational and training characteristics of TANF beneficiaries and the projected job growth in the state's labor markets before debating how well economic prosperity will facilitate the transition to work among welfare recipients.

## RESEARCH METHODS

### Sources of Data

The data for this study come from several different sources: administrative records of the Mississippi Department of Human Services for data on AFDC/TANF caseloads; administrative records from the Mississippi Department of Health for data on licensed child care facilities; and proprietary data obtained from Wessex, Inc., on estimates of county-level employment by occupational class for 1997 and projections through 2003. To protect the proprietary nature of these data, I do not report any detailed counts from the Wessex data set at the county level, but I have aggregated them to the multicounty Labor Market Area (LMA), given that an infinite number of combinations of the county-level estimates or projections could sum to the LMA estimate. Other spatial data were obtained from the U.S. Bureau of the Census TIGER database and the proprietary ESRI StreetMap database of streets and address ranges for locating physical address locations. More details can be found in Howell (2000).

### Measurement of Variables

#### TANF caseloads, by education

The numbers of TANF recipients by county during the 12 months of 1996 were obtained from the Mississippi Department of Human Services (DHS). Counts were received for each month by education level for adult recipients. Using the "peak-month" monthly count for each county, I collapsed educational levels into three categories: less than high school; high school only; and postsecondary school (including baccalaureate degrees or above).[1]

## Occupational groupings

Data on estimates and projections of employment by major occupational class were obtained from Wessex's proprietary database. Although it would be ideal to have detailed occupational classifications, such as either the three-digit Standard Occupational Classification used extensively by the Bureau of the Census or those found in the *Occupational Outlook Handbook* from the Department of Labor, such data in public-use form were unavailable. The major classes were collapsed to represent: a) "white-collar" jobs, composed of executives, professionals, technical, and sales; b) "skilled-worker" jobs, composed of clerical, protective services, production workers, and other services; and c) "unskilled-worker" jobs, composed of operators, materials handlers, unskilled laborers, and private household workers.

## Urban influence county code

This classification scheme was developed by the U.S. Department of Agriculture (USDA) Economic Research Service (ERS) and published in Ghelfi and Parker (1997). Its taxonomy classifies counties in terms of the level of "urban influence" as of 1990 and contains nine codes:

1) large metropolitan areas, with 1 million or more residents;
2) small metropolitan areas, with fewer than 1 million residents;
3) adjacent to a large metropolitan area with a city of 10,000 or more residents;
4) adjacent to a large metropolitan area without a city of 10,000 or more residents;
5) adjacent to a small metropolitan area with a city of 10,000 or more residents;
6) adjacent to a small metropolitan area without a city of 10,000 or more residents;
7) not adjacent to any metropolitan area but with a city of 10,000 or more residents;

8) not adjacent to any metropolitan area and with the largest city in the county between 2,500 and 9,999 residents; and

9) not adjacent to any metropolitan area with the population of largest city in the county under 2,500 residents.

The scheme is used as a base coverage for several maps used in the analysis of other data.

### Labor market area (LMA)

Using the concept of "labor market area," I constructed multicounty groups, which composed the LMAs designated through commuting-zone patterns by Tolbert and Sizer (1996) for 1990. The counties composing each LMA are illustrated in each map through a GIS procedure called a "polygon overlay" (LMA boundaries superimposed over constituent county polygons) and can be specifically identified in Tolbert and Sizer. In some maps, each LMA is labeled according to the rural-urban classification, ranging from "major metropolitan" to "small urban" labor market in Mississippi.

### Licensed child care facilities

The Mississippi Department of Health maintains a database of child care facilities in the state that are awarded licensed status under the terms of the state's requirements for licensure. I geocoded each facility using ESRI's Streetmap database, a version of GDT's Dynamap 1000 product (see Environmental Systems Research Institute 1997). For each facility, the maximum number of children who can be served under the terms of the license, the current number of children enrolled, the typical number of openings for additional children, and the number of employees at the facility were included into the final data set. These data were summarized at the county and LMA level in some portions of the analysis.

### Job-matching ratio

This is the ratio of TANF recipients in 1996 to the projected job growth over the period 1997–2002. This period matches the 60-month window set forth in PRWORA for maximum lifetime benefits available under TANF. The *raw job-matching ratio* is the sum of ratios of 1996

TANF recipients to the projected change in jobs during 1997–2002 for the three job classes of unskilled, skilled, and white-collar occupations. The *weighted job-matching ratio* is the raw job-matching ratio weighted by the proportions of 1996 TANF recipients in the three educational groups (less than a high school diploma, a high school diploma, and postsecondary education). The composite or weighted job-matching ratio is an estimated "absorption index" of the capacity of a local area to "absorb" TANF cohort members into jobs that match their educational credentials. An issue arises for both job-matching ratios when projected employment growth is negative; that is, a net job loss is forecast for the area. In these instances, the resulting job-matching ratio simply reflects the relative magnitude of TANF recipients to the projected *loss* in jobs over the period. Because this negative ratio does not follow the intended metric for the job-matching ratio, I simply label it as "job loss" in tables or maps.

## LABOR MARKET CAPACITY FOR ABSORBING WELFARE CASELOADS

### Cash Assistance Caseload Trends

I first examine trends in the AFDC/TANF caseload during most of the decade of the 1990s. Like most other states, Mississippi experienced a dramatic downturn in caseloads during welfare reform, and this decline began in virtually all labor market areas as early as 1993 (Howell 2000). However, the spatial nature of LMA-specific declines is important to note in the context of this study. In Figure 11.1, I compare the declines for the 1991–1998 period among LMAs for the state capital area, Jackson, with the Mississippi Delta region (including the Clarksdale and Greenville labor markets) and other metro and nonmetro labor markets. Two major findings can be drawn from Figure 11.1. The first is that the impoverished Delta region, comprising the Clarksdale and Greenville LMAs, is not where "most" of the TANF caseload was located in Mississippi, contrary to some public opinion. The Jackson metropolitan LMA by far held the single largest caseload

**Figure 11.1  Comparative Declines in Mississippi's TANF Caseloads, 1991–98**

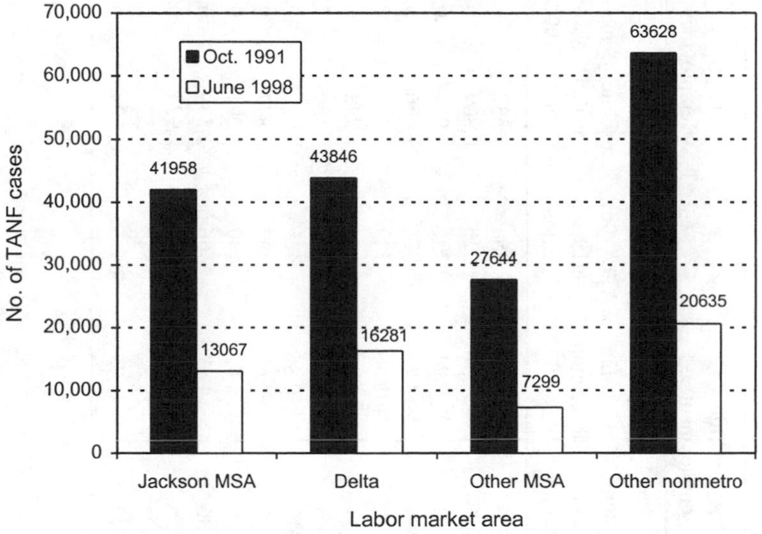

during the early 1990s.  In fact, the other various nonmetropolitan labor markets collectively had a far larger TANF caseload.

The second point is that the metropolitan LMA groups had the largest percent declines in caseloads over the 1991–1998 period (Jackson, –68.9%; Other MSA, –73.6%), although all four groups experienced TANF declines of about two-thirds (Delta, –62.9%; Other nonmetro, –67.6%).  Thus, the highly impoverished Delta labor markets had slightly smaller reductions in TANF caseloads, as a percentage of the 1991 base figure, and composed a moderate absolute size of the state's entire TANF caseload by 1998.  The single labor market area with the largest number of TANF recipients over this entire period was the Jackson metropolitan market.

**Supply Side: Education Levels and Available Jobs**

The distribution of 1996 TANF recipients by educational level across Mississippi's labor market areas is key to determining how effective the welfare-to-work transition will be.  Table 11.1 lists the num-

**Table 11.1  AFDC/TANF Caseload by Education Level, 1996, with Estimates of "Job-Matching" and the Capacity to Absorb 1996 TANF Beneficiaries during 1997–2002**

| Labor market area (1990) | AFDC 96: total caseload | AFDC 96: <H.S. education | "HS unskilled" employment Absolute growth, 1997 (est.) | "HS unskilled" employment Job-matching absorption, 1997–2002 | AFDC 96: HS education | "HS skilled" employment Absolute growth, 1997–2002 | "HS skilled" employment Job-matching absorption, 1997–2002 |
|---|---|---|---|---|---|---|---|
| Biloxi-Gulfport-Pascagoula MSA | 2,205 | 930 | 1,630 | 0.57 | 858 | 7,532 | 0.11 |
| Jackson MSA | 4,947 | 2,227 | 886 | 2.51 | 2,070 | 6,809 | 0.30 |
| Memphis, TN-AR-MS MSA | 903 | 412 | 1,708 | 0.24 | 391 | 4,974 | 0.08 |
| N-m[a] Clarksdale | 2,560 | 1,312 | 99 | 13.25 | 874 | 1,656 | 0.53 |
| N-m Columbus | 1,838 | 803 | −2[b] | −401.50[c] | 749 | 1,386 | 0.54 |
| N-m Corinth | 210 | 104 | 71 | 1.46 | 74 | 743 | 0.10 |
| N-m Greenville | 3,450 | 1,828 | −206[b] | −8.87[c] | 1,189 | 556 | 2.14 |
| N-m Hattiesburg | 951 | 349 | 412 | 0.85 | 425 | 2,035 | 0.21 |
| N-m Laurel | 551 | 244 | 52 | 4.69 | 237 | 877 | 0.27 |
| N-m McComb | 1,261 | 588 | 130 | 4.52 | 499 | 1,091 | 0.46 |
| N-m Meridian | 977 | 466 | 236 | 1.97 | 406 | 1,539 | 0.26 |
| N-m Tupelo | 602 | 343 | 756 | 0.45 | 214 | 2,923 | 0.07 |
| N-m Vicksburg | 1,388 | 603 | −32[b] | −18.84[c] | 529 | 578 | 0.92 |
| Statewide | 21,843 | 10,209 | 5,740 | 1.78 | 8,515 | 32,699 | 0.26 |

**Table 11.1  (Continued)**

| Labor market area (1990) | AFDC 96: post-HS education | "HS/white collar" employment | | | Absorption index, 1997–2002 | |
|---|---|---|---|---|---|---|
| | | Absolute growth, 1997–2002 | Job-matching absorption, 1997–2002 | | Crude | Composite job-matching |
| Biloxi-Gulfport-Pascagoula MSA | 417 | 7,400 | 0.06 | | 0.74 | 0.30 |
| Jackson MSA | 650 | 8,651 | 0.08 | | 2.89 | 1.27 |
| Memphis, TN-AR-MS MSA | 100 | 4,160 | 0.02 | | 0.34 | 0.15 |
| N-m[a] Clarksdale | 374 | 1,637 | 0.23 | | 14.01 | 7.01 |
| N-m Columbus | 286 | 1,497 | 0.19 | | -400.77[c] | -175.16[c] |
| N-m Corinth | 32 | 701 | 0.05 | | 1.61 | 0.77 |
| N-m Greenville | 433 | 519 | 0.83 | | -5.90[c] | -3.86[c] |
| N-m Hattiesburg | 177 | 2,296 | 0.08 | | 1.13 | 0.42 |
| N-m Laurel | 70 | 780 | 0.09 | | 5.05 | 2.21 |
| N-m McComb | 174 | 942 | 0.18 | | 5.17 | 2.32 |
| N-m Meridian | 105 | 1,443 | 0.07 | | 2.31 | 1.06 |
| N-m Tupelo | 45 | 2,820 | 0.02 | | 0.54 | 0.29 |
| N-m Vicksburg | 256 | 708 | 0.36 | | -17.57[c] | -7.77[c] |
| Statewide | 3,119 | 33,554 | 0.09 | | 2.13 | 0.95 |

[a] N-m = nonmetro.

[b] There is a projected job loss during the 1997–2002 period.

[c] These ratios are a function of the projected job loss during the period 1997–2002 (see note "a") and should not be interpreted substantively. Mathematically, they are the ratios of 1996 TANF recipients to the LMA's projected loss of jobs during the period.

SOURCE: Author's calculations based upon Mississippi Department of Human Services data and proprietary estimates from Wessex, Inc.

ber of 1996 AFDC/TANF recipients by education level for the 13 labor market areas in the state. These absolute counts are important in understanding the numbers of people who face the 60-month (lifetime) cut-off of cash assistance. These data are further summarized spatially in Figure 11.2, a map of the state's labor markets, the "urban influence" in their underlying counties, and the distribution of TANF education levels in the labor market area. In this map, each labor market area's TANF caseload by educational level is expressed as a percentage of the total caseload using a pie-chart symbol superimposed on each LMA. The raw counts in Table 11.2 and the percentages in Figure 11.2 each tell a different part of the story regarding the "supply-side" educational credentials of TANF beneficiaries across the state.

Table 11.1 shows that, in 1996, the LMAs of Jackson and Greenville had the largest pool of AFDC recipients. Jackson is a metropolitan-based labor market and the state capital, while Greenville is decidedly nonmetropolitan and in the heart of the Mississippi Delta. The nonmetro Clarksdale LMA, also in the Delta, and the metro Biloxi-Gulfport LMA, follow in rank order. In contrast to some assumptions about welfare beneficiaries (e.g., Blank 1997a; Leete and Bania 1996; Leete, Bania, and Coulton 1998), there are significant numbers of TANF recipients with post-high-school education. Other studies reviewed by McKernan et al. (in this volume, p. 257) suggest that between 9 percent and 26 percent of welfare recipients had postsecondary education. In fact, based on further analysis of data not shown in Table 11.1, a significant number of these recipients hold college degrees in several of these labor market areas.

Figure 11.2 contains a spatial visualization using pie-chart proportions of cases by educational level for each LMA. As the tabular numbers and the proportional pie-charts show, most welfare recipients in each labor market have less than a high school education, which is not surprising given the economic qualification requirements for AFDC/TANF and the fact that low education attainment is associated with lower income levels. What is surprising is the number of LMAs with at least one-fourth of the AFDC/TANF caseload with postsecondary education. Some of these are near the state's public universities or "high tech" government installations (e.g., NASA's Stennis Space Center in Hancock County).[2]    Thus, these data show that the AFDC/TANF program has also served as a support system for women

**Figure 11.2  TANF Recipient Education Levels by USAD Influence Code within Labor Market Areas**

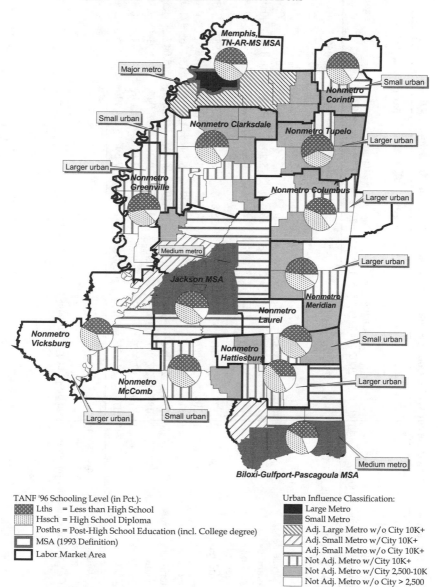

TANF '96 Schooling Level (in Pct.):

Lths   = Less than High School
Hssch = High School Diploma
Posths = Post-High School Education (incl. College degree)
MSA (1993 Definition)
Labor Market Area

Urban Influence Classification:

Large Metro
Small Metro
Adj. Large Metro w/o City 10K+
Adj. Small Metro w/City 10K+
Adj. Small Metro w/o City 10K+
Not Adj. Metro w/City 10K+
Not Adj. Metro w/City 2,500-10K
Not Adj. Metro w/o City > 2,500

SOURCE: U.S. Bureau of the Census; U.S. Dept. of Agriculture; Miss. Dept. of Human Services.

Table 11.2  Estimates and Projections of White-Collar, Skilled, and Unskilled Jobs in Mississippi, 1997–2002

| Labor market area (1990) | No. of white-collar jobs | | | No. of skilled jobs | | | No. of unskilled jobs | | |
|---|---|---|---|---|---|---|---|---|---|
| | 1997 | 2002 | Change (%) | 1997 | 2002 | Change (%) | 1997 | 2002 | Change (%) |
| Biloxi-Gulfport Pascagoula MSA | 67,686 | 75,086 | 10.93 | 71,057 | 78,589 | 10.60 | 27,327 | 28,957 | 5.96 |
| Jackson MSA | 108,021 | 116,672 | 8.01 | 100,026 | 106,835 | 6.81 | 41,694 | 42,580 | 2.13 |
| Memphis, TN-AR-MS MSA | 27,310 | 31,470 | 15.23 | 35,909 | 40,883 | 13.85 | 24,103 | 25,811 | 7.09 |
| N-m[a] Clarksdale | 28,362 | 29,999 | 5.77 | 28,875 | 30,531 | 5.74 | 18,455 | 18,554 | 0.54 |
| N-m Columbus | 25,758 | 27,255 | 5.81 | 26,643 | 28,029 | 5.20 | 16,438 | 16,436 | -0.01 |
| N-m Corinth | 9,577 | 10,278 | 7.32 | 11,495 | 12,238 | 6.46 | 10,414 | 10,485 | 0.68 |
| N-m Greenville | 18,526 | 19,045 | 2.80 | 18,235 | 18,791 | 3.05 | 10,856 | 10,650 | -1.90 |
| N-m Hattiesburg | 24,175 | 26,471 | 9.50 | 23,861 | 25,896 | 8.53 | 11,343 | 11,755 | 3.63 |
| N-m Laurel | 14,209 | 14,989 | 5.49 | 17,648 | 18,525 | 4.97 | 10,808 | 10,860 | 0.48 |
| N-m McComb | 16,519 | 17,461 | 5.70 | 19,516 | 20,607 | 5.59 | 13,026 | 13,156 | 1.00 |
| N-m Meridian | 21,626 | 23,069 | 6.67 | 24,300 | 25,839 | 6.33 | 14,811 | 15,047 | 1.59 |
| N-m Tupelo | 26,489 | 29,309 | 10.65 | 31,562 | 34,485 | 9.26 | 28,045 | 28,801 | 2.70 |
| N-m Vicksburg | 16,819 | 17,527 | 4.21 | 15,936 | 16,514 | 3.63 | 7,176 | 7,144 | -0.45 |
| Statewide | 405,077 | 438,631 | 8.28 | 425,063 | 457,762 | 7.69 | 234,496 | 240,236 | 2.44 |

NOTE: Values in all columns are estimates.
[a] N-m = nonmetro.
SOURCE: Author's calculations based upon proprietary estimates from Wessex, Inc.

with dependent children and who have more than minimal educational training and who live in labor markets with significant white-collar employment opportunities.

In summary, although most 1996 cash assistance recipients had less than a high school education, there is a significant variation in educational levels that most other studies of welfare reform have not empirically considered. Moreover, this variation in both the number and the relative share of post-high-school recipients occurs along spatial lines. This variation in human capital availability may well prove to be an important aspect of the welfare-to-work prospects of the state's TANF population.

**Demand Side: Employment**

To examine the employment, or "demand," side of the equation, I examine occupational composition, employment trends, and projected shifts in the 13 LMAs during 1997–2002. The projections in the net growth of jobs by occupational grouping are shown in Table 11.2. These include the number of jobs in 1997 and 2002, as well as the percentage change over the five-year period among white-collar, skilled, and unskilled workers. Figure 11.3 contains a spatial visualization of the percentage that each of these job classes contributes to the total projected employment growth within each LMA over the period. However, for slow-growth labor markets, the "small" total may appear magnified by this proportionate representation. Together, this table and figure summarize our estimate of the "demand side" of the differences among LMAs that vary along the rural-urban continuum.

In Table 11.2, there are different patterns of growth projected for white-collar, skilled, and unskilled jobs in Mississippi's labor market areas. First, there are relatively low levels of growth expected in jobs typically requiring unskilled workers, on the order of about 2.4 percent statewide. White-collar and skilled jobs are likely to grow at more than three times that rate—8.28 percent and 7.69 percent, respectively. Second, urban centers tend to fare better across the board in the projected growth rates *within* each of these three job sectors.

There are some key spatial differences among LMAs in these projected patterns of growth. Some labor markets will likely lose jobs with unskilled requirements. This sectoral decline is largely limited to

**Figure 11.3 Percent Growth in Job Types, 1997–2000, by USDA Urban Influence Code within Labor Market Areas**

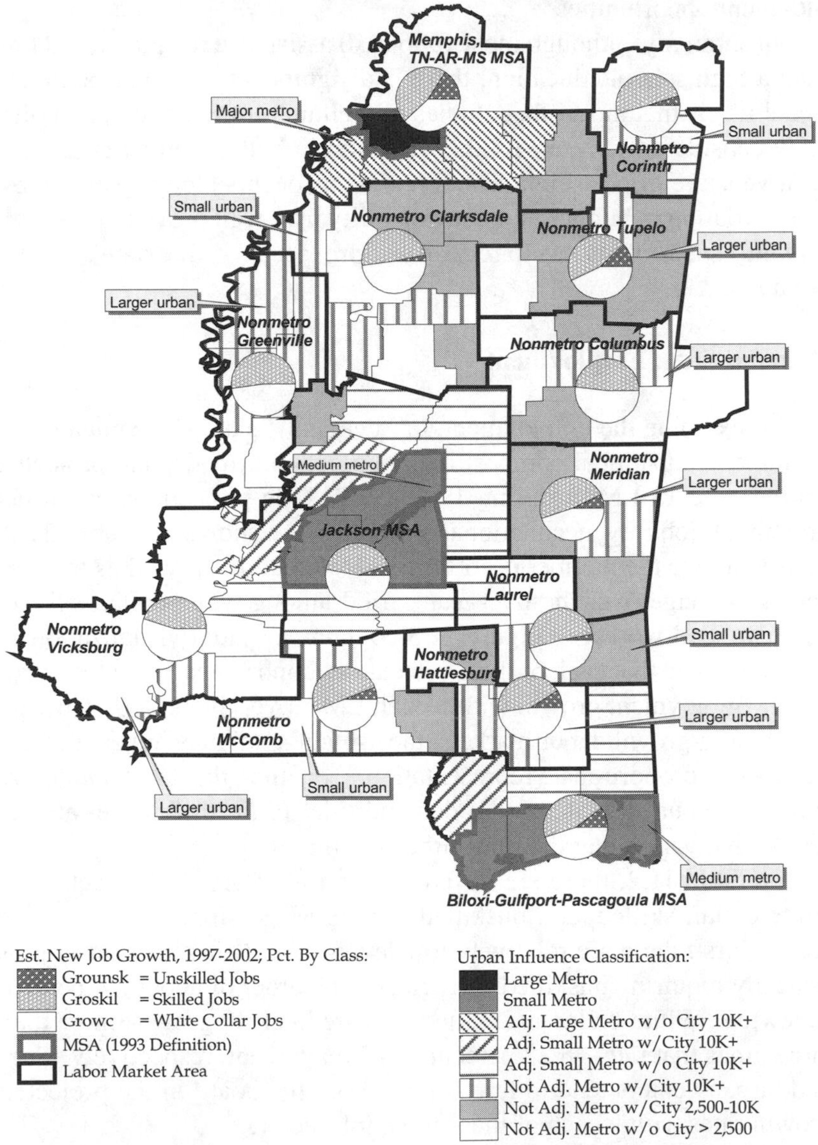
Memphis, TN-AR-MS MSA
Major metro
Small urban
Nonmetro Corinth
Small urban
Nonmetro Clarksdale
Nonmetro Tupelo
Larger urban
Larger urban
Nonmetro Greenville
Nonmetro Columbus
Larger urban
Nonmetro Meridian
Medium metro
Larger urban
Jackson MSA
Nonmetro Laurel
Nonmetro Vicksburg
Small urban
Nonmetro Hattiesburg
Larger urban
Nonmetro McComb
Small urban
Larger urban
Medium metro
Biloxi-Gulfport-Pascagoula MSA
Est. New Job Growth, 1997-2002; Pct. By Class:
Grounsk = Unskilled Jobs
Groskil = Skilled Jobs
Growc = White Collar Jobs
MSA (1993 Definition)
Labor Market Area
Urban Influence Classification:
Large Metro
Small Metro
Adj. Large Metro w/o City 10K+
Adj. Small Metro w/City 10K+
Adj. Small Metro w/o City 10K+
Not Adj. Metro w/City 10K+
Not Adj. Metro w/City 2,500-10K
Not Adj. Metro w/o City > 2,500

SOURCE: U.S. Bureau of the Census; U.S. Dept. of Agriculture; Miss. Dept. of Human Services.

the Delta region's Greenville LMA, although Columbus (–0.01 percent) to the east and Vicksburg (–0.45 percent) in the lower Delta also technically have negative growth projections for unskilled workers. For skilled workers, the job growth prospects are brightest in the Memphis and Biloxi-Gulfport-Pascagoula LMAs, as skilled jobs are expected to increase by 13 percent and 10 percent, respectively (see Table 11.2). For white-collar workers, these same LMAs are showing growth projections of 15 percent and 11 percent over the 1997–2002 period. The Tupelo and Hattiesburg labor markets are likely to also register white-collar job growth of about 10 percent during this period. Thus, although metropolitan labor markets tend to have brighter prospects for employment growth over the initial period of the welfare-to-work transition, there are pockets of growth by type of job in more rural labor markets.

Some understanding of how new job growth composition is spatially distributed can be found in Figure 11.3. Recall that, in the pie-charts, projected growth in each job type is a proportion of total job growth. The consistent result here is that very little job growth will be in unskilled positions, and this includes both rural and urban labor markets. For instance, in the Clarksdale LMA, situated in the northern portion of the impoverished Delta region, projected new job growth will consist largely of white-collar and skilled-workers (about 50 percent each for the projected new job growth), but almost no new growth in unskilled positions. A similar pattern is found in the Greenville labor market as well as the nonmetropolitan Columbus and Vicksburg LMAs. The only areas where an appreciable proportion of unskilled new job growth is likely to occur are the metropolitan centers of Memphis, the Gulf Coast (Biloxi-Gulfport-Pascagoula), and the smaller urban labor markets of Tupelo and Hattiesburg.[3] Thus, the rural-urban continuum in Mississippi is an important factor in the prospects that most AFDC/TANF beneficiaries face for obtaining continued employment.

It is clear that Mississippi's labor markets vary in ways that may affect the welfare-to-work transition, yet these rural-urban patterns may well parallel those seen nationally (see Gibbs, in this volume, p. 51). These patterns represent a type of socioeconomic "kaleidoscope," in which the composition of educational credentials among TANF recipients varies from labor market to labor market, and the projected employment growth patterns vary spatially, with different labor markets offering different occupational and growth trajectories. It is the spatial dimension within this kaleidoscope that is the most critical aspect of this study. The extent of the spatial mismatch between TANF recipients' educational credentials and the general occupational requirements of employers who are experiencing new job growth represents the "job-matching" outcomes in these LMAs.

## Spatial Mismatch between Education of TANF Recipients and Available Jobs

The approach used in this study is the "absorption index" based on the ratio of AFDC/TANF recipients in 1996 to the projected job growth over the succeeding three years, as illustrated in Howell (1997c) and described above. Thus, the higher the ratio, the more welfare recipients per projected available jobs in the immediate future and, therefore, a bleaker picture for a successful transition from welfare to work. A ratio of 1 indicates one net additional job available during the period being considered. A ratio less than 1 indicates more than one job per TANF recipient. If the ratio is greater than 1, there will be fewer than one new job per TANF recipient. I attempt to improve on my previous work by using the gross categories of white-collar, skilled, and unskilled job types "matched" with educational credentials of postsecondary school, high school only, and less than high school education levels, respectively.

Because the number of AFDC/TANF recipients in a labor market area varies across these three educational levels, a refined job-matching index was constructed by "weighting" the components of the crude job-matching index by the proportions of AFDC/TANF recipients within each educational level. This "composite" job-matching index reflects my best estimate of the absorption capacity of each labor market area for successfully merging welfare beneficiaries into the paid labor force.

The results are summarized in Table 11.1 and in Figure 11.4. Both the crude and composite job-matching ratios, as well as the individual crude ratios for each educational level, are shown in Table 11.1.[4] I first discuss the statewide results and follow by comparing them spatially.

Statewide, the 1996 cohort of AFDC/TANF recipients will out-number new job growth by a ratio of 2.13 or, put another way, there will be just over two TANF recipients from the 1996 cohort for each net

**Figure 11.4  Labor Market Absorption Capacity for Composite "Job-Matching" Educational Credentials of 1996 TANF Recipients to Employment Growth, 1997–2000**

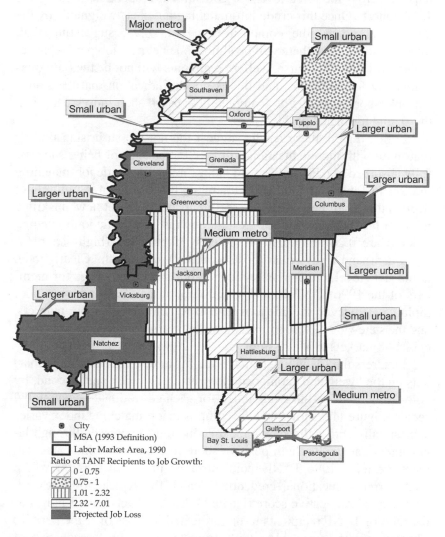

SOURCE: U.S. Bureau of the Census; Wessex Inc. (proprietary); Mississippi Department of Human Services.

new job created during the succeeding five years (see Table 11.1). This statewide, crude job-matching index does not take into account the imbalance across the three levels of educational credentials held by the 1996 cohort. Once this crude job-matching index is "weighted" by the educational levels, the composite index is 0.95, suggesting that, throughout the state, there will be almost one net new job per TANF recipient in 1996. Of course, welfare recipients will not be the only ones competing for such jobs, and this is not an indication that the state's various labor markets will "completely" absorb such individuals (i.e., the spatial mismatch problem).

In that regard, these results suggest the not-too-surprising finding that those with more education will face better odds of being successfully absorbed into the state's paid labor force. The crude job-matching indexes in Table 11.1 indicate that, among those without a high school degree, there will be 1.78 TANF recipients per each net new, unskilled job over the five-year period. In stark contrast, the crude job-matching indexes are 0.26 and 0.09, respectively, for skilled (high school or equivalent) and white-collar (postsecondary) job growth. Clearly then, at the state level, there are significant labor force challenges for members of the 1996 TANF cohort who do not at least hold a high school diploma. However, specific jobs tend to be held in local labor markets, and the statewide picture masks important spatial differences across local labor markets in Mississippi.

I address the spatial mismatch issue by, first, comparing labor markets on the "weighted" composite job-matching index and, second, by comparing them on the crude index for each educational-occupational sector. Figure 11.4 shows that the composite job-matching index varies substantially across the state's local economies, expressed through labor market areas. (A high positive score in Figure 11.4 indicates that there are more 1996 TANF recipients than projected jobs for which their current educational credentials match the typical job entry requirements. A negative score [labeled "Projected Job Loss"] indicates the ratio of TANF recipients to the projected job loss over the period.) The fate of the three LMAs with projected total job losses—two of which are in the Delta—is clearly negative. In the northern part of the Delta region, the Greenwood labor market area also has a bleak outlook, with a composite index of 7.01 TANF recipients per net new job. For the Delta region as a whole, either outright net job loss or a very stiff competition appears to face TANF recipients seeking jobs matching their existing training.

Elsewhere in Mississippi, the spatial matching is somewhat more promising. Areas of the state such as the urban LMAs of Jackson, McComb, Laurel, and Meridian have between one and two beneficiaries per new job during the period under review. The remaining LMAs, including Memphis, Tupelo, Hattiesburg, and the Gulf Coast, are all projected to fare much better. The composite job-matching indexes for these LMAs, as shown in Table 11.1, are all below 0.75, indicating that it is projected to be about 1.33 jobs (1/0.75) that "match" each TANF beneficiary's education level. The Corinth LMA has a composite index of 0.77, which effectively places it in a similar position to the pockets of relative optimism on the Gulf Coast and in the Memphis-Tupelo corridor. Thus, overall, the "job-matching" capacity of Mississippi is quite varied, depending on the area. The Delta and the Columbus areas face a bleak outlook for success in moving recipients into the labor force, while urbanized northern and southern extremes have reason to be relatively optimistic.

There appear to be two essential phenomena underlying these spatial patterns. One is simply the poor outlook for net employment growth in the larger urban Columbus, Greenville, and Vicksburg LMAs. The other is the spatial "mismatch" between the types of new jobs likely to be produced relative to their general education requirements. The Clarksdale LMA perhaps faces this challenge more than elsewhere in the state, but Jackson, McComb, Meridian, and Laurel LMAs are not far behind.

Examining the crude job-matching indexes for each education level held by TANF recipients helps identify where the most serious challenges exist for the welfare-to-work transition, given the projected new job growth described above (see Tables 11.1 and 11.2). The job-matching index for white-collar jobs and postsecondary education levels shows that in no case are there more welfare beneficiaries with postsecondary schooling than net new white-collar jobs. However, there is a familiar spatial pattern of inequality, even among the most educated TANF group. There is a more optimistic set of odds for those TANF beneficiaries with postsecondary credentials living in either the Memphis (effectively DeSoto County, Mississippi, in this case) or the Tupelo LMAs; there is projected to be 0.02 beneficiaries per new white-collar jobs (or 50 new jobs per TANF beneficiary).  By contrast, the Delta's Greenville labor market has a crude index value of less than 0.83 (or 1.2 jobs per beneficiary), suggesting that postsecondary TANF recipients living there face the most difficult challenge, owing largely to the relatively small number of white-collar jobs being forecast for 1997–2002.[5]  The familiar rural and/or Delta region labor markets, such as Clarksdale (0.23), Columbus (0.19), and Vicksburg (0.36), are more similar to the Greenville LMA, while more urban labor markets, such as Hattiesburg (0.08), Biloxi (0.06), and Meridian (0.07), tend to be nearer to the Memphis-Tupelo corridor's prospects.

The picture for skilled jobs and TANF recipients with high school diplomas tends to parallel that for white-collar jobs in terms of the spatial mismatch.  The Greenville LMA faces the most difficult odds in generating new skilled jobs relative to the TANF beneficiaries with high school diplomas or its equivalent.  In fact, these beneficiaries in the Greenville labor market hold about a 2:1 (index value of 2.14) margin over new growth in skilled positions.  The most optimistic odds are in the Memphis-Tupelo corridor because skilled jobs will outnumber TANF recipients by approximately 13 to 1 (the reciprocal of index values of 0.08 and 0.07, respectively).  The urbanized Gulf Coast region, including the Biloxi-Gulfport-Pascagoula and Hattiesburg labor market areas, and the Corinth area follow suit, with skilled jobs projected to range from 4 to 9 per welfare recipient with a high school education.  These results clearly parallel those for white-collar job growth and the "job-matching" absorption capacity of Mississippi's local labor markets.

Given that a preponderance of TANF recipients hold less than a high school education, the results for the unskilled job sector is nearly identical to that of the composite index itself.  In fact, the Spearman rank-order correlation between the composite index results and the crude index for the unskilled jobs sector is +0.974.  Thus, I will omit a repetitious review of these results shown in Table 11.1 since the spatial patterning is virtually the same as that described for the composite index displayed in Figure 11.4.

## Child Care Availability and Capacity in Labor Market Areas

Holding a paid job requires more than simply an available position. Job performance is a crucial aspect of permanent employment.  The vast majority of TANF mothers have dependent children and so the availability of quality child care is a potential barrier to a sustainable welfare-to-work transition.

I examined the availability and capacity of licensed child care using data from the Mississippi Department of Health's Child Care licensure database. Although the database does not include all child care arrangements, facilities licensed by the state have met certain child care accreditation standards and, therefore, are likely to render higher-quality care than others (see Howell and Wade 1990). My objective was to analyze the current operating capacity of the licensed child care facilities with respect to the labor market in which they operate. Namely, is there enough capacity in the existing child care system to accommodate those who would choose to make use of this system? Although I cannot fully answer this question, my analysis is perhaps a necessary beginning. I consider both the capacity and the proximity of licensed child care to the former TANF beneficiary.[6]

The results show that licensed child care is more concentrated in cities, but not all of these cities are in the most urban areas. As the level of urban influence declines so does the density of licensed child care establishments (Howell 2000). The three metropolitan areas in the state (circa 1993) have significantly greater concentrations of child care facilities, following a well-worn fact of business economics: markets drive service. These spatial patterns do not differ appreciably from the statewide study a decade earlier by Howell and Wade (1990).

The data were summarized by Labor Market Area (Table 11.3). The maximum licensed capacity reported by the Department of Health is 100,817 "slots" for children. At last count, these licensed "positions" were being used at 64 percent capacity (i.e., 64,519 children were occupying these 100,817 slots).[7] Theoretically, this leaves an estimated 36,298 openings in licensed child care facilities. Given that most 1996 TANF recipients had at least one dependent child, there was a potential "demand" among that population of at least 21,843 (or 60 percent of these openings), as shown in Table 11.3. If 1996 TANF recipients had more than one dependent child, an additional 20 percent more openings would be needed to fully meet the TANF demand. Although this exercise makes for an interesting initial assessment, the state-level analysis does not help us understand whether there is a "spatial match" between available child care and the welfare-to-work transition.

The variation across labor markets in the number of estimated

**Table 11.3  Current Operating Capacity of Licensed Child Care Facilities by Labor Market Area**

| Labor Market Area (1990) | Child care facilities | | | | | No. AFDC recipients, all education levels (1996) | Ratio of no. child care openings to no. AFDC recipients (1996) |
| | Total no. of facilities | Maximum licensed capacity | No. of openings | Current no. of children enrolled | Enrollment (% of rated capacity) | | |
|---|---|---|---|---|---|---|---|
| Biloxi-Gulfport-Pascagoula MSA | 151 | 11,371 | 5,262 | 6,109 | 53.72 | 2,205 | 2.39 |
| Jackson MSA | 401 | 29,885 | 10,157 | 19,728 | 66.01 | 4,947 | 2.05 |
| Memphis, TN-AR-MS MSA | 95 | 6,255 | 3,089 | 3,166 | 50.62 | 903 | 3.42 |
| N-m[a] Clarksdale | 147 | 8,027 | 2,321 | 5,706 | 71.00 | 2,560 | 0.91 |
| N-m Columbus | 130 | 6,895 | 2,924 | 3,917 | 57.59 | 1,838 | 1.59 |
| N-m Corinth | 50 | 1,852 | 638 | 1,214 | 65.55 | 210 | 3.04 |
| N-m Greenville | 133 | 7,443 | 2,696 | 4,747 | 63.78 | 3,450 | 0.78 |
| N-m Hattiesburg | 90 | 5,068 | 1,382 | 3,686 | 72.73 | 951 | 1.45 |
| N-m Laurel | 43 | 2,534 | 641 | 1,893 | 74.70 | 551 | 1.16 |
| N-m McComb | 82 | 4,308 | 1,526 | 2,782 | 64.58 | 1,261 | 1.21 |
| N-m Meridian | 71 | 4,647 | 853 | 3,794 | 81.64 | 977 | 0.87 |
| N-m Tupelo | 165 | 7,988 | 3,080 | 4,908 | 61.44 | 602 | 5.12 |
| N-m Vicksburg | 70 | 4,544 | 1,729 | 2,815 | 62.09 | 1,388 | 1.25 |
| Statewide | 1,628 | 100,817 | 36,298 | 64,519 | 64.00 | 21,843 | 1.66 |

[a] N-m = nonmetro.

SOURCE: Author's calculations based upon data from the MS Dept. of Health, MS Dept. of Human Services, and proprietary employment estimates from Wessex, Inc.

"openings" in licensed child care centers is considerable (Table 11.3) and these are related to being an urbanized area. For instance, the metropolitan Jackson LMA has twice the number of openings (greater than 10,000) than does the next nearest labor market, the metropolitan Biloxi-Gulfport-Pascagoula LMA, which has room for about 5,200 additional children. At the other end of the scale, the nonmetro Laurel (641 openings) and Corinth (638) labor markets have the lowest number of openings. When these openings are expressed as the percent of total licensed capacity, or the percent of operating capacity, a similar picture occurs. The LMAs with the lowest operating capacities are the metro Memphis (DeSoto County) at 51 percent and Biloxi-Gulfport-Pascagoula at 54 percent. However, the pattern varies somewhat irrespective of rural-urban status. For example, the next lowest operating capacity can be found in the rural Columbus labor market at 58 percent while the small urban Meridian LMA tops out at 81 percent. Thus, although the largest metropolitan labor markets in the state have the greatest number and share of child care openings, there is an irregular spatial pattern throughout the rest of the state on the remainder of openings by labor market.

The main issue for welfare reform, of course, is whether the vacancies are in proximity to TANF recipients. The ratios computed in Table 11.3 show a crude rate of vacancies in licensed child care facilities to the number of 1996 AFDC/TANF cohort members (assuming one child per adult). If this ratio is 1, then the number of vacancies matches estimated "demand." Fluctuations above 1 indicate a greater likelihood of meeting demand, and the converse is true for ratios less than 1. The LMAs of Greenville, Clarksdale, and Meridian all have ratios less than 1, similar to their employment absorption capacity. The Delta labor markets, in contrast, fall short of demand. The pattern is consistent with the even more dramatic results obtained by Howell and Wade (1990, p. 18) a decade ago, who identified the Delta region of the state as the area in which "there are at least 1,500 additional preschool children who need day care service but who are not currently in such a facility . . . a similar pattern . . . occurs for school-age children."

On the other end of the spectrum, the Tupelo LMA appears to be in the best position to accommodate TANF recipients' child care needs. With a ratio of vacancies to welfare recipients of 5.12, the Tupelo area substantially leads the Memphis (DeSoto County) LMA (3.42) and the Corinth LMA (3.04) in carrying capacity.

In summary, the need for additional carrying capacity in child care would not be obvious without examining the spatial coincidence of the child care system and the welfare reform process. There are clearly labor markets in which additional child care establishments are needed to complement the transition off the welfare rolls. This appears to be especially true in the impoverished Delta region. Although more careful analyses are needed, past studies (Howell and Wade 1990; Howell and Mason 1991a, b), combined with this preliminary assessment, strongly suggest that the child care system in Mississippi is an important part of building a sustainable welfare-to-work transition.

## DISCUSSION

The 1996 welfare reform act (PRWORA) instituted a maximum five-year lifetime benefit limit for TANF recipients. For Mississippi, a state both steeped in historically high poverty rates and the recent beneficiary of a growth economy, the success of the welfare-to-work transition constitutes an important social laboratory for the grand experiment that is the current welfare reform initiative. In many ways, the 1996 cohort of welfare recipients constitutes a vital part of the experiment, given that they are the first group to experience the welfare reform package. Thus, the time and the place offer an attractive space-time setting to examine the welfare-to-work transition.

The findings from this study offer some key insights in understanding the labor market areas in Mississippi and their capacity to successfully absorb welfare beneficiaries who must leave public support. Significant variation exists among the state's LMAs in their projected ability to effectively "absorb" this cohort of TANF recipients and a significant part of this result is linked to the spatial context of the labor market. The Delta labor markets around Greenville and Clarksdale and also in the Columbus area in the eastern part of the state face an especially clear challenge. These LMAs were projected to suffer net job losses, possibly requiring TANF beneficiaries to reach beyond their resident labor market areas to find employment.

The ability of these TANF beneficiaries to find employment that generally "matches" their educational skills is a vital part of the employment process. The findings suggest that there will be almost one net new job per member of the 1996 TANF cohort. However, welfare beneficiaries are not the only ones looking for work, and the methods used in this study are decidedly optimistic, favoring potential employment outcomes for TANF recipients.

The LMA comparisons perhaps tell a more realistic story about the prospects for successful welfare-to-work transitions. The major areas that will likely experience much easier transitions are the urban centers of Memphis, Tupelo, Hattiesburg, and Gulf Coast areas. The most challenging areas for generating jobs that "match" the educational credentials of TANF recipients are the more rural areas of Greenville, Clarksdale, and Columbus. The Jackson, McComb, Meridian, and Laurel labor markets, however, are not far behind.

How well the licensed child care system will facilitate welfare reform is also mixed and spatially dependent. In general, the core labor market areas in the Delta region—Greenville and Clarksdale—have a weaker capacity for licensed child care. By contrast, the Tupelo labor market area has much greater capacity relative to the potential needs of the TANF recipients. These results are generally compatible with the studies conducted by my colleagues and me at the beginning of the 1990s (Howell and Wade 1990; Howell and Mason 1991a, b). A significant expansion of the licensed child care system, especially in the core labor market areas of the Delta region, may significantly benefit the welfare-to-work transition.

There are several issues and limitations to this study. One is that I do not investigate racial patterns in the transition-to-work prospects of Mississippi TANF recipients. In a state with a large African-American population, and one with a poor history of race relations, this is a significant limitation.[8] A second issue involves the assumptions made in the simple index used in this study. It assumes that TANF recipients do not move across LMAs to seek employment, that only TANF recipients compete for new job growth, that TANF recipients are unwilling to be significantly underemployed (e.g., post-high-school educated TANF recipients not taking unskilled labor jobs), and that the crude classifications used adequately represent educational requirements of the job classes used for matching. A third issue is the need for geo-referenced microdata on TANF households, prospective employers, licensed child care centers, and microdata on TANF households regarding dependent children and other vital information.

In summary, labor market areas around the state vary widely in their apparent capacity to create net job growth that matches the educational credentials of this cohort. Moreover, the labor market areas of the state that are likely to be the most challenged by this spatial mismatch are also those with the weakest carrying capacity for licensed child care facilities (see Howell 2000). Public policy should pay close attention to creating investment opportunities for licensed child care establishments. Given the interwoven nature of the welfare-to-work process, policymakers should take heed and coordinate current programs that will reduce and alleviate these problems if the social contract embedded in PRWORA is to be fulfilled.

# Notes

This chapter was supported by a grant from the U.S. Department of Health and Human Services, the Administration for Children and Families, to the Mississippi Department of Human Services, and a subcontract to the Center for Applied Research at Millsaps College, Jackson, Mississippi. Dr. William Brister was the Principal Investigator. The author's collaboration with Lionel J. (Bo) Beaulieu, Lynn L. Reinschmiedt, and William Brister is gratefully acknowledged. The comments of Jill Findeis (Pennsylvania State University), Bonnie Thorton Dill (University of Maryland), Barbara Ray, and the editors are also sincerely appreciated. Proprietary data obtained from Wessex, Inc., were used in this study to make estimates for labor market areas in Mississippi. Every effort has been made to not disclose the proprietary county-level data in this aggregation process but we are not responsible for the actions of others. Any errors of fact or interpretation, however, are those of the author.

1. Using peak months allows us to examine the maximum potential TANF caseload, a conservative strategy for studying the labor market's capacity to absorb recipients into the labor force (Howell 1997c).
2. The county-level display of data in Howell (2000) shows even more detailed variation as certain counties have higher (and lower) levels of post-secondary education.
3. The Hattiesburg and Laurel areas achieved MSA-status in 1994 (Howell 2000), further evidence of the urban-centered growth in unskilled jobs.
4. As noted above, three LMAs are projected to experience a net job loss during the 1999–2002 period: Columbus, Greenville, and Vicksburg. This produces a negative job-matching ratio, of course, but one whose metric is essentially uninterpretable and only reflects the ratio of AFDC/TANF recipients to the projected job loss. In this event, I have labeled the spatial displays of the data shown in Table 11.1 as simply a "projected job loss" in these three LMAs.
5. This might, however, result in these recipients becoming underemployed rather

than not unemployed, and I do not take the underemployment issue into account in this simple labor market absorption model.

6. More detailed results regarding this portion of the analysis can be found in Howell (2000), including map displays of the spatial distribution of the licensed facilities.

7. Jill Findeis (University of Maryland) raised the question about the validity of these results since the 64 percent figure appeared to be low. I do not disagree that this "percent of capacity" figure appears low but, as with most administrative data, this is an estimate based upon the MS Department of Health's official licensure database. My previous work on the child care system in Mississippi (Howell and Wade 1990; Howell and Mason 1991a, b) showed that some modeled estimates of the demand suggested that in 1990 the supply would have to virtually double to meet estimated demand. These results a decade later would suggest an illogical conclusion, that demand has been "exceeded" since the licensure database suggests that the system is only operating at about two-thirds capacity. One hypothesis about these results is that the current enrollment estimates reported to the Department of Health may be systematically underestimated by licensed providers so as to protect their license status. I am unable to reconcile this matter but would caution the reader to the potential liabilities that such administrative data bring with them for scientific analysis.

8. At this writing, I have not reconciled how best to conduct this important aspect of the investigation. If the TANF caseload data were to simply be separated by race, into whites and African-Americans, and "amortized" against the projected employment as two separate labor market absorption indices, then the resulting ratios would effectively ignore the complementary racial group's competitive job-searching. That is, the separate indices would be artificially inflated by ignoring the other race-specific TANF number in the numerator portion of the job-matching ratio. There appears no practical means by which we can compute race-specific ratios since the projected job growth data are not race-specific. Despite these challenges, the issue of how race influences the welfare-to-work transition is a vital one to understanding welfare reform.

# References

Blank, Rebecca M. 1997a. *It Takes a Nation: A New Agenda for Fighting Poverty.* Princeton, New Jersey: Princeton University Press.

————. 1997b. "What Causes Public Assistance Caseloads to Grow?" Working paper no. 6343, National Bureau of Economic Research, Cambridge, Massachusetts.

Blank, Rebecca M., and Patricia Ruggles. 1996. "When Do Women Use Aid to Families with Dependent Children and Food Stamps? The Dynamics of Eligibility versus Participation." *Journal of Human Resources* 31(1): 57–89.

Bureau of the Census. 2000. *Small Area Income and Poverty Estimates*. December 13. Available at <http://www.census.gov/hhes/www/saipe.html>, January 2001.

Congressional Budget Office. 1993. "Forecasting AFDC Caseloads, with an Emphasis on Economic Factors." Staff memorandum. Congressional Budget Office, Washington, D.C.

Environmental Systems Research Institute, Inc. 1997. *ArcView StreetMap: Address Matching and Street Mapping for the USA*. Redlands, California: ESRI.

Ghelfi, Linda, and Timothy Parker. 1997. "A County-Level Measure of Urban Influence." *Rural Development Perspectives* 12(2): 32–41.

Howell, Frank M. 1997a. *Mississippi: (Barely) Poorest among Southern States*. Special Report Series, Social Science Research Center, Mississippi State University.

———. 1997b. *Mississippi: Leads Region in Work Disabled*. Special Report Series, Social Science Research Center, Mississippi State University.

———. 1997c. *Welfare Reform and Labor Market Capacity*. Special Report Series, Social Science Research Center, Mississippi State University.

———. 2000. *Prospects for Job-Matching in the Welfare-to-Work Transition: Labor Market Capacity for Sustaining the Absorption of Mississippi's TANF Recipients*. SRDC Publication no. 215. Southern Rural Development Center, Mississippi State University, and Center for Applied Research, Millsaps College, June.

Howell, Frank M., and T. David Mason. 1991a. *The Supply of Child Care in Mississippi: A Study of Program Cost, Organization and Quality*. Final report submitted to the Office of Children and Youth, Mississippi Department of Human Services from the Social Science Research Center, Mississippi State University.

———. 1991b. *The Child Care Equation in Mississippi: A Study of Public Priorities, Beliefs, and Usage*. Final report submitted to the Office of Children and Youth, Mississippi Department of Human Services from the Social Science Research Center, Mississippi State University.

Howell, Frank M., and Cynthia K. Wade. 1990. *The Need for Child Care Services in Mississippi: Estimates, Projections, and Public Support for Funding*. Social Research report series 90-1, Mississippi State University.

Kuhn, Betsey A., Michael LeBlanc, and Craig Gundersen. 1997. "The Food Stamp Program, Welfare Reform, and the Aggregate Economy." *American Journal of Agricultural Economics* 79(5): 1595–1599.

Leete, Laura, and Neil Bania. 1996. *The Impact of Ohio's Welfare Reform Plan on Local Labor Markets*. Briefing report no. 9602, Center on Urban Poverty and Social Change, Case Western Reserve University.

Leete, Laura, Neil Bania, and Claudia Coulton. 1998. *Welfare Reform: Using Local Labor Market Data for Policy and Analysis and Program Planning.* Briefing report no. 9804, Center on Urban Poverty and Social Change, Case Western Reserve University.

Martini, Alberto, and Michael Wiseman. 1997. "Explaining the Recent Decline in Welfare Caseloads: Is the Council of Economic Advisors Right?" Unpublished manuscript, The Urban Institute, Washington, D.C.

Tolbert, Charles M., and Molly Sizer. September 1996. *U.S. Commuting Zones and Labor Market Areas: A 1990 Update.* Economic Research Service, Staff paper no. 9614, U.S. Department of Agriculture, Washington, DC.

Ziliak, James P., David N. Figlio, Elizabeth E. Davis, and Laura S. Connolly. 1997. "Accounting for the Decline in AFDC Caseloads: Welfare Reform or Economic Growth?" Discussion paper 1151-97, Institute for Research on Poverty, University of Wisconsin, Madison.

# 12
# Whose Job Is It?
## Employers' Views on Welfare Reform

Ellen Shelton, Greg Owen, Amy Bush Stevens,
Justine Nelson-Christinedaughter, Corinna Roy, and June Heineman
*Wilder Research Center*

The employer viewpoint is an obvious, but often overlooked, aspect of rural welfare-to-work efforts and reforms. What do they see as the major barriers to successful employment of welfare recipients? Who do they believe should address these barriers? This chapter describes the experiences and opinions of 130 Minnesota employers who have demonstrated some degree of interest or involvement in hiring welfare recipients. Several clear themes emerge among the entire group, as do some important differences between rural and urban/suburban employers. In addition, because the survey is part of a broader study, this chapter contrasts employers' perceptions with those of welfare recipients.

## BACKGROUND

### Welfare Reform in Minnesota

When Congress passed the Personal Responsibility and Work Opportunity Reconciliation Act of 1996, Minnesota enacted the Minnesota Family Investment Program (MFIP) as its state Temporary Assistance for Needy Families (TANF) program. MFIP was intended to meet two goals: to reduce the number of people on welfare and to help families move out of and remain out of poverty. Key features of

MFIP include an emphasis on quick job placement, including some training and job support; relatively generous (38 percent) disregard of earned income in calculating assistance levels; continued eligibility until household income rises to about 120 percent of the poverty level; a maximum sanction of 30 percent; a full 60-month time limit; and a transitional child care subsidy and Medical Assistance (Minnesota's Medicaid program) for one year after leaving MFIP. (For initial outcomes of MFIP, see Gennetian and colleagues in this volume, p. 287.)

At the time of the transition from Aid to Families with Dependent Children (AFDC) to MFIP, roughly 50,000 persons were receiving welfare benefits in Minnesota. Over half of these recipients (60 percent) lived in the urban and suburban counties of the Twin Cities metropolitan area, while 30 percent lived in rural counties and 10 percent lived in counties with mid-sized cities (Minnesota Department of Human Services, 1999). Minnesota's unemployment rate dropped from 3.3 percent in 1997 to 2.8 percent in 1999, reflecting the state's significant economic growth.

## Rural Issues in Welfare Reform

Rural areas face special challenges in welfare-to-work efforts (Marks et al. 1999). Rural welfare recipients often travel longer distances between home, child care, work, and training opportunities, and services such as child care, public transportation, and workforce training are more scarce than in cities. Thus, it appears particularly important for public agencies to assist rural recipients with these services. Yet rural officials have fewer staff available to take advantage of state block grants for such purposes and to put welfare-to-work programs into action. In addition, public assistance appears to carry a greater stigma in rural areas, which reduces both recipients' willingness to seek help and others' awareness that help is needed.

Rural areas also have some advantages over metropolitan regions, including more personal relationships between service provider and recipient, the more informal nature of resource and support networks, and the smaller scale of human service agencies (Marks et al. 1999).

The types of jobs available in rural areas also differ. Jobs in manufacturing, which have traditionally supplied rural areas with higher wages, have decreased in the last three decades (RUPRI Rural Welfare Reform Initiative Panel 1999).  In their absence, rural employment opportunities are dominated by industries paying low wages, such as retail and service industries.  The employment boom in recent years has passed over many rural communities, which often have high unemployment rates (Marks et al. 1999).  To successfully move welfare recipients into the labor market without displacing current workers, rural communities with high unemployment must create new jobs.  At this time of economic prosperity, the necessity of job creation is unique to rural labor markets.

To place the requisite number of welfare recipients in jobs to satisfy new welfare-to-work requirements, efforts to involve businesses must reach beyond earlier business partnerships in three respects.  The first is *scale*; they must find ways to place and retain far more welfare recipients.  The second is *reach*; they must find ways to place and retain a far wider mix of recipients, including many with serious barriers to employment.  Finally, *retention and advancement* require that they help welfare recipients not only find jobs, but retain their jobs and advance into higher-paying jobs that can sustain their families without cash assistance (Brown, Buck, and Skinner 1998).

Mindful of these and other challenges to the successful implementation of a work-first model of welfare reform, the McKnight Foundation initiated 22 community partnerships throughout Minnesota, drawing together local welfare offices and the service providers who are helping welfare recipients make the transition from welfare to work, and strongly encouraging involvement from local employers.

## The McKnight Foundation's Welfare-to-Work Initiative

Minnesota's largest private philanthropy, the McKnight Foundation, was interested in helping families make a successful transition from the old welfare system to the new one.  McKnight was particularly concerned about potential gaps in service delivery and eager to learn the best ways to fill them.  To achieve these goals, the McKnight Foundation provided $20 million to 22 community partnerships serving MFIP families in 86 of Minnesota's 87 counties.  Funding for most partnerships began about the same time MFIP took effect statewide, January 1998, and was initially for a two-year grant period.

The community partnerships, many of which included multiple counties in rural areas, were encouraged to experiment with programs to accommodate the specific needs in their area. However, each partnership was expected to address transportation, child care, and the employment needs of MFIP families. Each partnership brought together a variety of organizations, often including county MFIP caseworkers and directors, government or nonprofit employment services providers, social service agencies, educational institutions, employers, faith-based groups, and other community members.

From their inception, the McKnight-funded partnerships were expected to involve employers. Employers had a vital resource for welfare recipients—jobs—and the recipients in turn made up a sizable potential workforce, which many employers needed. This chapter addresses the perceived barriers to the transition from welfare to work; who should do what to address those barriers; the role of employers in welfare reform; and how various stakeholders can best work with employers to support the transition from welfare to work. Thus, unlike many other chapters in this volume that explore the impact of welfare policies that emphasize work (such as McKernan et al. [p. 257] or Lichter and Jensen [p. 77]), this chapter investigates the context and effects of a program designed to supplement such policies with the support services that might help such a model work.

## STUDY APPROACH

The McKnight Foundation contracted with Wilder Research Center to examine the effectiveness of funded partnerships in increasing employment and self-sufficiency. Because each partnership was free to design its own approach within the relatively wide parameters laid out by McKnight, a controlled study design was not feasible. Instead, the study sought, through three separate methods, to describe the work of these partnerships. The first method involved interview-based case studies of 10 of the 22 partnerships.

The second approach involved telephone interviews with MFIP recipients residing in the 10 case study areas. Selected items from the survey are reported here; the complete results are found in Owen et al. (2000). The survey was conducted between July and November 1999 with 395 current and former MFIP recipients, who were selected at random from the list of all recipients in the 10 case study sites. The response rate was 62 percent. Because of the restriction to case study sites and English language interviews, the sample is not fully representative of the statewide MFIP population.

The third component of the study, and the one on which this chapter focuses, consisted of telephone interviews with 130 employers identified by local representatives in 21 of the 22 community partnerships. The interviews were conducted between August 1999 and February 2000. These employers likely overrepresent those most inclined to play a role in welfare reform and should not be taken to represent employers in general. Of 181 employers identified in the 21 sites, 130 completed the interview. Forty-one said they had not been involved in partnership activities and therefore declined to participate. When these employers are excluded from the sample, the response rate is 93 percent. Employers' views are presented and contrasted with the views of welfare recipients. In addition, employers' perceptions of barriers to employment are contrasted with recipients' perceptions of barriers to self-sufficiency.

The chapter also highlights rural/urban differences that emerged in the study. In this analysis, the urban/suburban grouping includes the core Twin Cities of Minneapolis and St. Paul and their three primary rings of suburbs, plus those in cities in the smaller Metropolitan Statistical Areas (MSAs) in the state. The rural grouping includes all non-metropolitan counties, those in the nonurban areas of the smaller MSAs, and those in independent growth centers at the fringes of the seven-county Twin Cities area. The rural group included 81 employers (62 percent of the total) and the urban/suburban group included 49 (38 percent). Because the group of employers surveyed was a purposive sample rather than a random one, no claims are made about the statistical significance of the findings. However, results of $\chi^2$ tests were used to determine differences worthy of mention and are reported here for rough guidance on the magnitude of the difference, recognizing that the necessary assumptions about random distribution cannot be met.

## STUDY FINDINGS

### The Employers

Of the 130 employers interviewed, 71 (55 percent) were in rural areas of the state; 35 (27 percent) were located in the Twin Cities area (Minneapolis and St. Paul and their primary suburbs); 14 (11 percent) were in other large cities; and 10 (8 percent) were in independent growth centers at the fringe of the seven-county Twin Cities metropolitan area. Most employers in this survey (58 percent) had more than 100 employees, including full-time and part-time workers. One-quarter of employers were mid-sized (20–100 employees). Only 15 percent had fewer than 20 employees. Smaller employers were more common in the rural sample; one-third of rural employers, compared with less than one-quarter of urban/suburban employers, had fewer than 50 employees.

In contrast to this sample, only 4 percent of all Minnesota employers had 100 or more employees in June 1999 (most recent statistics available), while 67 percent of all Minnesota employers had fewer than 10 employees, compared with only 10 percent of the sample and 12 percent of rural employers in the sample (Minnesota Department of Economic Security 1998). Compared with all Minnesota employers, the welfare-to-work partnerships heavily overrepresent manufacturing and services, while underrepresenting all other sectors. Just under one-third (30 percent) of all employers in this survey were in manufacturing, and 18 percent each were in trade and in health care services. All service categories combined (health, business to business, social services, other) totaled 47 percent.

Employers varied in the proportion of jobs available to low-skilled workers. For about one-third of the employers in the sample, 76 percent to 100 percent of the jobs required no more than a high school diploma. About half of the businesses required only a high school diploma for half or more of their jobs. However, almost 10 percent of employers had no jobs available for workers with only a high school diploma. These proportions are consistent across the state.

The average hourly wage for entry-level employees ranged from $5.30 to $13.00. The median entry pay was $7.59. Urban/suburban employers paid higher wages ($p \leq 0.001$). A rural worker earning the median full-time wage for this sample would earn $15,600 per year, or $1,300 per month. The median urban/suburban worker, also working full-time, would earn $16,640 per year, or $1,387 per month.

Most employers (79 percent) reported that entry-level workers qualified for health care benefits within three months after employment. Eleven percent of employers (more often the smaller ones) did not offer health care benefits at all. Among those who offered benefits, about half (48 percent) reported that at least some of their employees could not afford to take advantage of the benefits because of the cost. About one-quarter of employers (28 percent) estimated that one-quarter or fewer of their employees could not afford to use medical benefits, and about one-quarter (21 percent) of employers thought more than one-fourth of employees could not afford to participate in the benefits. There were no urban/rural differences in the availability of or participation in benefit plans.

Most employers—93 percent overall and 94 percent of rural employers—said that an entry-level worker who did a good job would be earning more money after one year. Among the 111 employers who would pay more, the amount of the raise ranged from $0.13 to $3.00 per hour. The median increase expected during a satisfactory first year was $0.70. Most employers expected to continue to have higher-paying opportunities available. They reported that if the same worker were still with the company after five years and still doing a good job, the median hourly wage would be $10.00 ($9.76 for rural workers). For 6 percent of the employers (8 percent of rural employers), the wage after five years would still be below $8.00 per hour. Only 23 percent of employers, and only 12 percent of rural employers, thought entry-level workers could reach more than $11.00 per hour in five years. Thirty-six employers were unable to estimate probable pay five years into the future.

The rural median wage of $9.76 after five years would yield an annual income of $20,301. Assuming an annual inflation rate of 2 percent, this would be about 133 percent of the federal poverty guideline for a family of three in 2004—enough to leave welfare—but only about 110 percent of poverty for a family of four, and thus not enough to leave welfare.

**The Welfare Recipients**

The study also interviewed a group of welfare recipients. The 10 case study sites included two suburban and two mainly urban communities in the Twin Cities area and six mostly rural communities in greater Minnesota. Overall, 55 percent of the recipients lived in rural areas and 45 percent lived in urban/suburban areas, including the Twin Cities and Moorhead. Comparisons of the basic demographic characteristics of the study sample and of the statewide MFIP population indicate that the study respondents are somewhat representative of the overall welfare population. The average ages, length of welfare use, and marital status among the two groups are very similar (Owen et al. 2000).

The vast majority of respondents (90 percent), regardless of geographic area, said that MFIP had helped them in some way. Help with basic needs, such as paying bills (31 percent), buying food (24 percent), getting medical coverage (16 percent), and paying for housing (15 percent), were cited as ways that MFIP had helped. Several respondents also mentioned that MFIP had helped them to stay in school (17 percent), find a job (17 percent), or get child care (15 percent).

About one-third of all respondents (37 percent) reported that MFIP had caused problems for them. The bureaucratic complexities of the system (20 percent), loss of benefits (14 percent), and poor service from MFIP workers (12 percent) were most often cited. The distribution of responses from rural and urban/suburban recipients was similar, although rural recipients were more likely to report a loss of benefits (19 percent, compared with 8 percent). Working respondents (26 percent) had more problems with program complexity and paperwork than did nonworking respondents (11 percent), reflecting the increased paperwork requirements associated with being employed. Those who were not working were more likely to say that their MFIP worker was insensitive or rude (27 percent) and that they were "forced" to work or look for work (22 percent). This compares with 16 percent and 1 percent of working respondents, respectively.

**Barriers to Hiring and Retaining Welfare Recipients**

Employers, current welfare recipients, and former welfare recipients held quite different views on which barriers to the transition from welfare to work were the most formidable. The only barrier that ranked among the top five for all three groups was the issue of child care.

### Employer perceptions of barriers

Employers were asked, "What do you see as the main barriers to hiring and retaining current and former welfare recipients?" Respondents had a wide variety of opinions. More than anything, they cited a lack of "soft skills." Soft skills are those work-related social and interpersonal skills needed to be successful on the job, such as general social skills, calling if one is going to be late or absent for work, and also staying with the job despite frustrations or disagreements. Forty-five percent of employers cited the lack of such skills as a barrier (Table 12.1). Past research confirms this sentiment. In a survey of 900 private businesses and public organizations in three Michigan cities, Holzer (1999) found that 90 percent of businesses wanted assurances that there would be no problems with absenteeism, tardiness, or work attitudes in hiring welfare recipients. These "soft skills" were mentioned more often than basic cognitive skills, and job-related skills were of least concern.

Employers in general did not see it as their responsibility to address the soft skills barrier. Their most common recommendation for welfare recipients was to improve their soft skills and attitudes: take more responsibility, be more dependable, develop a work ethic, "deal with their reasons for being late," be more realistic, balance work and family better, and so on (Table 12.2).

Problems with transportation and child care were also frequently cited by employers. About one-fourth of employers said recipients could help themselves by securing transportation, child care, or other basic supports. Among rural employers, transportation problems ranked second in frequency of mention and child care problems ranked third. Among urban/suburban employers, child care ranked second, and transportation tied for third place with poor attitude and motivation, which ranked fourth for the overall group. "Attitude and motivation" includes references to laziness, preferring welfare over work, or being unwilling to accept the wages or hours of the jobs that are available.

Prior research has found that few employers are willing to help

**Table 12.1  Employers' Views of Main Barriers to Hiring and Retaining MFIP Recipients (most common responses to an open-ended question)**

| Employers' views | Rural (N = 47) | | Urban/suburban (N = 79) | | Total (N = 126) | |
|---|---|---|---|---|---|---|
| | Number | % | Number | % | Number | % |
| Lack of "soft skills" | 36 | 46 | 21 | 45 | 57 | 45 |
| Transportation problems | 24 | 30 | 11 | 23 | 35 | 28 |
| Child care problems | 21 | 27 | 12 | 26 | 33 | 26 |
| Poor attitude/motivation | 15 | 19 | 11 | 23 | 26 | 21 |
| "Lifestyle" issues | 15 | 19 | 8 | 17 | 23 | 18 |
| Nothing; no barriers | 7 | 9 | 6 | 13 | 13 | 10 |
| System/structural problems[a] | 9 | 11 | 3 | 6 | 12 | 10 |

[a] System/structural problems include problems with medical insurance, loss of benefits, work-related costs, lack of support services, "can't earn enough to make it."

---

**Sample responses for Table 12.1 to the question,**
"What do you see as the main barriers to hiring and retaining current and former MFIP recipients?"

Their skill levels aren't good and neither is their work ethic. They don't understand about being on time, everyday basic common sense things. [Urban/suburban employer]

Lack of transportation. Unwilling to work second or third shift—due mostly to no child care available at that time. [Urban/suburban employer]

The primary one is work ethics. They just don't want to work. [Urban/suburban employer]

Some of these people (single moms) don't know how to juggle work and home life. They fizzle out after a month and they just can't hack it. [Rural employer]

Retaining [a job]—can they make it on the wages they are paid? They have new costs, for clothing, day care, transportation. Expenses are extra and unforeseen. [Urban/suburban employer]

Child care issues; children's issues such as sick children; big needs, like kids getting in trouble. They quit their jobs, because of their kids. They lack family support, transportation, a helpful environment. [Rural employer]

**Table 12.2  Most Common Responses to the Question, "What Do You Think MFIP Recipients Could Do to Address the Barriers They Face?"**

| Employers' responses | Rural (N = 40) | | Urban/suburban (N = 69) | | Total (N = 109) | |
|---|---|---|---|---|---|---|
| | Number | % | Number | % | Number | % |
| Improve their soft skills/ attitude/other life skills | 43 | 62 | 30 | 75 | 73 | 67 |
| Get transportation, child care, or other basic supports | 18 | 26 | 9 | 23 | 27 | 25 |
| Get education/training | 10 | 15 | 6 | 15 | 16 | 15 |
| Nothing; there's nothing they can do | 3 | 4 | 2 | 4 | 5 | 5 |
| Find a job (with a different employer) | 4 | 6 | – | – | 4 | 4 |
| Improve their psychological adjustment | 3 | 4 | 1 | 3 | 4 | 4 |

**Sample responses to the question in Table 12.2:**

Job preparation—have a safety net plan. If a car breaks down, can you get to work, by taxi, friend, how? Better to be late an hour than throw up your hands and not come at all. [Rural employer]

Be more open with employers, communicate their needs and concerns. Tell us when things come up in their lives. [Urban/suburban employer]

They need to get motivated and get responsible. They need to get moving—life is different when you have to work. [Rural employer]

Get technical skills and training, that builds their self-esteem. Also getting their relationships right, with family and friends. [Rural employer]

Find child care providers who will be flexible with nontraditional work hours. [Rural employer]

They don't have a lot of things they can do. It's a problem with society and the system. [Urban/suburban employer] with these supports.  In the above-noted Michigan study, Holzer (1999) found that only 7 percent of employers surveyed would help with child care, and only 8 percent would help with transportation, although more would help with basic skills (34 percent), and most would help with job skills (80 percent).  This is consistent with other studies (e.g., Regenstein, Meyer, and Hicks 1998) that found that employers want good attitudes and reliability and are willing to train employees to actually do their job.

Another general category of barriers is grouped here as "lifestyle issues," because they are sometimes perceived as resulting from welfare recipients' personal choices or those of their family members.  These included being a single parent, family crises (unspecified), drug abuse, domestic violence, or criminal history.  Eighteen percent of employers identified at least one of these issues as a main barrier to employment of welfare recipients.

Where employers *were* willing to help was in overcoming perceptions and creating a positive work environment for the new workers.  Over half (56 percent) offered suggestions that centered on employers' relationships with employees, such as trying to understand what they were going through, being open-minded or flexible or encouraging, communicating their expectations clearly, or "providing a positive work environment" (Table 12.3).  Nearly half (48 percent) suggested somewhat more tangible forms of support, including mentors; help with developing soft skills; help with child care, transportation, education, or training; and helping them "meet their needs."  These more concrete suggestions were more likely to come from rural employers (54 percent) than from urban/suburban employers (37 percent).  Thirteen percent of employers suggested some form of positive community participation, such as greater involvement with the partnership or with social service agencies, working on affordable housing issues in the area, or communicating to policymakers about the welfare-to-work process.

### Welfare recipients' perceptions of barriers

Welfare recipients themselves mentioned many of the same barriers as employers did, but ranked their importance quite differently (Table 12.4).  Respondents were asked to identify any barriers that

**Table 12.3  Most Common Responses to the Question, "What Do You Think Employers, Like Yourself, Could Do to Address These Barriers?"**

| Employers' responses | Rural (N = 41) | | Urban/suburban (N = 74) | | Total (N = 115) | |
|---|---|---|---|---|---|---|
| | Number | % | Number | % | Number | % |
| Understand their issues; communicate; encourage them; provide a supportive work environment | 40 | 54 | 24 | 59 | 64 | 56 |
| Help/support them; provide or link them to basic supports, mentors, soft skills, education/training | 40 | 54 | 15 | 37 | 55 | 48 |
| Civic involvement; work on policy/social environment | 10 | 14 | 5 | 12 | 15 | 13 |
| Employers could provide/improve pay, bonus, benefits, work hours | 9 | 12 | 4 | 10 | 13 | 11 |
| Hold the line; be tough with them; maintain standards; no special treatment | 5 | 7 | 3 | 7 | 8 | 7 |
| Nothing; "It's not our job." | 1 | 1 | 6 | 15 | 7 | 6 |
| Be willing to hire; match workers with suitable jobs (not necessarily at this business) | 5 | 7 | 1 | 2 | 6 | 5 |

**Sample responses to the question in Table 12.3:**

These people are not self-directed.  We need to be tougher on them.  Get them out of bed and on the telephone looking for work.  [Rural employer]

We could work with employees one-on-one, [tell them] "This is what's expected," tie the person to a mentor who can support them.  [Urban/suburban employer]

**Sample responses (continued)**

We are not positioned to do anything.  We don't have excess funds to provide what they need, like on-site child care. [Urban/suburban employer]

We could provide transportation and child care.  That would benefit us, that would cut the rate of days employees miss due to problems with transportation and child care.  [Urban/suburban employer]

Tolerance and patience, those are the two big things we have to give.  [Rural employer]

Nothing, we don't really have anything to offer, because they are so uneducated it's too much work to try to help them. [Urban/suburban employer]

Be as sensitive as possible to the needs of the employee.  Many haven't worked for a while, and be sensitive to their adjustment period. [Urban/suburban employer]

**Table 12.4  Welfare Recipients' Reported Barriers to Leaving and
Staying off Welfare (% of respondents)**

| Welfare recipients' responses | Rural (N = 219) | Urban/suburban (N = 176) | Total (N = 395) |
|---|---|---|---|
| Low paying jobs/cost of living compared with wages | 27 | 26 | 26 |
| Lack of education/couldn't go to school or finish degree/lack of skills | 18 | 22 | 20 |
| Lack of child care/can't find affordable, reliable, quality child care | 11 | 27 | 18 |
| Loss of health care coverage/can't afford insurance | 13 | 18 | 15 |
| Hard to find a job | 12 | 4 | 9 |
| Disability (physical or mental) | 9 | 4 | 7 |
| Lack of affordable housing/housing problems | 5 | 7 | 6 |

would make it difficult for them to get off or stay off welfare within the time limits.  Overall, about one-fourth of recipients (26 percent) cited the lack of livable wage jobs as a barrier to self-sufficiency.  Lack of education (20 percent), child care (18 percent), and health insurance (15 percent) were also cited by many respondents.  Rural and urban/suburban recipients did not vary much in reporting these barriers, although rural recipients (12 percent) were more likely than urban/suburban recipients (4 percent) to say that it was difficult to find a job, and urban/suburban recipients (27 percent) reported more problems with child care than did rural recipients (11 percent).

Overall, of the types of services typically offered by the partnerships, the following were most commonly used by rural respondents within the three months preceding the interview: help paying for child care (31 percent); help finding a job (24 percent); help at work from a mentor or someone else who supports and encourages you (21 percent); and soft skills training (20 percent).

Help to obtain and maintain a car was the dominant need for rural respondents. Overall, the most common areas of unmet need for rural recipients were help with car repairs (44 percent); an affordable car (free or low-cost) (37 percent); help paying for child care (26 percent); emergency money for living expenses (26 percent); help getting a car loan (25 percent); other car-related expenses (24 percent); and help getting car insurance or clearing a record (23 percent).

Although the majority of respondents said they were receiving food stamps (67 percent) and medical assistance or other medical coverage (85 percent), these were still areas of significant unmet need. Of those who did not have these benefits, 53 percent said they needed health insurance, and 38 percent said they needed food stamps. Rural and urban/suburban recipients reported almost identical rates of food stamp use and insurance coverage. Of those who did not have these supports, urban/suburban respondents (47 percent) were significantly more likely than their rural counterparts (31 percent) to report that they needed food stamps ($p \leq 0.05$).

## How Employers View the Community Partnerships

The role of service providers is changing as work demands increase under welfare reform. Employers in a nationwide random sample reported generally positive attitudes toward welfare recipients as prospective employees. Three-quarters of those who had already hired recipients were satisfied with their job performance, and 94 percent said they would hire recipients again (Regenstein, Meyer, and Hicks 1998). However, in another study, participants in focus groups in three major cities were not as positive. These employers believed that the many new applicants for entry-level positions, regardless of whether they received welfare, tended to have significant deficits in motivation, attitude, and life skills (Roberts and Padden 1998). Holzer (1999) found that employers had higher expectations for the advancement of welfare recipients who had been hired in the last two years than they had for welfare recipients they will hire in the future. Such findings point to the need to adjust business-involvement strategies as the characteristics of the welfare caseload change.

The employers participating in the partnerships under review here had a variety of opinions of what partnerships could do to strengthen the employability of recipients (Table 12.5). Nearly half (48 percent)

**Table 12.5  Most Common Responses to the Question, "What Do You Think the Partnerships Could Do to Help MFIP Recipients Address Those Barriers?"**

| Employers' responses | Rural (N = 40) | | Urban/suburban (N = 68) | | Total (N = 108) | |
|---|---|---|---|---|---|---|
| | Number | % | Number | % | Number | % |
| Provide/connect them with basic supports/resources | 35 | 52 | 17 | 43 | 52 | 48 |
| Help them develop soft skills | 23 | 34 | 12 | 30 | 35 | 32 |
| Help them get education/training | 9 | 13 | 10 | 25 | 19 | 18 |
| Provide services to employers/the community | 8 | 12 | 7 | 18 | 15 | 14 |
| Provide role models, mentors, coaching, counseling, support groups | 7 | 10 | 4 | 10 | 11 | 10 |
| Change/enforce the system | 9 | 13 | 1 | 3 | 10 | 9 |

**Sample responses to the question in Table 12.5:**

I think the MFIP recipients need the help of the partnership because they can't possibly do it on their own.  They need to develop job skills.  [Rural employer]

They could make sure the workers understand what's expected of them and teach them proper work expectations.  [Urban/suburban employer]

Follow up more on the placement with employees and also with employers about how it's working out.  More frequent communications between partnership entities.  [Rural employer]

Help them with their skill levels and their work ethics.  Many people don't have English skills so they need ESL classes.  Build relationships with recipients so they know resources.  [Urban/suburban employer]

Be strict.  Take away benefits right away [if they don't show up for work].  [Rural employer]

Provide people to work with new employees, to help them with adjustments.  [Urban/suburban employer] said partnerships could provide or connect recipients to basic supports and resources (such as child care, transportation, medical insurance, after-hours services, English as a second language classes, etc.), and nearly one-third (32 percent) said they could help them develop soft skills.   About 18 percent overall (13 percent of rural employers) thought they could help recipients get education or training.

In contrast, there were fewer mentions (14 percent of employers) of services that the partnerships could offer to employers or to the community.   These included more information on available services, following up with employers after placing workers, and screening job seekers and matching them with employers' needs.   Among the top five suggestions of rural employers (but not urban/suburban employers) was the suggestion to change the system (advocate for policy or funding changes, enforce penalties for not working, or provide better incentives for working).

The survey asked employers whether local partnerships had helped them recruit, train, and retain employees, and whether partnerships had helped their employees balance their responsibilities to their job and to their children.   Employers who reported that they had been helped in any of these ways were asked to explain.   The responses allow us to explore the kinds of programs and services that employers consider useful, either for themselves or for their workers.

Three-quarters of urban-suburban employers had been helped to find and recruit new employees, compared with just over half of rural employers ($p \le 0.05$).   The kinds of services that were helpful were the same for rural as for urban/suburban employers.   In both cases, they mainly cited referrals of job applicants and visibility in the community (75 percent of rural employers, 92 percent of urban-suburban employers).   The visibility came mainly through advertising job opportunities, including job fairs for urban/suburban employers (but not for rural employers).   To a lesser degree, it also included more general visibility for the company and its activities.   Other help included various supports to workers themselves (transportation, child care, translation or English as a second language, mentors, etc.).   Just over 10 percent of employers cited help given to employers themselves (assessment of applicants' soft skills; help with training; and payment of wages for an initial employment period).

Almost the same proportion of urban/suburban and rural employers reported that the partnership had helped them with training new employees (40 percent and 42 percent, respectively). The majority mentioned help given directly to employees, mainly partnership-based training programs, but also counseling or mentoring, English language or translation help, and "help with problems" not further specified. Only 11 percent cited help given directly to employers. These kinds of help included screening, training of supervisors or otherwise helping employers develop their own training programs, and partnership payment of wages for an initial period.

Job retention was also noted. Rural employers reported receiving slightly more help with retention than did urban/suburban employers (48 percent of rural, 38 percent of urban; not statistically significant). For the most part (80 percent), those who were helped cited ongoing support from the partnership for new employees, including help with transportation, child care, and translation, as well as training programs (especially in rural areas) and counseling or mentoring. To a lesser degree (20 percent), employers cited the value of help given to employers, including screening employees, training supervisors, ongoing communication with employers (presumably about any problems the employee might be having), and payment of initial wages or a bonus for staying six months. A few employers (6 percent) mentioned ways in which the partnership had helped them to better help employees. These included being more aware of workers' problems, making accommodations for problems, or developing a program to meet their needs.

Helping employees to balance their work and outside lives was not cited by any employer as a concern that had led them to become involved in the partnership. However, when asked, slightly more than one-third (38 percent) were able to think of some way in which they or their employees had received such help. Two-thirds of this group cited nonmaterial help provided directly to workers by the partnership, including "they go over that in the training."

Other employers mentioned material help to workers (40 percent), including providing or helping them to find basic goods and services, such as clothing and shoes, child care, transportation, and even housing. Just a few employers (9 percent) cited ways in which their involvement had led them to better support the work-life balance: greater awareness of employees' problems, or accommodation to them; training that includes issues of balance; or even (in one company) hiring family coordinators to help employees address family problems.

Another insight into what employers find helpful is in their answers to a question about how effectively the partnership has balanced the different goals of social service agencies and businesses. A focus group study (Roberts and Padden 1998) found that employers believe that public agencies are out of touch with the needs of employers, especially their need to produce a product or service at a competitive cost. They need employees with basic work skills, and want agencies to help job-seekers acquire these skills.

In this study, however, a substantial minority (42 percent, slightly higher in rural areas) either believed there was no conflict between these goals or that the partnership was ensuring that both were being met. Next in frequency (18 percent) was the observation that partnerships were doing a good job of balancing the goals because they were meeting business needs. Some employers cited process factors such as realism, communication, or effort as ways in which the balance was being achieved (13 percent), and some cited the importance of business being involved in or understanding social issues (8 percent). Respondents who believed that the partnerships were not doing a good job of balancing tended to cite ways in which the partnership failed to meet business needs (e.g., "the workers they sent over both quit"; 13 percent), or faulted the partnership for asking business to do too much or not asking workers to do enough (7 percent), or for poor process, mainly follow-up and communication (7 percent).

**How Employers View Their Own Role**

Forty-one percent of both rural and urban/suburban employers said their company does something differently as a result of their contact with the partnership. The changes ranged from knowledge and attitudes, to relationships with the community, to actual business practices. Urban/suburban employers were significantly more likely to report that they had adopted more open, less restrictive hiring practices (Table 12.6). Rural employers were slightly more likely to mention greater involvement or participation in the community or with social service agencies. About one-quarter of employers said they better understand the needs of welfare recipients, but a greater percentage have begun do-

**Table 12.6  Most Common Responses about What Employers Do Differently as a Result of Contact with Partnership**

| Employers' responses | Rural (N = 29) | | Urban/suburban (N = 20) | | Total (N = 49) | |
|---|---|---|---|---|---|---|
| | Number | % | Number | % | Number | % |
| Provide supports (tangible, e.g., training, mentor program, child care, literacy program) | 10 | 35 | 6 | 30 | 13 | 33 |
| "Meet their needs," connect workers to supports (tangible, e.g., provide info on child care, housing, transp) | 8 | 28 | 5 | 25 | 13 | 27 |
| Understand workers; "supportive work environment" (intangible or unspecified) | 7 | 24 | 6 | 30 | 13 | 27 |
| More networking, involvement in the community | 9 | 31 | 2 | 10 | 11 | 22 |
| More open to hiring; post jobs at agencies; identify welfare employees** | 2 | 7 | 8 | 40 | 10 | 20 |
| Changed hours; more flexible | 4 | 14 | 1 | 5 | 5 | 10 |
| "Working on" child care, housing | 3 | 10 | – | – | 3 | 6 |

NOTE: ** = $p \leq 0.05$.

ing specific things to meet those needs or to connect workers with resources for meeting them.

Almost all employers (95 percent) said there is a role for employers
in welfare reform.  Rural and urban/suburban employers alike said their
role was to be open-minded and flexible and to consider hiring welfare
recipients (65 percent).  Other roles cited were to be good citizens (28
percent)—to help the community, work together, or be a resource for
social service agencies; and to provide various kinds of tangible sup-

port to their workers (28 percent), such as training, benefits, living wages, mentors; or help with transportation, child care, or career advancement. Fourteen percent mentioned more vague or intangible kinds of help, such as providing encouragement or support or "working with them" (14 percent).

Of the handful of employers who said there was no role for employers in welfare reform (three rural and four urban/suburban), the reasons were interesting in juxtaposition with each other. All three of the rural employers said that it was too much to ask (recipients need too much special treatment, or it is not the responsibility of business to take care of these needs), while the four urban/suburban employers were evenly split between that view and the opinion that nothing needs addressing (recipients do not need any special treatment, "there shouldn't be any welfare").

### How to Work with Employers

Based on the responses, employer involvement in promoting the goals of welfare reform is likely to be more successful if

- public agencies, nonprofit agencies, and employers all agree on clear and consistent goals;
- employers can count on service providers to deliver tangible and agreed on supports;
- reasonable emphasis is placed on the needs of the employer, and genuine attempts are made to understand employer expectations;
- employers are educated in what can realistically be expected from some welfare recipients, and the time it might take to help them become good employees.

Reports from community partnerships bear out employers' responses regarding the welfare-to-work transition: employers can be involved, especially if one is careful about good, clear, honest, ongoing communication. They are more likely to enter into the partnership if public and nonprofit service agencies make individualized contact with them, and when the contact is made by one specific agency with a track record in the community rather than by a new and untested collaboration (Owen et al. 2000). Responses to this study show that social service providers who ask and listen, and who make consistent efforts to follow through with the needed support, can become valued allies for employers.

## Differences between Rural and Urban/Suburban Employers

Consistent with previous research, this study shows that rural employers are not very different from urban and suburban employers in their views of welfare reform and welfare recipients. Although rural employers tend to be smaller, on average, and pay lower wages than urban and suburban employers, this sample of employers who have become involved with welfare reform did not otherwise show significant differences except that urban and suburban employers were much more hungry for workers and consequently demonstrated greater flexibility in hiring practices.

Previous literature and the case studies in this project both indicate that most rural employers are small. To maximize their efforts, the rural partnerships recruited a disproportionate number of large employers; therefore, the sample for this survey underrepresents the typical, smaller rural employers. To explore what difference, if any, size makes in rural employers' needs and attitudes, the rural sample was subdivided into smaller and larger employers (with fewer or more than 100 employees). Those with a $\chi^2$ $p$-value of $\leq 0.05$ are summarized below.

Smaller employers were more likely to have no jobs available to applicants with only a high school diploma or less; they were less likely to offer a raise of more than $1.00 to beginning workers after one year; they were more likely to have no medical benefits for their employees; and they were more likely to report that employees were unable to take advantage of medical benefits because of the cost. Almost half of each group was made up of organizations in the service sector (profit or nonprofit), but the large employer group included more health care services, and the smaller employer group included more services other than health care, business-to-business, and social.

Smaller employers were less likely to have expected to benefit from working with the partnership. However, among those who did have hopes, there was no difference between larger and smaller employers in the kinds of hopes they had.

Large employers were more likely to perceive transportation problems as a barrier to hiring and retaining welfare recipients. This was the only significant difference in the barriers perceived by large and small rural employers.  Large employers were more likely to say that employers could help to address barriers by providing help and support to their employees, including help with transportation, child care, or connection to community resources.  In other respects, size made almost no difference at all in the kinds of suggestions for what employers could do.

Smaller employers were no more or less likely to say they did anything differently as a result of their contact with the partnership.  However, of those employers who did make changes, small employers were more likely to say they had become more flexible or had changed their hours.

## DISCUSSION

### Role of Employers in Welfare-to-Work

In Minnesota, where the unemployment rate is extremely low (2.8 percent in 1999), on average, employers in all areas of the state appear to welcome help that will bring qualified employees to their door, support workers who encounter difficulty in entry-level positions, and coach workers toward long-term adjustment and stability.  For the most part, rural employers value the help of social service providers in coaching and mentoring their entry-level workers.  There are indications that rural employers in this study have needed and received less help in recruiting than urban and suburban employers, but more help in retaining employees on the job.  All employers, whether urban, suburban, or rural, see two main benefits from affiliation with welfare reform service providers: preparing new workers for employment and providing ongoing support following the initial hiring.  One employer summarized the ideal situation this way: "When someone doesn't show up, I can call Sue and she will follow up with the worker and tell them to get back to work."  Nonetheless, a small number of employers say that they appreciate services provided by social service agencies to the employers themselves, for example through training, communication to employers, and suggestions on how best to support the transportation and child care needs of their employees.

Employer involvement in the welfare-to-work partnerships result-ed in little direct employer help to new workers. Employers continued to report that their role in welfare reform is to offer jobs, salary, and (sometimes) benefits, as well as "to tell (or dictate to) the welfare de-partment what we're looking for, so they can provide people who al-ready have the training they need for the job." If employers changed their practices, the change was most likely to "have a greater under-standing of employee issues, or to have a more open mind about the employees we are willing to hire." Most employers did not feel re-sponsible for helping employees deal with child care, transportation, or housing. Those that did were the exception rather than the rule.

Employers are most likely to remain involved in welfare-to-work activities when they see clear benefits through recruitment, hiring, and retention of new employees and when they find that social service agencies are clearly prepared to provide consistent back-up support to help new workers sort out problems and avoid ongoing crises. They want to be treated as a customer with needs to be filled, not as a way of filling someone else's needs; they appreciate that some partnerships are "starting to listen more to our needs and concerns." Other than recruit-ment, areas in which employers have clearly benefited include work-place mentoring of new employees, resolution of work behavior issues, and support for solving child care, transportation, and—occasionally—housing problems.

The wide variety of services offered by partnerships, and the equal-ly wide variety of reactions from employers, point to the need for flex-ible and individualized approaches to meeting employers' and recipi-ents' needs. In fact, it may be useful for social service providers to think of employers similarly to the way they think of recipients. Like recipients, some employers have it easier than others. Each is dealing with a unique set of circumstances while governed by fairly uniform rules and expectations, and each operates in a climate of scarcity and under significant stress, with little room for reflection or experimenta-tion or frills.

## Perceived Barriers to the Transition from Welfare to Work

Most employers in this study entirely overlooked two other sets of barriers that are of significant concern to the partnerships. One set of barriers mentioned repeatedly by recipients and partnerships, but only very rarely by employers, are those economic issues arising out of the imbalance between the low wages in low-skill jobs and the high costs of housing, child care, transportation, and medical insurance. One urban/suburban employer expressed this concern, which from their point of view appears as a problem with retention: "Can they make it on the wages they are paid? [They have] new costs for clothing, day care, transportation. Expenses are extra and unforeseen." For most employers, however, the assumption is that if people work (or work hard), they do not need any welfare. In contrast, recipients expressed significant worries about the most basic family support issues: paying for food, housing, medical insurance, and other unavoidable bills. One-quarter of all respondents worried about finding a job that pays enough to allow them to get by. One-eighth of rural recipients worried about finding any job at all. The lower pay among rural and small employers is consistent with Lichter and Jensen's finding (p. 77 in this volume) that although rural single mothers are more likely to "play by the rules" and work, they are also more likely to be poor.

The other set of barriers of growing concern to partnerships, but rarely mentioned by either employers or recipients, are those of welfare recipients with multiple problems or more serious problems. These problems include depression, learning disabilities, substance abuse, domestic violence, homelessness, or children with disabilities. The new welfare laws require most such recipients to work, but most employers are not ready to accommodate such needs in their workplaces: "I'll be honest, some just don't fit into the employment realm . . . (such as, severe depression). Be careful of placement of some individuals. Not everyone is made to work 8-to-5. How to help [them] is the next goal." Service providers cited by McKernan and coauthors (in this volume, p. 257) speak of the lack of services to address these needs. The failure of either employers or recipients in our study to even mention such needs illustrates one of the major difficulties in delivering vital services.

On the positive side, the survey suggests that employers' successful experiences with the first phase of welfare-to-work could help to lay the foundation for the next necessary steps. Some employers are currently taking what they perceive to be risks by hiring the more job-ready recipients and investing enough effort to help them adjust to the workplace, with the help of support services from the social service providers. Most employers are not prepared to do more than two things: "Give people without a job history an opportunity to build one and develop soft skills. Also we can be a resource for them in getting plugged into other services." If employers find this experiment successful, they may be willing to take slightly greater risks with slightly more challenging employees, provided they are assured of yet more support.

However, this study also suggests that most employers will not take even small risks unless forced by a tight labor market. If the economy takes a downturn before people with more serious barriers have been absorbed, it may be difficult indeed to persuade an employer to hire someone who requires substantially more accommodation. This is already true in regions with higher unemployment rates. To accomplish such a change in practices, employees may need supported work models, similar to community rehabilitation programs that serve adults with disabilities.

Lower-paying jobs are the rule in rural areas, and the cost of living is not comparatively low enough to enable most single parents with limited education, or even two-parent families with more than a few children, to earn the amount needed for self-sufficiency. For half the employers surveyed, even five years of successful work experience would not yield earnings high enough for an entry-level worker in a family of four to leave welfare in Minnesota. This study does not suggest any solutions for these barriers. Almost no employer believes they can increase their pay to help welfare recipients. These findings are echoed in a report of a recent employer survey in Wisconsin (Jacobson and Green 2000), which also found little interest in supporting employees beyond a paycheck and some job-specific training.

**Suggestions for Supporting the Welfare-to-Work Transition**

Employers' assessment of partnership benefits appears to reflect a traditional view of the roles of employers and workers, in which employers see themselves as responsible for recruiting, but see workers, once hired, as responsible to maintain or develop the needed skills and work-life accommodations. The few employers who mention the value of services to themselves in training, retention, or work-life balance may reflect the beginning of change in these assumptions, possibly as a result of changing labor force dynamics. Or they may represent a subset of employers with a high sense of civic and social responsibility who have been there all along, and who would naturally be among the first to respond to the call to participate in the McKnight partnerships. Until more employers are prepared to accept some role in assisting their employees with difficulties in training, retention, and family issues, it is unlikely that more than the "first third" of welfare recipients will be able to make a lasting transition into the workforce. Employment support services from public and nonprofit agencies could make a significant difference in persuading employers to begin to accept this role. Evidence from other components of this study (Owen et al. 2000) suggests that the involvement of a diverse array of private non-profit organizations alongside the public agencies in the community partnerships strengthened the support available both to recipients and to employers.

Information from recipients and partnerships yields a different perspective on the "lack of soft skills" than one might get from reviewing only the employers' comments. What many employers perceive as unreliability or lack of soft skills appears substantially related to problems with unavailable or unreliable child care or transportation. In other words, when an employee's child care arrangement falls through, causing the employee to miss work, the employee views this as a child care problem, while the employer is likely to see it as a reliability problem. In addition, some recipients reported that they were obliged by their welfare caseworkers to take time off from work to come to the welfare office to prove they were working, or to take care of other required paperwork. Employers seem to have no idea their employees have such demands on them.

Employers' suggestions for solutions to soft skills deficits emphasized that partnerships "could make sure the workers understand what's expected of them and teach them proper work expectations." In the participant survey, approximately one-fifth of respondents reported receiving such soft skills training, and most rated it somewhere between "somewhat useful" and "very useful." This rating, while clearly positive, was somewhat lower than the average rating for more tangible services, such as help paying for child care or help getting a low-cost car loan.

One can conclude that soft skills training is helpful for many recipients, but that it does not solve many of the underlying problems. Some partnerships have worked to educate employers about the shortages in child care, or have asked them to help develop solutions for transportation barriers. A few employers have become deeply involved in such problem-solving, and the survey suggests that a few more have increased their awareness of the underlying difficulties their employees are dealing with. Most employers, however, are only interested in efforts that affect the actual on-the-job performance of their workers. They are more interested in learning about community resources that can assist their employees with their child care or transportation problems. Getting to the job and ensuring that one's family responsibilities are met while one is at work are considered the employee's responsibilities. If anyone shares the responsibility, it is more likely to be the social service agencies in the community, not the employers. As one urban/suburban employer said, the employer's role is "Not much. It should be their responsibility—the program [partnership] and the employee. We just train them for the job."

From the employer's perspective, the best support for the welfare-to-work transition is to ensure that people are working and to provide them with ongoing help to deal with any problems that might interfere with their work. Employers mainly want such support to be provided directly to the worker, but some employers welcome services that help them as employers help their workers. Mentorship programs, including training supervisors to be job coaches, seems an especially promising approach for employers willing to undertake something new themselves. One employer said a mentoring workshop "provided knowledge how to bring out the best in others, and how to treat each other using a feedback system."

Smaller employers, underrepresented in this sample but predominant in the statewide population of employers, pose special challenges to social service providers who hope to assist rural welfare recipients move toward self-sufficiency. This study found that smaller employers have a lower proportion of jobs accessible to workers with a limited education, are likely to pay lower wages and offer smaller raises, and are less likely to provide medical benefits. There is some evidence that they may be harder to persuade to partner with social service providers, because they expect fewer benefits from such a partnership. On the positive side, although small businesses are less likely to feel that they can provide any additional supports to their workers, they do appear more likely to be "innovative, flexible, and make changes when they make sense, [such as] restructuring work and hours of work."

## Note

The Wilder Research Center is located in St. Paul, Minnesota.

## References

Brown, A., M.L. Buck, and E. Skinner. 1998. *Business Partnerships: How to Involve Employers in Welfare Reform.* New York: Manpower Demonstration Research Corporation.

Holzer, H.J. 1999. "Will Employers Hire Welfare Recipients? Recent Survey Evidence from Michigan." *Journal of Policy Analysis and Management* 18: 449–472.

Jacobson, R., and G. Green. 2000. *Who's Hiring Whom for What?* Madison, Wisconsin: Wisconsin Council on Children and Families.

Marks, E.L., S. Dewees, T. Ouellette, and R. Koralek. 1999. *Rural Welfare to Work Strategies: Research Synthesis.* Calverton, Maryland: Macro International, Inc.

Minnesota Department of Economic Security. 1998. Unpublished administrative data.

Minnesota Department of Human Services. 1999. Unpublished administrative data.

Owen, G., C. Roy, E. Shelton, and A.B. Stevens. 2000. *How Welfare-to-Work Is Working: Welfare Reform through the Eyes of Minnesota Employers, Welfare Participants, and Local Community Partnerships.* St. Paul, Minnesota: Wilder Research Center.

Regenstein, M., J.A. Meyer, and J.D. Hicks. 1998. *Job Prospects for Welfare Recipients: Employers Speak Out.* Washington, D.C.: The Urban Institute.

Roberts, B., and J.D. Padden. 1998. *Welfare to Wages: Strategies to Assist the Private Sector to Employ Welfare Recipients.* Chevy Chase, Maryland: Brandon Roberts and Associates.

RUPRI Rural Welfare Reform Initiative Research Panel. 1999. *Rural America and Welfare Reform: An Overview Assessment.* Publication no. 99-3, Columbia, Missouri: Rural Policy Research Institute.

# 13
# The Short-Term Impacts of Welfare Reform in Persistently Poor Rural Areas

Mark Harvey
*University of Wisconsin–Madison*

Gene F. Summers
*University of Wisconsin–Madison*

Kathleen Pickering
*Colorado State University*

Patricia Richards
*University of Texas at Austin*

Current welfare reform policy is based on the premise that persons who receive welfare are avoiding work and that requiring them to work will end "welfare dependency." This policy further assumes that employment opportunities are sufficient to absorb welfare participants into local labor markets. Thus, unemployment is equated with labor market inexperience and willful failure to take advantage of available employment opportunities.

This chapter reports findings on the short-term impacts of welfare reform in persistently poor rural areas of central Appalachia, the Mississippi Delta, the Lower Rio Grande Valley, and Indian reservations in South Dakota. These regions, often referred to as "pockets of rural poverty," have had substantial labor demand deficiencies for several decades. The persistence of poverty in these areas contradicts the assumption that sufficient employment opportunities are available to absorb all decanted welfare participants. These "pockets of poverty" are also characterized by an active and extensive informal economy, which undermines the notion that unemployment can be equated with economic inactivity.

The implementation of welfare reform policy based on faulty assumptions about the economies of these persistently poor areas raises questions concerning the likelihood of achieving the expressed policy goals.  In the face of insufficient labor demand in the formal economy, welfare participants will be severely challenged to secure adequate employment to replace cash welfare assistance.  Moreover, applying Temporary Assistance for Needy Families (TANF) eligibility criteria and time limits, which are based on participation in the formal economy, could result in many participants leaving TANF.  These "leavers" may become more dependent on other programs or family networks of support to meet their basic needs, and their ability to continue participating in the informal economy may be threatened.  Thus, official statistics that show declines in TANF participation and unemployment rates may mask the reality of continued or exacerbated social and human welfare deficiencies among low-income families in these pockets of rural poverty.  We therefore examine data on employment outcomes, labor force participation and unemployment, changes in rates of participation in public assistance programs, and changes in levels of dependence of unofficial sources of financial support, particularly food banks, to assess this probability.

Our findings indicate that the implementation of welfare reform in these persistently poor rural counties has resulted in rapid caseload decline and an increase in the day-to-day hardship faced by poor residents.  This is, in large part, owing to the fact that welfare reform has proceeded in a "backwards manner" in these places.  The refrain of community leaders, TANF participants, and program administrators across all counties was, there aren't any jobs.  The data suggest that many former welfare participants are making ends meet by working in informal labor markets and the downgraded service sector, at or near minimum wage.  They are also drawing more heavily on the already stretched resources of extended family, friends, and local food pantries to replace the loss of public assistance.  Most families that have left TANF probably remain well below the poverty threshold.

## BACKGROUND: RURAL LABOR MARKETS
## AND WELFARE REFORM

The reforms initiated by the Personal Responsibility and Work Opportunity Reconciliation Act of 1996 (PRWORA) encourage states to implement programs emphasizing immediate labor force participation. A review of the literature on rural labor markets highlights the importance of understanding how welfare systems operate in particular labor market contexts and presents a number of concerns regarding the ability of rural labor markets to absorb large numbers of former welfare participants. The first issue is the importance of accounting for the "opportunity structures" that exist in rural areas and how they differ from metro labor markets. A second issue is the crucial role that households play as a unit of analysis in understanding the labor market strategies of rural women. The central roles that the informal economy and "informalization" play are also key to understanding how rural labor markets operate. Finally, the operation of rural labor markets is subject to inefficiencies and a lack of meritocracy stemming from entrenched local power structures and historical underinvestment in workforce development programs. This chapter provides an initial look at the disjuncture between TANF policy and rural conditions to substantiate the importance of labor market differences between rural and urban contexts.

### Theories of Rural Labor Markets

The literature on rural labor market outcomes acknowledges the importance of human capital but emphasizes that local opportunity structures cannot be overlooked when studying rural labor markets. Tickamyer (1992) argued that place is a significant structural factor in labor market outcomes and critiques standard labor market theory for conceptualizing labor markets as if they operated outside the constraints of time and space. She advocated studying "local labor market areas" to account for specific opportunity structures (Tickamyer 1992, p. 43). Tickamyer and Bokemeier (1993, p. 57) assumed that rural labor markets differ from urban markets to the extent that "inequality of experience is systematically affected." Lobao (1993, p. 23) also stressed the importance of spatial analysis, noting that studies of local labor markets have shown that "the organization of economic production has developed unevenly over space and time resulting in different contexts of opportunity" and variations by place in "types of industries, firms and jobs."

The literature also cites the need for "multi-level models" that use households as a unit of analysis. Tickamyer and Bokemeier (1993, p. 52) cited the household as "the social structure" in which economic decisions, including labor allocation, migration, and consumption, are negotiated. Housing arrangements and kin networks in poor rural areas constitute an opportunity structure that influences the labor-market participation and mobility of household members (Halperin 1990, pp. 98–99; Tickamyer and Bokemeier 1993, p. 57). Household analysis is crucial in understanding how poor rural households employ strategies that pool the resources of family and nonfamily members to make ends meet. Household analysis also enhances our understanding of how gender relates to poverty, inequality, and the different experience of women workers (Fernandez-Kelly and Garcia 1989, p. 248; Nelson 1999, p. 20; Thornton and Williams 1992, p. 106; Tickamyer and Bokemeier 1993, p. 51).

Informal activities and "informalized" work are two related theoretical issues also raised in the literature. Castells and Portes (1989, p. 26) maintained that both the informal economy and processes of informalization are expanding under globalization. They argued that informal economies must not be reduced to the "survival strategies of marginalized groups," but rather be conceptualized as integral parts of national economies that develop under the "auspices of state tolerance." The informal economy is a specific form of relationships of production that cuts across the entire social structure and is articulated with formal activities. The defining feature of informal labor markets is that they are "unregulated by the institutions of society in a legal and social environment in which similar activities are regulated" (Castells and Portes 1989, p. 12).

The informalization of work is an equally salient issue. "Informalization" denotes the undoing of the employment relationship established between labor and capital under Fordism. The Fordist production paradigm was characterized by Keynesian demand-side management of the domestic economy. Fordism transformed workers into consumers, spurring the upward spiral of investment, production, and consumption that produced historically unprecedented growth from World War II through the early 1970s (see Legborne and Lipietz 1992). Jessop (1994), among others, argued that we have entered a new era of economic accumulation and social regulation that is post-Fordist. The post-Fordist employment relationship in the United States is marked by the flexibility of the employment relationship and the decline of labor unions and collective bargaining processes. The result is a downgrading of work for many without formal higher education or training (Legborne and Lipietz 1992; Streeck 1997). Lifelong, semi-skilled employment secured through unions and the internal labor markets of firms has been replaced for many by a series of temporary jobs offering less pay, fewer benefits, and fewer protections from the vagaries of the market (Castells and Portes 1989; Gringeri 1994; Nelson 1999, pp. 18–20; Peck 1996). The processes of informalization and the downgrading of work were inherent in the movement of manufacturing to rural areas in the 1960s and 1970s and defines the new rural low-wage service sector (see Gringeri 1994; Nelson and Smith 1999).

Finally, the operation of rural labor markets is often distorted by market imperfections. These include the ability of local political elites to manipulate the distribution of jobs and public benefits; a lack of diversified employment; discriminatory values regarding the role of women; spatial isolation; and inefficiencies in institutional mechanisms both for disseminating job-related information and for administering human resource development programs. All contribute to a lack of meritocracy and low returns on human capital investments (Duncan 1992, 1999; Gringeri 1994; Hofferth and Iceland 1998; Lichter and Costanzo 1987).

### Findings on Rural Employment and Welfare Dynamics

Empirical studies of rural labor markets, rural poverty, and rural welfare establish four significant characteristics of rural employment opportunity structures and welfare dynamics. The first is that rural labor markets are becoming more dependent on informalized and downgraded service-sector work. There is substantial evidence in the literature that rural labor markets have undergone major structural change as their industrial bases have been transformed from agricultural, extractive, and manufacturing to services (Duncan and Sweet 1992, p. xxii; Miller and Bluestone 1988; Nelson 1999, pp. 22–23; Summers et al. 1976). Seventy-five percent of overall employment growth in non-metro areas during the 1970s was in the service sector, while only 17 percent was in manufacturing (Gringeri 1994, p. 35). Moreover, the service-sector employment that emerged in rural areas was more labor oriented than in metro areas (Gorham 1992, p. 24; Miller and Bluestone 1988). Government employment accounts for a substantial proportion of total earnings in rural areas, where local school systems and government are often the largest employers (Pickering 2000, p. 153; Tickamyer 1992, p. 42). This is acutely so in the persistently poor rural pockets of poverty, which are the focus of this chapter.

The second characteristic of rural employment is that the restructured rural economy is marked by "employment hardship" in the form of low wages, low hours, and lack of benefits such as sick leave and health insurance (Findeis and Jensen 1998; Gorham 1992; Lichter 1989). Employment hardship creates working poverty. Research using households as a unit of analysis shows that the rural poor are largely working poor, given that the largest share of income in poor rural households—even among those with the most restricted labor market opportunities—comes from wages of household members (Bloomquist, Jensen, and Teixeira 1988). Deavers and Hoppe (1992) found that nearly 20 percent of poor rural householders worked full-time, year-round, and Bryant et al. (1985) found that 33 percent of rural workers held more than one job. The persistently poor rural areas examined in this chapter also are home to many "discouraged workers," those able-bodied persons who are not counted among the unemployed because they have given up trying to find an official job (Summers, Horton, and Gringeri 1995).

The third characteristic is that poor rural households combine the activities of household members in a "household survival strategy" composed of official earnings, unofficial activities, in-kind assistance from kin, and welfare (Fitchen 1981; Nelson and Smith 1999; Pickering 2000, p. 159; Rank and Hirschl 1988; Shapiro 1988). As noted above, the most significant component of household income among the rural poor comes from official earnings. Income from unofficial activities is also crucial, however, and not unrelated to a household's official labor market status. Nelson and Smith (1999) found that the type of official work done by the head of the household affects the ability of the household to sustain a multi-earner strategy and engage in unofficial activities.

Reciprocal support among kin and friends is also crucial to sustaining poor rural households (see Fitchen 1981; Halperin 1990; Ruiz 1987; Ruiz and Tiano 1987). Adams and Duncan (1992, p. 83) used data from the 1980 Panel Study of Income Dynamics (PSID) to analyze the extent to which persons could rely on their networks for emergency assistance. Three-fifths of the long-term rural poor stated that they had friends or relatives who could provide several hundred dollars more than they had available or could borrow from an institution. An even greater percentage said they had contacts who could be counted on to help out during an emergency. Housing is perhaps the most important form of network support, as families often double-up with parents or in-laws in times of crisis (see Fitchen 1981; Nelson and Smith 1999).

Welfare also plays an important part in the household survival strategies in rural areas among families with children. The rural poor typically go on and off cash assistance as a last resort in situations of unemployment or absence of a male earner (Adams and Duncan 1992; Fitchen 1981, p. 72). In contrast to metro areas, studies by Fitzgerald (1995) and O'Neill, Bassi, and Wolf (1987) found that rural welfare participants have shorter welfare spells, while Rank and Hirschl (1988) found that rates of program participation among welfare recipients are lower in rural areas. Finally, Meyer and Cancian (1998) found that those leaving welfare among rural recipients have lower earnings than their metro counterparts. A study by Adams and Duncan (1992) that focused on the long-term, nonmetro poor found that, between 1976 and 1985, the vast majority used some form of public assistance.

Finally, in addition to structural transformation, employment hardship, and household survival strategies, rural economies are characterized by a deliberate underinvestment in programs to upgrade the workforce. In contrast to metro areas, few efforts have been made to improve the human capital of the rural workforce or to move rural welfare participants into employment. Because agribusiness and other extractive industries historically required mainly unskilled labor, rural employers had little interest in human resource development, and the programs that existed functioned ultimately to meet the seasonal labor needs of producers (Marshall 1974, pp. 30, 89–90; Pickering 2000, pp. 154–55; Saenz and Ballejos 1993, p. 116). Instead, those interested in skilled labor have migrated to urban centers, creating a gradual decline in the rural population.

Demonstration projects by the Women's Bureau of the U.S. Department of Labor (1985) found few training and employment opportunities available to women in rural areas and pointed to a lack of qualified personnel to run programs, inadequate space, lack of transportation, and lack of child care services as key barriers to rural women's employment. Gringeri (1994, p. 31) noted that the Manpower Development and Training Act has spent $47 per capita in metro areas compared with $18 in rural areas. Although welfare-to-work programs have existed since the early 1970s, they were not extensively implemented in metro areas until the establishment of the Job Opportunities and Basic Skills (JOBS) program in 1988 and were only marginally implemented in the rural areas included in this study.

These theoretical and empirical studies of labor market issues illustrate that a national welfare reform policy based on assumptions of a robust labor market will face considerable challenges when imposed in rural areas.

## METHOD

In examining the short-term impact of welfare reform in persistently poor rural areas, we used data from national data archives such as the U.S. Census of Population and Housing, state and local government administrative records, records of nongovernmental organizations, and interviews with community leaders and welfare participants. To make the research project feasible within the limits of budget and time, we selected a sample of persistently poor rural counties for study.[1] Four states were selected to represent the four major pockets of rural poverty: Kentucky (Central Appalachia), Mississippi (Lower Mississippi River Delta), Texas (Lower Rio Grande Valley), and South Dakota (Indian reservations). Because welfare reform is state-specific in its implementation, it was necessary to select states to represent regions rather than use a random sample of counties in each region. Second, within each of the four states, we selected a cluster of contiguous counties, all of which were persistently poor. South Dakota is an exception to this selection rule. For that state, we selected all rural counties con-

taining an Indian reservation, even though some counties are not contiguous. These clusters of counties are assumed to represent the four
pockets of rural poverty. (See the appendix for the counties contained
in each of the four clusters.)

In addition to the clusters of counties, we selected two counties in
each state for more intensive case study. We conducted interviews with
community leaders and welfare participants to add depth and nuance to
the data available from secondary sources. Within each state, the two
counties with the highest poverty rate in 1990 were chosen as case
study sites. The case study counties are McCreary and Owsley (Kentucky), Holmes and Sunflower (Mississippi), Shannon and Todd (South
Dakota), and Maverick and Starr (Texas).

We used administrative and archival data to construct a database
for each cluster for the period 1990–1999, including the case-study
counties. This data design allows a short-term assessment of conditions in the counties before and after welfare reform. Interview data for
the case studies were collected over a period of several months using
face-to-face interviews. We conducted interviews with roughly 15
community leaders in each county between March 1999 and May 1999.

Interviews with welfare participants were conducted by county residents. All of the interviewers had experience working with welfare
participants. However, none of the interviewers was employed by a
state or county welfare agency at the time of the interviews. Some of
the interviewers were former welfare participants. All the interviewers
were given instructions, which included the objectives of the research
project, the principles of interviewing, and a structured interview
guide. Ten current or former recipients were interviewed in seven of
the eight counties, yielding a total of 70 participant interviews. Interviews were not conducted in Starr County, Texas, because we could not
locate an appropriate interviewer. The interviews with community
leaders and welfare participants were tape-recorded and used as refer-
ents by the authors.


## FINDINGS: CASELOAD DECLINE


The implementation of welfare reform in these counties encouraged many participants to leave the cash assistance rolls quickly. Case-

load data clearly indicate that participation in the AFDC/TANF "Basic" program peaked in the early to mid 1990s and had begun to decline in all four clusters by 1996. In 1996, the year immediately preceding the implementation of TANF, the Kentucky cluster had 18,540 TANF cases. By October 1999, only 11,524 remained, a 38 percent decline (Figure 13.1). In the Mississippi cluster, the caseload fell from 12,996 in 1996 to 4,842 in October 1999, a 63 percent decline. In the South Dakota cluster, the caseload dropped 42 percent, from 2,248 to 1,299. In Texas, it fell from 4,603 to 2,805, a 39 percent decline. Percentage declines among Unemployed Parent Program (UPP) cases in Kentucky and Texas were even sharper.[2]

According to respondents, there are five main reasons behind the rapid caseload decline. The first is that the counties are located in low-benefit states, in which cash welfare assistance functions as a supplemental source of income. Second, many participants had other forms of support, including participation in the informal economy and reciprocal networks of support among friends and kin. Third, because official labor markets provide few opportunities and the TANF program requires formal work participation, there is little positive incentive to participate in welfare-to-work programs. Fourth, the reforms increased the bureaucratization of welfare. Given the lack of employment opportunities, programs often are perceived by participants as ineffective, a "hassle," punitive, and "a waste of time." Finally, implementation

**Figure 13.1  Change in TANF Caseloads, 1996 to October 1999**

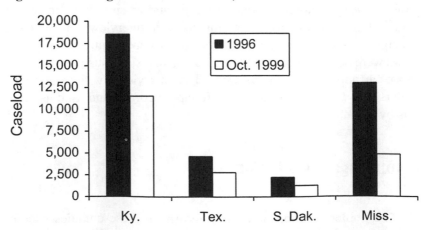

failed to provide the support services necessary to allow participation. Each of these reasons will be explained in more detail below.

## Low Benefits

Mississippi and Texas are among the states offering the lowest cash assistance benefits in the country. Prior to welfare reform, Mississippi offered a maximum benefit of $120 per month for a family of three. Under the reforms, the state raised the benefit to about $180 a month, approximately equivalent to that of Texas. The average grant for a family of three in Kentucky is $220 per month, while South Dakota offers $294. Given that the most generous of these states offers the average participant household a little over $70 a week, it is not surprising that many participants found the new work participation requirements of TANF "not worth the hassle."

## Other Sources of Support

Local TANF administrators explain the large caseload declines as a result of many recipients having other means of subsistence on which to draw. They are well aware that their service populations do not survive on public assistance alone and that income is garnered through other sources, including work (see Edin and Lein 1997). One Texas administrator estimated that at least 60 percent of his county's pre-reform caseload had been working informally while receiving welfare. According to administrators, when time-consuming work requirements were implemented under TANF, many chose to forfeit cash assistance in order to maintain unofficial activities. In areas where official work is available, others found it less of a hassle to seek work on their own. Although no data are available on those who dropped out of TANF, administrators and community leaders in counties experiencing job growth reported that these people are "doing the jobs that other people wouldn't take," including work in fast food establishments, hotel domestic services, and home health care.

These statements are supported by data from the Texas Workforce Commission for Maverick County, Texas, which record the employment status of those who obtained work through TANF. These data show that 125 TANF participants were placed in nonsubsidized employment between October 1998 and November 1999. Of those placed, 79 (63 percent) were still employed in November 1999. Among those still employed, 32 percent were working as nurses' aides or home health care assistants, 19 percent were working in fast food, 10 percent were in canning, 8 percent in pottery-making, and 8 percent were working in retail. Other jobs, constituting fewer than 5 percent of those still working, were housekeeper, custodian, clerk, laborer, caregiver, security guard, electrical helper, and truck driver. No data were available on the 37 percent who failed to maintain employment or the hundreds of leavers who did not obtain employment through the program. Excluding the wages of the two participants who found jobs as a truck driver and an electrical helper, the average starting wage was $5.34 per hour.

In areas where such jobs are unavailable, persons have reportedly become more economically dependent on informal work and assistance from family and friends. Informal employment is another important source of household income. The informal labor markets in these areas are described as "huge," and activities vary by region. In Kentucky, forestry work and seasonal tobacco cultivation and harvesting are widespread. In Texas, seasonal picking, gardening, day labor, construction, the drug trade, and trading in used goods across the border were common informal economic activities. In South Dakota, women make traditional clothing and beadwork, which they exchange for cash or in-kind services. It is estimated that 83 percent of the households in Pine Ridge engage in micro-enterprise and that 75 percent of households in Pine Ridge rely on some form of hunting, fishing, or gathering (Sherman 1988, p. 5).

Current and former TANF participants reported very high levels of reliance on their families for housing, food, essential baby items, including diapers and clothing, transportation, and child care. This shift of support from the government to extended families increases the vulnerability of working poor households when their limited resources are stretched to cover the needs of former TANF participants.

## Labor Market Deficiency

The number and types of jobs available in the counties provide little incentive for those looking for work, or employers in need of labor to participate in TANF welfare-to-work programs. In many of these counties, there are simply very few jobs to be had. In others, there is job growth, but labor markets are split between low-level service jobs and jobs with local school systems and government, which generally require higher education.

Earnings data from the U.S. Department of Commerce's Regional Economic Information System from 1977–1996 show strong growth in the government and service sectors (U.S. Department of Commerce 1997). Data on the Kentucky cluster show that the proportion of earnings from mining fell from 40 percent of total non-farm earnings to 15 percent, while earnings from services more than doubled, from 11 percent to 23 percent (Figure 13.2). The share of earnings from government also grew from 10 percent to 18 percent. In the Mississippi cluster, the proportion of total nonfarm earnings from service grew from 17 percent to 30 percent, while the government share remained steady at 19 percent. The South Dakota cluster exhibited the least change; the share of government jobs remained at about 39 percent of total earnings and services grew from 29 percent to 34 percent. Finally, the Texas cluster also saw growth in the share of earnings from services, rising from 14 percent to 19 percent, while government earnings jumped 12 percentage points, from 27 percent to 39 percent. Mississippi is the

**Figure 13.2  Earnings from Service Sector, 1977–96**

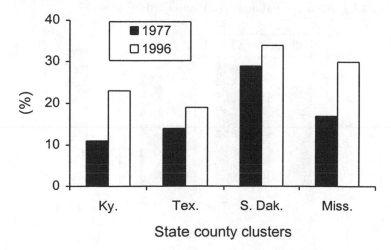

only cluster in which a substantial proportion of total nonfarm earnings were gained from manufacturing, roughly 20 percent.

Data from the U.S. Bureau of the Census and the U. S. Department of Labor's Bureau of Labor Statistics show that women in these counties are not faring well despite the economic growth. Rates of women's official labor force participation in these areas are substantially below national and state averages. Estimated women's labor force participation in the Kentucky cluster remained constant from 1990–1999 at only 46 percent (Figure 13.3).[3] Estimated unemployment rates among women declined over the same period from 8 percent to 5.8 percent. The South Dakota cluster saw little change in women's labor force participation, inching up from 51.6 percent in 1990 to 52.3 percent in 1999, while women's unemployment rate fell from 10.2 percent to 7.9 percent. In Texas, women's labor force participation declined steadily from 56.7 percent in 1990 to 50.4 percent in 1999, as unemployment among women fell from 23.9 percent to 17.4 percent. Mississippi exhibited the highest rate of women's labor force participation among the clusters. Between 1990 and 1999, the rate declined, however, from 63.4 percent to 61.1 percent, while the estimated women's unemployment rate dropped slightly from 11.9 percent to 10.3 percent.

The relatively low unemployment rates in Kentucky and South Dakota are, according to local residents, underestimated due to the

**Figure 13.3  Women's Labor Force Participation, 1990–99**

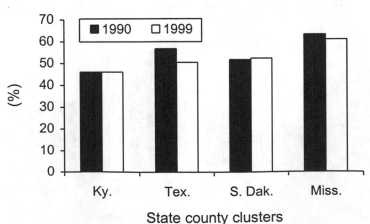

presence of a large number of "discouraged workers" who are in need of work but have given up looking for employment in the official labor force. For example, the Bureau of Indian Affairs calculated the overall unemployment rate on the Pine Ridge Reservation to be 73 percent, in contrast to the state's figure of less than 8 percent. The difference is largely due to different definitions of who is in the labor force.

These data indicate that there are few opportunities for women to participate in the official labor markets in these areas. Moreover, the data presented above on the employment and wages of TANF participants in Maverick County provide direct evidence that few jobs are available that may be expected to lead to economic self-sufficiency. According to community leaders in all of our sample counties, when jobs do appear, competition is fierce and selection between qualified candidates often comes down to politics. This is particularly so as regards good jobs in the public sector. Alternatively, good positions are often filled by "outsiders" with more formal qualifications than local residents.

## Increased Bureaucracy

PRWORA made it more difficult to apply for welfare assistance and placed tighter restrictions on eligibility, particularly for new immigrants and Legal Permanent Residents. Increased bureaucratization has contributed to the substantial declines in both the TANF and food stamp caseloads. These declines have been accompanied by a substantial increase in the use of nongovernment assistance, specifically, food banks.

The TANF programs implemented in these areas are based on the "work first" philosophy, that is, they emphasize "immediate labor market participation" in "whatever job is available." The primary, and in some counties singular, component of the welfare-to-work programs initiated in these areas is a six-week job search, at the end of which most participants are to have found a job. Because so few jobs are available, local administrators have resorted to placing large numbers of participants in voluntary community service positions so that they may remain eligible for benefits and administrators may meet federally mandated participation rates. The majority of these placements are with local school systems, county administrative offices, and county hospitals. Fewer numbers have been placed with private companies and local non-government organizations.

Mandatory six-week job-search programs were established in all but one county, Starr County, Texas. Participants who dropped out of TANF described these programs as a "hassle," a "waste of time," and an experience from which they "did not learn anything." One high school-age participant quit both school and TANF because she became confused and frustrated with the participation requirements that conflicted with school. In response to the question, "Did welfare help you?" she replied: "Well, not really. It was helping me buy things for my baby but I had to stop going to school because it conflicted with orientation [the six-week job search program]. Orientation was a waste of time . . . not training, just signing a lot of papers."

Participants and employers alike complained of bureaucratic irrationality. Participants report frustration and disappointment with volunteer work assignments in which it is clear that the organizations they are placed in do not have the resources to hire them as permanent employees. Some complained that too many participants are often assigned to the same site, resulting in a lack of work and training for all. Others expressed resentment about being forced to work for subminimum wages alongside regular employees paid higher wages for doing the same work. Reliance on such voluntary placements in which participants feel that they are merely "wasting time" has also contributed to caseload decline.

Some employers with whom TANF participants have been placed also criticized the process. They complained that lack of support services, particularly, child care and transportation, resulted in unreliability among some participants. Some employers were sympathetic to the difficulties faced by participants and were hesitant to report absences, even though they are mandated to do so, because they did not believe they should be sanctioned.

Local TANF administrators complained of a "lack of concern" among the private sector with the potential long-term negative effects of welfare reform. A complicated application process and demand for unskilled labor were cited as reasons why private employers have shown little interest in participating in TANF wage subsidy programs. These programs use TANF and food stamp benefits to subsidize the wages of participants as they are trained in the job-specific skills needed by specific employers. Rather than pay the small price associated with these programs, employers were reported to be "waiting in line" to accept TANF participants as free "unpaid volunteer labor." Some administrators expressed concern that employers may seek to exploit TANF work requirements and participants by using the program as a source of free labor.

### Effect of increased bureaucracy on Medicaid eligibility

Participants also complained that services are cut off too quickly after obtaining employment. The premature cut-off of services was seen as especially problematic in the case of health care for children. The children of TANF recipients who find employment may remain eligible for Medicaid for up to one year. Unfortunately, many of the jobs secured by TANF recipients provide no health insurance coverage for children of workers, and often not the workers themselves. When Medicaid eligibility has been exhausted, the family is faced with a choice of either forgoing health insurance and depending on emergency room care or quitting the job and returning to TANF. According to caseworkers, many participants choose the latter alternative.

Data on the Medicaid program from Kentucky, South Dakota, and Texas do not exhibit the same drastic decline as TANF and Food Stamp program participation. In fact, it appears that the extension of coverage for one year after leaving TANF in combination with state outreach efforts to enroll working poor families in "low income" Medicaid programs has substantially buffered declines in Medicaid.

Administrative data from Kentucky show that the percentage of children eligible for Medicaid declined only slightly between 1996 and 1998 (the last year for which Medicaid data are available), from 39 percent to 37.8 percent. Although the number of children eligible through TANF dropped sharply, the decline was largely offset by strong growth in the numbers of children eligible through Kentucky's Medical Assistance Case (MAC) program. Adults also experienced a decline in Medicaid eligibility of about 2 percentage points over the same period, from 7.8 percent to 5.7 percent.

South Dakota changed its method of reporting Medicaid data over the course of our study; thus, two measures are presented. From 1990–1998, data on Medicaid eligibility were reported for TANF eligibles and for Low Income Women and Children (LIWC). Comparisons show that the percentage of women (ages 18–64) and children eligible for Medicaid through TANF declined from 29.2 percent in 1992 to 24.9 percent in 1998. As in the Kentucky cluster, this decline was offset by an increase in the percentage of women and children eligible for Medicaid through the LIWC program, which rose from 4 percent in 1992 to 10.2 percent in 1998. There was, therefore, a net increase in Medicaid eligibility among women and children of about 2 percent between 1992 and 1998. The distinction between TANF and LIWC was replaced in 1999 with "child" versus "adult" eligibles. These data show an increase in child Medicaid eligibles, from 48.2 percent of children in 1997 to 54.3 percent in October 1999. The percentage of all adults (ages 18–64) eligible for Medicaid also increased during the period, from 18 percent to 22.9 percent.

Texas data on Medicaid eligibles is reported by "families and children" and "aged and disabled." The Medicaid eligibility rate for families and children (women ages 18–64 plus children) reached 30.3 percent in 1996 before falling to 26.1 percent in October 1999.

As of March 2000, the Mississippi Division of Medicaid had yet to release its 1998 annual report. A state Medicaid administrator stated that data problems would likely result in the joint publication of the 1998 and 1999 reports sometime in late 2000. Lack of post-1997 data precludes any inference regarding the effect of welfare reform on Medicaid eligibility in the Mississippi cluster.

Although the Kentucky and South Dakota data indicate that declines in TANF Medicaid eligibility have been largely offset by increases in the numbers eligible for expanded state low-income programs, particularly those serving children, it should be noted that transitional Medicaid assistance is available for only one year. Thus, over time, eligibility rates may be expected to decline. Medicaid eligibility is also not a direct indicator of use of or access to medical care. The increased bureaucratization of social service eligibility determination under TANF may make it more difficult for persons who are eligible for Medicaid to actually make use of the program. Moreover, the problem of health care in these areas is further compounded by a lack of health care providers.

### Effect of bureaucracy on food stamps

Although the bureaucratization accompanying TANF has not had a negative impact on Medicaid eligibility in the short-term, data on Food Stamp program participation indicate a major negative effect. With the exception of Texas, where the substantial decline in participation is directly related to changes in the eligibility status of the large population of legal permanent residents (LPRs), declines in food stamp participation are noteworthy because eligibility for food stamps is not linked to TANF eligibility.

Data on food stamp participation are presented as total numbers of recipients and as a food stamp participation rate, which reflects the percentage of estimated persons in poverty receiving food stamps.[4] The data indicate that the number of food stamp recipients in the Kentucky cluster fell 13 percent between 1996 and October 1999, while the food stamp participation rate among persons in poverty fell from 77.6 percent to 66.9 percent (Figure 13.4). In the Mississippi cluster, the number of food stamp recipients declined 35 percent, while the food stamp participation rate among the poor fell nearly 28 percentage points, from 87.8 percent to 60 percent. In South Dakota, the number of recipients declined by only 4.8 percent, while the participation rate fell from 80.1 percent to 74.4 percent. In Texas, the number of recipients fell 34 percent and the participation rate declined from 104.2 percent to 65.7 percent.

It is telling that the percentage decline in the number of persons receiving food stamps was roughly equal in the Mississippi and Texas clusters. A significant proportion of the decline in the Texas caseload is undoubtedly explained by the loss of benefits among the large population of LPRs. There is no comparable explanation for the Mississippi decline.

### Increasing food insecurity

Data on the pounds of food distributed by food banks in these counties indicate that reforms may be substantially increasing food insecurity. The data show that as food stamp rolls have declined, food bank distributions have risen sharply, suggesting that families that lost government food assistance have migrated to private charities for support.

**Figure 13.4  Food Stamp Participation Rates, 1996 and 1999**

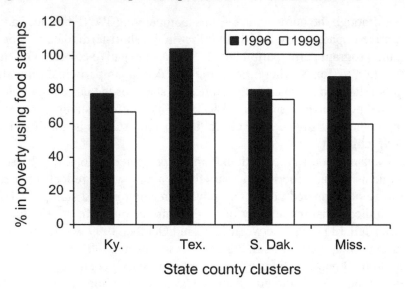

Annual figures on pounds of food distributed show that God's Pantry Food Bank in Lexington, Kentucky, distributed 119,917 pounds of food in McCreary County in 1997. This figure grew to 299,604 pounds in 1998, and stood at 230,769 in 1999 (Figure 13.5). The U.S. Department of Agriculture (USDA) commodities composed 75 percent to 80 percent of the food distributed. Food bank distribution also increased in the tri-county area of Owsley, Breathitt, and Jackson counties, from 174,568 pounds in 1997 to 221,258 pounds in 1998 and 208,201 pounds in 1999.

In Holmes County, Mississippi, the Mississippi Food Network of Jackson distributed 93,829 pounds of food in 1997, 96,017 pounds in 1998, and 110,589 pounds in 1999 (Figure 13.5). In Sunflower County, distribution grew from 97,549 pounds in 1997 to 104,479 pounds in 1998 before falling to 93,382 pounds in 1999. According to the director, about half of the poundage distributed was USDA commodities (Temporary Emergency Food Assistance Program).

The data from The Second Harvest Food Bank of South Dakota for 1995–1999 show tremendous growth in pounds of food distributed in the two case study counties. In 1995, Shannon County (the Pine Ridge

Figure 13.5  Food Bank Use in Selected Areas (lb.)

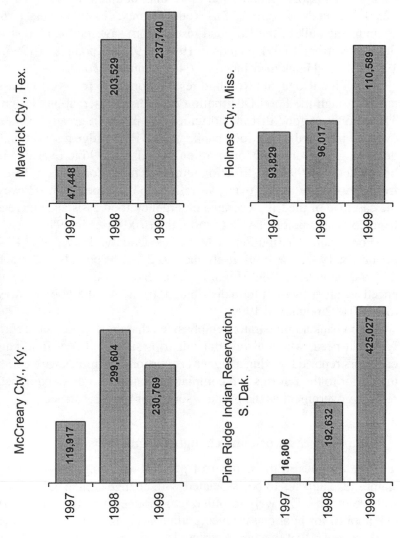

Indian Reservation) received 21,502 pounds of food. Ten times that amount, or 200,930 pounds, was distributed in 1996 before dropping back down to 16,806 pounds in 1997. In 1998, the poundage jumped back up to 192,632 pounds, and more than doubled in 1999, reaching 425,027 pounds (Figure 13.5). Todd County, South Dakota (which contains the bulk of the Rosebud reservation) saw food bank distributions grow from 46,991 pounds in 1995 to198,744 pounds in 1996. In 1999, the food bank distributed 377,490 pounds of food.

The Pine Ridge and Rosebud reservations also receive food assistance through the Food Distribution on Indian Reservations Program. The amount of food distributed under this program greatly overshadows that provided by the food bank. On the Pine Ridge reservation, the quantity grew from over four million pounds in 1996 to over five million pounds in 1999. Distribution remained fairly constant on Rosebud from 1994–1999 at just over two million pounds per year. However, the caseload of the tribe-operated emergency food assistance increased from 250 cases before TANF to more than 700 cases in 1999.

Food bank distribution in Maverick County, Texas, was 47,448 pounds in 1997. In 1998, it climbed to 203,529 pounds and reached 237,740 pounds in 1999 (Figure 13.5). Starr County, Texas, experienced steady growth in food distributed, from 341,795 pounds in 1996 to 1,780,092 pounds in 1999.

Food bank administrators emphasized that the data do not accurately reflect need, which always far outstrips supply. Local food pantry operators reported serving a higher proportion of families with children than prior to the reforms and complained that they are not equipped to replace government as the primary source of food assistance.

### Changing casework and changing regulations

The declines in the number of persons receiving TANF and food stamps also appears to be associated with changes in the culture of the welfare office. The welfare office is no longer merely a place where one applies for public assistance; rather, it is also a job center. Caseworkers report that they are instructed to treat participants as job seekers rather than persons entitled to government assistance. Their new role is to encourage self-sufficiency and divert applicants from applying for TANF assistance "if at all possible." Caseworker emphasis on diversion, as well as general confusion among the poor regarding the changes under PRWORA, has likely contributed to declines in food stamp participation.

Participants' accounts of interactions with caseworkers varied. Some caseworkers were described as "domineering." One participant stated that under the new system, caseworkers "ask you too many things to apply for TANF. They act as if the money is theirs." Another stated that the local social services workers "practically want to know the color of your underwear each day." Experience clearly varied, however. Other participants described caseworkers as "very helpful."

Finally, interviews with participants indicate a general lack of information and confusion about TANF regulations, programs, and benefits. Many of the state TANF plans offer new programs designed to meet the specific needs of particular individuals, such as diversion programs offering lump-sum payments of approximately $1,000 to individuals deemed highly responsible in lieu of a year's worth of monthly checks. Participants and, in some cases, administrators were completely unaware of such programs. In addition, directors of community-based organizations in several counties reported that recipients who lost eligibility for TANF mistakenly believed they also lost eligibility for other programs, including food stamps, WIC, and utilities programs such as the Low Income Heating Assistance Program. There was widespread concern among leaders of helping organizations that fear associated with the punitive nature of the new welfare system had resulted in some needy residents not seeking services for which they remained eligible.

## Inadequate Work Support Services

Working frequently requires basic services and resources including transportation, child or elder care, and the appropriate clothing, tools, and so forth. We found such services to be grossly lacking in the eight case-study counties. There are a variety of reasons for this, including labor market dynamics and the historical underinvestment in job assistance programs; a lack of basic infrastructure, including paved roads and buses; insufficient child and elder care facilities; and the persistence of a division of labor in which women are expected to stay home and take care of other family members.

Lack of services has contributed to caseload declines in two ways. First, it has made it practically impossible for those lacking informal supports, such as friends with vehicles or parents who can provide child care, to participate in TANF. Although participants who cannot obtain publicly provided child care may be exempted from work requirements under PRWORA, few are aware of this exemption and have simply dropped out. Second, because neither skills-training nor education are provided, those with some resources chose to seek work on their own.

TANF participants and community leaders expressed great disappointment with the lack of services accompanying the reform. Many held high expectations stemming from the promises of the rhetoric of welfare reform. One director of a community-based organization expressed her disdain with the new "punitive" approach, stating, "Yes, there is a lot of abuse. But we must focus on meeting the needs of the children. The services are not being provided. We thought that was what welfare reform was going to be." At the time of the interviews, the lack of services and real opportunities for training and work had left participants and community leaders alike disillusioned with the reforms and concerned about the long-term impact.

The problems of child care, elder care, and transportation in these areas cannot be overstated. Although some counties have contracted with transportation providers, these services are largely reserved for emergencies and are fully inadequate to address the daily problems that many participants face, especially those living in remote neighborhoods that may be 20–40 miles from the welfare office or the nearest place of employment. Participants without vehicles are encouraged to find rides with family and friends and apply for reimbursement from the TANF office at a later date. One social worker described this policy as insensitive to the reality of life on welfare, where recipients often do not have cash on hand to pay for transportation, gas, and car repairs. She reported the case of one participant whose car broke down in the middle of her six-week mandatory job search. As a result, she never completed the training, was sanctioned for nonparticipation, and was never reimbursed for the money she had spent on gas and lunch traveling 20 miles daily from her home to the training center for three weeks. Moreover, the caseworker described the reimbursement form as so complicated that even she had trouble filling it out.

Interviews with participants indicate that finding reliable child care is a major barrier to employment and that most rely primarily on family and friends. Although such supports are strong, they are not always reliable. One woman reported losing a job because her child was ill and she could not find anyone to take care of him while she went to work. She was fired and told by her employer that he needed someone without children. Official providers of child care are scarce, and the systems connecting them to welfare participants are patchwork.

Postemployment services to help participants obtain better jobs were all but nonexistent in these areas as of spring 1999. Work First programs were implemented in all but one of our case study counties (Starr County, Texas). In theory, Work First is shorthand for a policy orientation geared toward immediate labor force attachment combined with subsequent education and training if desired by the participant. Thus, participants are placed in whatever job is available "if at all possible." In the words of one local administrator, if at all possible means "if work is available and the recipient has a ninth-grade education." The reality as of October 1999 in the counties studied here was that, while Work First has been vigorously implemented, the postemployment education and training services that were to accompany it did not exist.

## Administrative Strategies

Although states and localities exercised substantial discretion in administering welfare under Aid to Families with Dependent Children, PRWORA (and the Work Force Investment Act of 1998) devolved even more responsibility to the local level. Under the Workforce Investment Act (WIA), authority over all regional workforce development programs, including welfare-to-work, is vested in New Area Workforce Boards (NAWBs). These boards are responsible for the design and oversight of all job-training programs, including TANF welfare-to-work programs (National Governors' Association 1998).

During the period of data collection, the NAWBs in the areas studied had either just been formed or were in the process of being created. Responsibility for TANF is only one among many tasks these boards are charged with carrying out. According to an executive of one of the Texas boards, their first and foremost concern is to "create jobs," and this goal is pursued "by serving the needs of business."

The economic problems plaguing these areas are described as affecting everyone, "not just welfare recipients." Serving the needs of welfare participants in transition to work is clearly secondary to the overarching goal of regional economic development and job growth. To the welfare program administrators, developing the services necessary to allow participants to take part in work activities of any kind is clearly subordinate to creating opportunities for work. Regarding transportation, one administrator stated, "If they get a job, we'll get them there." Yet the evidence indicates that this work support is seldom available.

Economic growth is therefore the primary concern of the bodies responsible for implementing TANF. The NAWBs spend much effort working with local development corporations to attract new employers to their regions and garner economic development grants from state and federal sources. Most of the counties in this study are in regions granted Empowerment Zone/Enterprise Community (EZ/EC) status under the USDA's EZ/EC program. The funds made available under these programs have been focused on increasing economic development and meeting general community needs, such as paving the streets of the "colonias" (unincorporated neighborhoods) in the Texas counties. As of 1999, these initiatives had produced variable results depending on whether an area was designated EZ or EC and the year in which the respective status was granted. In most areas, goals had merely been identified, while in a few others, a number of new businesses had started up as a result of the EZ initiative.

Other problems faced by local administrators related to the implementation of welfare-to-work programs in these counties is a lack of funds to participate in federal match grant programs, such as the competitive U.S. Department of Labor welfare-to-work grants. Even though such programs may be desirable and potentially beneficial, they cannot be implemented in communities that lack the financial resources to meet the federally required match.

Economic development is a long-term goal. In the short-term, administrators have sought to cope with the dilemma of implementing welfare-to-work programs in areas where there is no work by encouraging participants to move to other regions where demand for low-skilled labor is higher. Administrators acknowledge that this approach

has been unsuccessful in the past, due in large part to welfare participants' reluctance to move to urban locations and forfeit their kin support systems and other ties.  There is no evidence to suggest that encouraging such migration has been more successful in recent years.
Nonetheless, a number of counties have held job fairs to try to connect
regional employers with local residents in need of work.  Administrators report that some residents commute 150 miles or more each day to
work in order to remain in the area.  Obviously, exercising this option
requires a reliable vehicle.

Because the labor markets offer few positive incentives to find official work, administrators have turned to increased surveillance and
sanctioning to meet their federally mandated participation rates.  One
administrator looked forward to the implementation of the Food
Stamps Employment and Training Program in his region because it
would allow him to sanction the food stamp grants of persons who re-
fused to participate in TANF work activities.  He referred the Food
Stamps Employment and Training Program as providing the "hammer"
needed to force program participation.  Another metaphor used in describing sanctions was a "tightening of the noose" around clients.

Data from Texas and Kentucky show a substantial increase in sanctions between 1997 and 1998 in McCreary County, Kentucky, and
Maverick County, Texas.  The number of cases under sanction in Mc-
Creary County grew from 67 in September of 1997 to 103 in September of 1998 (Kentucky Youth Advocates 1999).  Data provided by the
Texas Workforce Commission show that in Maverick County, the average number of cases under sanction grew from 38 in 1997 to 94 in
1998.  At the same time, the number of cases sanctioned in Owsley
County, Kentucky, fell from 12 to 3.  Sanctions are not applied in Starr
County, Texas, because it is a "minimum service" county and participation in TANF work activities is voluntary.  Data on sanctions from Mississippi and South Dakota were unavailable.  Although administrators
in South Dakota expressed the desire to avoid imposing sanctions,
TANF participants spoke of the hardships caused when sanctions were
applied for missing an appointment, class, or community service hours
because of transportation problems, lack of child care, family illness, or
personal crisis.  Administrators report that their use of home visits has
increased as well.

## CONCLUSION

Program administrators and community leaders alike in the study counties are concerned with the potential negative long-term impact of welfare reform in the absence of job growth. State time limits have been suspended in most of these counties because of high unemployment rates; thus, no families have exhausted their time-limited eligibility for assistance. Leaders are concerned, however, with the approaching federal five-year lifetime limit on assistance, which they believe will not be waived. They are particularly worried about the ability of the counties to absorb the health care costs of those who lose Medicaid when lifetime limits on assistance take effect. Some also expressed concern that those left with no other alternative will turn to illegal activities, particularly the drug trade.

One hypothesis concerning the impact of welfare reform was that persons losing cash assistance in areas where employment was unavailable would migrate to other programs. Our findings indicate that, rather than migrating to other government programs such as food stamps, WIC, or Supplemental Security Income (SSI) Disability, people have turned to their families and to food banks. Regarding health insurance, the data indicate migration from one category of eligibility, that is, "TANF eligible," to another, "low income eligible." This change suggests that the jobs most TANF participants are obtaining do not provide affordable private health insurance and lends weight to local leaders' fears concerning the long-term ramifications.

Our interview data indicate that the overall short-term impact of welfare reform in these areas has been to create "more hardship for people with nothing." Nonetheless, it has also produced some positive results. These include increased emphasis on education, the attainment of job skills, student retention, and interagency planning and coordination. There also appears to be improved self-esteem among those who have found jobs and increased motivation to obtain education. At the same time, interagency coordination as of March 1999 was more rhetorical than real. Moreover, directors of local charitable agencies and nongovernmental organizations complained that their organizations are an inadequate substitute for government assistance, and that they are facing difficulties in meeting increased demand. One director expressed the concern that helping organizations may "begin to see more people in really desperate straits."

In addition, the emphasis on immediate employment has resulted in the gradual exclusion of General Equivalency Diploma (GEDs), training, and college courses as substitutes for the hours of work activity required by TANF. Although aspirations of education have risen among those who have found work, others have been disappointed by the lack of services available under TANF.

We chose to monitor the impact of welfare reform in the poorest rural counties under the assumption that if serious negative impacts were to follow from PRWORA, they would surely appear in these counties. The data indicate that although there have been substantial problems associated with the short-term implementation of welfare reform, widespread, drastic, negative effects have not occurred. Extensive participation in informal labor markets, strong networks of family support, relatively low costs of living in some areas, as well as the suspension of time limits in most counties, have buffered the potentially severe impacts that were predicted by some reform critics.

The overall effect of welfare reform in the rural areas studied has been the disruption of the survival strategies of households by removing an important source of income and failing to replace it with the promised alternative of a job and the support services needed to maintain it. TANF caseloads have fallen rapidly because the low payments offered in these states are not worth the hassle of meeting new program requirements, participants have other sources of support, and because the new welfare bureaucracy encourages diversion and has failed to deliver necessary supports. The caseload decline has resulted in increased reliance on nongovernment and non-market sources of support. These supports, primarily family networks and food pantries, are unlikely to be effective replacements for government assistance in the long-term.

Limited data collection efforts by the states and the unwillingness of state administrators to share employment data (particularly Mississippi and South Dakota) leave us little direct quantitative evidence of the employment status of TANF participants. The interview data indicate that it is likely that many of those who left welfare in these areas have found work in either formal or informal labor markets. Although some are undoubtedly better off, it is likely that many, even among families in which the head obtained formal employment, are worse off due to the type of work, loss of benefits, and lack of supports.

## Notes

This research was supported by USDA Cooperative Agreement No. 43-3-AEN-7-80065 and the Wisconsin Agricultural Experiment Station, Gene Summers, Principal Investigator.

1. We follow Cook and Meiser (1994) in defining "persistently poor" counties as those exhibiting poverty rates of 20 percent or more for the last four decennial censuses.
2. The Unemployed Parent Program is a cash assistance program under the AFDC/TANF umbrella that supports two-parent families in which one of the parents is unemployed.
3. Data from the Department of Labor's Bureau of Labor Statistics (BLS) and the Census Bureau were used to estimate women's labor force participation and unemployment for the clusters from 1990 through 1999. The women's labor force participation rate was obtained by dividing the estimated number of women in the labor force by census estimates of the population of working age women age 16–64 (U.S. Bureau of the Census 1999). The estimated number of women in the labor force was computed by applying the percentage of the total labor force comprised of women from the 1990 Census (U.S. Bureau of the Census 1990) to BLS estimates of overall labor force participation from 1991–1999 (U.S. Department of Labor 1999). Similarly, estimated women's unemployment rates for the clusters were obtained by applying the ratio of unemployed women to total unemployed from the 1990 Census to BLS estimates of unemployment from 1991 to 1999 and dividing this figure by estimated women's labor force participation rates.
4. The Food Stamp program participation rate for 1995 was obtained by dividing the average monthly number of food stamp recipients by the estimated number of persons below poverty using 1995 census estimates (http://www.census.gov/population/www/estimates/popest.html). Income adjustments used in TANF are not accounted for in the census income data used to estimate poverty. Thus, poverty rates are only rough proxies for those eligible for food stamps. The denominator for the 1996–1999 rates was estimated by applying the ratio of persons below poverty to population in 1995 to census estimates of population for 1996–1999. Eligibility for food stamps requires income below 130 percent of the federal poverty line. Thus the denominator in our food stamp rate (persons at or below 100 percent of poverty) underestimates the number of persons potentially eligible for food stamps and therefore produces an inflated participation rate. This explains why the Texas rate was over 100 percent in 1996.

# APPENDIX

## CLUSTER COUNTIES

| Appalachia, Kentucky | The Delta, Mississippi | Reservations, South Dakota | The Valley, Texas |
|---|---|---|---|
| Bell | Boliver | Bennett | Brooks |
| Breathitt | Carrol | Corson | Dimmit |
| Clay | Coahoma | Dewey | Jim Hogg |
| Floyd | Holmes | Jackson | Kinney |
| Harlan | Humphries | Shannon | Lasalle |
| Jackson | Issaquena | Todd | Maverick |
| Knott | LeFlore | Zeibach | Starr |
| Knox | Quitman | | Uvalde |
| Laural | Sharkey | | Zapata |
| Lee | Sunflower | | Zavala |
| Leslie | Tallahatchie | | |
| Letcher | Tunica | | |
| McCreary | Washington | | |
| Owsley | Yazoo | | |
| Perry | | | |
| Pike | | | |
| Pulaski | | | |
| Rock Castle | | | |
| Wayne | | | |
| Whitley | | | |

# References

Adams, Terry K., and Greg J. Duncan 1992. "Long-Term Poverty in Rural Areas." In *Rural Poverty in America*, Cynthia M. Duncan, ed. New York: Auburn House, pp. 63–93.

Bloomquist, Leonard, Leif Jensen, and Ruy Teixeira. 1988. "Too Few Jobs for Workfare to Put Many to Work." *Rural Development Perspectives* 5(1): 8–12.

Bryant, Clifton D., Charles J. Dudley, Donald J. Shoemaker, and Peggy A. Shifflet. 1985. "Rural Occupational Diversity: Impact of Multiple Job Holding on Job Satisfaction and Traditional Life." In *The Rural Workforce: Nonagricultural Occupations in America*, Clifton D. Bryant, Donald J. Shoemaker, James K. Skipper, Jr., and William E. Snizek, eds. Amherst, Massachusetts: Bergin and Garvey Publishers, pp. 223–240.

Castells, Manuel, and Alejandro Portes. 1989. "World Underneath: The Origins, Dynamics, and Effects of the Informal Economy." In *The Informal Economy: Studies in Advanced and Less Developed Countries*, Alejandro Portes, Manuel Castells, and Lauren A. Benton, eds. Baltimore: Johns Hopkins University Press, pp. 11–37.

Cook, Peggy, and Karen Meiser. 1994. "The Revised County Typology and Overview." *Rural Development Research Report No. 89*. Washington D.C.: U.S. Department of Agriculture, Economic Research Service.

Deavers, Kenneth L., and Robert A. Hoppe. 1992. "Overview of the Rural Poor in the 1980s." In *Rural Poverty in America*, Cynthia M. Duncan, ed. New York: Auburn House, pp. 3–20.

Duncan, Cynthia M. 1992. "Persistent Poverty in Appalachia: Scarce Work and Rigid Stratification." In *Rural Poverty in America*, Cynthia M. Duncan, ed. New York: Auburn House, pp. 111–133.

Duncan, Cynthia M. 1999. *Worlds Apart: Why Poverty Persists in Rural America*. New Haven, Connecticut: Yale University Press.

Duncan, Cynthia M., and Stephen Sweet. 1992. "Introduction: Poverty in Rural America." In *Rural Poverty in America*, Cynthia M. Duncan, ed. New York: Auburn House, pp. xix–xxvii.

Edin, Kathryn, and Laura Lein. 1997. *Making Ends Meet: How Single Mothers Survive Welfare and Low-Wage Work*. New York: Russell Sage.

Fernandez-Kelly, M. Patricia, and Anna M. Garcia. 1989. "Informalization at the Core: Hispanic Women, Homework, and the Advanced Capitalist State." In *The Informal Economy: Studies in Advanced and Less Developed Countries*, Alejandro Portes, Manuel Castells, and Lauren A. Benton, eds. Baltimore: Johns Hopkins University Press, pp. 247–264.

Findeis, Jill, and Leif Jensen. 1998. "Employment Opportunities in Rural Areas: Implications for Poverty in a Changing Policy Environment." *American Journal of Agricultural Economics* 80(5): 1000–1007.

Fitchen, Janet M. 1981. *Poverty in Rural America: A Case Study*. Prospect Heights, Illinois: Waveland Press.

Fitzgerald, John R. 1995. "Local Labor Markets and Local Effects on Welfare Duration." IRP reprint series 724. Institute for Research on Poverty, University of Wisconsin–Madison.

Gorham, Lucy. 1992. "The Growing Problem of Low Earnings in Rural Areas." In *Rural Poverty in America*, Cynthia M. Duncan, ed. New York, Auburn House, pp. 21–39.

Gringeri, Christina. 1994. *Getting By: Women Homeworkers and Rural Economic Development*. Lawrence: University of Kansas Press.

Halperin, Rhoda. 1990. "Karl Polanyi's Concept of Householding: Resistance and Livelihood in an Appalachian Region." *Research in Economic Anthropology* 13: 93–116.

Hofferth, Sandra, and John Iceland. 1998. "Social Capital in Rural and Urban Communities." *Rural Sociology* 63(4): 574–598.

Jessop, Bob. 1994. "Towards a Schumpeterian Workfare State? Preliminary Remarks on Post-Fordist Political Economy." *Studies in Political Economy* 40: 7–39.

Kentucky Youth Advocates. 1999. *A Reality Check: How Children Are Faring under Welfare Reforms in Kentucky*. Louisville: Kentucky Youth Advocates.

Legborne, D., and A. Lipietz. 1992. "Conceptual Fallacies and Open Questions on Post–Fordism." In *Pathways to Industrialization and Regional Development*, M. Storper and A.J. Scott, eds. London: Routledge, pp. 332–348.

Lichter, Daniel T. 1989. "Race, Employment, Hardship, and Inequality in the American Nonmetropolitan South." *American Sociological Review* 54: 436–446.

Lichter, Daniel T., and Janice A. Costanzo. 1987. "Nonmetropolitan Underemployment and Labor Force Composition." *Rural Sociology* 52: 329–344.

Lobao, Linda. 1993. "Renewed Significance of Space in Social Research: Implications for Labor Market Studies." In *Inequalities in Local Labor Market Areas*, Joachim Singelmann and Forrest A. Deseran, eds. Boulder, Colorado: Westview Press, pp. 11–31.

Marshall, Ray. 1974. *Rural Workers in Rural Labor Markets*. Salt Lake City: Olympus Publishing.

Meyer, Daniel, and Maria Cancian. 1998. "Economic Well-Being Following an Exit from Aid to Families with Dependent Children." *Journal of Marriage and Family* 60: 479–492.

Miller, James P., and Herman Bluestone. 1988. "Prospects for Service Sector Employment Growth in Non-Metropolitan America." *Review of Regional Studies* 18: 28–41.

National Governors Association. 1998. *Workforce Investment Act of 1998 (H.R. 1385): Summary and Description of Final Compromise.* Available at <http://www.reg10.doleta.gov/wia_nga.htm>.

Nelson, Margaret K. 1999. "Economic Restructuring, Gender, and Informal Work: A Case Study of a Rural County." *Rural Sociology* 64(1): 18–43.

Nelson, Margaret K., and Joan Smith. 1999. *Working Hard and Making Do: Surviving in Small Town America.* Berkeley: University of California Press.

O'Neill, J.A., L.J. Bassi, and D.A. Wolf. 1987. "The Duration of Welfare Spells." *The Review of Economic Statistics* 69: 241–247.

Peck, Jamie. 1996. *Work Place: The Social Regulation of Labor Markets.* New York: Guilford.

Pickering, Kathleen. 2000. "Alternative Economic Strategies in Low-Income Rural Communities: TANF, Labor Migration, and the Case of the Pine Ridge Indian Reservation." *Rural Sociology* 65(1): 148–167.

Rank, Mark R., and Thomas A Hirschl. 1988. "A Rural Urban Comparison of Welfare Exits: The Importance of Population Density." *Rural Sociology* 53(2): 190–206.

Ruiz, Vicki L. 1987. "By the Day or the Week: Mexican Domestic Workers in El Paso." In *Women on the U.S.–Mexico Border: Responses to Change*, Vicki L. Ruiz and Susan Tiano, eds. Boulder, Colorado: Westview Press, pp. 61–76.

Ruiz, Vicki L., and Susan Tiano. 1987. "Conclusion." In *Women on the U.S.–Mexico Border: Responses to Change*, Vicki L. Ruiz and Susan Tiano, eds. Boulder, Colorado: Westview Press, pp. 233–242.

Saenz, Rogelio, and Marie Ballejos. 1993. "Industrial Development and Persistent Poverty in the Rio Grande Valley." In *Forgotten Places: Uneven Development in Rural America*, Thomas A. Lyson and William W. Falk, eds. Lawrence: University of Kansas Press, pp. 102–134.

Shapiro, Isaac. 1988. *The Minimum Wage and Job Loss.* Washington, D.C.: Center on Budget and Policy Priorities.

Sherman, R. 1988. "A Study of Traditional and Informal Sector Micro-Enterprise Activity and Its Impact on the Pine Ridge Indian Reservation Economy." Unpublished paper, Aspen Institute for Humanistic Studies, Washington, D.C.

Streeck, Wolfgang. 1997. "Beneficial Constraints." In *Contemporary Capi-*

*talism: The Embeddedness of Institution*, J. Rogers Hollingsworth and Robert Boyer, eds. Cambridge: Cambridge University Press, pp. 197–219.

Summers, Gene F., Sharon D. Evans, Frank Clemente, E.M. Beck, and Jon Minkoff. 1976. *Industrial Invasion of Nonmetropolitan America: A Quarter Century of Experience.* New York: Praeger.

Summers, Gene F., Francine Horton, and Christina Gringeri. 1995. "Understanding Trends in Rural Labor Markets." In *The Changing American Countryside: Rural People and Places*, Emery N. Castle, ed. Lawrence: University Press of Kansas, pp. 197–210.

Thornton, Bonnie Dill, and Bruce Williams. 1992. "Race, Gender, and Poverty in the Rural South: African American Single Mothers." In *Rural Poverty in America*, Cynthia M. Duncan, ed. New York: Auburn House, pp. 97–109.

Tickamyer, Ann R. 1992. "The Working Poor in Rural Labor Markets: The Example of the Southeastern United States." In *Rural Poverty in America*, Cynthia M. Duncan, ed. New York: Auburn House, pp. 41–61.

Tickamyer, Ann R., and Janet Bokemeier. 1993. "Alternative Strategies for Labor Market Analysis: Multi-Level Models of Labor Market Inequality. In *Inequalities in Local Labor Market Areas*, Joachim Singelmann and Forrest A. Deseran, eds. Boulder, Colorado: Westview Press, pp. 49–68.

U.S. Bureau of the Census. 1990. Available at <http://homer.ssd.census.gov/cdrom/lookup/CMD=LIST/DB=C90STF3A/LEV=State>.

U.S. Bureau of the Census. 1999. Available at <http://www.census.gov/population/www/estimates/popest.html>.

U.S. Department of Commerce. 1997. Available at <http://govinfo.library.orst.edu>.

U.S. Department of Labor. 1999. Available from the Bureau of Labor Statistics at <http://146.142.424/cgi-bin/surveymost?la>.

U.S. Department of Labor, Office of the Secretary. 1985. *Employment Programs for Rural Women.* Washington, D.C.: USDL, Women's Bureau.

# Part 4

# Food Assistance and Hunger:
# The Rural Dimension

# 14

# Food Stamps in Rural America

## Special Issues and Common Themes

Sheena McConnell and James Ohls
*Mathematica Policy Research, Inc.*

The Food Stamp Program (FSP) is a federally administered assistance program and has, since its inception, had a high degree of uniformity in its administration. Given that the program is so centralized and serves a predominantly urban population, an important question is how successfully the program meets the special needs of rural, low-income populations. This chapter addresses this issue by examining rural-urban differences in characteristics of FSP participants, FSP participation rates, and experiences of low-income populations with the program. The chapter also contributes to the policy debate on the wider question of how best to structure assistance programs when different geographic areas have different needs.

We find that, overall, the FSP serves rural populations at least as well as urban populations. The participation rate—the proportion of persons eligible for food stamps who receive them—is higher in rural areas than in urban areas. Although the food stamp caseload has fallen since 1994 in both rural and urban areas, the sharp decline in participation rates that occurred is an urban phenomenon. Although the fall in the urban FSP caseloads is due to both a decline in the number of people eligible for the program and the rate at which those who are eligible participate, the fall in the rural FSP caseloads can be fully explained by the decline in the number of people eligible for the program.

Evidence from both survey research and focus groups suggests that rural and urban low-income populations face somewhat different issues in the decision to participate in the FSP. In rural areas, lack of information about eligibility for the program and information about where and how to apply are more significant barriers to participation than in urban areas. On the other hand, more complaints about disrespectful and unhelpful caseworkers are heard in urban areas than rural ones. A picture emerges from our data of large, impersonal, urban food stamp offices and smaller, more user-friendly, rural offices. This distinction may explain at least some of the rural/urban difference in participation rates. In rural areas, the caseworkers in the smaller offices may be more likely to ensure that people who are no longer eligible for cash assistance benefits know that they may still be eligible for food stamps. Surprisingly, we find relatively little evidence that transportation difficulties are an important deterrent to participation in either rural or urban areas.

Before describing our data sources and the distinctions between rural and urban welfare populations, we provide some background on the differences between the food stamp and cash welfare programs and how the programs were treated differently in the 1996 welfare reform legislation. We follow with a discussion of the differences in food stamp participation rates in rural and urban areas and present evidence from a survey and focus groups on the different barriers to participation in these areas.

## BACKGROUND

Since the 1970s, food stamps and cash welfare have been two of the three cornerstones of America's low-income assistance policy (the third being Medicaid). Interestingly, although FSP and cash assistance have close coordination at the local level, their overall structures and administrative approaches at the federal and state levels have differed.

Even prior to welfare reform in 1996, states, and some counties, were given high degrees of autonomy in setting the major parameters of their cash assistance programs. Even under the previous Aid to Families with Dependent Children (AFDC) system, program benefit levels for similar households could, and did, vary dramatically across states, and states had significant leeway in setting rules for determining such program parameters as benefit level, the countable income construct used in establishing eligibility, and work requirements.

By contrast, FSP policies since the 1970s have been closely set by federal legislation and regulation.  The *Code of Federal Regulations* has more than 400 pages of fine print, specifying in minute detail the programmatic and operation rules that states and local FSP offices must follow in determining and issuing benefits under the program.

This difference in the level of federal control between the two programs has reflected, at least in part, a belief that the uniformity built into the FSP was important because the program provided a partial safety net with which to mitigate potential problems caused by state disparities in levels of cash benefits.  This safety net function is readily apparent in available data on benefit levels.  For a typical AFDC family in states with relatively generous AFDC benefit levels, such as California, food stamp benefits amounted to less than one-third of the household's combined AFDC and food stamp benefits, while for a similar family in low-benefit states, such as Texas, food stamp benefits constituted well over half of the household's combined benefits (U.S. House of Representatives 1998).

In its deliberations over welfare reform, Congress explicitly decided to preserve the centralization of the FSP while decentralizing the cash assistance system.  The 1996 Personal Responsibility and Work Opportunity Reconciliation Act (PRWORA) transformed cash assistance into a block grant, essentially increasing the discretion afforded to the states in shaping their own welfare systems.  However, proposed legislation to transform food stamps funding into block grants was emphatically rejected.  A reading of the policy debate from the time makes it clear that there was a desire by much of the policy community to mitigate any potentially harmful effects of the increased decentralization of welfare policy by retaining federal uniformity in the FSP.

This same tension remains in the policy debate over many assistance policies today.  In recent years, states have regularly asked for more control over the Food Stamp Program to more thoroughly integrate food stamp and cash assistance policies, while policymakers at the federal level have reacted to these requests with considerable caution.  An important issue in this debate is the extent to which the FSP can serve the diverse needs of populations in different states.  This chapter addresses this issue by examining how well the program serves two quite different low-income populations: those in rural areas and those in urban areas.

## DATA SOURCES

We use data from four sources to compare how well the Food Stamp Program serves rural and urban populations. First, data on the number and characteristics of FSP participants were obtained from program administrative data. Second, data on the number of persons eligible for food stamps were obtained from the Current Population Surveys (CPS). Information on reasons for nonparticipation and experiences with the program was obtained both from a survey and from focus groups of low-income persons.

Our estimates of the number and characteristics of food stamp participants are from fiscal years 1996 and 1998 Food Stamp Program's Quality Control (FSPQC) sample. The FSPQC, designed to detect payment errors, consists of an annual review of national probability samples of about 50,000 food stamp cases. These program data provide better estimates of participation than do household survey data, owing to the considerable underreporting of program participation in household surveys (Ross 1988; Trippe, Doyle, and Asher 1992).

Our estimates of the number and characteristics of households that are eligible for food stamps are based on data from the March 1997 and March 1999 CPS. The food stamp eligibility of people and households in the CPS was simulated using information on the demographic and economic characteristics of the household.[1]

Both the FSPQC and CPS data use definitions of "urban" and "rural" aggregated at the county level and based on Office of Management and Budget definitions of Metropolitan Statistical Areas (MSAs). However, because the FSPQC data do not include data on the place of residence of the food stamp household, we define a household as "urban" if the local office that administers its food stamp case is located in a county that is in an MSA.[2] If the household's food stamp office is outside an MSA, it is defined as a "rural" household. The CPS defines a household as "urban" if its place of residence is within an MSA.

Third, quantitative information on satisfaction with the FSP and experiences applying for and using food stamps of both participants and eligible nonparticipants was obtained from the National Food Stamp Survey (NFSS), conducted in 1996 and 1997 for the U.S. Department of Agriculture, Food and Nutrition Service (FNS). It inter-

viewed national probability samples of more than 2,000 FSP participants and approximately 450 nonparticipants to obtain information
about their experiences with the program, as well as on other issues.
(Results of this survey are presented in Ponza et al. 1999 and Ohls et al.
1999.)

Fourth, qualitative information on the experiences of both participants and eligible nonparticipants was also collected in a study examining the reasons for low participation rates among working and elderly
people, *Reaching the Working Poor and Poor Elderly*, also conducted
for FNS. As part of this study, 12 focus groups were conducted with either food stamp participants (four groups) or low-income persons who
did not participate in the program (eight groups).[3] The groups were
evenly divided between groups of elderly and working people. The focus groups occurred in six sites. Of these sites, two were located in urban areas (Baltimore, Maryland, and Houston, Texas), two in suburban
areas (Baltimore County, Maryland, and around Eugene-Spring-
field, Oregon), and two in rural areas (Polk County, Texas, and Lincoln
County, Oregon). The focus group discussions focused on barriers
to participation, reasons why nonparticipants chose not to participate,
and reasons why participants could overcome the barriers to participation.

## URBAN/RURAL DIFFERENCES IN THE CHARACTERISTICS OF FOOD STAMP PARTICIPANTS

Although the FSP serves a predominantly urban population, a significant minority of recipients live in rural areas. In fiscal year 1998,
just under one-quarter of food stamp participants (measured as either
households or individual participants) lived in rural areas, while just
over three-quarters of food stamp participants lived in urban areas.
About 77 percent of all food stamp benefits were paid to people in urban areas, and 23 percent of all benefits were paid to people in rural
areas.

Rural and urban food stamp participants differ in terms of both demographic composition and economic characteristics (Table 14.1).
Rural households are less likely to contain children (54 percent of food

**Table 14.1  Characteristics of 1998 Food Stamp Households
by Urban/Rural Location**

| Household characteristic | Urban | Rural | All households |
|---|---|---|---|
| Composition (%) | | | |
| Households with children | 59.7 | 54.0 | 58.3 |
| Households with elderly | 16.6 | 23.0 | 18.2 |
| Households with children and single parent | 41.7 | 33.1 | 39.6 |
| Other | 24.8 | 24.5 | 24.7 |
| Race/ethnicity (%) | | | |
| White non-Hispanic | 38.9 | 65.8 | 45.6 |
| Black non-Hispanic | 38.8 | 23.8 | 35.1 |
| Hispanic | 18.6 | 6.6 | 15.6 |
| Asian or Pacific Islander | 2.9 | 1.1 | 2.5 |
| Other | 0.7 | 2.8 | 1.2 |
| Gross income relative to the poverty guideline (%) | | | |
| Below 50% of poverty level | 38.4 | 34.3 | 37.4 |
| 50% to 100% of poverty level | 52.0 | 55.1 | 52.8 |
| Above 100% of poverty level | 9.5 | 10.6 | 9.8 |
| Income, by type (%) | | | |
| Earned income | 25.4 | 28.9 | 26.3 |
| Unearned income | 79.8 | 75.5 | 78.8 |
| No income | 8.6 | 9.3 | 8.8 |
| Average household size (persons) | 2.42 | 2.44 | 2.42 |
| Average gross income as % of the poverty threshold | 59.9 | 61.8 | 60.3 |
| Average shelter expense ($) | 322 | 258 | 307 |
| Average monthly benefit ($) | 168 | 157 | 165 |
| Average monthly benefit per person ($) | 70 | 65 | 68 |
| Sample size | 31,430 | 15,666 | 47,145[a] |

[a] The metropolitan status of 49 households was unknown.
SOURCE: Fiscal year 1998 Food Stamp Quality Control Sample.

stamp households in rural areas contain children compared with 60 percent of food stamp households in urban areas). In addition, urban food stamp households with children are more likely to be single-parent households compared with rural food stamp households. Rural food stamp households are more likely to contain an elderly person. Approximately 23 percent of food stamp households in rural areas contain an elderly person compared with 17 percent in urban areas. The racial and ethnic composition of food stamp households also varies between urban and rural areas. The majority (66 percent) of food stamp households in rural areas are white and not of Hispanic origin, compared with only 39 percent of food stamp households in urban areas. In contrast, the majority of food stamp households in urban areas are black or Hispanic (57 percent), compared with less than one-third of food stamp households in rural areas (30 percent).

On average, food stamp households in rural areas are slightly better off financially than their counterparts in urban areas (see average values at the bottom of Table 14.1). Average income before any deductions for expenses (gross income) is 62 percent of the poverty threshold in rural food stamp households compared with 60 percent in urban households. A slightly higher proportion of households in rural areas have gross income above the poverty threshold (11 percent in rural areas compared with 10 percent in urban areas). Rural FSP households are more likely to receive income from the employment of a household member.

Average food stamp benefits per person are lower in rural areas. Average monthly benefits are $65 per person in rural areas compared with $70 per person in urban areas (Table 14.1). Rural food stamp households have lower average food stamp benefits because they have higher average income and slightly larger average households.[4] Shelter expenses are, on average, 25 percent higher in urban areas than rural areas for food stamp households.

## URBAN/RURAL DIFFERENCES IN FOOD STAMP PARTICIPATION RATES

The FSP was designed to provide food assistance to all people that need it, irrespective of where a person lives. An important indication of how well the program is fulfilling this mission is the participation rate—the rate at which persons eligible for the program participate in it. Low participation rates suggest that the FSP may not be meeting the needs of the low-income population.

### Urban/Rural Differences in 1998

Table 14.2 presents estimates of the participation rates in rural and urban locations.[5] About 73 percent of rural residents who are eligible for food stamps participate in the program compared with only 63 percent of urban residents eligible for food stamps. The overall participation rate is 65 percent. The higher participation rates in rural areas are somewhat surprising, given the differences in demographic characteristics of low-income households in urban and rural areas. It is well documented that participation rates are relatively low among households containing elderly persons, those with working household members, and households without children (Castner and Cody 1999; McConnell and Nixon 1996). As noted above, these populations with low participation rates—the elderly, the working, and people without children—are more highly concentrated in rural areas. Thus, on the basis of demographic characteristics alone, we might expect rural areas to have lower participation rates.

The urban/rural difference in participation rates is primarily due to higher proportion of participating households with children in rural ar-

**Table 14.2  Food Stamp Participation Rates by Household Composition and Location, 1998 (%)**

| Household composition | Urban | Rural | All areas |
|---|---|---|---|
| All individuals | 63.1 | 73.3 | 65.3 |
| Individuals in households with children | 72.4 | 90.0 | 75.9 |
| Nonelderly individuals in households without children | 53.7 | 58.8 | 54.8 |
| Elderly individuals in households without children | 28.6 | 34.0 | 30.0 |

SOURCE: Fiscal year 1998 Food Stamp Program Quality Control Sample and the March 1999 Current Population Survey.

eas. Table 14.2 reports the participation rates of people in three different types of households. Although the FSP participation rate is higher in rural areas for people in each type of household, the largest urban/rural difference is found in the participation rate for people in households with children—90 percent in rural areas and only 72 percent in urban areas.

## Changes over Time in Rural and Urban FSP Participation Rates

The rural/urban difference in the trends over time in the participation rate is quite striking. Table 14.3 presents estimates of the number of food stamp participants, the number of persons eligible for food stamps, and the FSP participation rates in urban and rural areas in 1996

**Table 14.3  Number of Food Stamp Participants, Eligibles, and Participation Rates, 1996 and 1998**

| Location | 1996 | 1998 | Change 1996–1998 (%) |
|---|---|---|---|
| Urban | | | |
| Food stamp participants (000s) | 20,002 | 15,087 | −24.6 |
| Food stamp eligibles (000s) | 27,947 | 23,898 | −14.5 |
| Participation rate (%) | 71.6 | 63.1 | −8.5[a] |
| Rural | | | |
| Food stamp participants (000s) | 5,857 | 4,858 | −17.1 |
| Food stamp eligibles (000s) | 8,211 | 6,627 | −19.3 |
| Participation rate (%) | 71.3 | 73.3 | 2.0[a] |
| All areas[b] | | | |
| Food stamp participants (000s) | 25,874 | 19,969 | −22.8 |
| Food stamp eligibles (000s) | 36,239 | 30,586 | −15.6 |
| Participation rate (%) | 71.4 | 65.3 | −6.1[a] |

[a] Values are percentage points.
[b] The number of participants and eligibles in the urban and rural areas do not add up to the total in all areas because the urban/rural location is unknown for some people.
SOURCE: Fiscal years 1996 and 1998 Food Stamp Program Quality Control Sample and the March 1997 and 1999 Current Population Surveys.

and in 1998.[6]  As we had anticipated based on data on overall case-loads, the FSP participation rate in urban areas fell dramatically between 1996 and 1998, from 72 percent to 63 percent.  However, the FSP participation rate in rural areas actually increased slightly, from 71 percent to 73 percent.  Hence, whatever has caused the decrease in FSP participation rates in urban areas has apparently not affected participation rates in rural areas.

We found this result sufficiently surprising that we spent considerable effort checking its accuracy.  Because the participation rates are determined by combining estimates derived from two separate databases, the FSPQC and the CPS, we initially were concerned that some subtle difference or change over time in how these data sets defined "urban/rural" could be affecting the results.  However, a careful review of the relevant documentation revealed no evidence of this.  More convincingly, to further examine the robustness of the participation rate results, we redid the analysis dividing the data into two groups of states—the 19 most urban states and the 31 remaining most rural states.  The logic is that this state-based analysis makes no direct use of the indicator for whether an area is urban or rural and could, therefore, not be sensitive to changing urban-rural definitions.  Again, in this version of the analysis (not shown), the finding remains that the overall decrease in participation rates is essentially an urban phenomenon.

We also examined patterns over time and between states in FSP participation as measured by the CPS.  The QC data, which are based on administrative records, are in general a much stronger data set for examining trends in participation because of the problems of undercounting in survey data, because of the richness of the QC data, and because the QC data are weighted to sum to known national program participation counts.  However, a reviewer of an earlier draft of this chapter noticed that the rural participation rate calculated using CPS data as the numerator *fell* between 1996 and 1998, contrary to our finding using QC data (see Nord, in this volume, p. 433).  If the QC data on participation are approximately correct, the different findings from CPS data would suggest that the well-documented "undercount" of food stamp cases in the CPS must have been increasing (getting worse) in rural areas between 1996 and 1998.  To ensure that this trend was not limited to some idiosyncratic problem in just one or two states, we calculated the undercount by state using the ratio of the number of participants in the CPS to the number of participants in the QC data. As expected, we found that the undercount was increasing more in relatively rural states, but there was no individual state or small number of states that accounted for most of the difference.

So what accounts for the overall decline in participation and the fact that it is largely an urban phenomenon? Although we lack a complete understanding of the mechanisms causing the overall decline in the FSP participation rate, it has frequently been attributed to either the strong economy or factors related to welfare reform (Dion and Pavetti 2000). FSP caseloads have declined steadily since 1994, and FSP participation rates historically have fallen as the economy improved (Castner and Cody 1999). However, this cannot explain the urban/rural difference in FSP participation rates, given that the number of persons in poverty has fallen faster in rural areas. Although the poverty rate is still higher in rural areas than in urban areas (the 1998 poverty rate was 14 percent in rural areas compared with 12 percent in urban areas), between 1996 and 1998, the number of people in poverty decreased by 10.1 percent in rural areas compared with only 4.3 percent in urban areas (U.S. Census Bureau 2000).

We have also considered the possibility that the larger drop in the number of food stamp–eligible people in rural areas might be due to the changes in FSP eligibility rules introduced by PRWORA. However, the available data do not support this hypothesis. PRWORA made two major changes in FSP eligibility rules: most permanent resident aliens became ineligible for food stamps; and most able-bodied adults without dependents (ABAWDs) were limited to only three months of benefits in a 36-month period unless they worked or participated in a workfare or another approved employment and training program.[7] Evidence suggests that a greater proportion of the people affected by the changes in eligibility rules live in urban areas.[8] In 1994, nearly 14 percent of food stamp–eligible people in urban areas were noncitizens compared with fewer than 4 percent in rural areas. The urban/rural difference in the number of people affected by the ABAWD provision is smaller but in the same direction—a slightly smaller proportion of people eligible for food stamps were affected by the ABAWD provision in rural areas.[9]

Welfare reform may have affected FSP participation rates in four ways. First, food stamp participants leaving welfare (because they find work, are sanctioned, or reach the time limit) may think they are no longer eligible for food stamps. Second, food stamp participants may believe it is not worth the hassle to continue to receive only food stamp benefits. Third, diversion programs that discourage people from applying for welfare may also discourage applications for food stamps. Fourth, welfare reform, by placing a greater emphasis on self-sufficiency, may have increased the stigma of receiving food stamps. Evidence concerning how welfare reform may have affected FSP participation rates is discussed below.

## URBAN/RURAL DIFFERENCES IN EXPERIENCES WITH THE FOOD STAMP PROGRAM

The opinions and experiences of the FSP clientele are also important indicators of how well the program is serving those in need of food assistance. Table 14.4 shows the responses of FSP participants in the NFSS to questions about their experiences with the FSP. The participants are distinguished by those residing in urban areas, those residing in rural areas, and those residing in areas that have both rural and urban components.

The most striking finding is the high degree of overall satisfaction with the program in all areas. More than 85 percent of respondents were satisfied with the overall program, and similarly high rates of satisfaction were expressed with the application and recertification procedures. Satisfaction is at least as great in rural areas as it is in urban areas. For each of the three measures of satisfaction examined in the top panel of the table, the percent of respondents who were satisfied was at least as high in rural areas as it was in urban areas.

Food stamp participants in rural areas seem to be more satisfied with their treatment by caseworkers than in urban areas. In rural areas, 96 percent of respondents said that their caseworkers treated them respectfully compared with 90 percent of respondents in urban areas. Similarly, a higher proportion of rural respondents said they thought that the caseworkers provided the needed services.

These survey results are consistent with our findings from focus group discussions among low-income working and elderly people conducted for the Ponza and McConnell (1996) study. Focus group mem-

**Table 14.4  Participants' Experiences with the Food Stamp Program by Participant Location (% of participants)**

|  | Urban | Rural | Mixed |
|---|---|---|---|
| Satisfaction with Food Stamp program |  |  |  |
| Satisfied with application process | 84.5 | 84.5 | 85.9 |
| Satisfied with recertification process | 85.8 | 87.3 | 88.8 |
| Satisfied with overall program | 86.7 | 88.9 | 88.5 |
| Participants indicating perception of stigma |  |  |  |
| Avoided telling people that they received food stamps | 22.1 | 18.2 | 25.0 |
| Perceived disrespectful treatment by store clerks, others | 24.4 | 17.2 | 22.3 |
| Replied "yes" to at least one of six stigma-related questions | 39.9 | 36.6 | 40.5 |
| Participants satisfaction with caseworkers |  |  |  |
| Believed caseworker treats them respectfully | 90.1 | 96.2 | 91.8 |
| Believed caseworker provides the needed services | 86.4 | 91.7 | 91.1 |
| Sample size | 1,234 | 325 | 728 |

NOTE: Survey respondents were classified as urban if the census reported that at least 90% of the households in their zip code lived in urban areas, they were classified as rural if at least 90% of the households in their zip code did not live in urban areas, and were otherwise classified as mixed.

SOURCE: 1996 National Food Stamp Survey, weighted data; see Ohls et al. (1999).

bers in urban areas emphasized problems with food stamp office staff attitudes and the rude and disrespectful way they often treated food stamp clients. The following comment was typical of members of the urban focus groups: "It's the attitude of the people that work there. You know . . . they act like they don't really care whether they help you or not." Members of the focus groups in rural and suburban areas complained much less about the food stamp office staff. According to focus group members, the food stamp offices that people in rural and suburban areas visited were smaller operations and staff were more personable and had a greater sense of community.

To shed additional light on the rural/urban differences in the FSP participation rates, we examined differences in the reasons given for nonparticipation by both NFSS survey respondents and Ponza and McConnell (1996) focus group members who were not receiving food stamps at the time they participated in the data collections. In the analysis of both the survey and focus groups, we examined four main groups of reasons for not participating in the program.

1. Some people lack information about the program. They may think they are ineligible or do not know how or where to apply.
2. Some people say that they do not need food stamp benefits. A frequent response given by nonparticipants when asked in focus groups or surveys why they do not participate was, "I can get by without them."
3. Problems related to the administration of the program may deter participation. Problems cited in surveys and focus groups include difficulty getting to the food stamp office, an application process that is too long and complicated, the need to provide too much personal information, food stamp staff who are perceived to be disrespectful, and a food stamp office that is viewed as unpleasant or unsafe.
4. People frequently cite embarrassment in applying for and using food stamp benefits.

The most common reason given, by far, for not applying for food stamps was that the respondent did not think he or she was eligible (Table 14.5). This perception of ineligibility was more prevalent in rural areas than in urban areas (79 percent vs. 70 percent in urban locales). Lack of information was more frequently mentioned as a reason for nonparticipation among the Ponza and McConnell focus groups in rural and suburban areas than in the urban areas. Several members of an elderly nonparticipant focus group in a rural county in Oregon reported that, although they knew about food stamps, they did not know how to apply for them, and many thought, erroneously, that they were ineligible because they did not receive welfare. This was also true for working and elderly focus groups in suburban areas. In contrast, in urban areas, the members of the nonparticipant focus groups were very aware of food stamps and knew where the office was. Indeed, many had previously either applied for or received benefits. It is important to note that both the survey and focus groups were conducted prior to the

**Table 14.5  Reasons for Not Applying for Food Stamps by Eligible
Nonparticipants, by Location (% of nonparticipants)**

| Reasons for nonparticipation | Urban | Rural | All |
|---|---|---|---|
| Information problems | | | |
| Not aware that they may be eligible | 69.6 | 79.2 | 71.7 |
| Do not know where or how to apply | 1.8 | 0 | 1.4 |
| Perceptions of need | | | |
| Do not need food stamps | 7.9 | 7.4 | 7.8 |
| Program administration | | | |
| Too much paperwork | 2.9 | 2.4 | 2.8 |
| Transportation is a problem | 1.6 | 1.2 | 1.5 |
| Benefit too small for effort required | 2.9 | 2.4 | 2.8 |
| Psychological/stigma | | | |
| Do not like to rely on government assistance | 5.3 | 1.2 | 4.4 |
| Do not want to be seen shopping with food stamps | 0.9 | 0 | 0.7 |
| Do not want peers to know need help | 0.9 | 0 | 0.7 |
| Too proud to ask for assistance | 0.5 | 0 | 0.4 |
| People treat you badly | 0.9 | 0 | 0.7 |
| Questions too personal | 0.6 | 0 | 0.5 |
| Previous bad experience with the program | 2.4 | 2.4 | 2.4 |
| Other reasons | | | |
| Never got around to applying | 1.4 | 0 | 1.1 |
| Don't feel like it | 2.1 | 3.6 | 2.4 |
| Other | 3.3 | 0.6 | 2.7 |
| Missing data | 2.0 | 1.2 | 1.8 |
| Sample size | 325 | 125 | 450 |

NOTE: Percentages may sum to more than 100% because respondents could give
more than one reason for not applying.
SOURCE: 1996 National Food Stamp Program Survey, weighted data. See Ohls et
al. (1999).

implementation of PRWORA, and the proportion of persons who think
they are ineligible may now have increased in urban areas.

A second common reason given for nonparticipation is that the respondent does not need food stamp benefits. This reason was given
slightly more frequently by respondents in urban areas than in rural areas. To the extent that the nonparticipants really do not need assistance,

a low participation rate should not be a concern. However, discussions in the Ponza and McConnell focus groups suggested that at least some people who said they did not need food stamp benefits showed signs of food insecurity, such as visiting food banks and having to go to friends or relatives for meals.

It is commonly stated that transportation difficulties in rural areas are barriers to FSP participation. However, problems with transportation were rarely raised in either the rural or urban focus groups. Also, in the NFSS, transportation problems were rarely given as reasons for not applying for food stamps in either rural or urban areas. Transportation problems were cited slightly more frequently as reasons for not applying for food stamps in urban areas.

We also examined whether people in rural areas are more affected by the stigma of receiving food stamp benefits than are people in urban areas; however, the evidence is mixed. NFSS respondents in rural areas perceived less stigma than did those in urban areas. In rural areas, 37 percent of respondents replied "yes" to one of six stigma-related questions, compared with 40 percent in urban areas (see Table 14.4). Also, a slightly higher proportion of urban nonparticipants gave stigma-related reasons when asked why they did not participate (see Table 14.5). On the other hand, stigma-related issues were mentioned by members of the working and elderly focus groups more often in rural areas. Typical comments among rural residents were: "It's pride"; "I want to be independent"; "I would find it very embarrassing"; "I would feel a failure." The reported sources of embarrassment were mainly related to using food stamps in grocery stores. Although in urban areas, people were often shielded by anonymity in grocery stores, rural residents believed that it was unlikely they could go to a store without meeting someone they knew. As one focus group member in Lincoln County, Oregon, said, "You go to the grocery store behind somebody that uses food stamps and the clerks and all the other people around you kind of look down on you because you are using food stamps."

Members of the rural focus groups suggested that they would be more likely to use food stamps if the benefits could be accessed by using an Electronic Benefit Transfer (EBT) card—a card that looks like a credit card and automatically debits the customer's food stamp account. In Polk County, Texas, where EBT was used, focus group members claimed it made using food stamps less embarrassing, although they noted that people could still tell.  The use of EBT, which is now mandated by law, is increasing rapidly.


## CONCLUSION


Several useful conclusions about how the Food Stamp Program is operating in rural areas emerge from our analysis.  We review them here and then attempt to generalize to the larger issues of public assistance strategy mentioned in the introduction.  First, our analysis suggests that the characteristics of the urban participants differ quite significantly from the rural participants.  Second, contrary to expectations, it appears that participation rates are actually higher in rural areas than in urban areas.  The differentials vary substantially according to household characteristics, with the largest difference observed for households with children.

Third, the recent decline in FSP participation rates occurred primarily in urban areas.  In studying the fall in FSP participation rates, it may be useful to researchers to focus on urban-rural differences.  An understanding of why the FSP participation rates did not fall in rural areas may suggest ways to raise the participation rates in urban areas.  Fourth, the focus group and survey data suggest several reasons why rural participation rates may not have fallen in line with those in urban areas.  Although lack of program knowledge seemed to be greater in rural areas in 1996, this may no longer be the case.  The confusion about FSP eligibility may have increased in urban areas given the changes in welfare programs.  The confusion may be lesser in smaller rural offices, where the overall quality and "user-friendliness" of administration may be better and where a smaller proportion of the clients are affected by the changes in the welfare programs.

Fifth, it appears that transportation is not as strong a barrier to participation as might have been expected in either rural or urban locations.  Although distances to the offices are clearly greater in rural areas, most eligible households appear to be able to find the necessary transportation, either with their own cars or by finding a ride.

So how do these observations relate to the appropriate levels of centralization in public assistance programs?  Our interpretation is that the FSP, with its relatively centralized structure and policy-setting process, has been quite successful in meeting the needs of different types of localities, as reflected in the urban-rural distinction. Our data suggest that, overall, the program appears to be meeting the needs of the rural low-income populations at least as well as those of the urban low-income populations.

To be sure, the FSP has well-known limitations in both rural and urban settings. In both rural and urban areas, there is concern about participation rates and levels of program access. Issues surrounding administrative error rates are present in both areas. Further, there may well be unique problems associated with the FSP in rural areas. For instance, although our evidence suggests that they are probably few in number, there may be some households for whom transportation barriers posed by rural distances are significant. There does seem to be a lack of understanding of the FSP eligibility rules in rural areas. However, our general point is that, overall, the apparent obstacles to operating the program successfully appear to be no worse in rural areas than in urban areas.

Parsing the data by urban versus rural location represents a strong test of whether a single assistance program can meet the diverse needs of many different local areas given that the urban/rural distinction would appear to be one of the most significant in differentiating localities across the country. Our argument is that the relatively centralized structure of the FSP passes this test.

# Notes

The authors would like to thank Mark Nord and Carole Trippe for helpful comments on an earlier draft of the paper and Mark Brinkley, Melynda Ihrig, Dan O'Connor, Catherine Palermo, Bruce Schechter, and Amy Zambrowski for providing programming and research assistance.

1.  This simulation was conducted using a model constructed under contract to the Food and Nutrition Service of the U.S. Department of Agriculture. The model is discussed in detail in Castner and Cody (1999), Cody and Castner (1999), and Trippe, Doyle, and Asher (1992).
2.  In the 15 states where the Food Stamp Program is county-administered, an office in the household's county of residence administers its case. In the other states, it is

possible, but not likely, that the office that administers a household's case is located in a county that is not their county of residence.

3.  The design of, and findings from, the focus groups are discussed in Ponza and Mc-Connell (1996).

4.  Based on an assumption of economies of scale in food purchases, household food stamp benefits are set so that benefits per person fall as the number of people in the household increases.

5.  Estimates of FSP eligibles are derived from the CPS data using methods that essentially parallel those used by the Food and Nutrition Service of the U.S. Department of Agriculture in producing official estimates of participation rates. Our figures differ slightly from the official participation rates reported by the Food and Nutrition Service (Castner and Cody 1999) because they are calculated from the average annual number of participants and eligibles, rather than the number of participants and eligibles for a particular month. The official rates are also adjusted for payment errors and adjusted so that the number of households and participants are the same as reported in program operations data.

6.  Comparisons of 1994 and 1998 data show larger changes in the same direction in the number of FSP-eligible people and the FSP participation rates.

7.  Eligibility was restored to some permanent resident aliens in the 1998 Agricultural Research, Extension, and Education Reform Act. The Balanced Budget Act of 1997 increased the availability of exemptions for ABAWDs.

8.  Because neither the FSPQC nor the CPS contain all the information necessary to model the complex eligibility rules for these two groups, the estimates on the number of persons affected by the eligibility changes are based on a substantial number of assumptions that are not fully tested.

9.  These estimates do not take into account that states can apply for waivers from the ABAWD provision for areas that have unemployment rates greater than 10 percent or are considered to have insufficient jobs. It is possible that states applied for more waivers for the urban areas, although this is not obvious from a casual observation of the list of waivers.

# References

Castner, Laura, and Scott Cody. 1999. *Trends in FSP Participation Rates: Focus on September 1997*. Alexandria, Virginia: U.S. Department of Agriculture, Food and Nutrition Service.

Cody, Scott, and Laura Castner. 1999. *Characteristics of Food Stamp Households Fiscal Year 1997*. Alexandria, Virginia: U.S. Department of Agriculture, Food and Nutrition Service.

Dion, M. Robin, and LaDonna Pavetti. 2000. *Access to and Participation in Medicaid and the Food Stamp Program*. Washington, D.C.: Mathematica Policy Research, March.

McConnell, Sheena, and Lucia Nixon. 1996. *Reaching the Working Poor and the Poor Elderly: Report on Literature Review and Data Analysis*. Washington, D.C.: Mathematica Policy Research, March.

Ohls, James, Michael Ponza, Lorenzo Moreno, Amy Zambrowski, and Rhoda Cohen. 1999. *Food Stamp Participants' Access to Food Retailers*. Princeton, New Jersey: Mathematica Policy Research, July.

Ponza, Michael, and Sheena McConnell. 1996. *Reaching the Working Poor and Poor Elderly: Interim Report on Focus Groups*. Washington, D.C.: Mathematica Policy Research, December.

Ponza, Michael, James C. Ohls, Lorenzo Moreno, Amy Zambrowski, and Rhoda Cohen. 1999. *Customer Service in the Food Stamp Program*. Princeton, New Jersey: Mathematica Policy Research, July.

Ross, Christine. 1988. *The Food Stamp Program: Eligibility and Participation*. Washington, D.C.: Congressional Budget Office.

Trippe, Carole, Pat Doyle, and Andrew Asher. 1992. *Trends in Food Stamp Program Participation Rates: 1976 to 1990*. Alexandria, Virginia: U.S. Department of Agriculture, Food and Nutrition Service.

U.S. Census Bureau. 2000. *Historical Poverty Tables*. Available at <http://www.census.gov/hhes/poverty/histpov/hstpov8.html>, May.

U.S. House of Representatives. 1998. *Background Material and Data on Programs within the Jurisdiction of the Committee on Ways and Means*. Washington, D.C.: U.S. Government Printing Office.

# 15

# The Decline in Food Stamp Use by Rural Low-Income Households

## Less Need or Less Access?

Mark Nord

*Economic Research Service, USDA*

The Food Stamp program is the largest federal food assistance program and a mainstay of the federal safety net. In 1994, prior to the recent declines in food stamp participation, more than 1 in every 10 Americans, some 27.5 million people, benefited from the program.

From 1994–1998, food stamp caseloads declined dramatically, falling 34 percent in four years (Genser 1999; Wilde et al. 2000). Cash welfare caseloads also declined dramatically during this period. In nonmetropolitan areas, declines were substantial, although somewhat smaller than in metropolitan areas, at least in the early part of the period (RUPRI 1999; Reinschmiedt et al. 1999).

A great deal of research has looked at the causes of these declines, especially the role of the economy, and intended and unintended effects of welfare reform. Fewer studies have assessed whether the changes in cash welfare use have resulted in improved or worsening economic well-being of potential users. These studies have generally found that economic well-being has not improved and may have deteriorated for these households (Primus et al. 1999). To date, there has been no such assessment of the changes in food stamp use on household well-being. In this chapter, we analyze data on household food insecurity and hunger in 1995 and 1999 to assess whether the decline in food stamp use was associated with an improvement or a deterioration in the food security of U.S. households. The analysis is carried out at both the national level and in nonmetro areas to explore the possibly different welfare outcomes in these two areas (RUPRI 1999).

433

## LESS NEED FOR FOOD ASSISTANCE,
## OR LESS ACCESS TO FOOD STAMPS?

Much of the decline in food stamp caseloads from 1994–1998 resulted from the economic expansion, which lowered unemployment and raised incomes, thus reducing both eligibility and the perceived need for food stamps among eligible households (Wilde et al. 2000). However, food stamp participation declined even among lower-income households, most of which were eligible for food stamps.[1] At the national level, about 55 percent of the overall decline in food stamp caseloads from 1994–1998 resulted from a decline in participation among low-income households (Wilde et al. 2000).

This chapter takes a closer look at those low-income households. Did fewer households apply for food stamps because fewer believed they needed food assistance? Or was it because they found it more difficult or less socially acceptable to get food stamps? This is a question of some importance to the U.S. Department of Agriculture (USDA), which is responsible for ensuring that food stamps are readily available to all eligible households. States and local communities also want to know if needy households are receiving the food assistance available to them.

The decline in food stamp use among low-income households does not, by itself, demonstrate that access to food stamps has become more restricted or difficult. There are several reasons why an improved economy could lower participation even among eligible households. For example, eligible households may have more stable income, even though still below the eligibility level, and may therefore perceive less need for food assistance. They may, on average, have higher income, and therefore be eligible for a smaller total food stamp benefit, thus reducing their incentive to apply for food stamps. They may be more confident of their ability to secure a job in the near future and may, therefore, spend down assets or borrow to meet immediate food needs rather than apply for food stamps.

Nevertheless, changes in the Food Stamp program under the Personal Responsibility and Work Opportunity Reconciliation Act of 1996 (PRWORA) did tighten access to food stamps for some groups, especially for aliens and for able-bodied working-age persons without de-

pendents, and the act slightly reduced benefit levels available to most
eligible persons.  Further, there is evidence that changes in cash welfare
programs have indirectly reduced access to the Food Stamp program
because families losing cash welfare assistance, or not qualifying for
cash assistance, do not always know they are eligible for food stamps
(Zedlewski and Brauner 1999).

These two forces—declining need for and access to food stamps—
both likely to reduce food stamp participation, converged in the latter
half of the 1990s.  Assessing the role of changing access in the caseload
decline during a period when these two forces converged poses a difficult analytic challenge.  However, data on household food security can
shed light on this issue.  The USDA sponsors an annual survey, conducted by the Census Bureau, that collects information about food security, food insecurity, and hunger in U.S. households (Bickel, Carlson,
and Nord 1999).  The household food security scale, which is calculated from these data, is a direct measure of conditions that the Food
Stamp program is designed to ameliorate—food insecurity and hunger.
Food security status can be used as a measure of households' perceived
need for food assistance, thus providing an analytic tool to answer the
"less need versus less access" question.

The analysis focuses on low-income (most of whom are eligible for
food stamps) families not receiving food stamps.  On the one hand, if
households that were eligible for (but not receiving) food stamps were
"food secure," then it may reasonably be inferred that they did not believe they needed food assistance.  On the other hand, if such households were food insecure or, especially, if household members went
hungry, these households likely needed food assistance but found it difficult, impossible, or socially unacceptable to get food stamps.

Similarly, changes in the food security status of low-income households not receiving food stamps during a period of rapidly declining
caseloads shed light on the reasons for the decline.  If food stamp use
declined among low-income households because their perceived need
declined, either due to improved economic situations or for other reasons, then the prevalence rate of food insecurity and hunger among
low-income households not receiving food stamps would have remained unchanged (or perhaps declined).  Alternatively, if food stamp
use declined among low-income households because they found it
more difficult to get food stamps, or because some of them were ineli-

gible or were unaware they were eligible, then the prevalence rate of food insecurity and hunger among low-income households not receiving food stamps would have increased.

This chapter also analyzes changes in the prevalence of food insecurity among low-income food stamp–recipient households. However, it is less clear what the changes for these households imply about the roles of "less need" and "less access" in the caseload decline. Improvements in the economy would be expected to improve incomes among those still receiving food stamps, thus reducing average food insecurity and hunger. Reduced access to cash welfare would lower incomes, increasing food insecurity and hunger. Program changes that reduce the value of food stamps might also tend to increase food insecurity and hunger among recipients. However, all of these effects are likely to be swamped by changes due to the characteristics of households that left the food stamp rolls. Given that the least needy are most likely to have left the program, those left behind are likely to have greater levels of food insecurity and hunger, thus increasing the prevalence of these conditions among food stamp recipients.

Alternatively, if there was less access to food stamps, those leaving (or not applying) may not have been the least needy; they could include a substantial number of more needy households as well. Because of these uncertainties, it is impossible to clearly link changes in food security among food stamp recipients to reduced need versus reduced access to food stamps. This analytic difficulty is partially overcome by assessing changes over time in food insecurity and hunger among food stamp recipients and nonrecipients while controlling for changes in income distribution. However, this only partly controls for well-being, and the meaning of the observed changes for food stamp recipient households remains somewhat ambiguous.

## Data and Methods

Data used in this analysis are from the April 1995 and April 1999 Current Population Survey (CPS) Food Security Supplements and the associated labor force "core" survey. The Food Security Supplements are sponsored by USDA and conducted by the Census Bureau along with the CPS once each year. The CPS includes a nationally representative sample of some 50,000 households, about 44,000 of which complete the Food Security supplements. The supplements include questions about household food expenditures, sources of food assistance, food insecurity, and hunger.

The food insecurity and hunger questions ask about a wide range of experiences and behaviors that are known to characterize households having difficulty meeting their food needs. A scale based on 18 of these questions has been developed to measure the severity of food insecurity and hunger, ranging from food secure to severe hunger (Hamilton et al. 1997a, b; Price, Hamilton, and Cook 1997; Bickel et al. 2000). All the scale questions refer to the 12 months prior to the survey and include a qualifying phrase reminding the respondent to report only those occurrences due to limited financial resources. Restrictions to food intake due to dieting or busy schedules are excluded. For analytic purposes, each household is classified into one of three categories based on their food security scale score: 1) food secure, 2) food insecure with no hunger evident, and 3) food insecure with hunger (Hamilton et al. 1997a; Bickel et al. 2000).

Households were classified by income (below, or at or above, 130 percent of the poverty line) and by household composition (two-parent families with children, single-mother families, multi-adult households without children, men living alone, and women living alone). Households in which the reference person was not a U.S. citizen were analyzed as a separate category, irrespective of their household composition because most noncitizens became ineligible for cash assistance and food stamps during the period under study as a result of welfare reform.

Food stamp receipt was referenced to the previous 30 days in the 1995 CPS but to the previous year in the 1999 CPS. To make the 1999 classification comparable, receipt and nonreceipt of food stamps in the prior 30 days was calculated based on month and date of last food stamp receipt.

Prevalence of food insecurity (with or without hunger) and of hunger was calculated for categories defined by income, food stamp receipt, and household composition. These prevalences were compared between 1995 and 1999. Appropriate household weights were used for calculating prevalence rates, and standard errors of the estimates were calculated based on the number of unweighted cases and an assumed design factor of 1.6 for national prevalence and 2.4 for nonmetro prevalence.[2]

## FINDINGS

### National Level: Food Stamp Caseload Decline

The important contribution of rising incomes to the decline in food stamp use that was reported by Wilde et al. (2000) is also observed in the Food Security Supplement data. The proportion of households with incomes below 130 percent of the poverty line declined from 24 percent in 1995 to 19 percent in 1999 (Table 15.1). Adjusted for population growth, this represented a decline of 21 percent in the low-income, generally food-stamp-eligible, population.

Even among low-income households, food stamp use declined by more than one-third (also consistent with Wilde et al. 2000). Declines were largest for noncitizens (57.3 percent) and for two-parent families with children (41.2 percent) and were smallest for women living alone (23.8 percent). In absolute terms, the decline was largest for single mothers (21.0 percentage points). This large decline is of particular interest analytically because single mothers represented about 40 percent

**Table 15.1  Changes in Household Income and Food Stamp Use, 1995–99**

| Household characteristic | 1995 (%) | 1999 (%) | Change Pct. pt. | % |
|---|---|---|---|---|
| Share with income below 130% of poverty | 24.2 | 19.1 | −5.1 | −21.0 |
| Share of low-income hh. that received food stamps in prior month | | | | |
| All low-income hh. | 32.2 | 20.2 | −12.0 | −37.4 |
| Aliens | 33.1 | 14.1 | −19.0 | −57.3 |
| Citizens | 32.1 | 20.9 | −11.2 | −34.8 |
| Two-parent with children | 31.5 | 18.5 | −13.0 | −41.2 |
| Single mother with children | 63.5 | 42.5 | −21.0 | −33.2 |
| Multi-adult with no children | 15.8 | 10.1 | −5.7 | −36.2 |
| Men living alone | 18.2 | 11.2 | −7.0 | −38.5 |
| Women living alone | 21.8 | 16.6 | −5.2 | −23.8 |

SOURCE: Calculated by ERS using data from Current Population Survey Food Security Supplements, April 1995 and April 1999.

of all low-income households that received food stamps in 1995. Further, there is concern that some of these families stopped receiving food stamps because they did not know they were still eligible after leaving cash welfare (Zedlewski and Brauner 1999).

## National Level: Changes in Food Insecurity and Hunger

At the national level, food insecurity declined by 1.7 percentage points from 1995 to 1999 (Table 15.2). Food insecurity is closely linked to income, and the decline in food insecurity from 1995 to 1999 can be accounted for entirely by higher incomes in 1999. The association between income and food insecurity was virtually unchanged from 1995 to 1999 (Figure 15.1). In fact, the small change that did occur would have resulted in a slight increase (about 0.1 percentage point; analysis not shown) in food insecurity during the period, but this was more than offset by the upward shift in the income distribution.

The important role of higher income in the decline of food insecurity is reflected also by the changes in food insecurity at different income levels (Table 15.2). The prevalence of food insecurity declined slightly among medium-income and higher-income households (income more than 130 percent of the poverty line), and registered a sta-

**Figure 1  Food Insecurity by Income (1995 and 1999 estimated independently)**

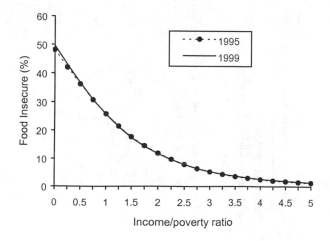

**Table 15.2  Changes in Household Food Insecurity and Hunger, 1995–1999**

| Household characteristic | Food insecurity (with or without hunger) | | | Hunger | | |
|---|---|---|---|---|---|---|
| | 1995 (%) | 1999 (%) | Change (pct. pt.) | 1995 (%) | 1999 (%) | Change (pct. pt.) |
| All households | 11.8 | 10.1 | -1.7* | 4.2 | 2.9 | -1.3* |
| Medium- and high-income | 6.2 | 5.6 | -0.6* | 1.9 | 1.3 | -0.6* |
| Low-income | 31.5 | 32.4 | 0.9 | 11.9 | 10.7 | -1.2* |
| Low-income hh. not receiving food stamps in prior month | 23.2 | 28.2 | 5.0* | 8.8 | 8.9 | 0.1 |
| Aliens | 33.3 | 34.2 | 0.9 | 12.1 | 9.3 | -2.8 |
| Citizens | 22.1 | 27.4 | 5.3* | 8.4 | 8.8 | 0.4 |
| Two-parent with children | 26.6 | 32.0 | 5.6* | 6.4 | 6.1 | -0.3 |
| Single mother with children | 36.3 | 41.4 | 5.1 | 14.9 | 11.1 | -3.8* |
| Multi-adult with no children | 16.8 | 20.9 | 4.1* | 6.3 | 8.3 | 2.0 |
| Men living alone | 23.9 | 29.7 | 5.8* | 12.8 | 12.1 | -0.7 |
| Women living alone | 16.9 | 19.9 | 3.0* | 6.7 | 8.0 | 1.3 |

| Low-income hh. receiving food stamps in prior month | 48.9 | 48.8 | -0.1 | 18.6 | 17.9 | -0.7 |
|---|---|---|---|---|---|---|
| Aliens | 51.5 | 52.7 | 1.2 | 17.3 | 17.7 | 0.4 |
| Citizens | 48.6 | 48.5 | -0.1 | 18.8 | 17.9 | -0.9 |
| Two-parent with children | 49.5 | 52.4 | 2.9 | 17.4 | 10.9 | -6.5 |
| Single mother with children | 51.3 | 47.5 | -3.8 | 19.0 | 15.3 | -3.7 |
| Multi-adult with no children | 46.8 | 43.6 | -3.2 | 16.7 | 23.6 | 6.9 |
| Men living alone | 54.9 | 55.6 | 0.7 | 33.8 | 24.7 | -9.1 |
| Women living alone | 38.6 | 50.2 | 11.6* | 15.3 | 24.6 | 9.3* |

NOTE: * = change was significant at a 90% confidence level.
SOURCE: Calculated by ERS using data from Current Population Survey Food Security Supplements, April 1995 and April 1999.

tistically insignificant increase of 0.9 percentage point among low-income households (income less than 130 percent of the poverty line). Clearly, the major factor in the improved food security was the reduced proportion of households falling in the low-income category.

It is unclear *a priori* how, or to what extent, the distribution of income within the low-income category may have changed from 1995 to 1999. On the one hand, an improved economy might generally raise incomes throughout the lower end of the distribution. On the other hand, the improved economy might primarily benefit those who were most attached to the labor market and thus falling not too far below the low-income cutoff. If those "escaping" from low-income status were primarily from among this less needy group, the remaining low-income households might have lower average income in 1999 than in 1995. Analysis of the relation between income and food insecurity (not shown) indicated that, in fact, the overall incomes in the low-income category improved slightly from 1995 to 1999. Holding constant the relation between income and food insecurity as observed in 1995, increases in income from 1995 to 1999 would have resulted in a small decline in food insecurity (–0.31 percentage point). This decline was more than offset by other factors so that food insecurity registered a small (not statistically significant) increase of 0.9 percentage point.

For low-income households not receiving food stamps, the prevalence of food insecurity increased by 5 percentage points (Table 15.2). This represented an increase in food insecurity of 21.6 percent (5.0 as a percentage of 23.2). This rather large increase in food insecurity suggests that much of the decline in food stamp receipt by low-income households resulted from decreased access to food stamps, not from lessening need for food assistance. Income distribution changed little within this group, and only 0.32 percentage point of the increase in the prevalence of food insecurity was due to the change in income distribution (analysis not shown).

The increase in food insecurity among low-income households not receiving food stamps was widespread, affecting all household types (Table 15.2). Among U.S. citizens, increases in the prevalence of food insecurity were substantial and similar in magnitude for all household types, except women living alone. Even for this latter category, observed food insecurity increased by 3 percentage points. Women living alone also experienced the smallest proportional decline in food stamp receipt (Table 15.1), which may explain the smaller deterioration in food security observed.

Among households not receiving food stamps, noncitizens registered a smaller, and statistically insignificant, increase in food insecurity compared with citizen households. This is unexpected given that noncitizens were affected more by welfare program changes than were citizens, and they experienced a sharper decline in food stamp receipt.

Changes in the prevalence of hunger were less consistent than changes in food insecurity. The prevalence of hunger declined among low-income households by 1.2 percentage points (Table 15.2). Low-income households not receiving food stamps registered almost no change in hunger rates. The largest, and only statistically significant, change in the hunger rate among low-income households not receiving food stamps was for single-mother families (a decline of 3.8 percentage points). The combination of widespread increases in food insecurity, but little or no change (or even declines) in hunger among low-income households not receiving food stamps suggests that the most needy households—those facing hunger without food assistance—were still able to access food stamps. Even so, it is a sobering thought that in 8.8 percent of low-income households not receiving food stamps, people were hungry at some time during the year because they could not afford enough food.

Among low-income households that received food stamps, there was almost no change in the prevalence of food insecurity, and the slight reduction in the prevalence of hunger was not statistically significant. Interpreting changes in food security for households receiving food stamps is complicated by uncertainty about how changes in Food Stamp program participation might have affected the makeup of the population still receiving food stamps in 1999. Of particular interest is the extent to which less needy households may have exited the program, leaving behind only the more needy households. However, analysis of the association of income and food insecurity indicates that incomes rose slightly among low-income food-stamp-recipient households from 1995 to 1999 and would have reduced food insecurity among these households by 0.25 percentage points in the absence of any other changes. Thus, to the extent that income stands as a proxy for overall need, either changes in composition of the food stamp population due to the smaller caseload were small, or they were offset by changes in income owing either to the improved economy, or to changes in cash welfare programs, or to the combined effects of both.

The most remarkable change among food stamp recipients was the large increase in the prevalence of both food insecurity and hunger among low-income women living alone. Low-income women living alone registered a smaller decline in receipt of food stamps than other groups (Table 15.1), so change in composition seems unlikely to account for these large increases. This is confirmed by the fact that the income distribution of low-income women living alone who received food stamps changed little from 1995 to 1999, and the small change that did occur was positive; that is, it would have resulted in a slight reduction in food insecurity in the absence of any other changes (analysis not shown). The reduction in food stamp benefit levels required by PRWORA could be a partial explanation of the increase in food insecurity and hunger among women who received food stamps, but that reduction also was relatively small.

## Nonmetropolitan Households: Food Stamp Caseload Decline

In nonmetro areas, as at the national level, increasing incomes contributed substantially to the decline in food stamp use. The proportion of nonmetro households with incomes below 130 percent of the poverty line declined from 30.7 percent in 1995 to 25.1 percent in 1999 (Table 15.3). Adjusted for population change, this represented a decline of 18.1 percent in the size of the nonmetro low-income population—a decline somewhat smaller than that for the nation as a whole (21 percent; see Table 15.1).[3]

As at the national level, food stamp use among low-income, nonmetro households also declined substantially. For citizen-headed households, the observed decline in nonmetro areas was somewhat smaller than at the national level (33.9 percent in nonmetro areas compared with 37.4 percent at the national level), but this nonmetro/national difference was not statistically significant. In all citizen-headed household categories, the differences between nonmetro and national declines were small and not statistically significant. The large decline in food stamp use registered for nonmetro, low-income, noncitizen households should be interpreted with caution given that this sample was quite small ($N = 69$ households).

**Table 15.3  Changes in Income and Food Stamps in Nonmetropolitan Households, 1995–99**

| Household characteristic | 1995 (%) | 1999 (%) | Change Pct. pt. | % |
|---|---|---|---|---|
| Proportion of households with income below 130% of poverty | 30.7 | 25.1 | –5.6 | –18.2 |
| Proportion of low-income hh. that received food stamps in prior month | | | | |
| All low-income hh. | 30.3 | 20.0 | –10.3 | –33.9 |
| Aliens | 27.4 | 1.9 | –25.5 | –93.2 |
| Citizens | 30.4 | 20.6 | –9.8 | –32.3 |
| Two-parent with children | 30.2 | 20.9 | –9.3 | –30.7 |
| Single mother with children | 59.8 | 40.1 | –19.7 | –32.9 |
| Multi-adult with no children | 17.5 | 9.2 | –8.3 | –47.4 |
| Men living alone | 16.7 | 13.9 | –2.8 | –16.7 |
| Women living alone | 24.9 | 19.0 | –5.9 | –23.8 |

SOURCE: Calculated by ERS using data from Current Population Survey Food Security Supplements, April 1995 and April 1999.

## Nonmetropolitan Households: Changes in Food Insecurity and Hunger

Food insecurity and hunger declined somewhat among nonmetro households from 1995–1999 (Table 15.4). This was primarily a result of improved incomes. Among low-income, nonmetro households, food insecurity was unchanged, and the slight decline in hunger was not statistically significant. As at the national level, income distribution changed very little within the low-income category, and its effect on food insecurity in nonmetro areas was negligible.

Food insecurity increased among nonmetro, low-income households not receiving food stamps, and the increase for citizen-headed households in this category (4.7 percentage points) was similar in magnitude to the corresponding increase at the national level (5.3 percentage points). The increase in food insecurity was less consistent across household types in nonmetro areas than it was at the national level. Increases in food insecurity for households with children were smaller

**Table 15.4  Changes in Food Insecurity and Hunger in Nonmetropolitan Households, 1995–99**

| Household characteristic | Food insecurity (with or without hunger) | | | Hunger | | |
|---|---|---|---|---|---|---|
| | 1995 (%) | 1999 (%) | Change (pct. pt.) | 1995 (%) | 1999 (%) | Change (pct. pt.) |
| All households | 12.1 | 10.2 | -1.9* | 4.1 | 2.7 | -1.4* |
| Medium- and high-income hh. | 5.8 | 5.1 | -0.8 | 1.6 | 1.0 | -0.6* |
| Low-income | 28.1 | 28.2 | 0.1 | 10.1 | 8.8 | -1.3 |
| Low-income hh. not receiving food stamps in prior month | 19.6 | 23.9 | 4.3* | 6.4 | 6.6 | 0.2 |
| Aliens | 32.2 | 23.1 | -9.1 | 13.5 | 5.0 | -8.5 |
| Citizens | 19.2 | 23.9 | 4.7* | 6.3 | 6.7 | 0.4 |
| Two-parent with children | 26.8 | 28.1 | 1.3 | 5.8 | 2.9 | -2.9 |
| Single mother with children | 38.0 | 39.8 | 1.8 | 10.3 | 10.8 | 0.5 |
| Multi-adult with no children | 14.9 | 18.1 | 3.2 | 5.0 | 4.6 | -0.4 |
| Men living alone | 20.0 | 24.8 | 4.8 | 11.8 | 12.0 | 0.2 |
| Women living alone | 10.0 | 17.1 | 7.1* | 3.8 | 6.6 | 2.8 |

| | | | | | | |
|---|---|---|---|---|---|---|
| Low-income hh. receiving food stamps in prior month | 47.8 | 45.4 | -2.4 | 18.6 | 17.5 | -1.1 |
| Aliens | NA[a] | NA | NA | NA | NA | NA |
| Citizens | 48.1 | 45.5 | -2.6 | 18.5 | 17.5 | -1.0 |
| Two-parent with children | 52.0 | 55.2 | 3.2 | 17.1 | 6.8 | -10.3 |
| Single mother with children | 51.7 | 45.1 | -6.6 | 20.5 | 17.4 | -3.1 |
| Multi-adult with no children | 47.6 | 36.9 | -10.7 | 13.0 | 25.3 | 12.3 |
| Men living alone | 55.5 | 54.3 | -1.2 | 36.5 | 29.1 | -7.4 |
| Women living alone | 36.8 | 42.8 | 6.0 | 14.3 | 21.7 | 7.4 |

NOTE: The nonmetro sample of alien-headed, low-income, food-stamp-recipient households was too small for reliable estimates of food insecurity and hunger prevalences. * = change was significant at 90% confidence level.

[a] NA = not applicable.

SOURCE: Calculated by ERS using data from Current Population Survey Food Security Supplements, April 1995 and April 1999.

in nonmetro areas than in the nation as a whole, while the reverse was true for women living alone. For multi-adult households without children and for men living alone, increases in food insecurity were similar in nonmetro and metro areas. However, these differences across household types in nonmetro areas may be mainly an artifact of higher sampling variation due to the small nonmetro sample sizes in the CPS.

The change from 1995 to 1999 in the prevalence of hunger among low-income households not receiving food stamps was small and statistically insignificant in nonmetro areas, as it was at the national level. The observed increase among nonmetro households amounted to only 0.4 percentage points for citizen-headed households and to 0.2 percentage points when noncitizens are included. Among nonmetro, citizen-headed households, the largest observed changes were a decline in hunger among two-parent families with children (2.9 percentage points) and an increase in hunger among women living alone (2.8 percentage points). These were not statistically significant, but were large enough to merit further consideration. The corresponding changes at the national level were in the same direction, but were smaller and also not statistically significant. The substantial decline in hunger for single-mother families at the national level was not observed among nonmetro households.

Changes in food insecurity and hunger among nonmetro low-income households that received food stamps were not statistically significant (Table 15.4). The large observed decline for two-parent families with children and increase for multi-adult households without children merit further examination, however.

## SUMMARY

Much of the overall decline in the food stamp caseload from 1995 to 1999 resulted from rising income, which lowered the proportion of households eligible for food stamps. However, a substantial part of the caseload decline resulted from decreased food stamp use among low-income households, and much of this decline appears to have resulted from less access to food stamps, rather than less need for food assistance.

Reduced access to food stamps is suggested by the substantial increase in food insecurity among low-income households that did not receive food stamps. At the national level, this pattern was consistent for all household types, with the exception of households headed by non-citizens, for whom the increase in food insecurity was smaller and not statistically significant. In nonmetro areas, the same general pattern of increased food insecurity was observed for citizen-headed, low-income households not receiving food stamps. Increases were less consistent across household types in nonmetro areas, likely due, in part, to the smaller sample sizes. Differences between nonmetro and national changes in food stamp use and food security were not statistically significant, and, in general, there is little evidence of important differences in causes and consequences of declining food stamp caseloads between nonmetro and metro areas. It should be noted, however, that the data and methods used would only register a nonmetro difference if the distinctive characteristic were quite widespread in nonmetro areas.

Changes in the prevalence of hunger among low-income households not receiving food stamps were small overall and inconsistent across household types, generally suggesting that the most needy households were still able to access food stamps. This was especially true for single mothers, among whom the prevalence of hunger declined significantly at the national level.

Food insecurity and hunger increased among low-income women living alone, both nationally and in nonmetro areas. This did not appear to be associated with changes in food stamp participation, however. Food stamp receipt by low-income women living alone declined less sharply than for most other groups, and food insecurity and hunger increased among both food stamp recipients and nonrecipients.

## Notes

1. Income information used in the Wilde (2000) study, as well as for the present study, refers to annual income. Food stamp eligibility is based on income during the previous month, and there are asset tests for eligibility as well. This means that some households with annual incomes above 130 percent of the poverty line were eligible for food stamps in some months. Conversely, some households with annual incomes below 130 percent of the poverty line were ineligible because of asset holdings.
2. The design factor is an adjustment that must be applied when calculating sampling

variance based on data from a complex sample such as the CPS, rather than from a simple random sample. The design factors used here are consistent with information provided by the Census Bureau.

3. The proportion of nonmetropolitan households with low income (below 130 percent of the poverty line) was above the national average in both years, consistent with the higher poverty rate registered in nonmetro areas.

# References

Bickel, Gary, Mark Nord, Cristofer Price, William Hamilton, and John Cook. 2000. *Guide to Measuring Household Food Security—Revised 2000*. Arlington, Virginia: Office of Analysis, Nutrition, and Evaluation, Food and Nutrition Service, United States Department of Agriculture.

Bickel, Gary, Steven Carlson, and Mark Nord. 1999. *Household Food Security in the United States 1995–1998 (Advance Report)*. Washington, D.C.: Office of Analysis, Nutrition, and Evaluation, Food and Nutrition Service, United States Department of Agriculture.

Genser, Jenny. 1999. "Who Is Leaving the Food Stamp Program? An Analysis of Caseload Changes from 1994 to 1998." Paper presented at the annual conference of the National Association of Welfare Research and Statistics, August.

Hamilton, William L., John T. Cook, William W. Thompson, Lawrence F. Buron, Edward A. Frongillo, Jr., Christine M. Olson, and Cheryl A. Wehler. 1997a. *Household Food Security in the United States in 1995: Summary Report of the Food Security Measurement Project*. Arlington, Virginia: Office of Analysis, Nutrition, and Evaluation, Food and Nutrition Service, United States Department of Agriculture.

———. 1997b. *Household Food Security in the United States in 1995: Technical Report*. Arlington, Virginia: Office of Analysis, Nutrition, and Evaluation, Food and Nutrition Service, United States Department of Agriculture.

Price, Cristofer, William L. Hamilton, and John T. Cook. 1997. *Guide to Implementing the Core Food Security Module*. Arlington, Virginia: Office of Analysis, Nutrition, and Evaluation, Food and Nutrition Service, United States Department of Agriculture.

Primus, Wendell, Lynette Rawlings, Kathy Larin, and Kathryn Porter. 1999. *The Initial Impacts of Welfare Reform on the Incomes of Single-Mother Families*. Washington, D.C.: Center on Budget and Policy Priorities.

Reinschmiedt, Lynn, Mark Henry, Bruce A. Weber, Elizabeth E. Davis, and Willis Lewis. 1999. *Welfare and Food Stamps Caseloads in Three States:*

*Rural-Urban Contrasts.*  Report P99-10, Rural Policy Research Institute, Columbia, Missouri.

RUPRI.  1999.  *Rural America and Welfare Reform: An Overview Assessment.* Report P99-3, Rural Policy Research Institute, Columbia, Missouri.

Wilde, Parke, Peggy Cook, Craig Gundersen, Mark Nord, and Laura Tiehen. 2000.  *The Decline in Food Stamp Program Participation in the 1990s.* Food and Rural Economics Division, Economic Research Service, U.S. Department of Agriculture.

Zedlewski, Sheila R., and Sarah Brauner.  1999.  "Declines in Food Stamp and Welfare Participation: Is There a Connection?"  Discussion paper 99-13, The Urban Institute, Washington D.C.

# Part 5

# Lessons Learned

# 16
# Lessons Learned
## Welfare Reform and Food Assistance in Rural America

Greg Duncan
*Northwestern University* and *Joint Center for Poverty Research*

Leslie A. Whitener
*Economic Research Service, U.S. Department of Agriculture*

Bruce A. Weber
*Oregon State University* and *Rural Policy Research Institute*

The Personal Responsibility and Work Opportunity Reconciliation Act (PRWORA) of 1996 ended cash assistance as a federal entitlement and imposed time limits and work requirements as a condition of assistance. It also gave state governments more flexibility in designing welfare policy while imposing new accountability requirements on the states. This increased flexibility was intended to allow states to "respond more effectively to the needs of families within their unique environments."

Some states responded to this devolution of authority by giving counties more leeway in designing welfare policies to meet local conditions. Most states, however, implemented uniform programs statewide. The existence of uniform, statewide programs and federally imposed universal time limits and work requirements have led some to wonder how disadvantaged areas and families headed by persons with multiple barriers will fare. There has been a particular interest in how welfare reform might affect the one-fifth of the U.S. population that lives in nonmetropolitan areas (Stangler 2000; Blum et al. 2000; Rural Policy Research Institute 1999).

The chapters in this volume provide an empirical basis for some preliminary judgments about how welfare reform is working in rural areas during its first five years and about what kinds of changes might make the Temporary Assistance for Needy Families (TANF) and Food Stamp programs more successful in both rural and urban areas.  In this concluding chapter, we attempt to summarize the lessons from the volume about the rural-urban differences in welfare reform outcomes and suggest some implications for future welfare policy.  We begin by briefly reviewing some reasons why welfare reform might be expected to have different impacts in rural areas.  We then review the evidence from the chapters in this volume about the impact of welfare reform on caseloads, employment, earnings, and family well-being in rural and urban areas and derive some lessons from this evidence.  These lessons suggest some general implications for future antipoverty policy, and some specific ideas related to reauthorization of PRWORA.  We conclude with a reflection on the spatial implications of welfare policy.

## WHY MIGHT WELFARE REFORM EFFECTS DIFFER IN RURAL AND URBAN AREAS?

Rural areas are exceedingly diverse.  Some are growing rapidly and have high rates of in-migration; others are economically stagnant and are losing population.  Some have high concentrations of agriculture and forestry; others have no significant presence of these industries.  Some have high concentrations of African American, Hispanic, and Native American populations.  Some are adjacent to metropolitan areas and others are isolated from large cities.

Yet all rural areas share one common characteristic: relatively low population densities.  This characteristic shapes the economic prospects of rural communities and regions, and the capacity of the local public and nonprofit sectors to provide community services.  Local economic conditions and community services, in turn, affect the well-being of the residents of rural areas, and the ways rural people might respond to a given set of federal and state policies.  To the extent that rural and urban areas differ in their local labor markets and support services, one might expect the impact of a policy change to differ as well.  Therefore, the question is, how are rural labor markets and support services different from those in urban areas?

## Local Labor Markets

When compared with urban areas, local rural labor markets generally offer fewer job options.  Average wage levels are lower in rural than urban areas, although lower costs of living in rural areas may offset these disadvantages somewhat.[1]  The types of jobs available in rural areas are not as likely to provide steady employment at high wages because employment in rural areas is more concentrated in minimum-wage and part-time jobs and more likely to involve routine work.  In some rural and agricultural areas, employment is more seasonal.

On the supply side of the labor market, rural residents have personal characteristics that may make it harder for them to become and to stay employed, relative to urban residents.  In particular, rural residents have lower average levels of formal education than their urban counterparts.  Unemployment rates are, on average, higher in rural than urban areas, and the unemployment gap between rural and urban areas is growing; unemployment rates for single female-headed families with children (those most affected by welfare reform) are also higher in rural than in urban areas.  Underemployment rates (the underemployed include the unemployed, as well as discouraged workers, involuntary part-time workers, and low-income workers) are also higher in nonmetropolitan areas than in metropolitan areas, and higher even than in central cities (Findeis and Jensen 1998).

## Availability of and Access to Work and Family Support Services

The sheer fact of greater distances to jobs and support services introduces a greater access barrier for rural residents.  Access to jobs, child care, training, and other support services requires reliable personal transportation and, often, more time and money in rural than urban areas.

On one hand, lower population densities in rural areas make it more difficult to support some specialized support services.  Services that support work, such as public transportation and specialized education and job training, are often not present in rural communities.  Formal, paid child care is less available in rural areas.  Family supports, such as health and mental health services, emergency services, and services for those with disabilities, are also often only available in larger central places.  On the other hand, rural residents often have more extensive and stronger informal personal support networks, which can compensate to some extent for the weaker formal support services in helping single mothers make the transitions into paid employment.

In sum, rural welfare recipients have lower levels of formal education, poorer access to high-quality employment opportunities, and poorer access to services and infrastructure to support work and family (job training and education, child care, transportation, health care, and emergency services). These barriers for rural residents suggest that welfare reform could well be less successful in moving low-income adults into the workforce and out of poverty.


## RESEARCH ON RURAL/URBAN DIFFERENCES IN WELFARE REFORM EFFECTS

### TANF and Food Stamp Participation

TANF and food stamp caseloads declined dramatically in both rural and urban areas over the past seven years. TANF caseloads declined 47 percent between 1994 and 1999, while the food stamp caseload declined 30 percent over this same period. TANF caseload declines were fueled by a mixture of booming economic conditions and welfare reform changes, as well as expansion of the Earned Income Tax Credit, with most, but by no means all, former recipients securing at least a temporary foothold in the labor market.

Food stamp declines are more troubling, given that most families leaving TANF retain eligibility for food stamps. It is clear that state policies have a significant impact on food stamp participation. For example, in Ohio between 1994 and 1999, the TANF caseload fell by 53 percent, a decline not much greater than the food stamp caseload decline of 45 percent. In contrast, South Carolina made special efforts to promote food stamp use, and its TANF caseload decline over this period (64 percent) was much greater than the 13 percent fall in food stamp caseloads.

Overall, food stamp participation rates appear to have declined more in urban than rural areas. More generally, though, patterns of TANF and food stamp caseload declines differ between rural and urban areas, but with the differences varying considerably from one state to the next. It is difficult to draw general conclusions that apply to all or even most states. Thus, state policies must be developed with an eye toward the unique features of the given state.

## Employment and Earnings

Reducing caseloads is a major goal of welfare reform, but it is not the only goal. One issue that has not been resolved in the few years since PRWORA was enacted is how recipients who have left the rolls are faring in the labor market, and whether this experience differs in rural and urban areas. Can welfare recipients find work? Is the transition more difficult in rural areas? How interested are employers in hiring recipients? What kinds of jobs are they getting? How much are they earning? Can former welfare recipients escape poverty through work? The tight labor markets and low unemployment rates nationwide throughout the late 1990s provided the best possible environment for welfare recipients entering the labor market. Reductions in caseloads, however, do not mean that all rural and urban families that leave the rolls are making ends meet.

### Can rural welfare recipients find work?

National-level studies have suggested that welfare reform and expansion of the Earned Income Tax Credit are playing important roles in raising the employment rates of single mothers (Meyer and Rosenbaum 2000), with some research finding that more than half of mothers leaving the welfare rolls are employed at some time after ending their welfare participation (Cancian et al. 1999; Brauner and Loprest 1999). A high work response to welfare reform has occurred in both metro and nonmetro areas. McKernan and her coauthors (in this volume, p. 257) find few differences in the effect of welfare reform in metro and nonmetro areas for all single mothers, although the more disadvantaged group of low-educated, single mothers in rural areas has not shared the employment gains of their urban counterparts. A more detailed comparison of nonmetro and central-city residents shows lower employment gains between 1989 and 1998 for nonmetro single mothers with children than for central-city mothers. However, the data do not support the early, dire predictions that rural mothers and their children would be left behind in job attainment under the new welfare policy and economic environment (see in this volume, Danziger, p. 25; Lichter and Jensen, p. 77).

Assessments of welfare reform at the state level suggest more variable effects. Minnesota implemented an experimental welfare waiver program with complementary components of financial incentives to encourage work and mandatory participation in employment-focused services for long-term welfare recipients. In their chapter (p. 287) on the effects of this welfare program, Gennetian and colleagues find that employment among long-term, single-parent recipients increased in both urban and rural counties during the two years after selection for study in 1994–1996. However, in contrast to the large and lasting employment increases in urban counties, average employment increases were much smaller in rural counties, and the effects on employment faded considerably by the last year of follow-up.

### Is the welfare-to-work transition more difficult in rural areas?

Most national-level research in this volume suggests that obstacles to employment for single mothers leaving welfare are no greater in rural areas than in urban areas. Rural areas are becoming more culturally, politically, and economically integrated, and many issues related to low-wage service economies are relevant for both rural and urban areas.

State-level analyses, however, suggest that barriers to work can vary widely by labor market area. Howell's Mississippi labor market analysis (in this volume, p. 313) quantitatively demonstrates that labor market areas differ in their capacity to create net job growth that matches the educational credentials of TANF recipients. Moreover, the labor market areas that are likely to be the most challenged by this spatial mismatch are also those with the worst access to licensed child care facilities. The nonmetropolitan labor market area in the Delta region appears to hold the bleakest outlook for TANF recipients to find jobs that will match their educational credentials. Areas of the state with the highest levels of urban influence hold the brightest prospects for job-matched employment. The availability of regulated child care facilities also follows this pattern of urban influence.

Similarly, interviews with welfare families and community informants in seven Iowa communities ranked by population density suggest that differential effects of welfare reform policies hinge on differences in the proximity of jobs and access to support services (see Fletcher, in this volume, p. 201). Urban centers offer more job opportunities and support a scale of auxiliary social services that cannot be matched in rural communities. Welfare recipients who live in or adjacent to urban areas have potential access to more jobs, and jobs that pay higher wages compared with recipients who live in remote rural communities. However, capitalizing on local jobs requires access to reliable, affordable transportation. The feasibility of establishing cost-effective mass transit systems depends, in part, on population density and, therefore, is more likely to exist in urban areas. Families making the transition from welfare to work need an array of support services that include job training, health care, child care, or a range of emergency services.

### Have employment transitions improved the economic well-being of rural recipients?

National-level analyses show that welfare-to-work transitions resulted in significant gains in total per-capita earnings between 1993 and 1999 for nonmetro, single, female-headed families with children, larger than the gains seen for their metro counterparts (Mills, Alwang, and Hazarika 2000). The status of heads shifted from "not in the workforce and on welfare" to the more remunerative state of "in the workforce and not on welfare" is often used as an indicator of program success. This shift accounted for nearly all of the gains in total per capita income between 1993 and 1999. However, these welfare-to-work shifts and the resulting economic gains are largely due to increases in the education and ages of single mothers and improvements in area economies rather than to structural shifts related to welfare reform.

Assessments at the state level also point to limited effects of welfare reform on earnings in rural areas, although the effects are more positive for urban areas. Gennetian and coauthors (in this volume, p. 287) find that the waiver program in Minnesota had no statistically significant effect on the average earnings of rural welfare recipients, although it increased the average earnings of urban recipients. The program increased income (measured by welfare and earnings) for both urban and rural recipients because it allowed recipients to maintain their welfare income as their earnings increased. Differences in recipients' prior marital history and changes in family structure, particularly, explain the programs' different effects on rural and urban recipients.

### Can former welfare recipients escape poverty through work?

Although most former recipients can find some work, many cannot get or keep full-time, year-round work. As a result, many welfare recipients return to the welfare system for economic support. Jensen and coauthors, in their chapter, explore returns to welfare in Iowa and find, for example, that among welfare recipients, those in metro areas were less likely to leave welfare compared with those in nonmetro areas. Once they left, however, metro residents were less likely to return right away. After the first two quarters, there was little difference in the likelihood of returning to welfare between metro and nonmetro residents. Iowa's experience suggests that human capital, child support, and the presence of children are major determinants of welfare dependence and cycling.

Additional analysis suggests that the impacts of welfare-to-work transitions are likely to vary systematically by type of county. Brady and coauthors, in their chapter (p. 147), argue that welfare use patterns in California's rural and agricultural counties differ from those in urban counties, owing largely to variation in employment patterns. The average welfare recipient in either a rural or agricultural county has more, and shorter, welfare spells than the average welfare recipient in an urban county. A person in these rural or agricultural counties is, therefore, more likely to begin receiving welfare in a given year. However, once on welfare, he or she is more likely to exit welfare before an urban welfare recipient who began welfare at the same time. Significant seasonality exists in the nonurban caseload. The average California welfare recipient in an agricultural or rural county is more likely than the average welfare recipient in an urban county to exit in the summer months than in the winter months.

Over one-third of working, rural female heads are in poverty, a rate higher than at any time since 1989 (see Lichter and Jensen, in this volume). The problem for most rural, poor adults is less one of finding a job than of finding a job that pays a living wage. Harvey and coauthors, in their chapter (p. 375), analyze the short-term impacts of welfare reform in the persistently poor rural areas of central Appalachia, the Mississippi Delta, the Lower Rio Grande Valley, and Indian reservations in South Dakota. They find that personal and policy adjustments have buffered the severity of negative impacts predicted by many reform critics. Personal adjustments include extensive participation in informal labor markets, and reliance on strong networks of family support. An institutional response in these areas has been to suspend time limits in some counties. It is likely that many of those who left the welfare rolls have found work in either the formal or informal labor market. Welfare reform may have reduced the ability of poor adults to combine welfare assistance with informal work.

## Poverty

Poverty rates are higher in nonmetropolitan areas than in metropolitan areas, and they have declined more over the last decade. Public assistance has had a modest effect in moving single mothers with children out of poverty, moving them out of deep poverty, and closing the "poverty gap" (the gap between their incomes and the poverty line for their family). Welfare reform and a strong economy combined to reduce poverty among single mothers with children since 1996. For the most part, welfare reform did not differ greatly in rural and urban areas in its effect on poverty. Yet there is some indication that this "ameliorative effect" has been greater in metropolitan areas than in nonmetropolitan areas. As Lichter and Jensen report in their chapter, this ameliorative effect of public assistance for single mothers with children declined since 1996, and it decreased more in nonmetro areas.

## Food Insecurity and Hunger

There was no substantial difference between metropolitan and nonmetropolitan areas in levels of hunger and food insecurity during the late 1990s. Food insecurity remained the same but hunger rates declined significantly between 1995 and 1998 in both nonmetropolitan areas and nationally.

The substantial declines in food stamp use during the late 1990s may have been because of decreases in program access or because of less need. Nord's chapter (in this volume, p. 433) shows that food insecurity increased substantially in the late 1990s among low-income households not participating in the Food Stamp program. He concludes that much of the decline in food stamp use by low-income households "appears to have resulted from less access to food stamps, rather than less need for food assistance." Because there was no corresponding increase in hunger, however, it appears that the most needy households, those facing hunger without food assistance, were generally still able to access food stamps.

## LESSONS LEARNED

The chapters in this volume provide some insight into the spatial variation in welfare reform outcomes and the differences in context, opportunities, and barriers that shape the different outcomes. Four lessons emerge from these studies:

- Both work-oriented welfare policy and a strong national economy have reduced the welfare caseload and resulted in increased incomes and lower poverty for both urban and rural single-parent families. When viewed from the national level, nonmetropolitan outcomes related to welfare use, poverty, and employment of single-parent families are not significantly different from metropolitan outcomes. As one looks at specific states, and regions within those states, however, enormous variation emerges within and among urban and rural areas in the structure of opportunities and in outcomes.
- Both personal characteristics and structural conditions hinder the success of low-income people making the transition from welfare to work. Low-income people in rural areas generally face substantial structural barriers: fewer and lower-wage jobs, long distances to services and jobs, low automobile access (a greater barrier because of the distances and no public transportation), and lack of child care options. Personal barriers, however, are more ubiquitous in both rural and urban areas: a lack of soft skills (work-related social and interpersonal skills), lack of edu-

cation (although rural single mothers are somewhat better educated than their urban counterparts), and personal stress.

- Participation in the informal economy is an important element of
  the economic strategies used by low-income people to make
  ends meet, perhaps particularly in rural areas.  Because welfare
  reform's work mandates do not recognize informal work, rural
  residents in severely depressed regions have experienced economic hardship from losing a welfare income without being able
  to replace it through work in the formal economy.
- Welfare participants, employers, and welfare administrators
  have quite different views on why people participate in welfare
  programs and what prevents them from getting jobs that move
  them to self-sufficiency.  Welfare participants stress low wages,
  their own lack of education, and local child care availability as
  major barriers to self-sufficiency.  Employers stress the lack of
  soft skills, transportation, child care problems, and the lack of a
  "work ethic" among the welfare recipients. Welfare administrators point to both personal issues (generational dependence on
  welfare, lack of education and motivation, substance abuse) and
  structural barriers (lack of jobs and transportation, expense of
  owning a car) as impediments to self-sufficiency.  Where welfare policy implementation is devolved to the local level, local
  administrators appear to be energized by the increased responsibility to attempt innovations.

These lessons suggest that antipoverty policy will be more effective if
it recognizes the diversity in context, resources and opportunities in
different places.


## POLICY IMPLICATIONS


The 2002 reauthorization of the Personal Responsibility and Work
Opportunity Reconciliation Act of 1996 will provide an opportunity to
make adjustments in the federal welfare regulations and in state programs.  The chapters in this volume point to five ways in which welfare
policy could be redirected to make it more effective in improving the
work opportunities and well-being of rural and urban families.

## Making Work Pay

As TANF caseloads have fallen sharply, most but not all families that leave welfare are gaining at least a temporary foothold in the labor market. National studies suggest that the effects of welfare reform are no different in nonmetro areas than in metro areas. However, too many families leaving welfare remain poor, and not all are receiving the work-based supports they need to gain permanent economic independence.

Our findings suggest that states and the federal government would do well to increase their efforts to make work pay for low-wage workers. Macroeconomic policy aimed at maintaining a full-employment economy can provide the underpinning for specific tax and human investment policies. Some of these policy options include

- expanding the federal Earned Income Tax Credit to further support the work efforts of low-income families;
- initiating or expanding state Earned Income Tax Credit supplements;
- expanding coverage of and participation rates in health insurance and child care assistance programs for low-wage families;
- increasing the minimum wage to keep up with general wage levels; and
- taking advantage of resources in the Workforce Investment Act to help match workers and jobs.

In addressing these policy areas, it is important to preserve work incentives for families and job-creation incentives for firms.

## Addressing the Unique Work Barriers in Sparsely Settled Places

Although the overall impact of welfare reform does not seem to differ greatly between metropolitan and nonmetropolitan areas at the national level, some studies of specific state welfare programs and specific policy provisions have found that welfare reform has had a less favorable impact on earnings and employment in rural areas.

People who live in sparsely settled rural areas face unique barriers to working that are associated with low-population densities: long distances to jobs and services and limited options for services such as health and child care. States can facilitate access to reliable cars for rural, low-income workers and seek creative ways of providing or subsidizing services that are needed for successful transitions to work.  Of special importance to rural areas are state welfare reforms that

- address the less favorable opportunities (low-wage jobs) and high unemployment of rural labor markets;
- recognize the transportation needs of rural residents by enabling them to own reliable cars while at the same time maintaining eligibility for assistance programs;
- address service delivery problems caused by the geographic dispersion of people in need of program services; and
- increase access to affordable and flexible child care that provides an adequate level of quality.  Family-based financial incentives for child care are not effective if lack of base funding for child care facilities prevents development of formal child care facilities in rural areas.  Improving child care choice in rural areas would require additional base funding.

## Maintaining the Safety Net

Many low-income families that need supports from food stamps do not realize that they remain eligible for these programs even if they lose eligibility for cash assistance.  Some states have been quite successful in getting the message out; others much less so.  Increased state efforts to ensure that families eligible for food stamps and other in-kind programs are, in fact, enrolled in the program would strengthen the safety net for low-income families.

## Helping Multiple-Barrier Families

As TANF caseloads fall, families remaining on the rolls will increasingly be characterized by multiple barriers to work, including low skill levels, drug dependence, mental health problems, and family members (children and/or adult relatives) with disabilities.  This suggests that states need to experiment with intensive demonstration programs aimed at multiple-barrier families, and to be creative in assisting families that face TANF work requirement and time limits by rewarding postsecondary schooling and community-service activities, and considering selective use of state-financed, low-wage public-sector jobs.

## Helping Persistent High-Poverty Areas

Not all areas have benefited equally from the strong economy and welfare reforms.  Parts of the urban core of major metropolitan areas and rural areas in Appalachia, the Mississippi Delta, and the Rio Grande Valley have suffered from persistently high levels of poverty and unemployment.  Recipients in these areas may be more likely to "hit the time limits" and be economically dependent on informal work. State policy could be more flexible about time limits and work requirements in persistently poor areas, and they could put more effort into creating employment opportunities.  In states with high-poverty, high-unemployment areas, the work-oriented approach of welfare reform may not adequately address the needs of families in these areas.

Two underlying themes emerge from this discussion about the rural and urban dimensions of social and economic policy as it affects low-income populations.  First, some policy actions appear to be helpful in both rural and urban areas: tax policy, food stamps, and certain work-force investments.  Second, the diversity of circumstances among low-income people and between regions suggests the need for flexibility in regulation and differential investments in services (child care, education, and transportation, for examples), infrastructure, and job creation.

## A ROLE FOR PLACE-BASED ANTIPOVERTY STRATEGIES?

Work-oriented, family-based changes in welfare under the 1996 legislation and a healthy economy have resulted in increased incomes and lower poverty rates for rural and urban single mothers with children.  The choice of antipoverty strategy, however, has implications for population distribution between rural and urban areas.  Urban labor markets provide higher earnings and better and more varied work supports.  Policy that encourages work and enhances job-readiness but does not address rural barriers to working may induce more rural low-income people to move to the cities.

A recent study by the Brookings Institution, which analyzed welfare caseloads in the 89 urban counties containing the nation's 100 largest cities, found that caseloads are concentrating geographically in these cities, and are highly concentrated in the nation's largest cities (Allen and Kirby 2000). Some observers have concluded that this is because urban welfare recipients are "still stuck on the rolls . . . trapped by concentrated urban poverty" (*The Economist*, July 22, 2000, p. 31). The increasing concentration of caseloads in urban areas might well be due to rural recipients leaving the caseload at a greater rate than urban recipients, and to these rural welfare leavers remaining in rural areas with or without a job. It might also be that the increasing concentration of caseloads in urban areas is, in part, a result of rural-to-urban migration of former rural welfare recipients who cannot find work in rural areas. This speculation is a fruitful area for future research.

The long-standing policy debate continues about the proper balance between human investments and place-specific investments. Current antipoverty strategies emphasize human investments and family supports. There is a continuing need to provide financial incentives that "make work pay," to strengthen the safety net for those who cannot work, and to continue to invest in training and work support systems. However, employment, earnings, and poverty outcomes are not as favorable in areas in which job opportunities are lacking. Stimulating job investments in these areas would increase the likelihood of success of the current human-investment, work-oriented welfare policy for the residents of these areas and reduce incentives to move.

## Note

1.   This has always been a controversial area; see Nord (2000) and National Research Council (1995).

## References

Allen, Katherine, and Maria Kirby. 2000. *Unfinished Business: Why Cities Matter to Welfare Reform.* Survey Series, Center for Urban and Metropolitan Studies, Brookings Institution, Washington, D.C., July. Available at <http://www.brook.edu/es/urban/welfarecaseloads/2000report.htm>.

Blum, Barbara, Jennifer Farnsworth, Mary Clare Lennon, and Ellen Winn. 2000. *Welfare Research Perspectives: Past, Present, and Future, 2000 Edition.* National Center for Children in Poverty, Washington, D.C., August.

Brauner, Sarah, and Pamela Loprest. 1999. *Where Are They Now? What States' Studies of People Who Left Welfare Tell Us*. The Urban Institute, Washington, D.C.

Cancian, Maria, Robert Haveman, Thomas Kaplan, Daniel Meyer, and Barbara Wolfe. 1999. "Work, Earnings, and Well-Being after Welfare." In *Economic Conditions and Welfare Reform*, Sheldon H. Danziger, ed. Kalamazoo, Michigan: W.E. Upjohn Institute for Employment Research.

Findeis, Jill, and Leif Jensen. 1998. "Employment Opportunities in Rural Areas: Implications for Poverty in a Changing Policy Environment." *American Journal of Agricultural Economics* 80(5): 1000–1007.

Meyer, Bruce, and Dan Rosenbaum. 2000. "Making Single Mothers Work: Recent Tax and Welfare Policy and Its Effects." *National Tax Journal* 53(4, part 2): 1027–1062.

Mills, Bradford, Jeffrey R. Alwang, and Guatam Hazarika. 2000. "The Impact of Welfare Reform Nationally and in Nonmetropolitan Areas: A Nonparametric Analysis." Paper presented at the Joint Center for Poverty Research conference, "Rural Dimensions of Welfare Reform: A Research Conference on Poverty, Welfare, and Food Assistance," Washington, D.C., May 4–5.

National Research Council. 1995. *Measuring Poverty: A New Approach*. Washington, D.C.: National Academy Press.

Nord, Mark. 2000. "Does It Cost Less to Live in Rural Areas? Evidence from New Data on Food Security and Hunger." *Rural Sociology* 65(1): 104–125.

Rural Policy Research Institute, Rural Welfare Reform Panel. 1999. *Rural America and Welfare Reform: An Overview Assessment*. Rural Policy Research Institute, University of Missouri, Columbia.

Stangler, Gary. 2000. "Job Skills, Urban versus Rural Differences, and Translating Research into Policy." *Poverty Research News* 4(6), Joint Center for Poverty Research, Chicago.

# The Authors

Henry Brady is a professor of political science and public policy at the University of California, Berkeley and director of Berkeley's Survey Research Center and its data archive, UC DATA.

Sheldon Danziger is the Henry J. Meyer collegiate professor of social work and public policy and the director of the Center on Poverty, Risk and Mental Health at the University of Michigan

Greg J. Duncan is a professor of education and social policy and a faculty associate in the Institute for Policy Research at Northwestern University. He is also director of the Northwestern University/University of Chicago Joint Center for Poverty Research.

Cynthia Needles Fletcher is a professor in the Department of Human Development and Family Studies of Iowa State University.

Jan L. Flora is a professor of sociology and community extension sociologist at Iowa State University.

Barbara J. Gaddis is a research associate at Iowa State University, Department of Human Development and Family Studies Extension.

Steve Garasky is an associate professor in the Department of Human Development and Family Studies and is affiliated with the Iowa State University Center for Family Policy.

Lisa A. Gennetian is a senior research associate at Manpower Demonstration Research Corporation in New York.

Fredric C. Gey is assistant director of UC DATA at the University of California, Berkeley.

Robert Gibbs is a regional economist and head of the rural labor and

471

education research unit at the Economic Research Service, U.S. Department of Agriculture, in Washington, D.C.

Mark Harvey is a graduate student in the Department of Rural Sociology at the University of Wisconsin–Madison.

June Heineman is a research associate at the Wilder Research Center in St. Paul, Minnesota.

Debra A. Henderson is an assistant professor of sociology at Ohio University.

Mark Henry is a professor in the Department of Agricultural and Applied Economics at Clemson University.

Frank M. Howell is a professor of sociology in the Department of Sociology, Anthropology, and Social Work at Mississippi State University.

Darren Hudson is an associate professor in the Department of Agricultural Economics, Mississippi State University.

Helen H. Jensen is a professor of economics and head of Food and Nutrition Policy Research, Center for Agricultural and Rural Development (CARD), at Iowa State University

Leif Jensen is a professor of rural sociology and demography at Pennsylvania State University.

Shao-Hsun Keng is an assistant professor at the National Taichung Institute of Technology, Taiwan.

Robert I. Lerman is a professor of economics at American University and director of the Labor and Social Policy Center at the Urban Institute.

Willis Lewis, Jr., is a graduate student in the Department of Agricultural and Applied Economics at Clemson University.

Daniel T. Lichter is Robert F. Lazarus professor in population studies and a professor of sociology at The Ohio State University. He also is director of the University's Initiative in Population Research.

Jacquelyn S. Litt is an associate professor in the Women's Studies Program and Department of Sociology at Iowa State University. She is also chair of the University Committee on Women.

Sheena McConnell is a senior economist at Mathematica Policy Research, Inc.

Signe-Mary McKernan is an economist and senior research associate in the Labor and Social Policy Center at the Urban Institute.

Cynthia Miller is a senior research associate at Manpower Demonstration Research Corporation in New York.

Justine Nelson-Christinedaughter is a research associate at Wilder Research Center, St. Paul, Minnesota.

Mark Nord is team leader for the Food Stamps and Food Security Research Team of the Food Assistance and Rural Economy Branch, Economic Research Service, U.S. Department of Agriculture.

James Ohls is a senior fellow at Mathematica Policy Research, Inc.

Greg Owen is a consulting scientist at the Wilder Research Center, St. Paul, Minnesota.

Kathleen Pickering is an assistant professor at Colorado State University on the faculty of the Department of Anthropology and on the graduate faculty of the Department of Sociology.

Nancy Pindus is a senior research associate in the Urban Institute's Labor and Social Policy center.

Cindy Redcross is a research associate at Manpower Demonstration Research Corporation in New York.

Lynn Reinschmiedt is associate dean of the College of Agriculture and Life Sciences, Mississippi State University.

Patricia Richards is a doctoral candidate in the Department of Sociology and a Mellon Fellow in Latin American sociology at the University of Texas–Austin.

Corinna Roy is currently the housing coordinator for the Urban League of Rhode Island. She is also a research consultant for the Brown University Center for Alcohol and Addition Studies.

Ellen Shelton is a research scientist for Wilder Research Center, a private, nonprofit research and evaluation group based in Saint Paul, Minnesota.

Mary Sprague is a Ph.D. candidate in the Department of Political Science, University of California, Berkeley

Amy Bush Stevens is project coordinator for the Illinois Families Study at the Institute for Policy Research and Institute for Health Services Research and Policy Studies at Northwestern University

Gene F. Summers is a professor emeritus of the Department of Rural Sociology at the University of Wisconsin–Madison.

Barry Tadlock serves as a senior research associate/project manager for the Rural Welfare Reform Project (RWRP). He is also an adjunct professor in Ohio University's Department of Political Science.

Ann Tickamyer is a professor of sociology in the Department of Sociology/Anthropology at Ohio University and is an Ohio University Research Scholar.

Jesse Valente is an analyst at Abt Associates, Inc., in Cambridge, Massachusetts.

Bruce Weber is a professor of agricultural and resource economics at Oregon State University. He is currently serving as chair of the Rural Policy Research Institute Rural Welfare Reform Research Panel.

Julie White is an associate professor of political science at Ohio University.

Leslie A. Whitener is chief of the Food Assistance and Rural Economy Branch, Economic Research Service, U.S. Department of Agriculture in Washington, D.C.

Mary Winter is a professor of human development and family studies and Associate Dean for Research and Graduate Education in the College of Family and Consumer Sciences, Iowa State University.

Michael Wiseman is a research professor of public policy and economics at George Washington University.

# Cited Author Index

The italic letters *f*, *n*, and *t* following a page number indicate that the cited name is within a figure, note, or table, respectively, on that page.

Abramovitz, M., 234, 253
Acs, Gregory, 30, 48, 51, 75
Adams, Terry K., 381, 406
Administration for Children and
    Families, 222, 228
Albert, Vicky N., 150, 173
Allen, J.C., 203, 228, 469
Allen, Katherine, 469
Alwang, Jeffrey R., 461, 470
Andrews, David, 78, 106
Annie E. Casey Foundation, 80, 106
Asher, Andrew, 416, 430*n*1, 432

Ballejos, Marie, 381, 408
Bane, M., 233, 234, 253
Bania, Neil, 315, 316, 342, 343
Barkley, D., 135*n*2, 145
Bartik, Timothy J., 61, 73, 126, 135*n*3,
    135*n*7, 137*n*16, 139*n*25, 144
Bassi, Laurie J., 151, 174, 381, 408
Battese, G.E., 139–140*n*26, 144
Beale, Calvin L., 174, 182, 198
Beaulieu, Lionel J., 11, 19, 56, 74
Beck, E.M., 409
Beeler, Jesse D., 119, 144
Bensman, J., 201, 229
Bernstein, Jared, 68, 73
Besser, T., 206, 207, 228
Bickel, Gary, 435, 437, 450
Blank, Michael, 107
Blank, Rebecca M., 85, 86, 109, 127,
    135*n*7, 137*n*16, 138*n*19, 139*n*26,
    145, 150, 173, 276, 285, 286,
    315, 341
Bloomquist, Leonard E., 72*n*3, 73, 380,
    406
Bluestone, Barry, 150, 173

Bluestone, Herman, 380, 408
Blum, Barbara, 455, 469
Bokemeier, Janet L., 105, 109, 377, 378,
    409
Born, Catherine E., 180, 198
Bosley, Sarah, 257, 260, 280, 283
Brady, Henry E., 167, 173
Brady, Peter, 150, 173
Brandon, Peter David, 180, 198
Brauner, Sarah, 114, 116, 127, 133,
    136*n*15, 146, 435, 439, 451, 459,
    470
Brister, Bill M., 144
Brocht, Chauna, 68, 73
Brooks, K., 135*n*2, 145
Brown, A., 81, 82, 347, 374
Brown, C., 234, 253
Brown, David L., 107, 174
Brown, Lawrence A., 78, 108
Bryant, Clifton D., 380, 406
Buck, M.L., 229, 347, 374
Burke, Raymond, L., 78, 106
Burke, Sandra Charvat, 81, 107, 204,
    204*t*, 228, 229
Buron, Lawrence F., 450
Burtless, Gary, 61, 73
Burton, L., 201, 228
Butler, Margaret A., 182, 198

California Department of Social
    Services, 174
California Employment Development
    Department, 160, 174
Cancian, Maria, 10, 19, 381, 407, 459,
    470
Cao, Jian, 180, 198
Capps, Randy, 285

Card, David, 284
Carlson, Steven, 435, 450
Castells, Manuel, 378, 379, 406
Castner, Laura, 420, 423, 431, 431n5
Caudill, Pamela J., 198
Chambry, Sharon, 144
Cherlin, A.J., 228
Chernik, Howard, 137n18, 144
Citro, Constance F., 85, 107, 228
Clark, Sandra J., 262, 284
Clemente, Frank, 409
Cody, Scott, 420, 423, 431, 431n5
Coe, Norma, 48
Cohen, Rhoda, 432
Conger, Rand D., 81, 107
Congressional Budget Office, 150, 173,
    315, 342
Connolly, Laura S., 175, 181, 198, 286,
    343
Conoway, C., 303, 311
Cook, John T., 437, 450
Cook, N.M., 228
Cook, Peggy J., 1, 7, 20, 21, 139n27,
    144, 404n1, 406, 451
Cook, Steven T., 180, 199
Corcoran, Mary, 30, 48, 49
Cornwell, Gretchen T., 81, 82, 108
Costanzo, Janice A., 82, 108, 379, 407
Coulton, Claudia, 316, 343
Council of Economic Advisers, 60, 73,
    124, 136–137n16, 138n19,
    138n24, 139n26, 144, 150, 171,
    173
Cromartie, John B., 64, 65, 73

Dagata, Elizabeth, 1, 20, 84, 107
Dalaker, Joseph, 103, 107
Danzinger, Sandra K., 30, 34, 38, 48, 49
Danzinger, Sheldon, 27, 31, 48n9, 49
Davis, Elizabeth E., 145, 175, 181, 198,
    286, 343, 450
Deavers, Kenneth L., 259, 284, 380, 406
Dewees, Sarah, 108, 374
Dillman, D.A., 203, 228
Dion, M. Robin, 5, 20, 423, 431

Dodoo, M., 311
Doeringer, Peter B., 55, 73
Douglas, Toby, 284
Doyle, Pat, 416, 430n1, 432
Doyle, Patricia, 109
Dudley, Charles J., 406
Duke, Amy-Ellen, 259, 280, 281, 284
Duncan, Cynthia M., 78, 81, 103, 107,
    109, 379, 380, 406
Duncan, Greg J., 381, 406

Eathington, Liesl, 179, 180, 198, 205,
    228
Eberts, Randall W., 126, 135n3, 135n7,
    137n16, 139n25, 144
Economic Research Service (ERS), 6f,
    7, 12f, 18, 19n5, 20, 63f, 64, 66f,
    284
The Economist, 469
Edin, Kathryn, 229, 406
Eggebeen, David J., 83, 84, 95, 108
Eissa, N., 308, 311
Elder, Glen H., Jr., 81, 107
Ellwood, David T., 46, 49, 124, 129,
    135, 137n18, 144, 228, 233, 234,
    253
Environmental Systems Research
    Institute, Inc., 319, 342
Epstein, W., 233, 253
Evans, Sharon D., 409

Falk, William W., 80, 108
Farnsworth, Jennifer, 469
Ferguson, K., 234, 253
Fernandez-Kelly, M. Patricia, 378, 406
Figlio, David N., 115, 135n7, 137n16,
    139n26, 144, 175, 286, 343
Findeis, Jill L., 82, 105, 107, 152, 173,
    180, 181, 198, 341n7, 380, 407,
    457, 470
Fink, B., 229
Fitchen, Janet M., 81, 107, 203, 228,
    380, 381, 407
Fitzgerald, John R., 149, 151, 174, 381,
    407

Fix, Michael, 152, 175
Fletcher, C.N., 211, 228, 229
Flora, C., 203, 228
Flora, J.L., 228
Flynt, Wayne, 81, 107
Fortmann, Louise, 152, 174
Fossett, Mark A., 80, 107
Fraker, Thomas M., 183, 198
Francis, J., 228
Fraser, N., 234, 253
Friedman, Samantha, 103, 107
Frongillo, Edward A., Jr., 450
Fuguitt, Glenn V., 174
Fuller, W.A., 139n26–140n26, 144

Gaddis, B.J., 229
Gais, Thomas L., 4, 20
Gallagher, L. Jerome, 4, 20, 30, 49, 284, 285
Gallagher, Megan, 20, 49, 284
Garasky, Steven, 81, 107, 196, 199
Garcia, Anna M., 378, 406
Gardner, Erica L., 83, 108
Garfinkel, Irving, 93, 107
Garkovich, Lori, 68, 75
Garner, Thesia, 109
Geen, Rob, 262, 284
Gennetian, Lisa, 288, 311
Genser, Jenny, 433, 450
Gey, Fredric C., 173
Ghelfi, Linda M., 56, 65, 74, 116, 126, 144, 314, 318, 342
Giannarelli, Linda, 285
Gibbs, Robert, 1, 7, 20, 51, 64, 65, 73, 281
Gilder, G., 233, 253
Gingrich, N., 233, 234, 253
Glaeser, Edward, L., 56, 73
Gloecker, L.A., 197, 199
Goldstein, G.S., 55, 73
Gordon, Anne R., 198, 233
Gordon, L., 253
Gorham, Lucy, 380, 407
Gottschalk, Peter, 49, 51, 73
Goudy, Willis, 107, 204, 204t, 228, 229

Green, G., 371, 374
Greene, J.C., 210, 229
Greene, William H., 139n26, 144
Gringeri, Christina, 73, 379, 380, 382, 407, 409
Grogger, Jeff, 284
Gronberg, T.J., 55, 73
Gundersen, Craig, 21, 315, 342, 451

Halperin, Rhoda, 378, 407
Hamilton, William L., 437, 450
Handler, J., 233, 254
Hanson, Margaret, 107, 204, 229
Harris, Kathleen, 149, 174
Hasenfeld, Y., 233, 243, 254
Haveman, Robert, 19, 470
Hazarika, Guatam, 461, 470
Heflin, Colleen, 49
Henderson, D., 254
Henry, Mark S., 135n2, 145, 450
Hicks, J.D., 360, 374
Hirschl, Thomas A., 82, 107, 151, 174, 380, 381, 408
Hofferth, Sandra, 379, 407
Hoffman, Sandra, 152, 174
Holcomb, Pamela A., 177, 198
Holzer, Harry J., 10, 20, 352, 360, 374
Hoppe, Robert A., 259, 284, 380, 406
Horton, Francine, 380, 409
Howell, Frank M., 138n22, 283n16, 284, 314, 316, 317, 320, 335, 338, 339, 340n1–n3, 341n7, 342
Hoynes, H., 308, 311
Hoynes, Hilary Williamson, 149, 174
Hudson, Darren, 145
Hunter, J.A., 311

Iceland, John, 379, 407
Iowa Department of Human Services, 177, 179f, 199
Iowa Department of Workforce Development, 178, 199

Jacobson, Jonathan E., 198, 371
Jacobson, R., 374

Jantti, Markus, 27, 49
Jarrett, R., 228
Jensen, Helen H., 196, 199, 211, 228
Jensen, Leif, 81, 82, 83, 84, 95, 105,
     107, 108, 109, 152, 173, 180,
     181, 198, 380, 406, 407, 457, 470
Jessop, Bob, 379, 407
Johnson, David, 109
Johnson, Kenneth P., 126, 145
Johnston, Gail M., 81, 108, 151, 174
Jovanovic, Boyan, 65, 74

Kalil, Ariel, 48, 49
Kaplan, Thomas, 19, 20, 470
Katz, M., 233, 254
Kaye, Kelleen, 51, 74
Keng, Shao-Hsun, 196, 199
Kentucky Youth Advocates, 401, 407
Kiefer, Nicholas M., 197, 199
Killian, Molly Sizer, 56, 74
Kirby, Gretchen, 74, 284
Kirby, Maria, 469
Knox, Virginia, 311
Koralek, Robin, 108, 374
Kuhn, Betsey A., 315, 342
Kunz, John F., 198
Kurka, Robin, 74, 284

Lamborghini, Nita, 81, 107
Lampman, Robert J., 44, 49
Larin, Kathy, 450
LeBlanc, Michael, 315, 342
Leete, Laura, 315, 316, 342, 343
Legborne, D., 379, 407
Lein, Laura, 385, 406
Lennon, Mary Clare, 469
Lerman, Robert, 48, 61, 74, 259, 280,
     281, 282n9, 284, 285
Levine, Judith, 49
Lewis, Willis, 145, 450
Lichter, Daniel T., 81, 82, 83, 84, 85,
     103, 107, 108, 109, 151, 174,
     315, 379, 407
Liebschutz, Sarah F., 4, 19n2, 20
Lipietz, A., 379, 407

Litt, J., 211, 229
Lobao, Linda, 78, 108, 377, 407
Long, Sharon K., 51, 74, 259, 284
Loprest, Pamela, 61, 74, 282n9, 283n16,
     284, 459, 470
Lucas, Robert E., Jr., 56, 74
Luloff, A.E., 82, 109
Lurie, Irene, 20
Lyson, Thomas A., 80, 108

MaCurdy, Thomas, 151, 152, 174
Mancuso, David, 151, 152, 174
Maré, David C., 56, 73
Marks, Ellen L., 78, 80, 108, 346, 347,
     374
Marshall, Ray, 381, 407
Martin, Philip L., 152, 175
Martin, Thomas J., 198
Martini, Alberto, 315, 343
Mason, T. David, 338, 339, 341n7,
     342
Massey, Douglas S., 78, 108
Matthews, Stephen A., 81, 82, 109
McConnell, Sheena, 420, 424, 426, 428,
     431n3, 432
McDonald, Anne L., 144
McGranahan, David A., 56, 62, 64, 65,
     74
McGuire, Therese J., 137n18, 144
McKernan, Signe-Mary, 270t, 272t,
     275t, 277t, 282n8, 285
McLaughlin, Diane K., 81, 82, 83, 108,
     109, 151, 174
Meiser, Karen, 404n1, 406
Meyer, Bruce D., 263, 285, 459, 470
Meyer, Daniel, 19, 381, 407, 470
Meyer, J.A., 360, 374
Michael, Robert T., 85, 107, 228
Miller, Cynthia, 288, 308, 311
Miller, James P., 380, 408
Mills, Bradford, 257, 260, 280, 283,
     461, 470
Minkoff, Jon, 409
Minnesota Department of Economic
     Security, 350, 374

Minnesota Department of Human
    Services, 346, 374
Mississippi Department of Human
    Services, 145
Mizer, Karen L., 20, 139n27, 144
Moffitt, Robert A., 115, 135n5, 137n16,
    145, 180, 199, 285
Moreno, Lorenzo, 432
Munnell, A.H., 308, 311
Murray, C., 234, 254

Nathan, Richard P., 20
National Governors Association, 399,
    408
National Research Council, 469n1, 470
National Rural Development
    Partnership, 51, 74
Nelson, Margaret K., 378, 379, 380, 408
Nightingale, Demetra Smith, 4, 20, 51,
    74, 259, 285
Nixon, Lucia A., 198, 420, 432
Nord, Mark, 21, 53, 74, 82, 85, 109,
    435, 450, 451, 470
Norton, R.D., 56, 74

O'Brien-Strain, Margaret, 151, 152, 174
O'Connor, M., 225, 229
Oellerich, Donald, 93, 107
Office of Management and Budget,
    72n1
Ohls, James, 417, 425t, 427t, 432
Oliveira, Victor, 20
Olson, Christine M., 450
Olson, Krista, 284
Oltmans, Elizabeth, 49
O'Neill, June A., 151, 174, 381, 408
Otto, Daniel M., 179, 180, 198, 205, 228
Ouellette, T., 108, 374
Owen, G., 16, 352, 366, 372, 374

Padden, J.D., 360, 364, 374
Padilla, Y.C., 229
Parker, Timothy, 51, 73, 116, 126, 144,
    206, 229, 314, 318, 342
Parks, R.W., 139n26, 145

Parrott, S., 179, 199
Pavetti, LaDonna, 5, 20, 51, 75, 145,
    198, 283n16, 285, 423, 431
Peck, Jamie, 379, 408
Perese, Kevin, 20, 49, 284
Pickering, Kathleen, 380, 381, 408
Pindus, Nancy, 260, 262, 285
Ponza, Michael, 417, 424, 426, 428,
    431n3, 432
Porter, Kathryn, 450
Porterfield, Shirley L., 151, 152, 174,
    181, 199
Portes, Alejandro, 378, 379, 406
Prentice, R.L., 197, 199
President's National Advisory
    Commission on Rural Property,
    109
Price, Cristofer, 437, 450
Primus, Wendell, 433, 450
Purdy, Jedediah, 78, 109

Quane, J., 228
Quint, J., 201, 229

Rank, Mark R., 151, 174, 380, 381, 408
Ratcliffe, Caroline, 61, 74, 198, 282n9,
    283n16, 284, 285
Rauch, James E., 65, 75
Rawlings, Lynette, 450
Rector, Robert E., 136n16, 137n16, 145
Redcross, Cindy, 311
Reed, Deborah, 29f, 47n2
Rees, J., 56, 74
Regenstein, M., 360, 374
Regional Economic Information
    System, U.S. Department of
    Commerce, 409
Reichert, D., 225, 229
Reidy, Mairead, 181, 199
Reinharz, S., 237, 254
Reinschmiedt, Lynn, 123, 145, 433, 450
Riedinger, Susan, 198–199
Rob, Rafael, 65, 74
Roberts, B., 360, 364, 374
Rosen, Daniel, 49

Rosenbaum, Dan T., 263, 285, 459, 470
Ross, Christine, 416, 432
Ross, Peggy, 259, 284
Roy, C., 374
Rubin, Donald B., 183, 199
Rucker, G., 211, 229
Ruggles, Patricia, 315, 341
Ruiz, Vicki L., 381, 408
Rulli, Jamie, 78, 108
Rungeling, Brian, 55, 75
RUPRI Rural Welfare Reform Initiative
    Research Panel, 347, 374, 433,
    451
Rural Policy Research Institute, 1, 21,
    151, 174, 257, 259, 262, 263,
    285, 287, 311, 455, 470
Rural Sociological Society Task Force
    on Persistent Rural Poverty, 82,
    102–103, 109
Ryan, W., 202, 229

Saenz, Rogelio, 105, 109, 381, 408
Sandefur, Gary D., 180, 199
Sanders, Seth, 149, 174
Saunders, Milda, 285
Schoeni, Robert F., 85, 86, 109, 276,
    285
Schram, S., 233, 237, 254
Schreiber, Susan, 20, 49, 284
Scott, Loren C., 55, 75
Seefeldt, Kristin, 48, 49
Seibert, M. Therese, 80, 107
Shapiro, Isaac, 380, 408
Shelton, E., 374
Sherman, R., 386, 408
Sherwood, K.E., 227, 229
Shifflet, Peggy A., 406
Shoemaker, Donald J., 406
Short, Kathleen, 85, 109
Siefert, Kristine, 49
Simmons-Hewitt, O., 229
Sizer, Molly, 343
Skinner, E., 347, 374
Smith, David M., 134, 145
Smith, Joan, 380, 408

Smith, Lewis H., 55, 75
Smith, Robin, 285
South Carolina Department of Social
    Services, 144
Spade-Aguilar, Maggie, 68, 73
Spears, J.D., 228
Spera, Christopher, 198
Sprague, Mary, 173
Stangler, Gary, 455, 470
Stevens, A.B., 374
Streeck, Wolfgang, 379, 408
Struthers, Cynthia B., 105, 109
Sullivan, Daniel, 284, 282n11
Summers, Gene F., 380, 409
Sumrall, James, 150, 173
Swanson, Linda E., 105, 109, 228
Sweet, Stephen, 380, 406
Swenson, David A., 179, 180, 198, 205,
    228

Tadlock, B., 254
Taylor, J. Edward, 152, 175
Teixeira, Ruy, 380, 406
Teles, S., 232, 233, 245, 254
Thomas, John K., 105, 109
Thompson, William W., 450
Thornton, Bonnie Dill, 378, 409
Tiano, Susan, 381, 408
Tickamyer, Ann R., 103, 109, 148, 152,
    175, 234, 235, 244, 245, 252,
    254, 377, 378, 380, 409
Tiehen, Laura, 21, 451
Tienda, Marta, 105, 108
Tolbert, Charles M., 343
Tolman, Richard, 49
Tomaskovic-Devey, Donald, 73
Tönnies, F., 203, 229
Trippe, Carole, 416, 430n1, 432
Truelove, Cynthia, 73
Tweedie, J., 225, 229

U.S. Bureau of Labor Statistics, 79, 86,
    109
U.S. Bureau of the Census, 79, 81, 83,
    109, 172n3, 173, 204t, 228, 269,

283, 314, 325*f*, 328*f*, 331*f*, 342, 388, 404*n*3, 409, 423, 432
U.S. Department of Commerce, 204*t*, 229, 387, 409
U.S. Department of Health and Human Services, 10*t*, 283*n*16, 285, 286
Administration for Children and Families, 222, 228
U.S. Department of Labor, 382, 388, 404*n*3, 409
Office of the Secretary, 409
U.S. House of Representatives, 172*n*9, 294, 415, 432
Committee on Ways and Means, 175, 311
U.S. National Advisory Commission on Rural Poverty, 110, 79

Valente, Jesse, 259, 280, 281, 284, 285
Valmont, M.E., 229
Ver Ploeg, Michele, 135*n*5, 145
Vidich, A.J., 201, 229

Wade, Cynthia K., 335, 338, 339, 341*n*7, 342
Wallace, Geoffrey, 127, 135*n*7, 137*n*16, 138*n*19, 139*n*26, 145, 286
Warner, Milred, 81, 107
Waters, Shelley, 74, 284

Watson, Keith, 20, 48, 49, 284
Weber, Bruce A., 145, 181, 198, 450
Wehler, Cheryl A., 450
Weinberg, Daniel H., 81, 110
White, J., 254
Wilde, Parke, 5, 21, 433, 434, 438, 451
Williams, Bruce, 378, 409
Williams, C., 228
Williamson, O.E., 203, 211, 229
Winn, Ellen, 469
Winter, M., 229
Wiseman, Michael, 150, 173, 315, 343
Wolf, D.A., 381, 408
Wolf, Douglas A., 151, 174
Wolfe, Barbara, 19, 470
Woodbury, Stephen A., 134, 135*n*2, 145

Youssef, Sarah E., 136*n*16, 137*n*16, 145

Zambrowski, Amy, 432
Zedlewski, Sheila R., 114, 116, 127, 133, 136*n*15, 146, 284, 435, 439, 451
Ziliak, James P., 115, 135*n*7, 137*n*16, 139*n*26, 144, 150, 175, 286, 315, 343
Zimmerman, Julie N., 68, 75
Zimmerman, Wendy, 284

# Subject Index

The italic letters *f*, *n*, and *t* following a page number indicate that the subject information is within a figure, note, or table, respectively, on that page.

Absorption index, 316, 320, 330, 332–334
AFDC. *See* Aid to Families with Dependent Children
Agricultural Research, Extension, and Education Reform Act (1998), 431*n*7
Agricultural sector, seasonality of welfare participation, 152, 164*t*, 165–166, 165*f*, 167–170, 169*f*
Aid to Families with Dependent Children (AFDC), ix, 2, 77, 181, 232, 414
  child care support and, 290, 336*t*
  compared with MFIP, 289–290, 299–301, 300*f*, 302*t*, 303, 304*t*–305*t*, 306*f*
  participation rate, 8, 10*f*, 116, 117*f*, 120*f*, 179, 179*f*
  participation rate by education level, 322*t*–323*t*
  relationship to earnings, 66*f*
  relationship to unemployment rates, 63*f*, 117*f*, 120*f*
  *See also* TANF; Welfare
Alabama, 80
Alimony, 93
Appalachian Regional Commission (ARC), 236
Arkansas, 80
"Assessing the New Federalism" (Urban Institute), 260
*Assessing the New Federalism* (Urban Institute), 210

Balanced Budget Act (1997), 431*n*7
Beale codes, 157
Brookings Institution, 468–469

California
  county typology, 154–155, 156*f*, 157
  welfare participation, 153, 157–160, 159*t*, 160*f*, 161*f*, 172–173*n*9
  *See also* Welfare participation, seasonality of
California WORKS program, 148, 170–171
Cash assistance. *See* Welfare
Child care availability
  Iowa, 222–223, 226
  Mississippi, 319, 335, 336*t*, 337–338, 339, 341*n*7
  TANF participants, 334–335, 336*t*, 337, 339
  welfare reform and, 244
Child care support
  AFDC and, 290, 336*t*
  as employment barrier, 296, 359, 359*t*, 360, 398–399
  MFIP and, 290
Child support, 93
  Family Investment Program and, 185, 190
  MFIP and, 305*t*, 307
  return to welfare and, 192, 193*t*
Childhood poverty, 44, 80
  Iowa, 204*t*, 205
  rural/urban differences, 84
  *See also* Poverty
Children's Health Insurance Program (CHIP), 31, 226
Clinton, Bill, 31, 232
*Code of Federal Regulations*, 415
Combiner mothers
  defined, 35
  employment barriers, 36*t*, 37
  income, 40*t*, 41–42

Combiner mothers (continued)
    poverty rates, 40t, 42–43
    See also Single mothers
Community, unit of analysis in welfare
    reform, 202–203
Consumer Expenditure Survey (1998),
    85–86
Contract with America (Gingrich), 233,
    234
County typology
    California, 154–155, 156f, 157
    urban influence county code,
        318–319
Culture of poverty, 246, 253n2
Current Population Survey (CPS), 268
    Food Security Supplements, 436–437

Deep poverty
    female-headed families, 96f, 97
    measure of, 95–96
    welfare impact, 99
    See also Poverty
Dependent Care Credit (DCC), 46
Discouraged workers, 380, 389

Earned Income Tax Credit (EITC)
    antipoverty impact, 46, 88t, 89, 99,
        100t, 101
    expansion of, 31, 226, 258
    incentive to leave welfare, 137n18
Earnings, 77–78
    by education level, 67–68, 67t
    female-headed families, 89, 90t,
        91–94, 93f, 94f, 106n2
    by gender, 67–68, 67t
    Iowa, 180
    MFIP impact, 300–301, 300f, 306f
    by race, 67–68, 67t
    relationship to AFDC, 66f
    return to welfare and, 192, 193t
    rural labor markets, 64–65, 66f,
        67–68, 67t, 70
    rural/urban differences, 53–54, 53f,
        67–68, 67t, 82, 106n2, 180
    single mothers, 28, 29f, 31, 32t, 33,
        40t, 41–42

    urban labor markets, 67–68, 67t
    See also Income; Informal
        economy
Earnings disregard (Michigan), 43
EBT. See Electronic Benefit Transfer
    card
Economic function types (county
    typology), 157
Economic Research Service, ix–x,
    1–2
Economy
    FSP participation and, 434
    informal, 378–379, 380–381,
        385–386
    measures of, 137n16
    1990s, 11, 84–85
    welfare participation and, 11, 13,
        131, 136–137n16, 150–151
Education, exclusion through TANF,
    403
Education level
    earnings and, 67–68, 67t
    as employment barrier, 359, 359t
    by industry, 60t
    Mississippi welfare recipients, 321,
        322t–323t, 324, 325f, 327
    relationship to unemployment rates,
        61, 62t, 274, 275t, 276, 280
    rural labor markets, 56, 57t, 58,
        81–82
    rural/urban differences, 56, 57t, 58,
        81–82
    single mothers, 274, 275t, 276, 280,
        283n16
    spatial mismatch with job
        availability, 316, 330, 331f,
        332–334, 338–341
EITC. See Earned Income Tax Credit
Electronic Benefit Transfer (EBT) card,
    428–429
Employers
    exploitation of TANF participants,
        390–391
    perceived role in welfare reform,
        370–371
    perceptions of employment barriers,

16–17, 353, 354*t*, 355*t*, 356, 369–370, 465
perceptions on effectiveness of community partnerships in welfare reform, 360, 361*t*, 362–364
role in welfare reform, 366–367, 368–369
Employment barriers, 210–211, 370
child care availability, 222–223, 226, 319, 335, 336*t*, 337–338, 339, 341*n*7
child care support, 296, 353, 354*t*, 359, 359*t*, 360, 398–399
education level, 359, 359*t*
employers' perceptions, 16–17, 353, 354*t*, 355*t*, 356, 369–370, 465
health care benefits, 359, 359*t*, 360, 391
low wages, 359, 359*t*
persistently poor rural areas, 397–399
single mothers, 35*t*, 36*t*, 38*t*, 281
soft skills, 353, 354*t*, 372
transportation costs, 242–243, 260, 353, 354*t*, 359–360, 398
welfare administrators' perceptions, 231–232, 244, 465
welfare recipients' perceptions, 17, 244, 262, 356, 357*t*–358*t*, 359–360, 359*t*, 370, 465
*See also* Employment support services
Employment barriers, rural/urban differences, 114, 123, 236, 457–458, 464–465
child care support, 296, 353, 354I*t*, 359, 359*t*, 360
single mothers, 281
Employment distribution, by occupation, 61*t*
Employment responsiveness, rural/urban differences, 15–16
Employment support services
Iowa, 214*t*, 218–224
labor markets, 457–458

reduction of welfare participation, 227
*See also* Employment barriers
Empowerment Zone/Enterprise Community (EZ/EC) program, 400
Ethnicity. *See* Race

Family General Assistance Program (FGA), 289, 310*n*2
Family Independence Act (FIA), 115–116, 135–136*n*8
Family Investment Program (FIP), 177, 207–208, 209*f*, 210
participants' demographics, 183, 184*t*, 185, 187, 188*t*–189*t*, 190, 212*t*–213*t*
participants' mobility, 186–187, 186*t*
receipt of child support and, 185, 190
return to welfare and, 191–194, 193*t*, 194*f*
Family Well-Being and Welfare Reform project (Iowa), 202
Female-headed families
deep poverty, 96*f*, 97
economic well-being, 95–97, 95*f*, 96*f*, 98*t*, 99
impact of employment on economic well-being, 99, 100*t*, 101–102
income, 89, 90*t*, 91–94, 93*f*, 94*f*, 106*n*2
poverty income threshold, 95–96, 95*f*
poverty rates, 87, 88*t*, 89, 100*t*, 101–102, 103–104
PRWORA impact, 89, 90*t*, 91–92
rural/urban differences, 83, 90*t*, 91–93, 101–102, 103–104, 106*n*2
*See also* Single mothers
FGA. *See* Family General Assistance Program
FIA. *See* Family Independence Act
FIP. *See* Family Investment Program
Food Assistance and Nutrition Research Program, U.S. Department of Agriculture, x

Food banks, 393–394, 395*f*, 396,
     402–403
Food Distribution on Indian
     Reservations Program, 396
Food insecurity, 439, 439*f*, 442–444
     low-income households, 440*t*–441*t*,
          442
     rural areas, 446*t*–447*t*, 448
     rural/urban differences, 463–464
     welfare office procedural changes
          and, 396–397
Food Stamp Program (FSP). *See* FSP
Food Stamp Program's Quality Control
     (FSPQC), 416
Food Stamps Employment Training
     Program, 401
Fordism, 378–379
Forestry sector, welfare participation
     and, 152
FSP (Food Stamp Program)
centralization of, 414–415
     coordination with welfare, 414–415
     PRWORA provisions, 4–5, 116, 423,
          434–435
     vehicle asset limits of, 262, 282*n*7
FSP eligibility, 448–449, 449*n*1
     ABAWDS (able-bodied adults
          without dependents), 423, 431*n*7,
          431*n*9
     confusion over, 426, 435
     PRWORA provisions, 423,
          434–435
FSP participants
     rural/urban differences, 417, 418*t*,
          419, 424–429, 425*t*, 427*t*
FSP participation, 8, 10*f*, 17–18, 90*t*, 91,
     114, 433
     barriers to, 426–428, 427*t*, 429,
          430
     correlation with unemployment rates,
          118*f*, 119, 122*f*, 123
     economy and, 434
     income and, 418*t*, 419, 438, 438*t*
     Iowa, 179, 179*f*, 185
     Kentucky, 393, 394*f*

Mississippi, 118*f*, 119, 128*t*,
     132–133, 393, 394*f*
Ohio, 458
perception of ineligibility, 426, 435
race and, 418*t*, 419
reduced eligibility, 448–449
return to welfare and, 193, 193*t*
rural areas, 444–445, 445*t*
rural/urban differences, 133,
     413–414, 419–424, 420*t*, 421*t*,
     429–430, 458–459
single mothers, 438–439, 438*t*
South Carolina, 121, 122*f*, 123, 128*t*,
     132–133, 458
South Dakota, 393, 394*f*
stigma of, 425*t*, 428
TANF impact, 132–133, 393, 394*f*
Texas, 393, 394*f*
welfare reform and, 423–424
FSPQC. *See* Food Stamp Program's
     Quality Control

Gender
     earnings and, 67–68, 67*t*
     likelihood of wage progression and,
          70, 71
     unemployment rates, 61, 62*t*
Generational welfare. *See* Culture of
     poverty
God's Pantry Food Bank (Lexington,
     Kentucky), 394
Government sector, 380

Health care benefits
     as employment barrier, 359, 359*t*,
          360, 391
     Iowa, 220–221
     welfare-to-work transition and, 46,
          351, 391, 402
     *See also* Medicaid
Household analysis, 378
Household food security scale, 435–436,
     437
Household survival strategy, 380–381
Hunger. *See* Food insecurity

Income, 28
    female-headed families, 89, 90*t*,
        91–94, 93*f*, 94*f*, 106*n*2
    FSP participation and, 418*t*, 419,
        438, 438*t*
    Ohio, 238*t*
    poverty rates responsiveness to, 47*n*1
    single mothers, 28, 29*f*, 31, 32*t*, 33,
        40*t*, 41–42
    *See also* Earnings; Informal
        economy
Industry employment, seasonality of
        welfare participation and,
        162–163, 164*t*, 165–167
Informal economy, 378–379, 380–381,
        385–386
Iowa
    child care availability, 222–223,
        226
    childhood poverty, 204*t*, 205
    earnings, 180
    employment support services, 214*t*,
        218–224
    FSP participation, 179, 179*f*, 185
    health care benefits, 220–221
    job availability, 215–218
    job training and education, 218–220
    labor market shifts, 205–207, 206*t*
    Medicaid, 220–221
    population trends, 204–205, 204*t*
    poverty rates, 81
    rural/urban differences, 224–225
    unemployment rates, 79, 178–179,
        204*t*, 205, 206
    welfare participation, 179, 179*f*
    *See also* Family Investment
        Program
IPR. *See* Poverty income threshold

Job availability
    Iowa, 215–218
    Mississippi, 326*t*, 327, 328*f*,
        329–330, 338–341
    rural labor markets, 60–70, 69*t*,
        262–263, 347, 386–387

    rural/urban differences, 457–458
    spatial mismatch with education
        level, 316, 330, 331*f*, 332–334,
        338–341
    TANF participants and, 330, 331*f*,
        332–334
Job-matching ratio. *See* Absorption
        index
Job training and education, 218–220
Jobs, low-skill, 73*n*5
JOBS (Job Opportunities and Basic
        Skills) program, 382

Kentucky
    FSP participation, 393, 394*f*
    informal employment, 386
    labor markets, 387–388
    Medicaid eligibility, 391
    out-migration, 82
    unemployment rates, 388–389, 388*f*
    welfare benefits, 385
    welfare participation, 384, 384*f*
    welfare sanctions, 401
Kids Count project (1999), 80

Labor market areas (LMA), 319
Labor markets
    employment support services,
        457–458
    individuals' responsiveness to, 150
    Iowa, 205–207, 206*t*
    Kentucky, 387–388
    research studies on capacity to
        absorb welfare recipients,
        315–317
    rural/urban differences, 55–56, 114,
        457
    South Carolina, 130–131
    South Dakota, 387–388
    support services, 457–458
    welfare participation and, 149–151
    *See also* Rural labor markets; Urban
        labor markets
Labor markets, Mississippi, 130–131
    capacity to absorb welfare recipients,

Labor markets, Mississippi (continued)
    322*t*–323*t*, 326*t*, 327, 328*f*,
    329–330, 338–341
Living wage movement, 68, 69*t*, 70
Louisiana, 314
Low-education counties, 72–73*n*4
Low Income Women and Children,
    Medicaid eligibility, 392
Low-skill jobs, 73*n*5
Low-wage counties, 66*f*

MAC. *See* Medical Assistance
    Program
Manpower Development and Training
    Act (1962), 382
Manufacturing sector, seasonality of
    welfare participation, 164*t*, 166,
    167
March Current Population Survey, 31,
    32*t*, 84
Marital status, MFIP impact and, 305*t*,
    307, 308
Maryland Family Investment Program,
    180–181
McKnight Foundation community
    partnerships, 347–348
McKnight Foundation community
    partnerships, effectiveness study,
    348–349
    employers' perceptions, 360, 361*t*,
        362–364
    employers' perceptions of role
        in welfare reform, 364–366,
        365*t*
    employers' sample, 350–351
    welfare recipients' sample, 352
Medicaid, 46
    eligibility, 391–392
    frustration with, 220–221
    *See also* Health care benefits
Medical Assistance Case (MAC)
    program, 391
Metropolitan areas. *See* Urban areas
Metropolitan Statistical Areas (MSAs),
    416

MFIP (Minnesota Family Investment
    Program), 16, 289–291, 345–346
    child care support and, 290
    child support and, 305*t*, 307
    compared with AFDC, 289–290,
        299–301, 300*f*, 302*t*, 303,
        304*t*–305*t*, 306*f*
    recipients' demographics, 288–289,
        293*t*, 294, 309
    rural/urban differences among
        recipients, 294, 309
MFIP evaluation, 291–292
    basic empirical estimation,
        298–299
    expected effects, 297–298
    recipients' perceptions of, 294,
        295*t*–296*t*, 296, 309, 346
    sample, 292, 293*t*, 294
MFIP impact
    earnings, 300–301, 300*f*, 306*f*
    marital status and, 305*t*, 307, 308
    rural/urban differences, 288, 301,
        306–308
    by type of employment, 301,
        304*t*–305*t*
    unemployment rates, 299–300, 300*f*,
        301, 302*t*, 303, 309
Minimum wage, 30, 68
Minnesota
    STRIDE program, 289, 290, 310*n*1
    unemployment rates, 346
    *See also* McKnight Foundation;
        MFIP; Welfare reform,
        Minnesota
Minnesota Family Investment Program
    (MFIP). *See* MFIP
Mississippi
    child care availability, 319, 335,
        336*t*, 337–338, 339, 341*n*7
    determinants of welfare and FSP
        participation, 128*t*
    education level of welfare recipients,
        321, 322*t*–323*t*, 324, 325*f*, 327
    FSP participation, 118*f*, 119, 128*t*,
        132–133, 393, 394*f*

job availability, 326*t*, 327, 328*f*, 329–330, 338–341
labor markets, 130–131, 387–388
labor markets' capacity to absorb welfare recipients, 322*t*–323*t*, 326*t*, 327, 328*f*, 329–330, 338–341
Medicaid eligibility, 392
poverty rates, 80, 314
rural disadvantage, 130–131, 134
spatial mismatch of job availability with education level, 330, 331*f*, 332–334, 338–341
TANF Work Program (TWP), 136*n*9
unemployment rates, 117*f*, 118*f*, 119, 388, 388*f*
welfare benefits, 385
welfare participation, 116, 117*f*, 119, 320–321, 321*f*, 384, 384*f*
welfare sanctions, 401
Work First (work program), 136*n*9
Mississippi Welfare Restructuring Program Act (1993), 136*n*9

National Food Stamp Survey (NFSS), 416–417
Negative Income Tax experiments, 308
New Area Workforce Boards (NAWBS), 399–400
New Hampshire, 79
New Mexico, 80
Nonmetropolitan areas. *See* Rural areas
Northwestern University/University of Chicago Joint Center for Poverty Research, ix–x, 1–2

Ohio, 238*t*, 458
*See also* Welfare reform, Ohio
Ohio Works First (OWF), 237
Out-migration, rural labor supply, 81–82

Persistently poor rural areas, 9*t*, 80–81, 383–401, 384*f*
employment barriers, 397–399
informal economy, 385–386
labor market deficiency, 386–389

Medicaid eligibility, 391–392
short-term impact of welfare reform, 375–376, 402
support network of welfare recipients, 381
unemployment rates, 388–389, 388*f*
welfare administrative strategies for reduction of welfare participation, 399–401
welfare benefits, 385
welfare bureaucracy, 389–397
welfare participation, 383–401, 384*f*
welfare reform, 375–376, 397–399, 468
*See also* Rural areas; TANF bureaucracy; *specific states*
Personal Responsibility and Work Opportunity Reconciliation Act (PRWORA), ix, 1, 25, 232, 402–403
devolution of authority, 455
goals of, 8, 10, 83, 257
impact on female-headed families, 89, 90*t*, 91–92
impact on FSP, 4–5, 116, 415, 423, 434–435
impact on single mothers, 10, 30
key provisions, 2, 3*t*, 258, 313
time limit provision, 26, 44, 45, 104, 258, 402
welfare participation and, 14–15, 25, 77
Women's Employment Study, 39–44
*See also* TANF; Welfare reform
Pockets of poverty, rural. *See* Persistently poor rural areas
Post-Fordism, 379
Poverty
measures of, 85–86, 105
nonmetro counties, 6*f*
trends in, 86–89
welfare reform and, 79–84
*See also* Childhood poverty; Deep poverty; Persistently poor rural areas

Poverty income threshold (IPR), 85–86,
    95–96, 95*f*, 106*n*3
Poverty rates, 27–28
    Arkansas, 80
    EITC-adjusted, 86–87, 87*f*
    female-headed families, 87, 88*t*, 89,
        100*t*, 101–102, 103–104
    Iowa, 81
    Louisiana, 314
    Mississippi, 80, 314
    New Mexico, 80
    Ohio, 238*t*
    responsiveness to economic
        indicators, 47*n*1
    rural/urban differences, 7, 79, 86–87,
        87*f*, 100*t*, 101–102, 103–104,
        287, 463
    single mothers, 31, 32*t*, 33, 40*t*,
        42–43
    stability of, 13, 26, 29–30
    West Virginia, 80, 81
Private charities, 402–403
PROMISE JOBS (Promoting
    Independence and Self-
    sufficiency through Employment,
    Job Opportunities, and Basic
    Skills), 207, 208, 217, 218–220
PRWORA. *See* Personal Responsibility
    and Work Opportunity
    Reconciliation Act
Public assistance. *See* Welfare

Race
    earnings and, 67–68, 67*t*
    FSP participation, 418*t*, 419
    likelihood of wage progression and,
        70, 71
    rural/urban differences among
        female-headed families, 83
    TANF effects and, 276, 277*t*,
        278–279
    unemployment rates and, 61, 62*t*,
        276, 277*t*, 278–279
*Reaching the Working Poor and Poor*

    *Elderly* (USDA, Food and
        Nutrition Service), 417
Rural areas
    defined, 5, 6*f*, 7, 19*n*4, 227*n*1, 416
    diversity of, 456
    earnings and, 64–65, 66*f*, 67–68, 67*t*,
        70
    food insecurity, 446*t*–447*t*, 448
    FSP participation, 444–445, 445*t*
    public awareness of problems facing,
        78
    relationship to urban areas, 105–106
    return to welfare, 193–194, 194*f*
    underemployment, 82, 105, 152, 181
    unemployment rates, 61, 62*t*
    *See also* Employment barriers;
        Persistently poor rural areas;
        Rural-urban differences; *specific
        states*
Rural disadvantage, welfare reduction,
    130–131, 133, 134
Rural disadvantage hypothesis, test of,
    124–133
    food stamps model, 127
    opportunity cost variables, 124–125
    regions used, 126–127
    results, 127, 128*t*, 129–133
    TANF and economy variables,
        125–126
Rural ghetto communities. *See*
    Persistently poor rural areas
Rural labor markets, 51–72, 81–82, 457
    compared with urban labor markets,
        52
    earnings, 64–65, 66*f*, 67*t*, 68, 70
    education level, 56, 57*t*, 58, 81–82
    employment density, 54–56
    government sector, 380
    job availability, 60–70, 69*t*, 262–263,
        347, 386–387
    opportunity structures, 377–378
    out-migration, 81–82
    persistently poor rural areas,
        386–389

shift from manufacturing to service
    sector, 58–60, 71, 379–380, 387
skill requirements, 58–60, 60*t*
Texas, 387–388
theories of, 377–379
underinvestment in human resources
    development, 381–382
welfare reform and, 51–52, 70–72,
    377–382
*See also* Labor markets
Rural Policy Research Institute, ix–x,
    1–2
Rural/urban differences, ix
    childhood poverty, 84
    earnings, 53–54, 53*f*, 67–68, 67*t*, 82,
        106*n*2, 180
    education level, 56, 57*t*, 58, 81–82
    employers, 367–368
    employment responsiveness, 15–16
    female-headed families, 83, 90*t*,
        91–93, 101–102, 103–104,
        106*n*2
    food insecurity, 463–464
    FSP participants' characteristics,
        417, 418*t*, 419
    FSP participants' experiences,
        424–429, 425*t*, 427*t*
    FSP participation, 133, 413–414,
        419–424, 420*t*, 421*t*, 429–430,
        458–459
    Iowa, 224–225
    job availability, 457–458
    labor markets, 55–56, 59–60, 60*t*,
        114, 457
    MFIP impact, 288, 301, 306–308
    MFIP recipients, 294, 309
    poverty rates, 7, 79, 86–87, 87*f*, 100*t*,
        101–102, 103–104, 287, 463
    return to welfare, 462
    single mothers, 280–281
    TANF impact among single mothers,
        271–273, 272*t*
    underemployment, 82
    unemployment rates, 7, 53–54, 53*f*

unemployment rates of single
    mothers, 259, 269, 270*t*,
    271–273, 272*t*, 459–460
welfare dependency, 181
welfare impact, 99, 274, 275*t*, 276,
    280
welfare participation, 151, 464
welfare reform, 280–281, 456–458
welfare spells, 381, 462
welfare-to-work transition, 460–461
Rural/urban differences, employment
    barriers, 114, 123, 236, 457–458,
    464–465
    child care support, 296, 353, 354*t*,
        359, 359*t*, 360
    single mothers, 281

Seasonal workers
    agricultural sector, 164*t*, 165–166,
        165*f*, 167–170, 169*f*
    correlation of unemployment rates
        and welfare participation, 161,
        162, 162*f*
    manufacturing sector, 164*t*, 166, 167
    unemployment insurance, 171
    welfare participation, 147–148,
        162–163, 164*t*, 165–167
    welfare reform and, 148, 170–171
The Second Harvest Food Bank of
    South Dakota, 394, 396
Single mothers
    defined, 32*t*
    earnings, 28, 29*f*, 31, 32*t*, 33, 40*t*,
        41–42
    education level, 274, 275*t*, 276, 280,
        283*n*16
    employment barriers, 35*t*, 36*t*, 38*t*,
        281
    employment responsiveness, 15–16
    food insecurity, 440*t*–441*t*,
        446*t*–447*t*
    FSP participation, 438–439, 438*t*
    income, 28, 29*f*, 31, 32*t*, 33, 40*t*,
        41–42

Single mothers (continued)
poverty rates, 31, 32*t*, 33, 40*t*,
42–43
PRWORA impact, 10, 30
rural/urban differences, 280–281
*See also* Female-headed families;
Women's Employment Study
Single mothers, unemployment rates
education level and, 274, 275*t*, 276,
280
by race, 276, 277*t*, 278–279
rural/urban differences, 259, 269,
270*t*, 271–273, 272*t*, 459–460
TANF impact, 267*f*, 269, 270*t*,
271–272, 272*t*, 274, 275*t*, 276,
280
South Carolina
determinants of welfare
participation, 128*t*
Family Independence Act, 115–116,
135–136*n*8
FSP participation, 121, 122*f*, 123,
128*t*, 132–133, 458
labor markets, 130–131
rural disadvantage, 130–131, 134
unemployment rates, 120*f*, 121,
122*f*
welfare participation, 119, 120*f*, 121,
458
South Dakota
FSP participation, 393, 394*f*
informal employment, 386
labor markets, 387–388
Medicaid eligibility, 391–392
unemployment rates, 79, 388–389,
388*f*
welfare benefits, 385
welfare participation, 384, 384*f*
welfare sanctions, 401
Spatial inequality, 80–81
welfare participation and, 131
STRIDE (Minnesota employment and
training program), 289, 290,
310*n*1

TANF (Temporary Assistance for Needy
Families), ix, 2, 232, 282*n*1
employers' exploitation of
participants, 390–391
exclusion of education, 403
health care benefits, 391, 402
participation, 8, 10*f*, 136–137*n*16,
137–138*nn*18–19, 179, 179*f*, 458
time limit provision, 134–135, 148,
170–171, 195
*See also* Aid to Families with
Dependent Children; Personal
Responsibility and Work
Opportunity Reconciliation Act;
Welfare
TANF bureaucracy, 389–396
food insecurity, 393, 395*f*, 396
food stamps, 393, 394*f*
Medicaid eligibility, 391–392
TANF effects, 264–281
difference estimators as measure of,
264–266, 267*f*, 268
FSP participation, 132–133, 393,
394*f*
rural/urban differences among single
mothers, 271–273, 272*t*, 274,
275*t*, 276, 280
single mothers by race, 276, 277*t*,
278–279
single mothers' unemployment rates,
267*f*, 269, 270*t*, 271–272, 272*t*,
274, 275*t*, 276, 280
TANF participants
child care availability, 334–335,
336*t*, 337, 339
confusion among, 396–397
job availability, 330, 331*f*, 332–334
TANF Work Program (TWP), 136*n*9
Temporary Assistance for Needy
Families. *See* TANF
Texas
FSP participation, 393, 394*f*
informal employment, 386
Medicaid eligibility, 391, 392

rural labor markets, 387–388
  unemployment rates, 388, 388*f*
  welfare benefits, 385
  welfare participation, 384, 384*f*
  welfare sanctions, 401
Texas Workforce Commission, 385–386
Transportation costs
  as employment barrier, 242–243,
    260, 353, 354*t*, 359–360, 398
  FSP participation and, 428, 429

Underemployment
  rural areas, 82, 101, 105, 152
  rural/urban differences, 82
  *See also* Unemployment rates
*Understanding Rural America*
    (Economic Research Service,
    USDA), 18
Unemployed Parent Program (UPP),
    384, 404*n*2
Unemployment insurance (UI) ,
    seasonal workers and, 171
Unemployment rates, 27, 77
  AFDC and, 63*f*, 117*f*, 120*f*
  correlation with FSP participation,
    118*f*, 119, 122*f*, 123
  correlation with seasonality of
    welfare participation, 161, 162,
    162*f*
  correlation with welfare
    participation, 117*f*, 119, 120*f*,
    121, 159*t*, 161–162, 162*f*
  education level and, 61, 62*t*, 274,
    275*t*, 276, 280
  gender and, 61, 62*t*
  Iowa, 79, 178–179, 204*t*, 205, 206
  Kentucky, 388–389, 388*f*
  MFIP impact, 299–300, 300*f*, 301,
    302*t*, 303
  Minnesota, 346
  Mississippi, 117*f*, 118*f*, 119, 388,
    388*f*
  New Hampshire, 79
  Ohio, 238*t*

  persistently poor rural areas,
    388–389, 388*f*
  poverty rates responsiveness to, 47*n*1
  race and, 61, 62*t*, 276, 277*t*, 278–279
  rural areas, 61, 62*t*
  rural/urban differences, 7, 53–54,
    53*f*
  South Carolina, 120*f*, 121, 122*f*
  South Dakota, 79, 388–389, 388*f*
  Texas, 388, 388*f*
  variability of, 61–62, 62*t*
  *See also* Underemployment
Unemployment rates, single mothers
  education level, 274, 275*t*, 276,
    280
  rural/urban differences, 259, 269,
    270*t*, 271–273, 272*t*, 459–460
  TANF effects, 267*f*, 269, 270*t*,
    271–272, 272*t*, 274, 275*t*, 276,
    280
U.S. Department of Agriculture
  Economic Research Service (ERS),
    ix–x, 1–2
  Food and Nutrition Services, 416,
    417
  Food Assistance and Nutrition
    Research Program, x
U.S. Department of Labor, welfare-to-
    work grants, 400
U.S. National Advisory Commission on
    Rural Poverty, 79
UPP. *See* Unemployed Parent Program
Urban areas
  defined, 5, 7, 19*n*4, 227*n*1, 269,
    416
  relationship to rural areas, 105–106
  *See also* Rural/urban differences
Urban influence code, 318–319
Urban Institute, 210, 260
Urban labor markets
  compared to rural labor markets, 52
  earnings, 67–68, 67*t*

Vehicle asset limits, 260, 262, 282*n*7

Wage progression, likelihood among
    women and minorities, 70, 71
Wage-reliant mothers
    defined, 35
    employment barriers, 36t, 37
    income, 40t, 41–42
    poverty rates, 40t, 42–43
    See also Single mothers
Wage subsidies, 225–226
Welfare
    ameliorative effects, 95–97, 98t,
        99
    criticism prior to PRWORA, 45
    diversity of state policies, 2, 4
    FSP coordination, 414–415
    stigma of, 151, 201–202, 295t, 296
    See also Aid to Families with
        Dependent Children; Family
        Investment Program; FSP; MFIP;
        TANF
Welfare, return to, 181
    child support and, 192, 193t
    determinants, 192–194, 193t, 194f
    Family Investment Program,
        191–194, 193t, 194f
    FSP participation, 193, 193t
    rural/urban differences, 462
Welfare administrators, perceptions of
        employment barriers, 231–232,
        244, 465
Welfare benefits, persistently poor rural
        areas, 385
Welfare caseload analysis, rural/urban,
        114–116, 135n1
Welfare caseload regression model,
        141–144
Welfare dependency
    causes of, 233–234, 242–243,
        246–247
    character deficits and, 242,
        246–247
    determinants, 180–181, 196
    negative duration dependence, 180
    rural/urban differences, 181

Welfare participation
    defined, 172n6
    California, 153, 157–160, 159t, 160f,
        161f, 172–173n9
    correlation with unemployment rates,
        117f, 119, 120f, 121, 159t,
        161–162, 162f
    by county type, 157–160, 159t, 160f,
        161f
    determinants, 128t
    economy and, 11, 13, 131,
        136–137n16, 150–151
    interaction of TANF and local
        economic variables, 129–130
    Iowa, 179, 179f
    Kentucky, 384, 384f
    labor markets and, 149–151
    Mississippi, 116, 117f, 119, 320–321,
        321f, 384, 384f
    persistently poor rural areas,
        383–401, 384f
    PRWORA and, 14–15, 25, 77
    resource-based employment and,
        152–153
    rural/urban differences, 151, 464
    South Carolina, 119, 120f, 121, 458
    South Dakota, 384, 384f
    TANF regulations and, 136–137n16,
        137–138nn18–19
    Texas, 384, 384f
    urban concentration, 468–469
    wage subsidies, 225–226
Welfare participation, reduction of
    effective measures, 196
    employment support obstacle, 227
    incentives, 137n18–138n18
    rural disadvantage, 130–131, 133,
        134
Welfare participation, seasonality of,
        147–148
    agricultural sector, 152, 164t,
        165–166, 165f, 167–170, 169f
    correlation with unemployment rates,
        161, 162, 162f

by county type, 157–159
industry employment and, 162–163,
    164t, 165–167
manufacturing sector, 164t, 166,
    167
Welfare recipients
    classification, 245–246
    labor markets' capacity to absorb,
        315–317, 322t–323t, 326t, 327,
        328f, 329–330, 338–341
    network support in persistently poor
        rural areas, 381
    perceptions of employment barriers,
        17, 244, 262, 356, 357t–358t,
        359–360, 359t, 370, 465
    perceptions of welfare reform,
        244–245
Welfare recipients, education level, 274,
    283n16
    Mississippi, 321, 322t–323t, 324,
        325f, 327
    single mothers, 274, 275t, 276, 280,
        283n16
Welfare reform, 44–47, 386, 466–468
    child care availability and, 244
    community as unit of analysis,
        202–203
    devolution of authority, 235–236,
        259
    employer involvement, 366–367
    employers' perceived role, 364–366,
        365t, 370–371
    employers' role, 368–369
    false assumptions, 375–376
    FSP participation, 423–424
    household well-being, 461–462
    rational choice model, 234–235
    rural dimensions, 78, 79–84, 105,
        201–202, 346–347
    rural labor markets and, 51–52,
        70–72, 377–382
    rural/urban differences, 280–281,
        456–458
    seasonal workers and, 148, 170–171

transitional benefits, 46, 263, 351,
    391, 402
trends, 31, 32t, 33
See also Personal Responsibility and
    Work Opportunity Reconciliation
    Act; TANF; Women's
    Employment Study
Welfare reform, Minnesota, 281,
    345–346
    employer involvement, 366–367
    employers' perceived role,
        370–371
    employers' role, 368–369, 371–374
Welfare reform, Ohio
    administrators' perceptions,
        231–232, 239–242
    as community effort, 252
    devolution of authority, 248, 251
    funding, 249
    intervention model, 246–247
    organizational changes, 247–248
    problems of, 242–245, 251
    recipients' perceptions, 244–245
    time limits, 249–250
Welfare reform, persistently poor rural
    areas, 468
    lack of support services, 397–399
    short-term impact, 375–376
Welfare Reform Demonstration Project,
    136n9
Welfare-reliant mothers
    defined, 35, 37
    employment barriers, 36t, 37
    income, 40t, 41–42
    poverty rates, 40t, 42–43
    See also Single mothers
Welfare sanctions, 244, 249–251, 401
Welfare spells, rural/urban differences,
    381, 462
Welfare-to-work transition
    health care benefits, 46, 351, 391,
        402
    rural/urban differences, 460–461
West Virginia, 80, 81

WIC. *See* Women, Infants, and
    Children feeding program
Women, Infants, and Children (WIC)
    feeding program, 221
Women's Employment Study (WES)
    financial well-being following
        PRWORA, 39–44
methodology, 34–35, 37
results, 37–39
sample, 33–34
Work First programs, 136n9, 399
Workforce Investment Act (WIA),
    399

# About the Institute

The W.E. Upjohn Institute for Employment Research is a nonprofit research organization devoted to finding and promoting solutions to employment-related problems at the national, state, and local levels. It is an activity of the W.E. Upjohn Unemployment Trustee Corporation, which was established in 1932 to administer a fund set aside by the late Dr. W.E. Upjohn, founder of The Upjohn Company, to seek ways to counteract the loss of employment income during economic downturns.

The Institute is funded largely by income from the W.E. Upjohn Unemployment Trust, supplemented by outside grants, contracts, and sales of publications. Activities of the Institute comprise the following elements: 1) a research program conducted by a resident staff of professional social scientists; 2) a competitive grant program, which expands and complements the internal research program by providing financial support to researchers outside the Institute; 3) a publications program, which provides the major vehicle for disseminating the research of staff and grantees, as well as other selected works in the field; and 4) an Employment Management Services division, which manages most of the publicly funded employment and training programs in the local area.

The broad objectives of the Institute's research, grant, and publication programs are to 1) promote scholarship and experimentation on issues of public and private employment and unemployment policy, and 2) make knowledge and scholarship relevant and useful to policymakers in their pursuit of solutions to employment and unemployment problems.

Current areas of concentration for these programs include causes, consequences, and measures to alleviate unemployment; social insurance and income maintenance programs; compensation; workforce quality; work arrangements; family labor issues; labor-management relations; and regional economic development and local labor markets.